Characters

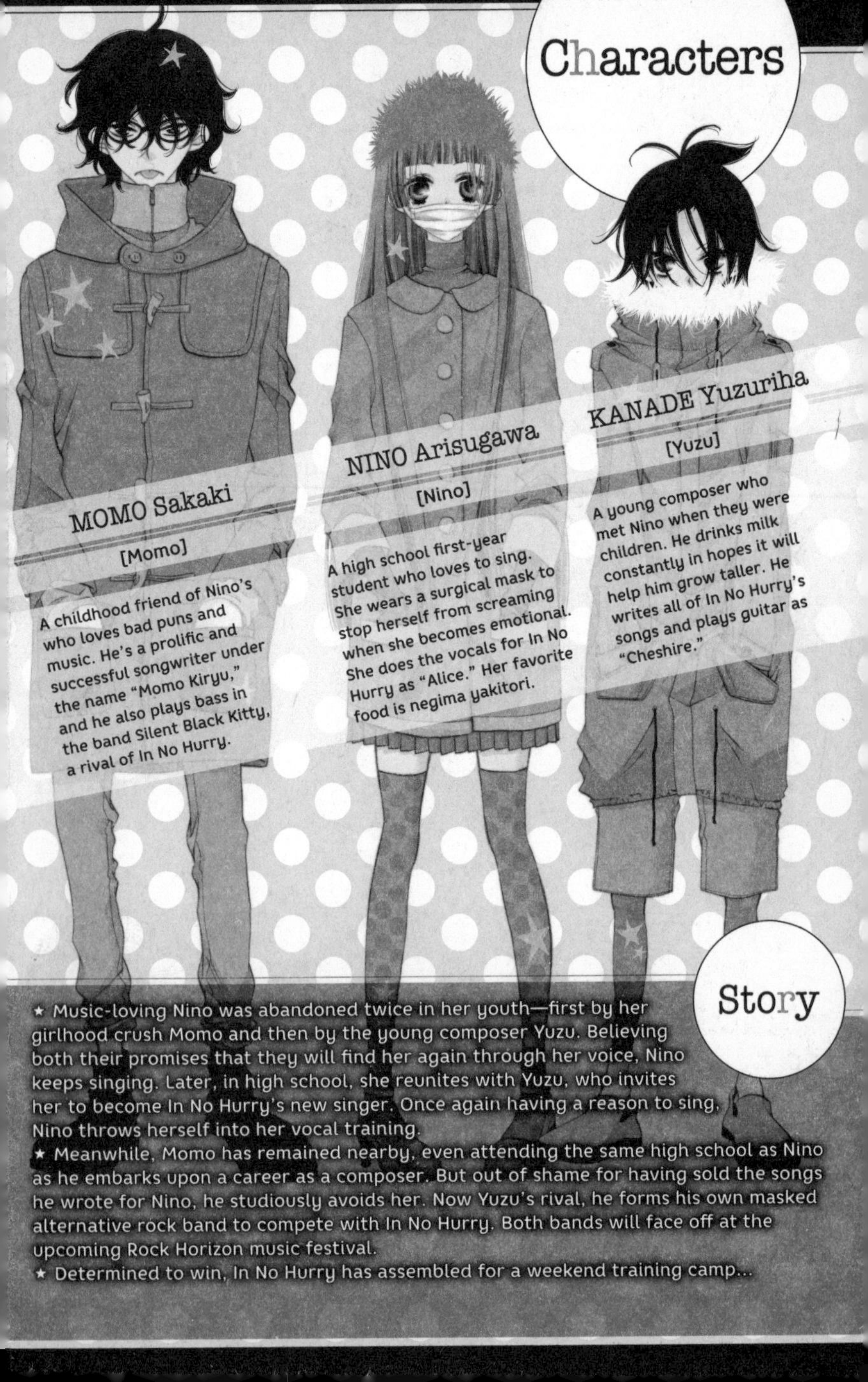

MOMO Sakaki
[Momo]

A childhood friend of Nino's who loves bad puns and music. He's a prolific and successful songwriter under the name "Momo Kiryu," and he also plays bass in the band Silent Black Kitty, a rival of In No Hurry.

NINO Arisugawa
[Nino]

A high school first-year student who loves to sing. She wears a surgical mask to stop herself from screaming when she becomes emotional. She does the vocals for In No Hurry as "Alice." Her favorite food is negima yakitori.

KANADE Yuzuriha
[Yuzu]

A young composer who met Nino when they were children. He drinks milk constantly in hopes it will help him grow taller. He writes all of In No Hurry's songs and plays guitar as "Cheshire."

Story

★ Music-loving Nino was abandoned twice in her youth—first by her girlhood crush Momo and then by the young composer Yuzu. Believing both their promises that they will find her again through her voice, Nino keeps singing. Later, in high school, she reunites with Yuzu, who invites her to become In No Hurry's new singer. Once again having a reason to sing, Nino throws herself into her vocal training.

★ Meanwhile, Momo has remained nearby, even attending the same high school as Nino as he embarks upon a career as a composer. But out of shame for having sold the songs he wrote for Nino, he studiously avoids her. Now Yuzu's rival, he forms his own masked alternative rock band to compete with In No Hurry. Both bands will face off at the upcoming Rock Horizon music festival.

★ Determined to win, In No Hurry has assembled for a weekend training camp...

Shojo Beat

ANONYMOUS NOISE

Ryoko Fukuyama

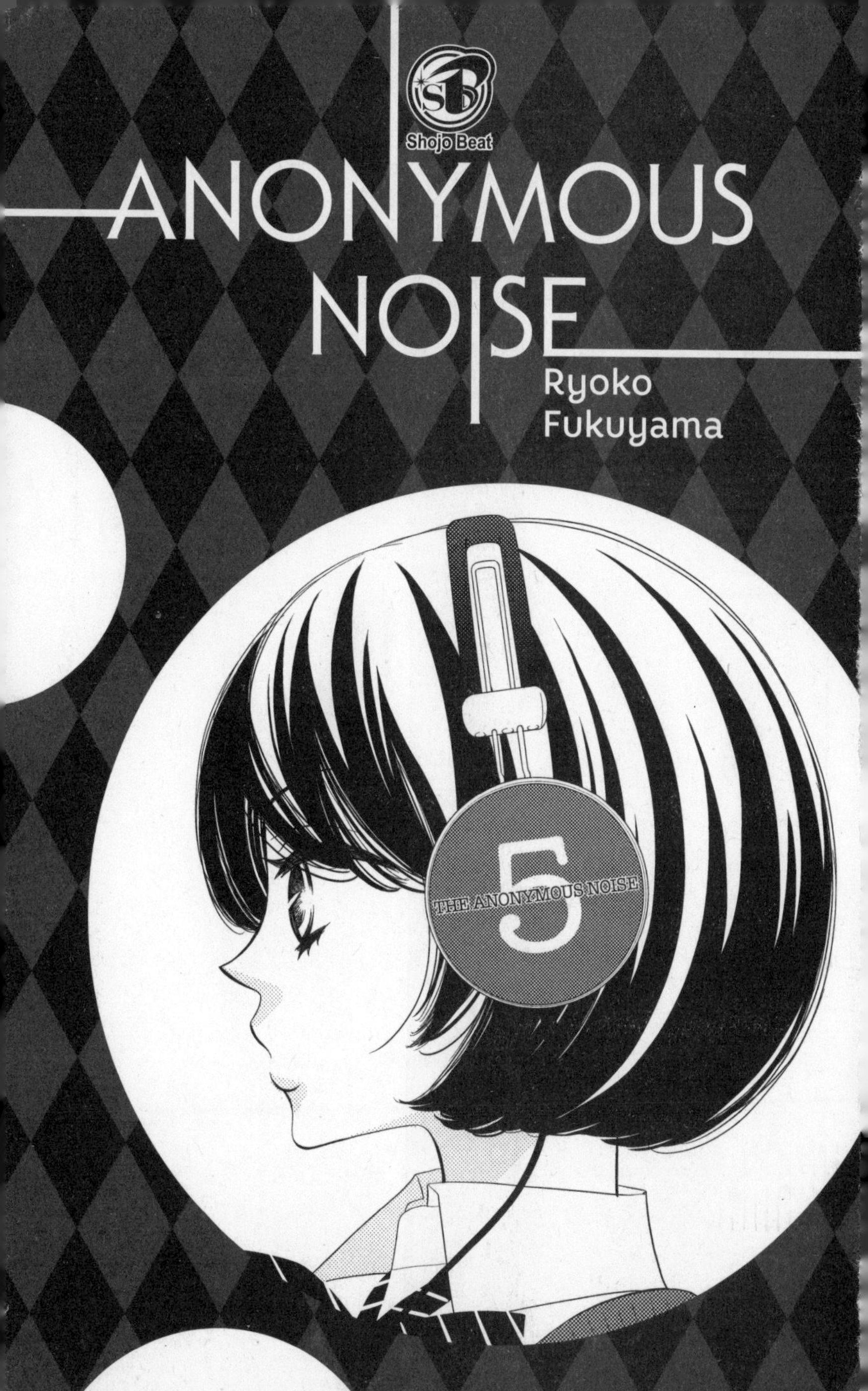
5
THE ANONYMOUS NOISE

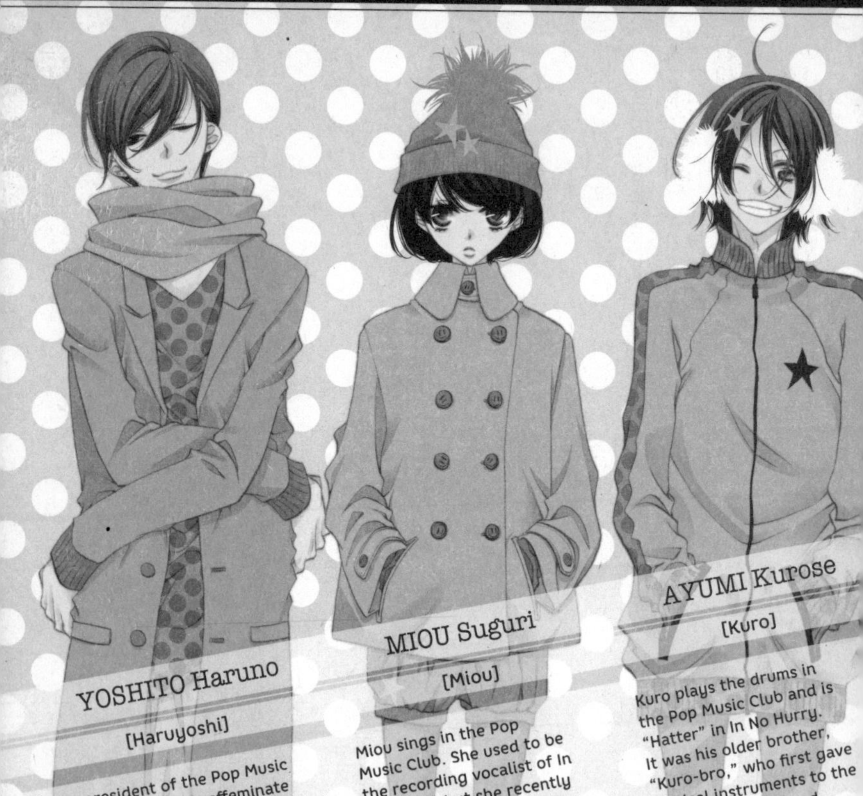

YOSHITO Haruno

[Haruyoshi]

The president of the Pop Music Club, known for his effeminate style of speech. He was the one who convinced Yuzu to join the club after Yuzu had tried to quit music. Haruyoshi plays the bass as "Queen" for In No Hurry.

MIOU Suguri

[Miou]

Miou sings in the Pop Music Club. She used to be the recording vocalist of In No Hurry, but she recently quit. She won an audition to become the vocalist for Silent Black Kitty.

AYUMI Kurose

[Kuro]

Kuro plays the drums in the Pop Music Club and is "Hatter" in In No Hurry. It was his older brother, "Kuro-bro," who first gave musical instruments to the members of the band.

in NO hurry to shout;

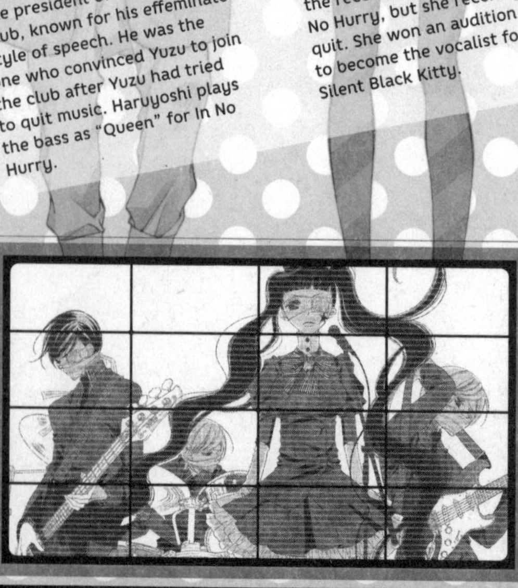

In No Hurry to Shout

A popular rock band whose members hide their identities with masks and eye patches.
Vocals: Alice
Guitar: Cheshire
Bass: Queen
Drums: Hatter

Anonymous
Noise
Volume 5

CONTENTS

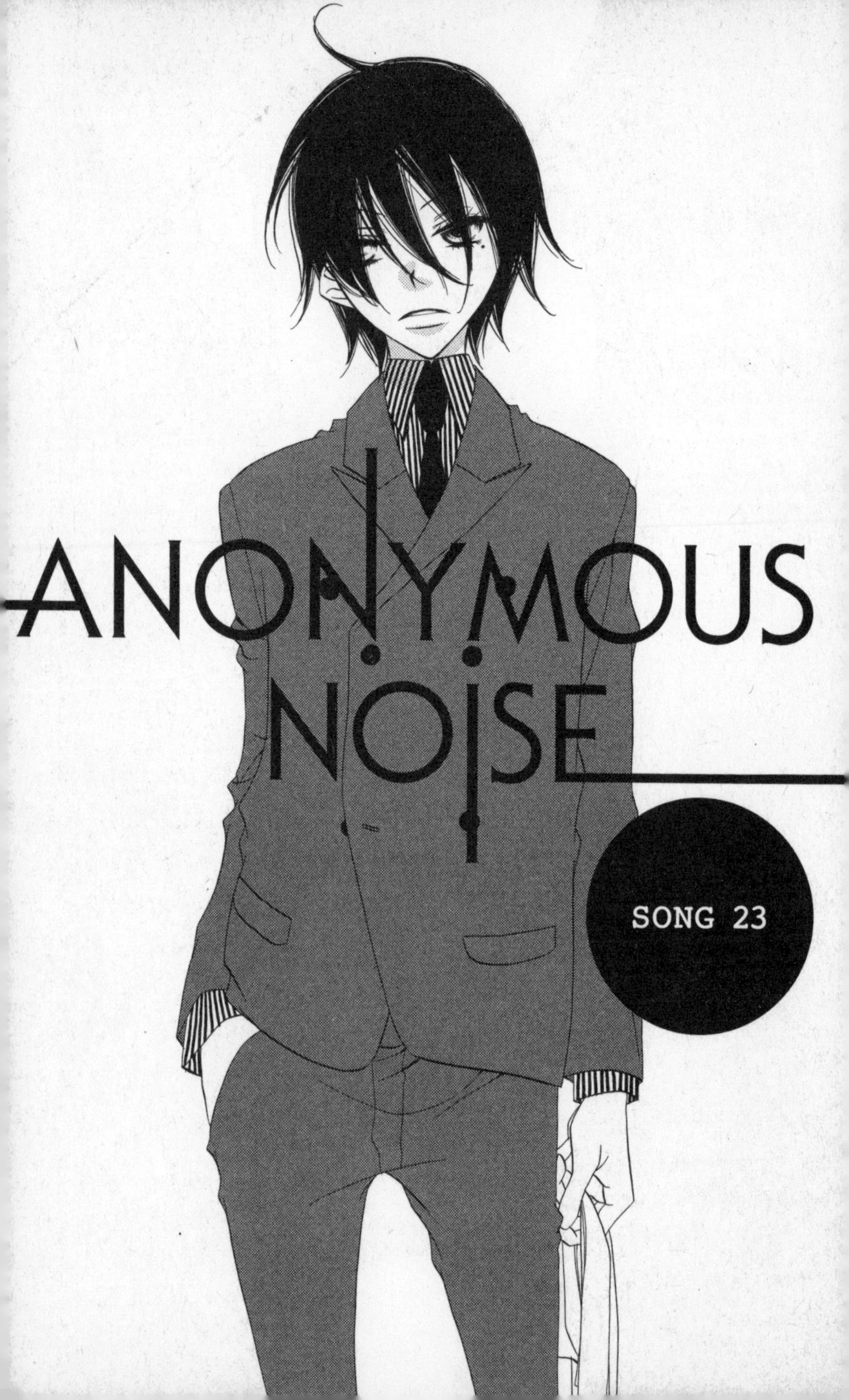
ANONYMOUS
NOISE
SONG 23

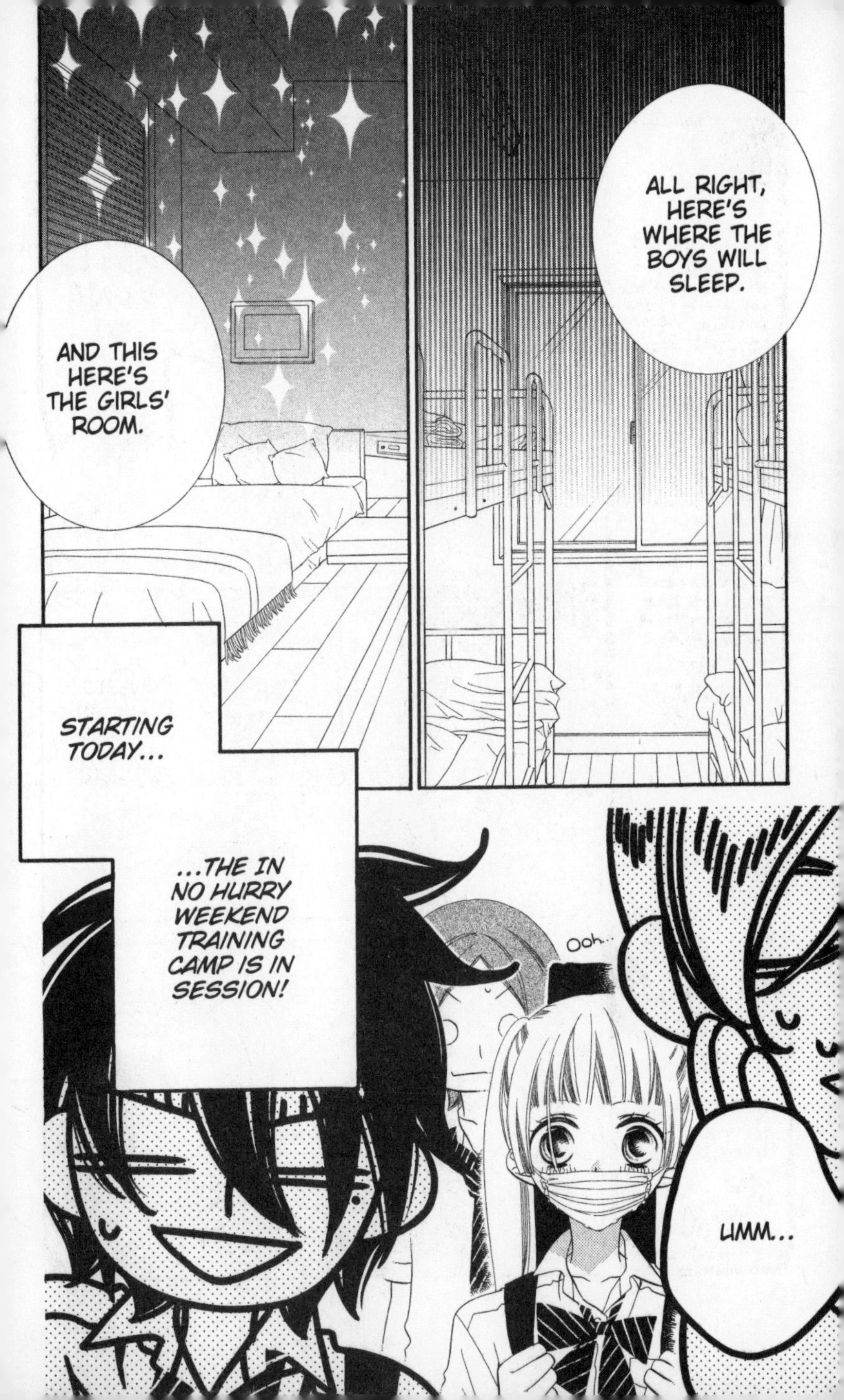
ALL RIGHT, HERE'S WHERE THE BOYS WILL SLEEP.
AND THIS HERE'S THE GIRLS' ROOM.
STARTING TODAY...
...THE IN NO HURRY WEEKEND TRAINING CAMP IS IN SESSION!
UMM...
Ooh...

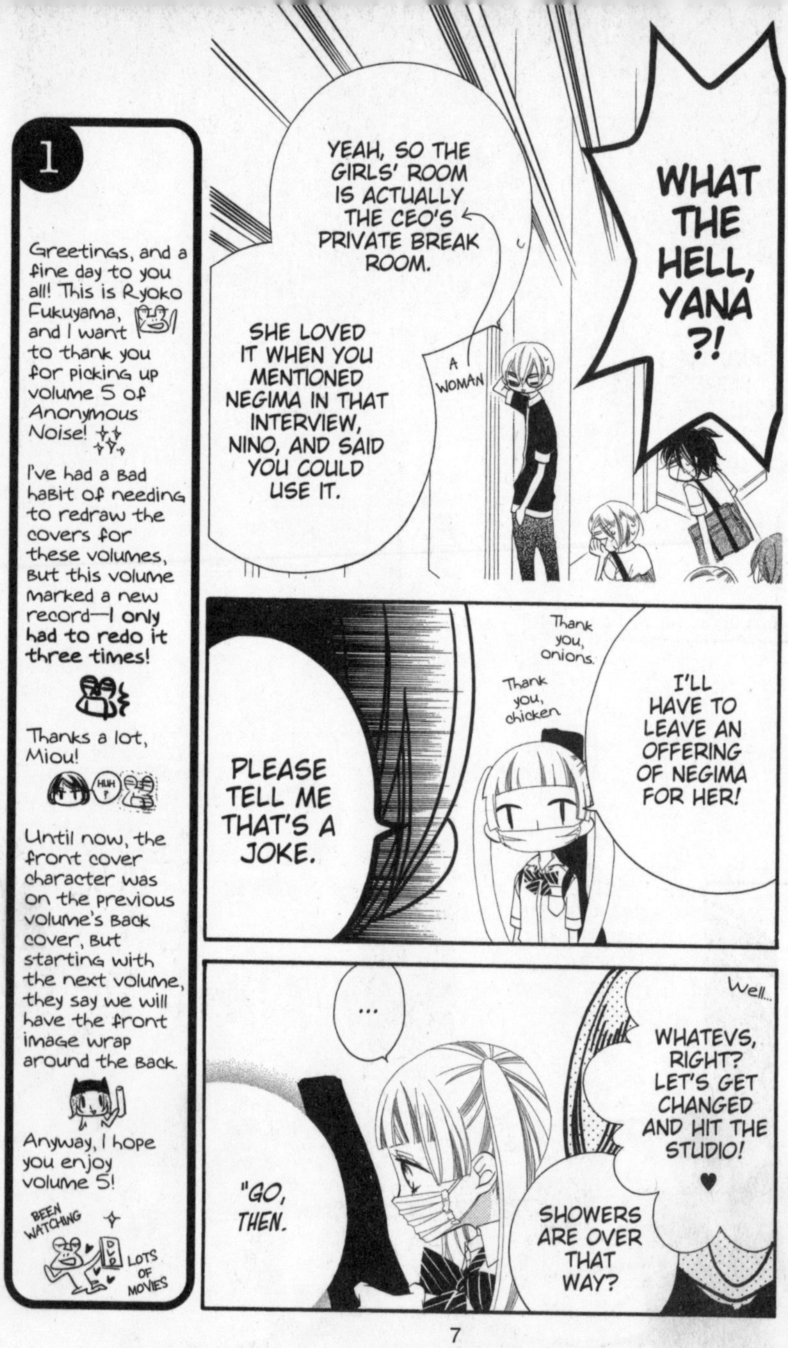
WHAT THE HELL, YANA?!
YEAH, SO THE GIRLS' ROOM IS ACTUALLY THE CEO'S PRIVATE BREAK ROOM.
A WOMAN
SHE LOVED IT WHEN YOU MENTIONED NEGIMA IN THAT INTERVIEW, NINO, AND SAID YOU COULD USE IT.
I'LL HAVE TO LEAVE AN OFFERING OF NEGIMA FOR HER!
Thank you, onions.
Thank you, chicken.
PLEASE TELL ME THAT'S A JOKE.
Well...
WHATEVS, RIGHT? LET'S GET CHANGED AND HIT THE STUDIO! ♥
SHOWERS ARE OVER THAT WAY?
...
"GO, THEN.

1

Greetings, and a fine day to you all! This is Ryoko Fukuyama, and I want to thank you for picking up volume 5 of Anonymous Noise!

I've had a bad habit of needing to redraw the covers for these volumes, but this volume marked a new record—**I only had to redo it three times!**

Thanks a lot, Miou!

HUH?

Until now, the front cover character was on the previous volume's back cover, but starting with the next volume, they say we will have the front image wrap around the back.

Anyway, I hope you enjoy volume 5!

BEEN WATCHING LOTS OF MOVIES

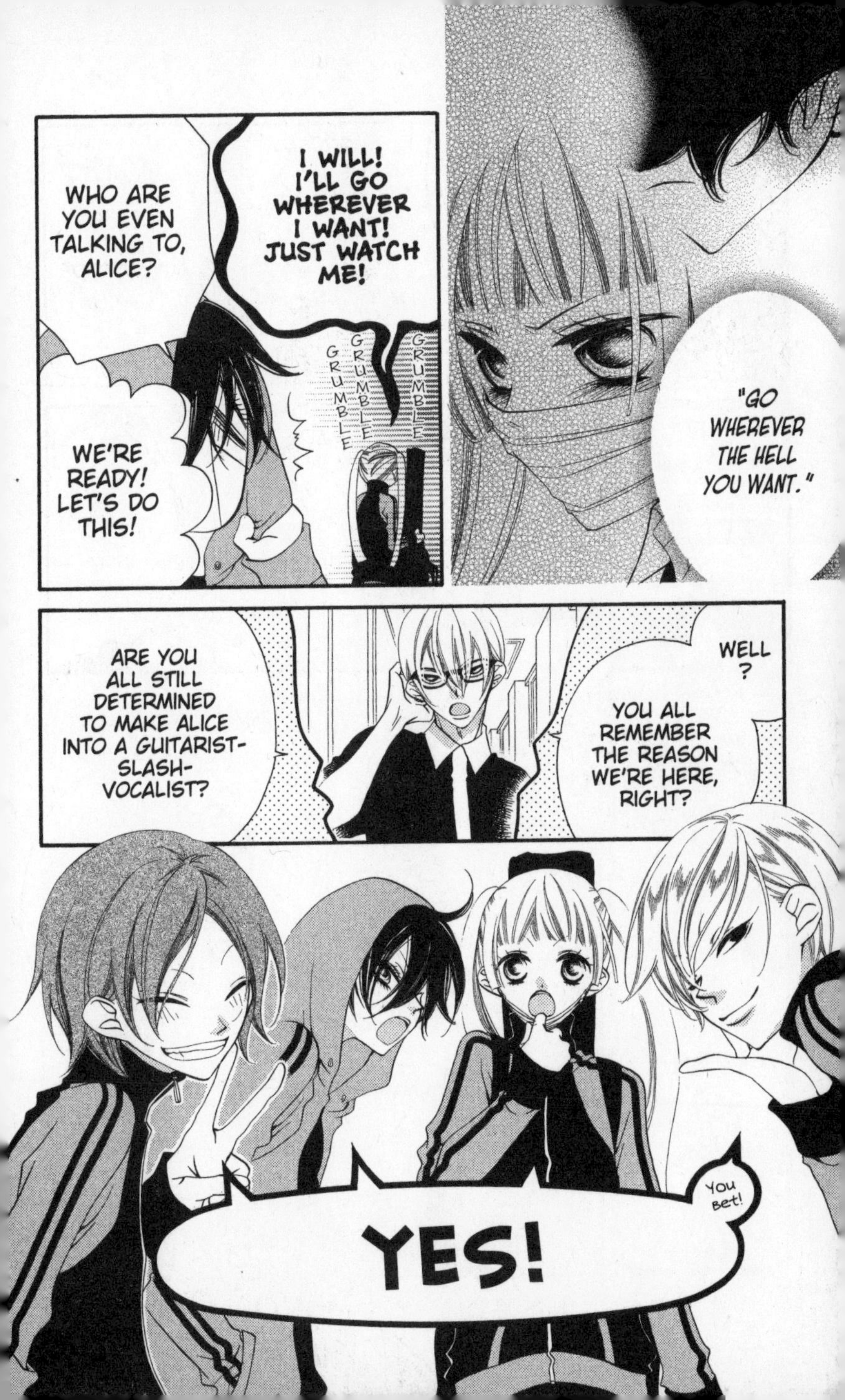
"GO WHEREVER THE HELL YOU WANT."
I WILL! I'LL GO WHEREVER I WANT! JUST WATCH ME!
WHO ARE YOU EVEN TALKING TO, ALICE?
GRUMBLE GRUMBLE GRUMBLE
WE'RE READY! LET'S DO THIS!
WELL?
YOU ALL REMEMBER THE REASON WE'RE HERE, RIGHT?
ARE YOU ALL STILL DETERMINED TO MAKE ALICE INTO A GUITARIST-SLASH-VOCALIST?
You bet!
YES!

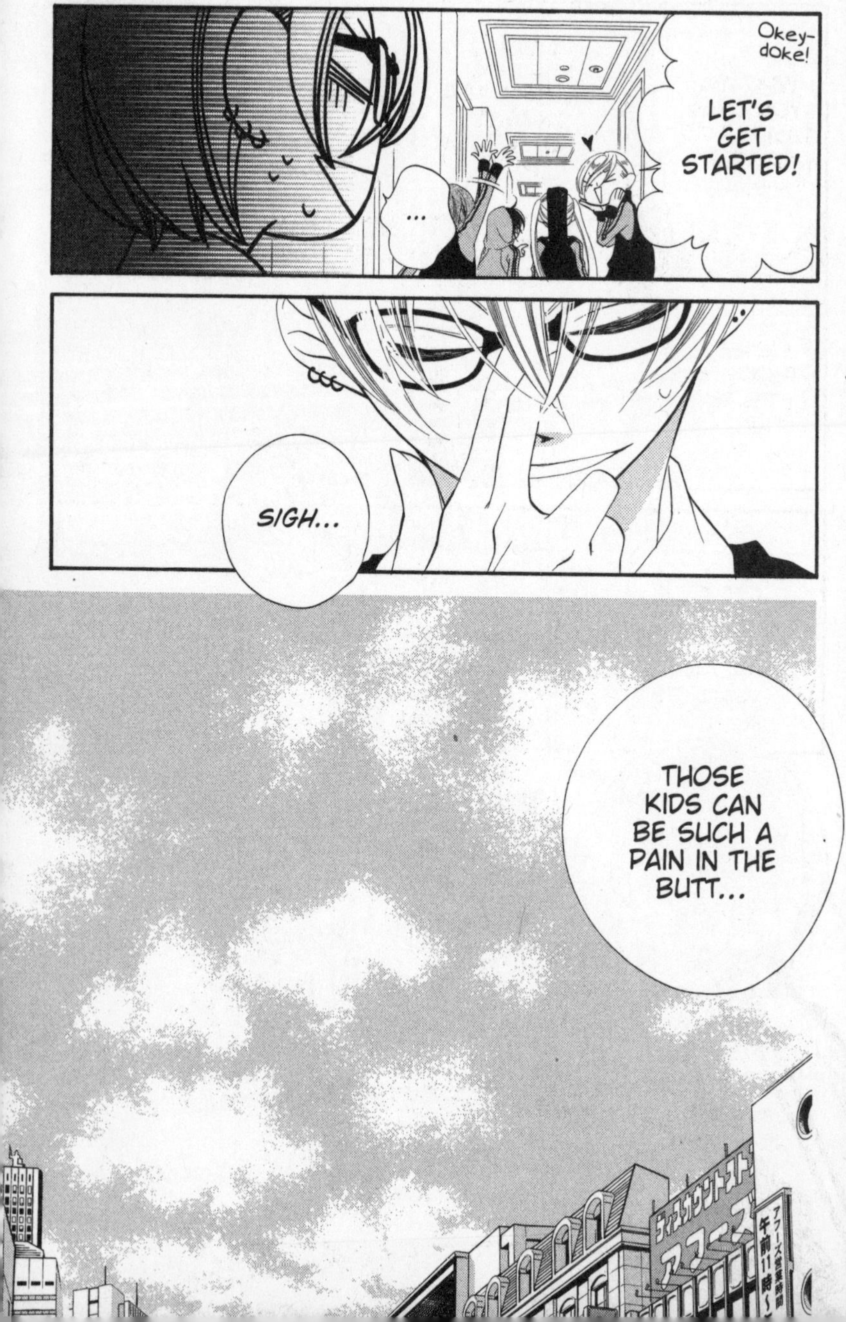
Okey-doke!
LET'S GET STARTED!
...
SIGH...
THOSE KIDS CAN BE SUCH A PAIN IN THE BUTT...

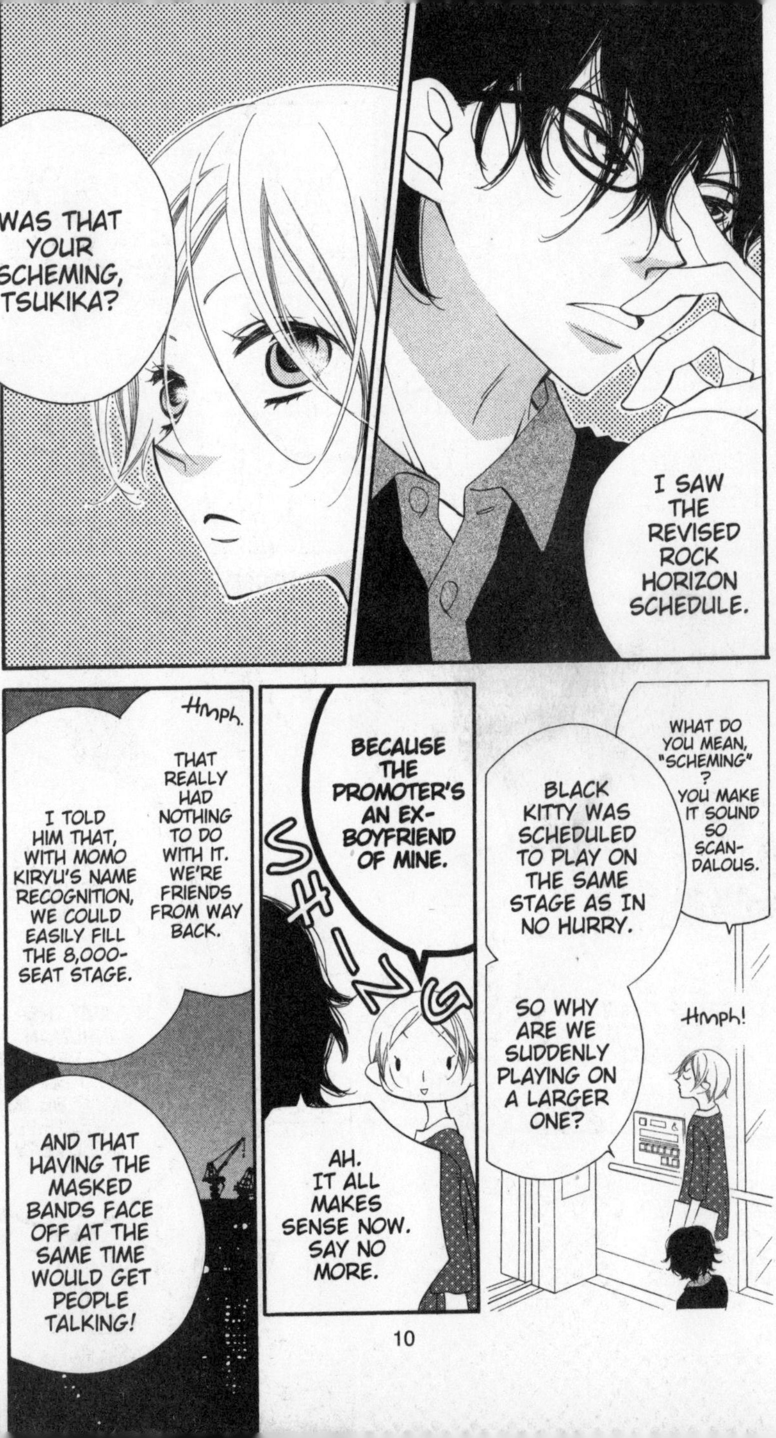
I SAW THE REVISED ROCK HORIZON SCHEDULE.
WAS THAT YOUR SCHEMING, TSUKIKA?
WHAT DO YOU MEAN, "SCHEMING" ? YOU MAKE IT SOUND SO SCAN-DALOUS.
BLACK KITTY WAS SCHEDULED TO PLAY ON THE SAME STAGE AS IN NO HURRY.
Hmph!
SO WHY ARE WE SUDDENLY PLAYING ON A LARGER ONE?
BECAUSE THE PROMOTER'S AN EX-BOYFRIEND OF MINE.
SHI-NG
AH. IT ALL MAKES SENSE NOW. SAY NO MORE.
Hmph.
THAT REALLY HAD NOTHING TO DO WITH IT. WE'RE FRIENDS FROM WAY BACK.
I TOLD HIM THAT, WITH MOMO KIRYU'S NAME RECOGNITION, WE COULD EASILY FILL THE 8,000-SEAT STAGE.
AND THAT HAVING THE MASKED BANDS FACE OFF AT THE SAME TIME WOULD GET PEOPLE TALKING!

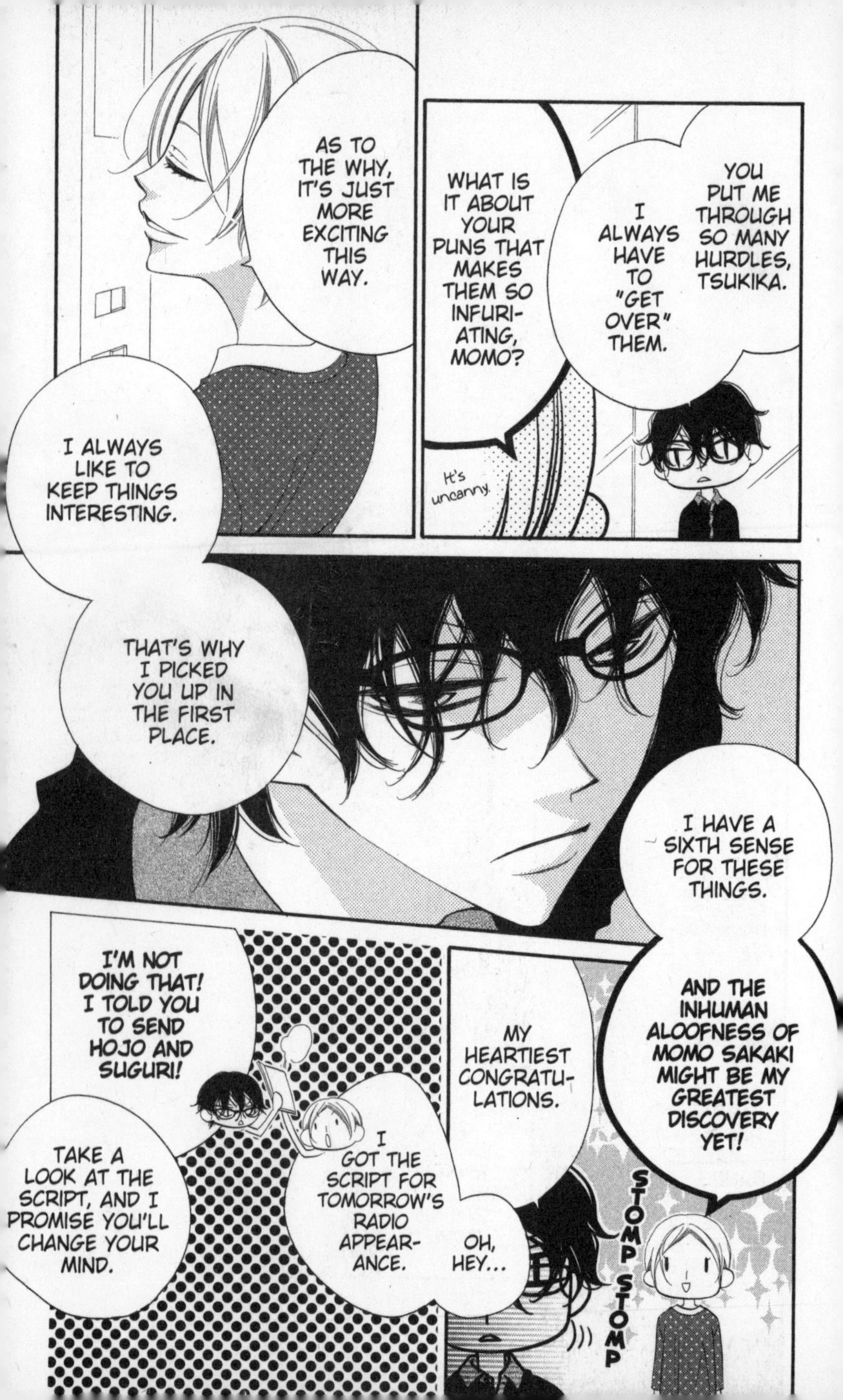
YOU PUT ME THROUGH SO MANY HURDLES, TSUKIKA.
I ALWAYS HAVE TO "GET OVER" THEM.
WHAT IS IT ABOUT YOUR PUNS THAT MAKES THEM SO INFURIATING, MOMO?
It's uncanny.
AS TO THE WHY, IT'S JUST MORE EXCITING THIS WAY.
I ALWAYS LIKE TO KEEP THINGS INTERESTING.
THAT'S WHY I PICKED YOU UP IN THE FIRST PLACE.
I HAVE A SIXTH SENSE FOR THESE THINGS.
AND THE INHUMAN ALOOFNESS OF MOMO SAKAKI MIGHT BE MY GREATEST DISCOVERY YET!
STOMP STOMP
MY HEARTIEST CONGRATULATIONS.
OH, HEY...
I GOT THE SCRIPT FOR TOMORROW'S RADIO APPEARANCE.
I'M NOT DOING THAT! I TOLD YOU TO SEND HOJO AND SUGURI!
TAKE A LOOK AT THE SCRIPT, AND I PROMISE YOU'LL CHANGE YOUR MIND.

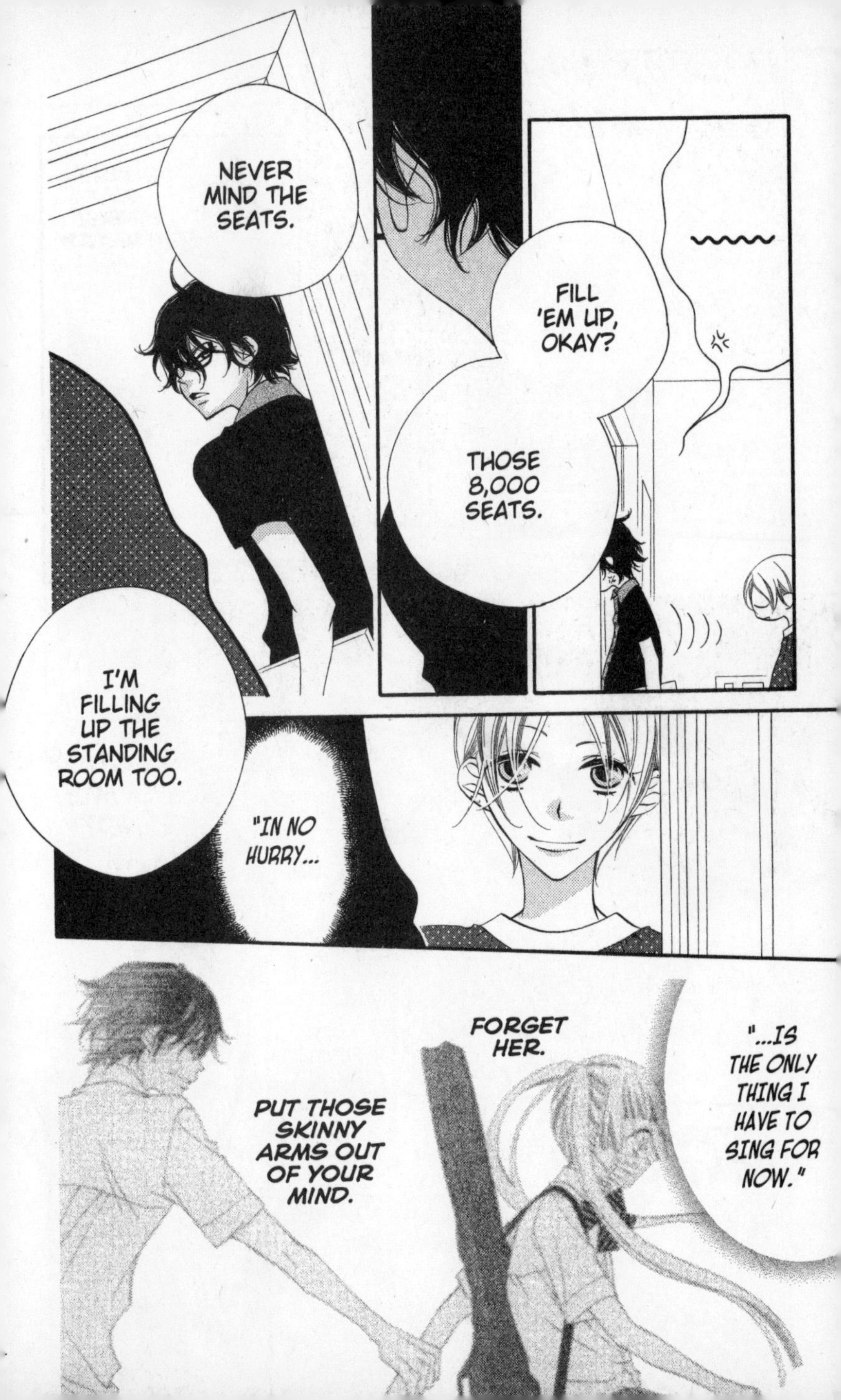

FILL 'EM UP, OKAY?
THOSE 8,000 SEATS.
NEVER MIND THE SEATS.
I'M FILLING UP THE STANDING ROOM TOO.
"IN NO HURRY...
"...IS THE ONLY THING I HAVE TO SING FOR NOW."
FORGET HER.
PUT THOSE SKINNY ARMS OUT OF YOUR MIND.

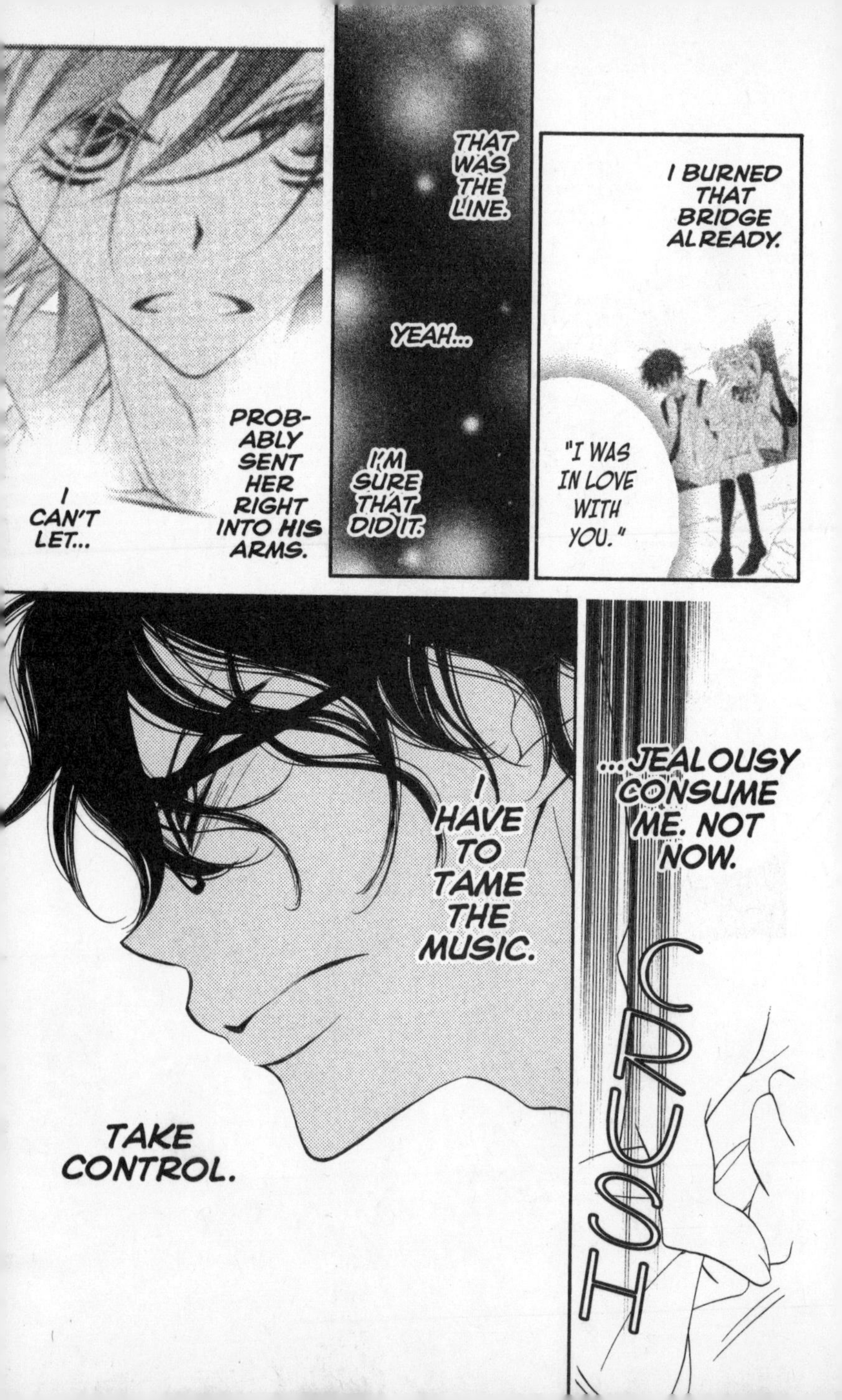
I BURNED THAT BRIDGE ALREADY.
"I WAS IN LOVE WITH YOU."
THAT WAS THE LINE.
YEAH...
I'M SURE THAT DID IT.
PROB-ABLY SENT HER RIGHT INTO HIS ARMS.
I CAN'T LET...
...JEALOUSY CONSUME ME. NOT NOW.
CRUSH
I HAVE TO TAME THE MUSIC.
TAKE CONTROL.

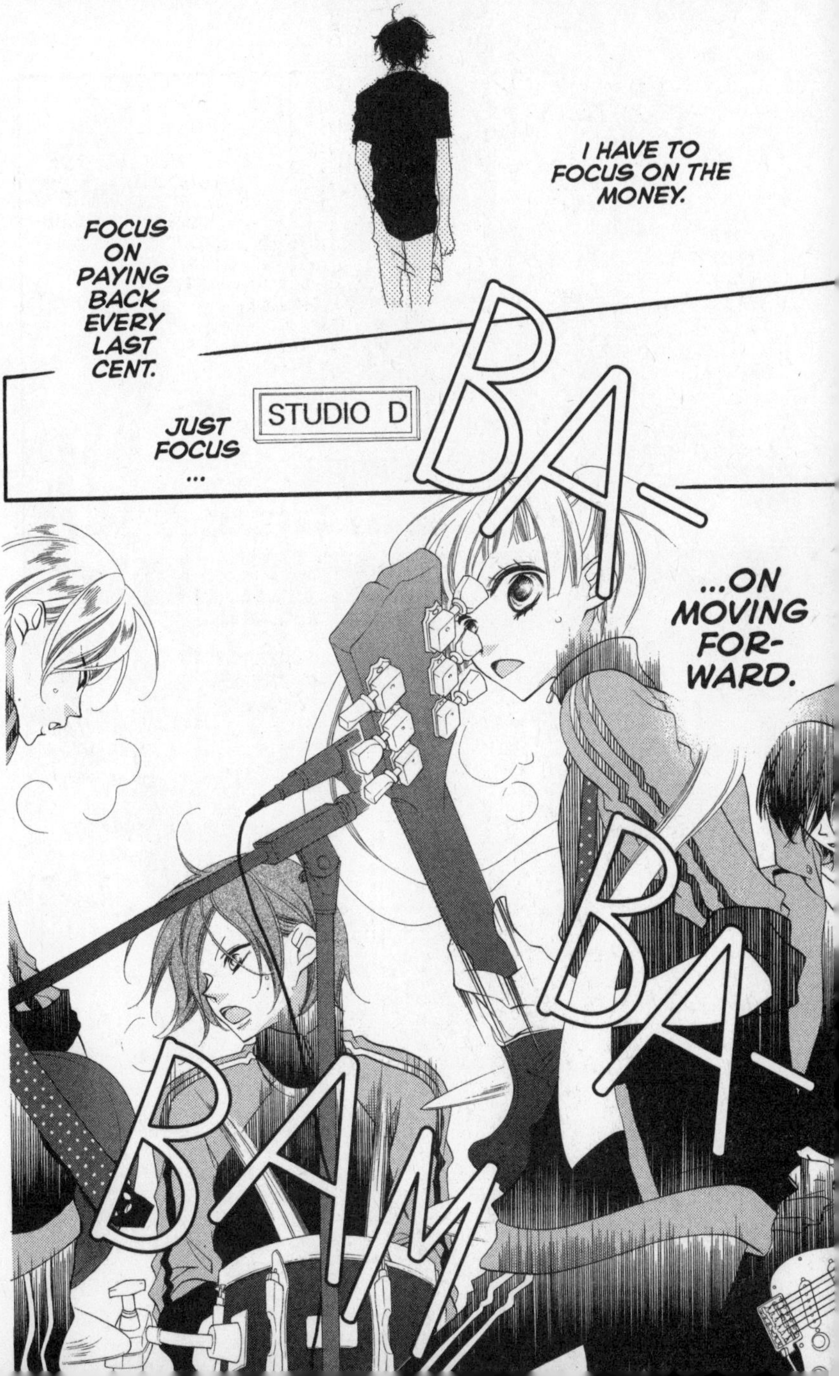
I HAVE TO FOCUS ON THE MONEY.
FOCUS ON PAYING BACK EVERY LAST CENT.
BA-
STUDIO D
JUST FOCUS ...
...ON MOVING FORWARD.
BA-
BAM

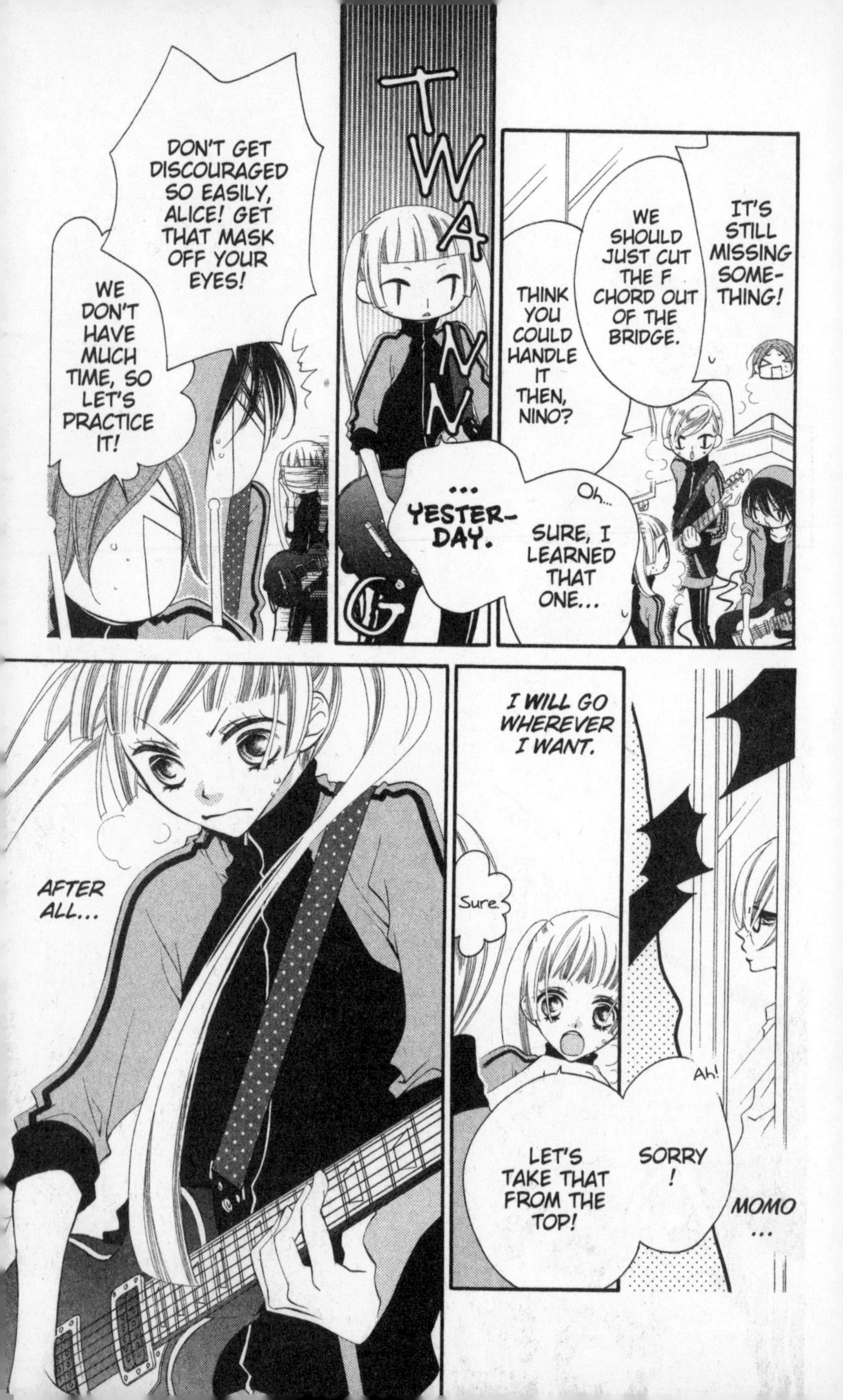
IT'S STILL MISSING SOME-THING!
WE SHOULD JUST CUT THE F CHORD OUT OF THE BRIDGE.
THINK YOU COULD HANDLE IT THEN, NINO?
Oh...
SURE, I LEARNED THAT ONE...
TWANG
... YESTER-DAY.
DON'T GET DISCOURAGED SO EASILY, ALICE! GET THAT MASK OFF YOUR EYES!
WE DON'T HAVE MUCH TIME, SO LET'S PRACTICE IT!
MOMO...
I WILL GO WHEREVER I WANT.
Sure.
Ah!
SORRY!
LET'S TAKE THAT FROM THE TOP!
AFTER ALL...

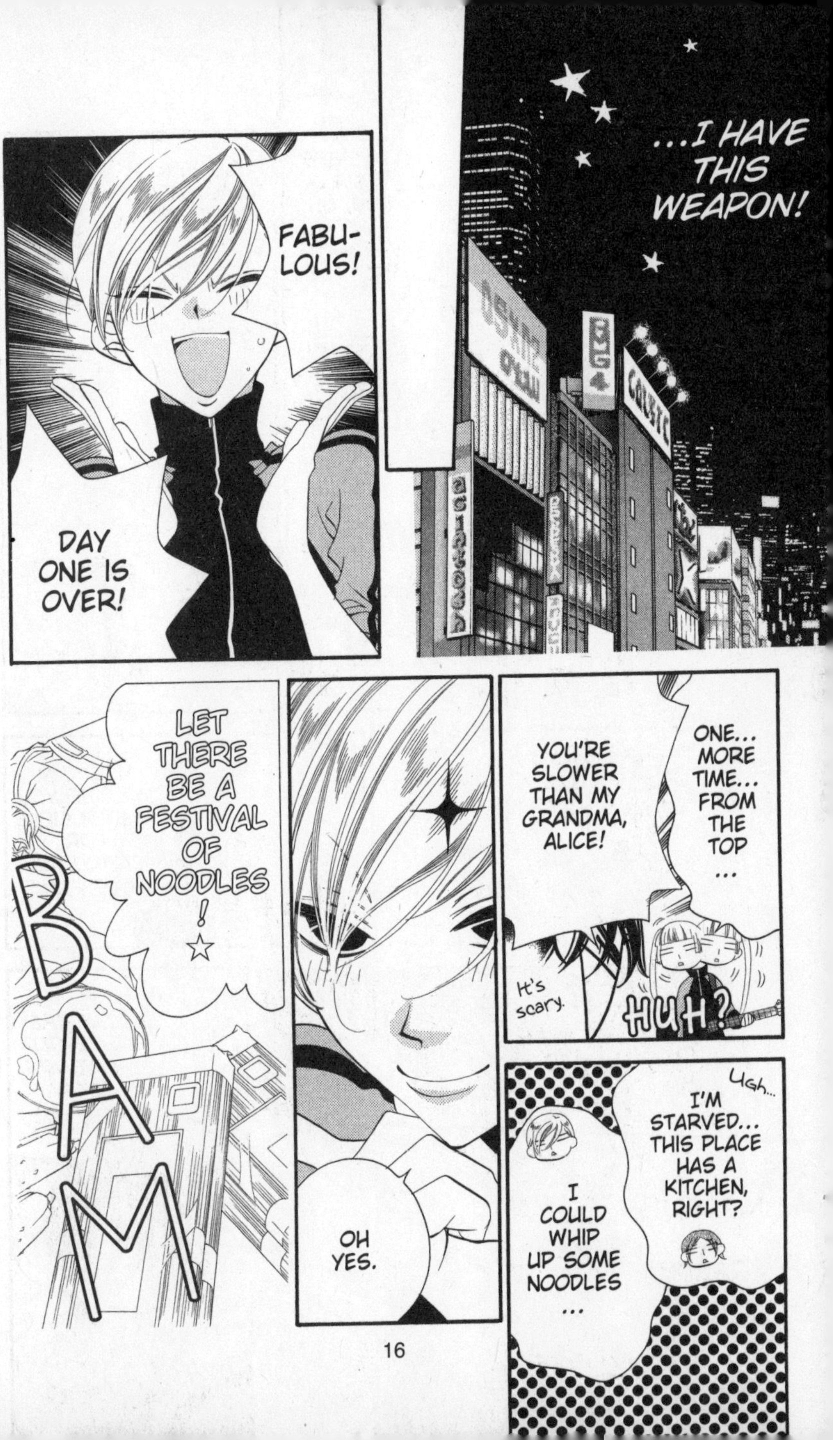
...I HAVE THIS WEAPON!
FABULOUS!
DAY ONE IS OVER!
ONE... MORE TIME... FROM THE TOP...
YOU'RE SLOWER THAN MY GRANDMA, ALICE!
It's scary.
HUH?
Ugh...
I'M STARVED... THIS PLACE HAS A KITCHEN, RIGHT?
I COULD WHIP UP SOME NOODLES...
OH YES.
LET THERE BE A FESTIVAL OF NOODLES! ☆
BAM

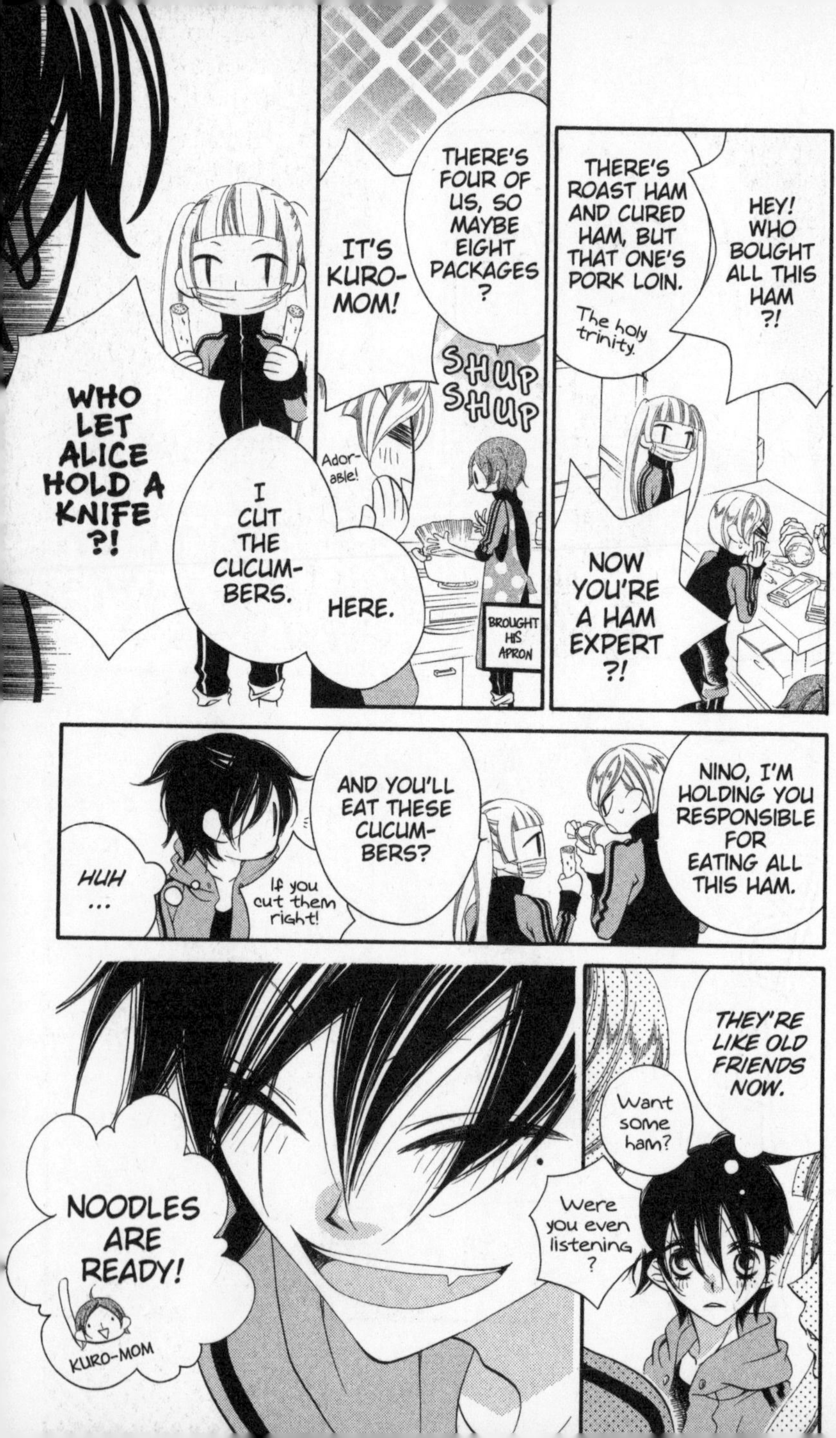
HEY! WHO BOUGHT ALL THIS HAM?!
THERE'S ROAST HAM AND CURED HAM, BUT THAT ONE'S PORK LOIN.
The holy trinity.
NOW YOU'RE A HAM EXPERT?!
THERE'S FOUR OF US, SO MAYBE EIGHT PACKAGES?
IT'S KURO-MOM!
SHUP SHUP
Adorable!
HERE.
BROUGHT HIS APRON
I CUT THE CUCUMBERS.
WHO LET ALICE HOLD A KNIFE?!
NINO, I'M HOLDING YOU RESPONSIBLE FOR EATING ALL THIS HAM.
AND YOU'LL EAT THESE CUCUMBERS?
If you cut them right!
HUH...
THEY'RE LIKE OLD FRIENDS NOW.
Want some ham?
Were you even listening?
NOODLES ARE READY!
KURO-MOM

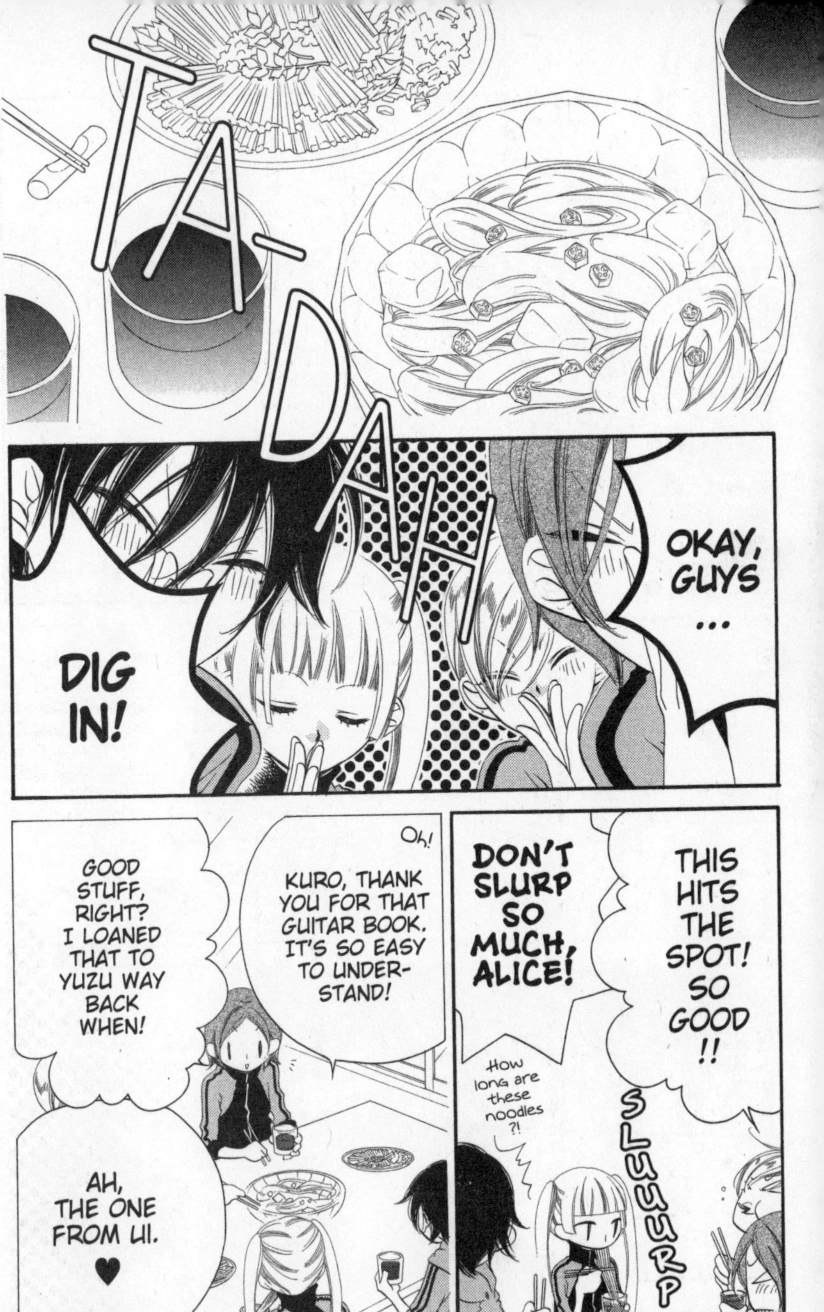
TA-DAH
OKAY, GUYS...
DIG IN!
THIS HITS THE SPOT! SO GOOD!!
DON'T SLURP SO MUCH, ALICE!
How long are these noodles?!
SLUURP
Oh!
KURO, THANK YOU FOR THAT GUITAR BOOK. IT'S SO EASY TO UNDERSTAND!
GOOD STUFF, RIGHT? I LOANED THAT TO YUZU WAY BACK WHEN!
AH, THE ONE FROM LII. ♥

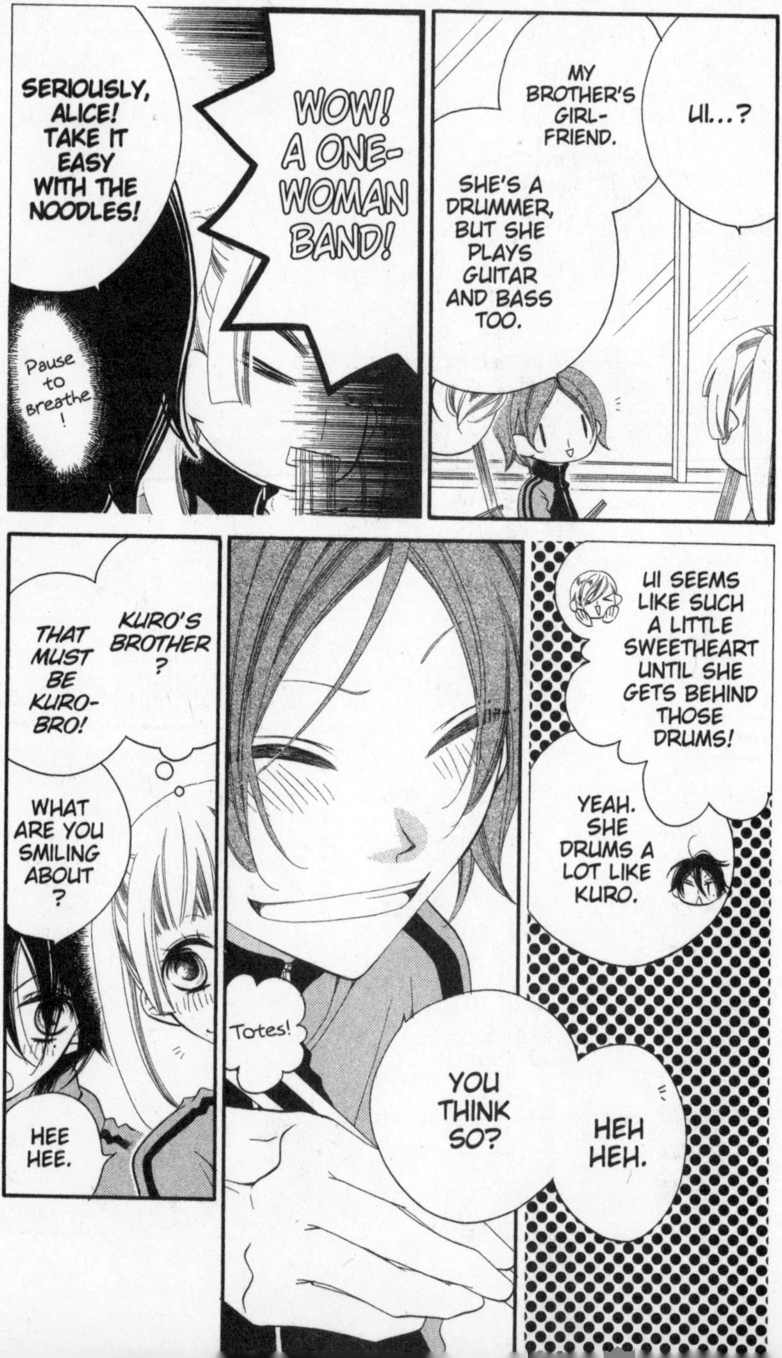
UI...?
MY BROTHER'S GIRL-FRIEND.
SHE'S A DRUMMER, BUT SHE PLAYS GUITAR AND BASS TOO.
WOW! A ONE-WOMAN BAND!
SERIOUSLY, ALICE! TAKE IT EASY WITH THE NOODLES!
Pause to breathe!
UI SEEMS LIKE SUCH A LITTLE SWEETHEART UNTIL SHE GETS BEHIND THOSE DRUMS!
YEAH. SHE DRUMS A LOT LIKE KURO.
YOU THINK SO? HEH HEH.
Totes!
KURO'S BROTHER?
THAT MUST BE KURO-BRO!
WHAT ARE YOU SMILING ABOUT?
HEE HEE.

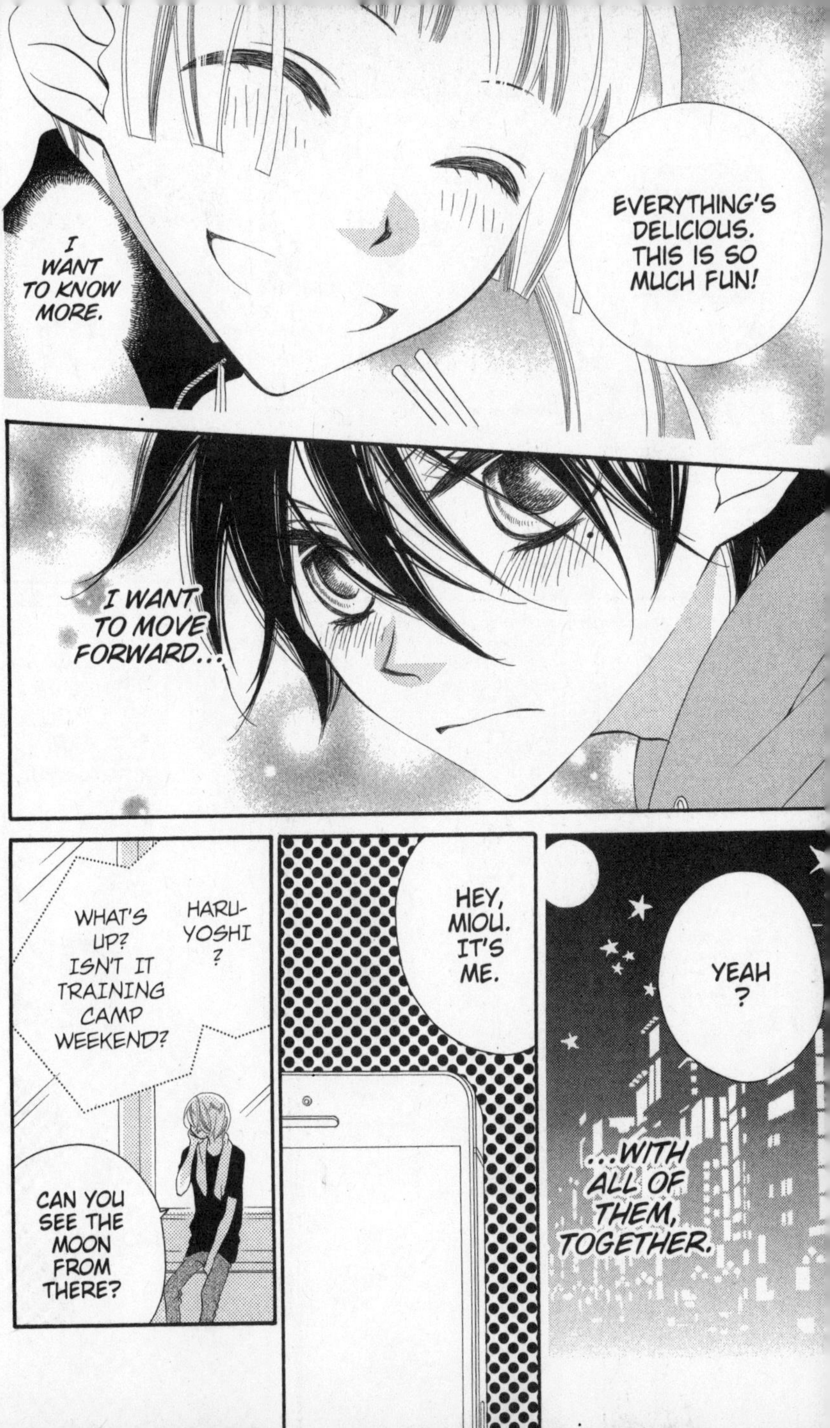
EVERYTHING'S DELICIOUS. THIS IS SO MUCH FUN!
I WANT TO KNOW MORE.
I WANT TO MOVE FORWARD...
YEAH?
...WITH ALL OF THEM, TOGETHER.
HEY, MIOU. IT'S ME.
HARU-YOSHI?
WHAT'S UP? ISN'T IT TRAINING CAMP WEEKEND?
CAN YOU SEE THE MOON FROM THERE?

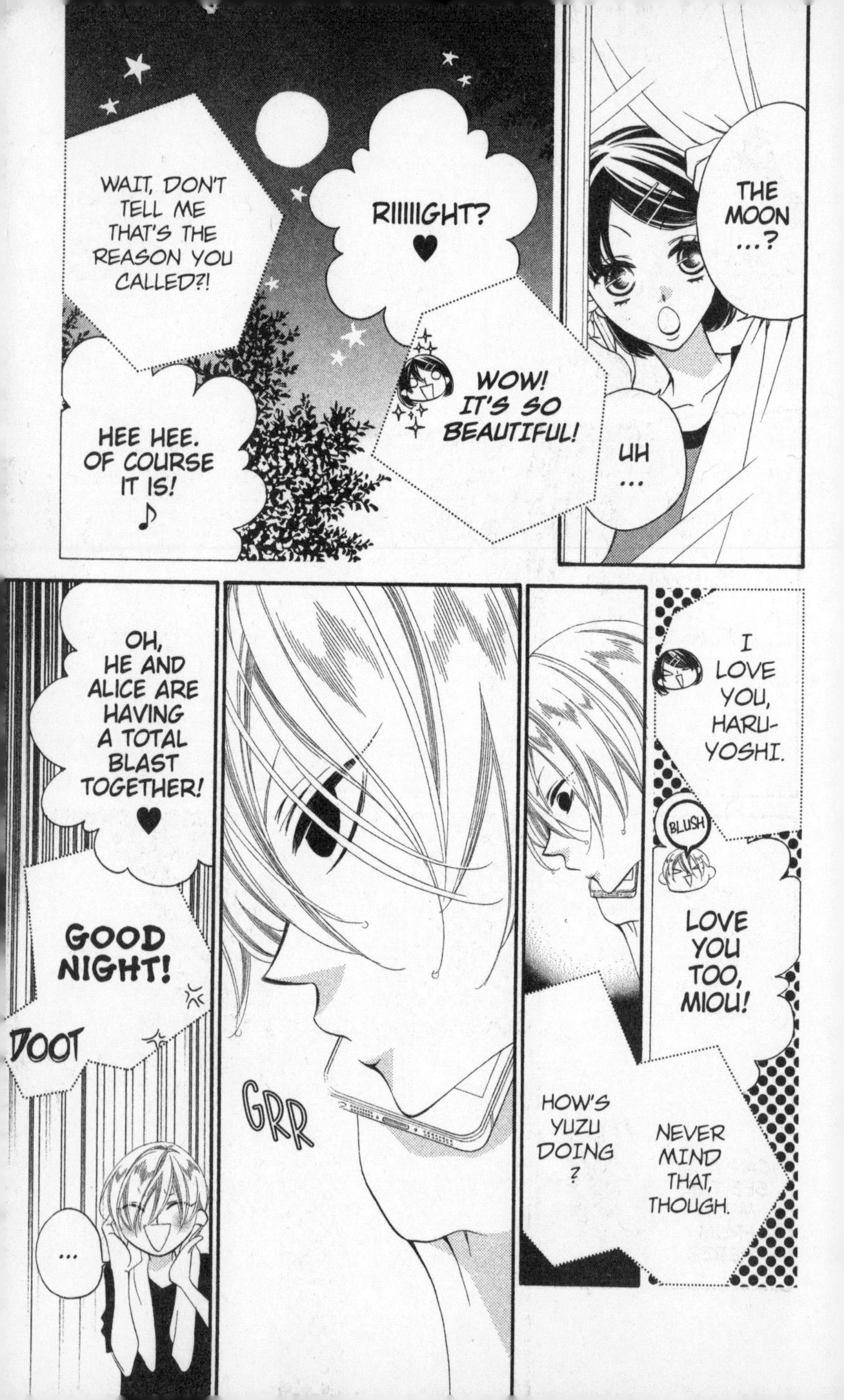
THE MOON ...?
UH ...
WOW! IT'S SO BEAUTIFUL!
RIIIIIGHT? ♥
WAIT, DON'T TELL ME THAT'S THE REASON YOU CALLED?!
HEE HEE. OF COURSE IT IS! ♪
I LOVE YOU, HARU-YOSHI.
BLUSH
LOVE YOU TOO, MIOU!
NEVER MIND THAT, THOUGH.
HOW'S YUZU DOING?
GRR
OH, HE AND ALICE ARE HAVING A TOTAL BLAST TOGETHER! ♥
GOOD NIGHT!
DOOT
...

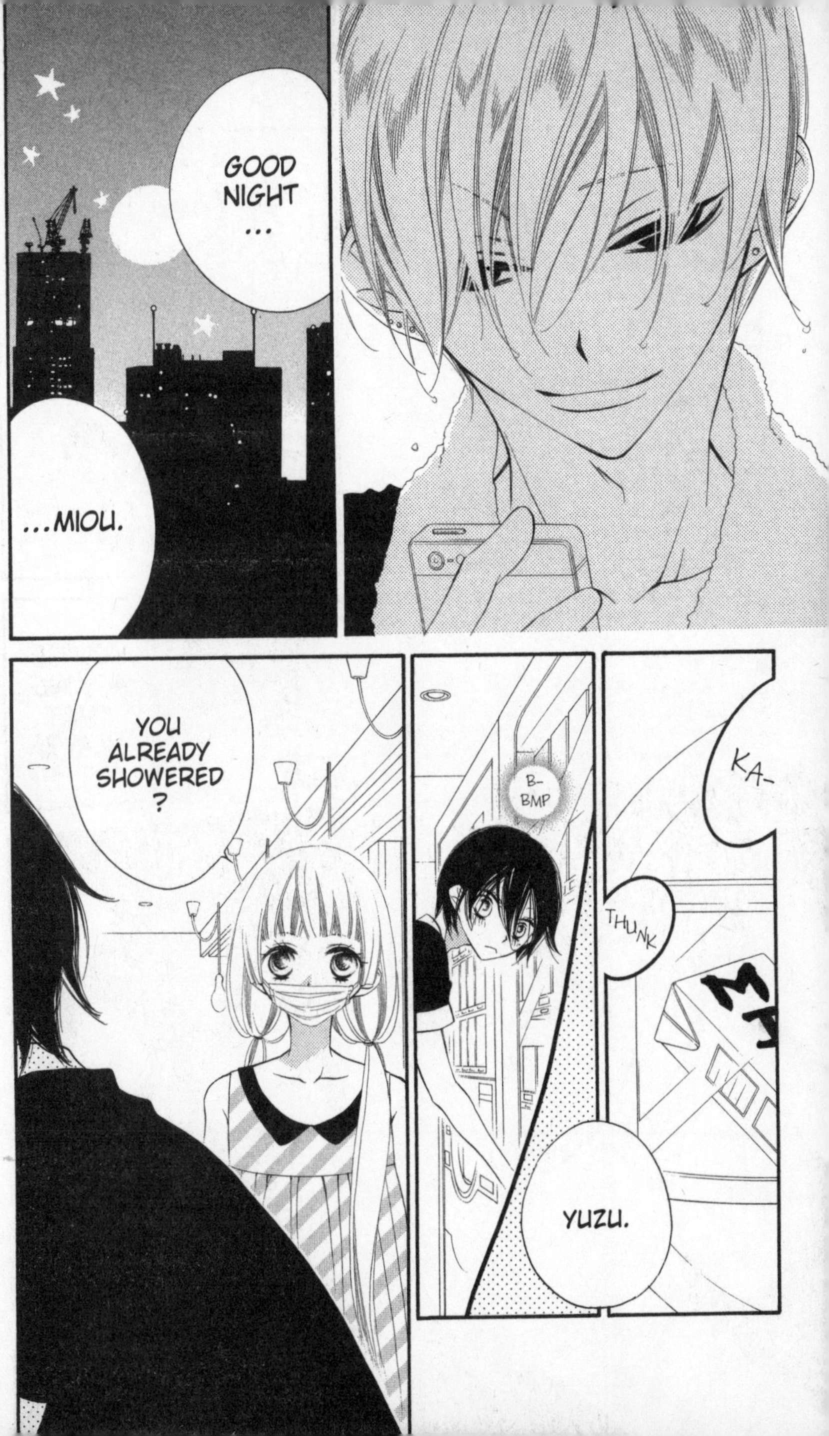
GOOD NIGHT ...
...MIOU.
KA-
THUNK
YUZU.
B-BMP
YOU ALREADY SHOWERED?

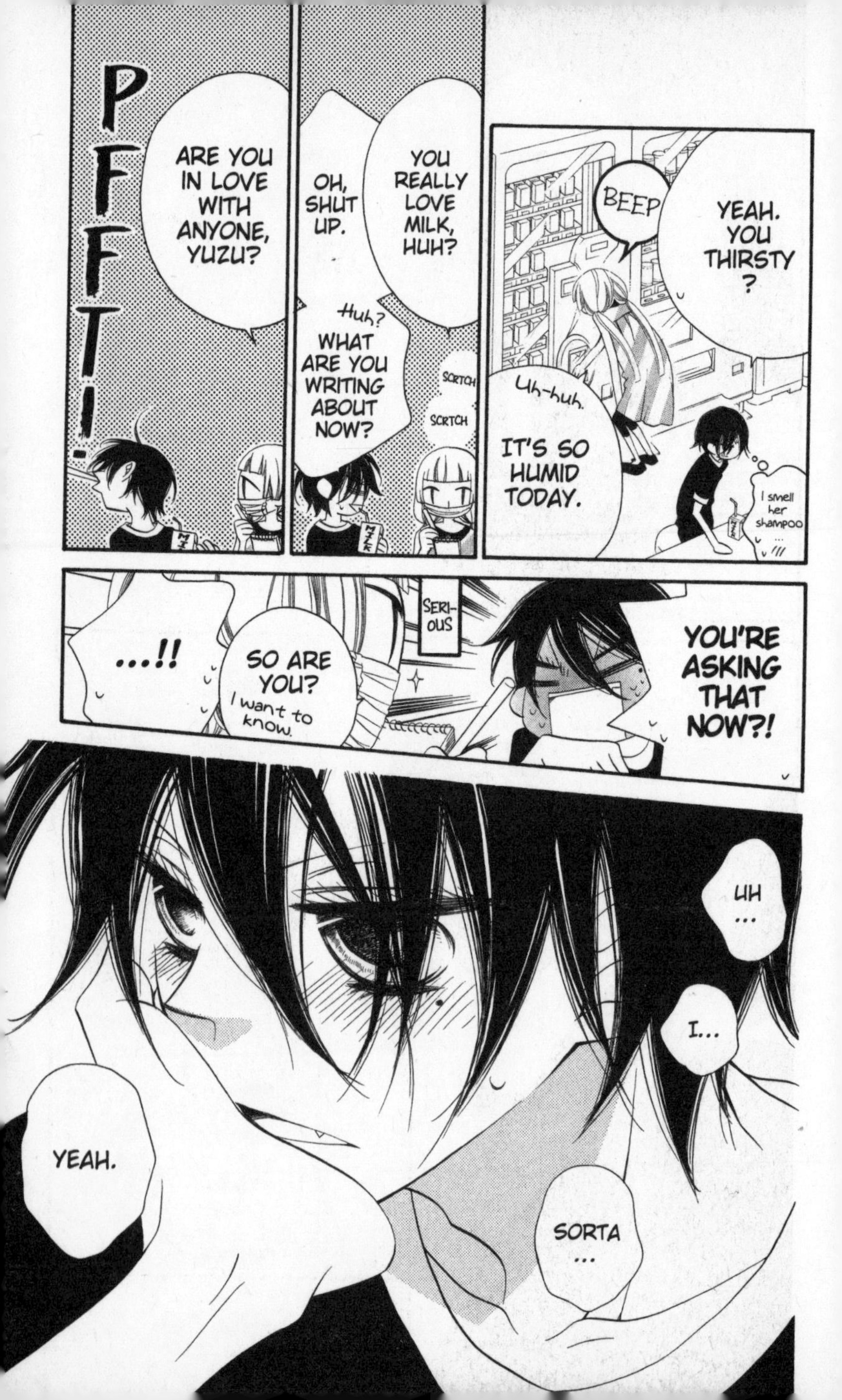
BEEP
YEAH. YOU THIRSTY?
Uh-huh.
IT'S SO HUMID TODAY.
I smell her shampoo ...
YOU REALLY LOVE MILK, HUH?
OH, SHUT UP.
Huh?
WHAT ARE YOU WRITING ABOUT NOW?
SCRTCH
SCRTCH
ARE YOU IN LOVE WITH ANYONE, YUZU?
PFFT!!
YOU'RE ASKING THAT NOW?!
SERI-OUS
SO ARE YOU?
I want to know.
...!!
UH ...
I...
SORTA ...
YEAH.

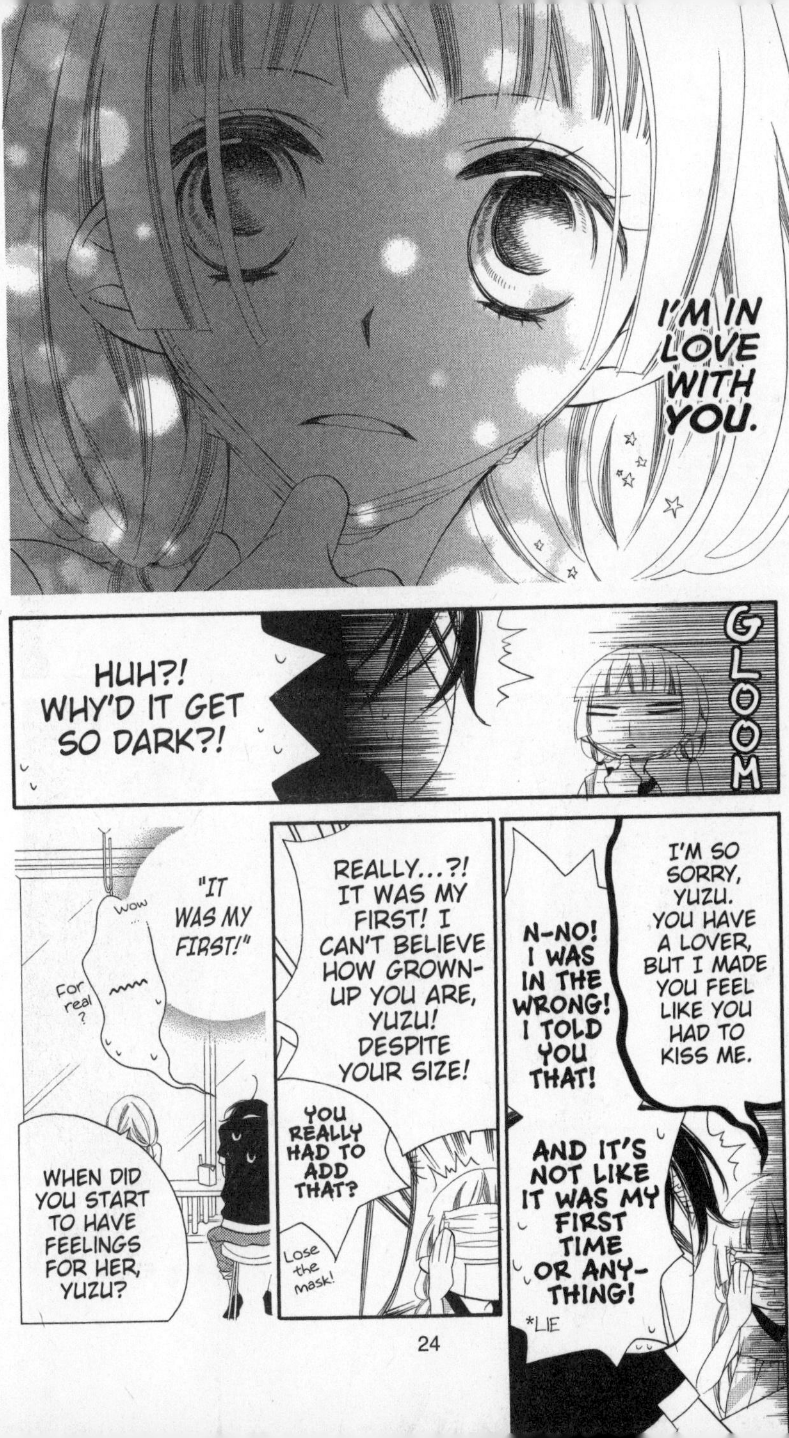
I'M IN LOVE WITH YOU.
GLOOM
HUH?! WHY'D IT GET SO DARK?!
I'M SO SORRY, YUZU. YOU HAVE A LOVER, BUT I MADE YOU FEEL LIKE YOU HAD TO KISS ME.
N-NO! I WAS IN THE WRONG! I TOLD YOU THAT!
AND IT'S NOT LIKE IT WAS MY FIRST TIME OR ANY-THING!
*LIE
REALLY...?! IT WAS MY FIRST! I CAN'T BELIEVE HOW GROWN-UP YOU ARE, YUZU! DESPITE YOUR SIZE!
YOU REALLY HAD TO ADD THAT?
Lose the mask!
"IT WAS MY FIRST!"
Wow...
For real?
WHEN DID YOU START TO HAVE FEELINGS FOR HER, YUZU?

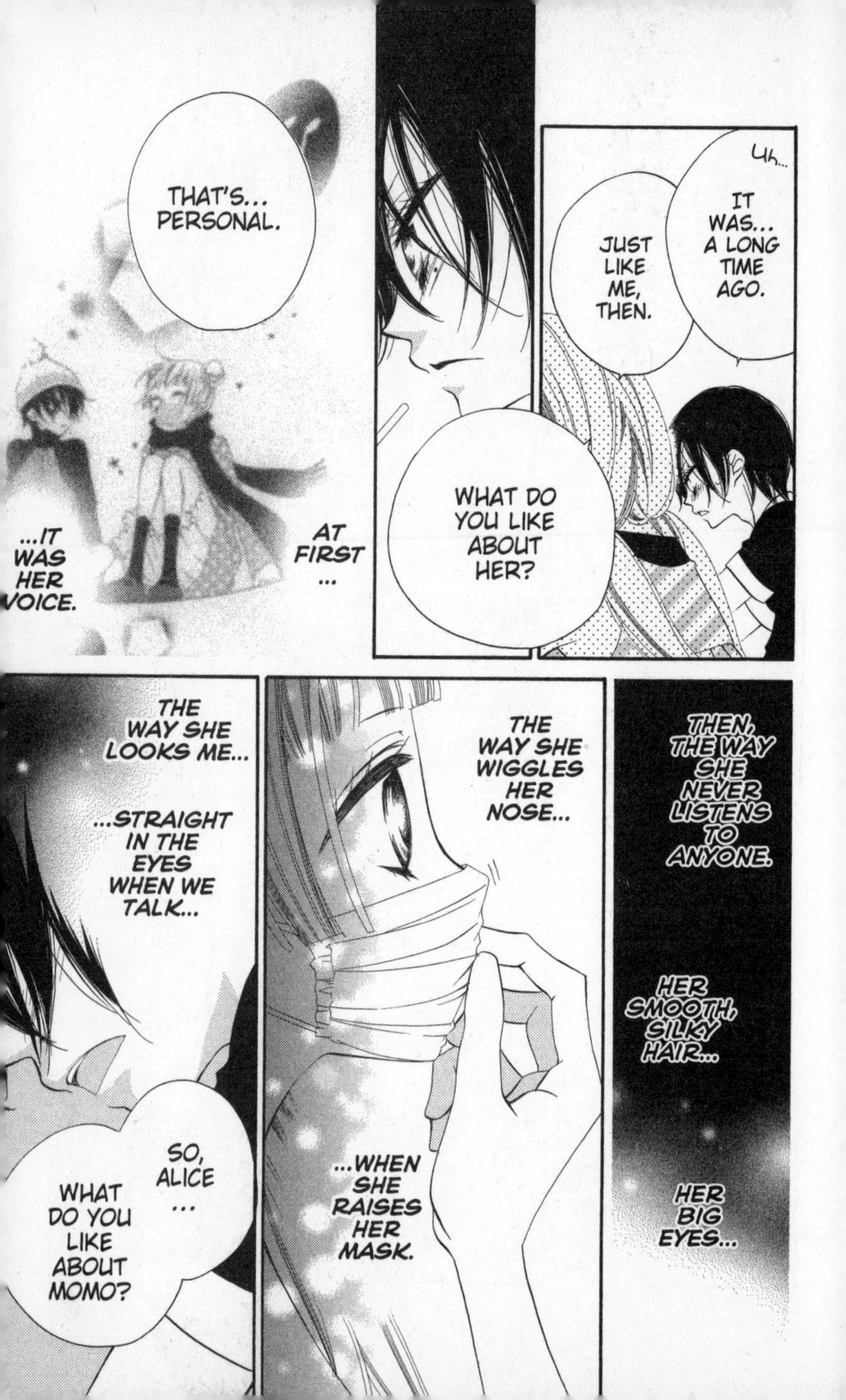
Uh...
IT WAS... A LONG TIME AGO.
JUST LIKE ME, THEN.
WHAT DO YOU LIKE ABOUT HER?
THAT'S... PERSONAL.
AT FIRST ...
...IT WAS HER VOICE.
THEN, THE WAY SHE NEVER LISTENS TO ANYONE.
HER SMOOTH, SILKY HAIR...
HER BIG EYES...
THE WAY SHE WIGGLES HER NOSE...
...WHEN SHE RAISES HER MASK.
THE WAY SHE LOOKS ME...
...STRAIGHT IN THE EYES WHEN WE TALK...
SO, ALICE ...
WHAT DO YOU LIKE ABOUT MOMO?

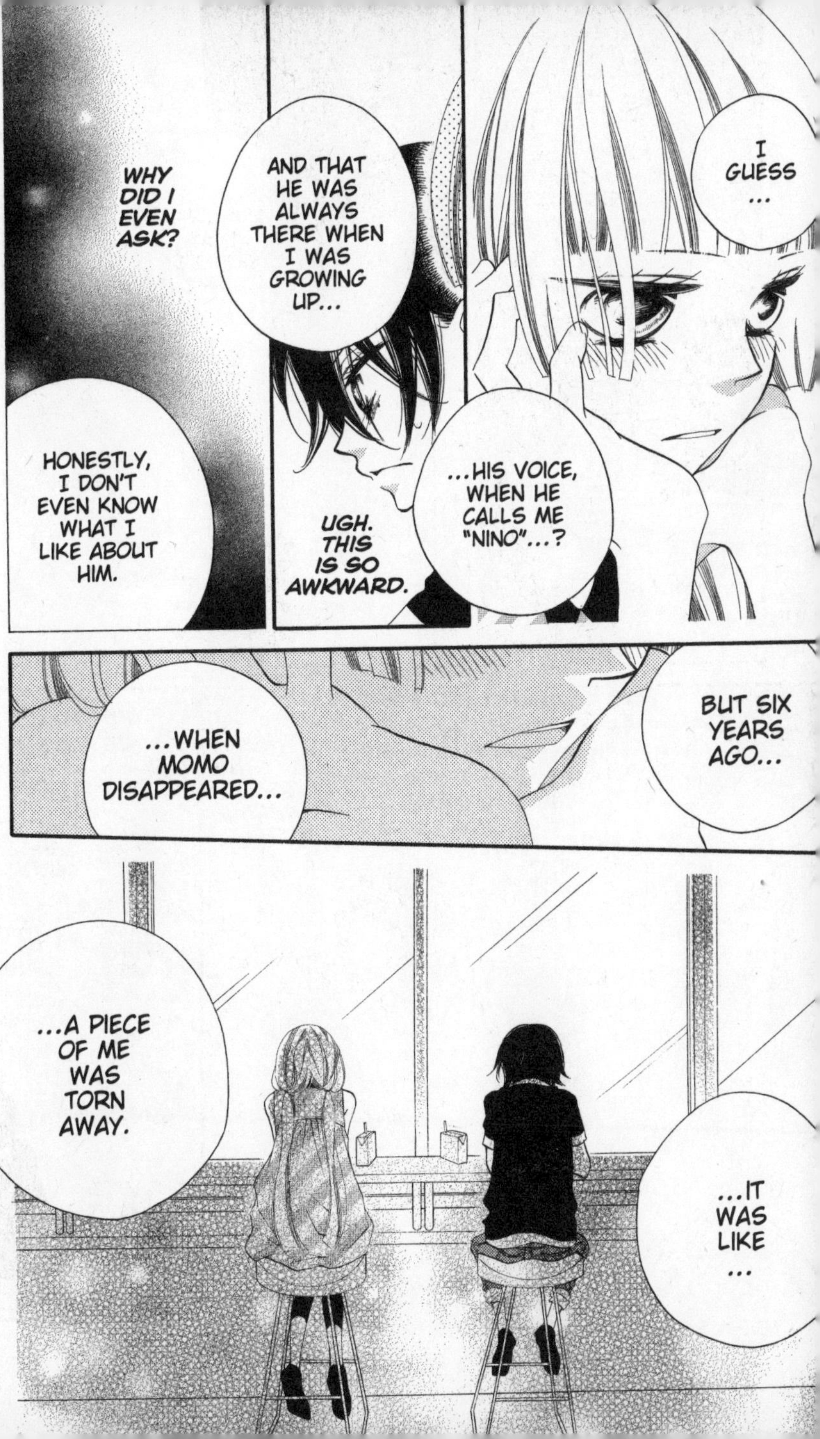
I GUESS...
...HIS VOICE, WHEN HE CALLS ME "NINO"...?
AND THAT HE WAS ALWAYS THERE WHEN I WAS GROWING UP...
UGH. THIS IS SO AWKWARD.
WHY DID I EVEN ASK?
HONESTLY, I DON'T EVEN KNOW WHAT I LIKE ABOUT HIM.
BUT SIX YEARS AGO...
...WHEN MOMO DISAPPEARED...
...IT WAS LIKE...
...A PIECE OF ME WAS TORN AWAY.

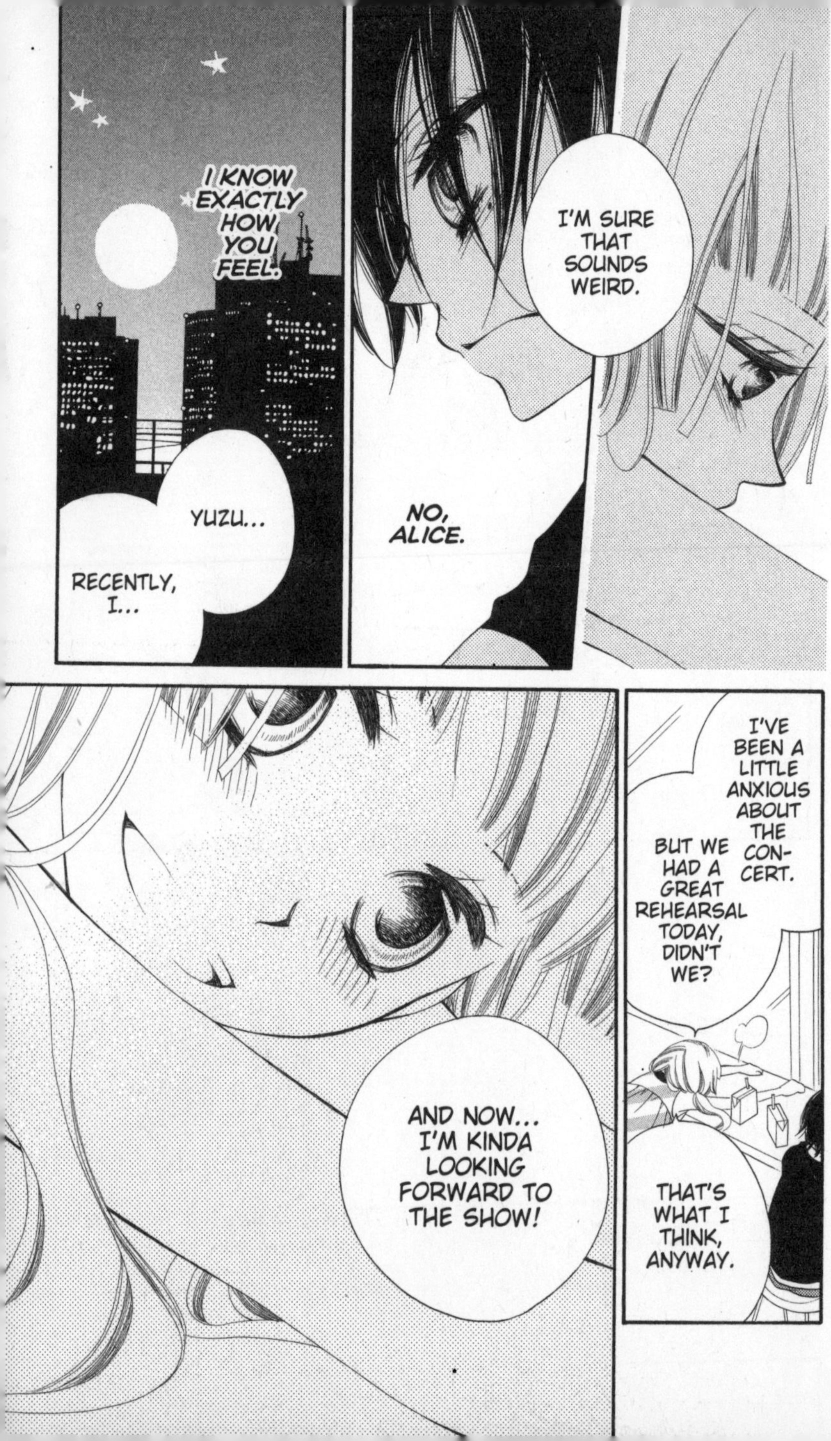
I'M SURE THAT SOUNDS WEIRD.
NO, ALICE.
I KNOW EXACTLY HOW YOU FEEL.
YUZU...
RECENTLY, I...
I'VE BEEN A LITTLE ANXIOUS ABOUT THE CONCERT.
BUT WE HAD A GREAT REHEARSAL TODAY, DIDN'T WE?
THAT'S WHAT I THINK, ANYWAY.
AND NOW... I'M KINDA LOOKING FORWARD TO THE SHOW!

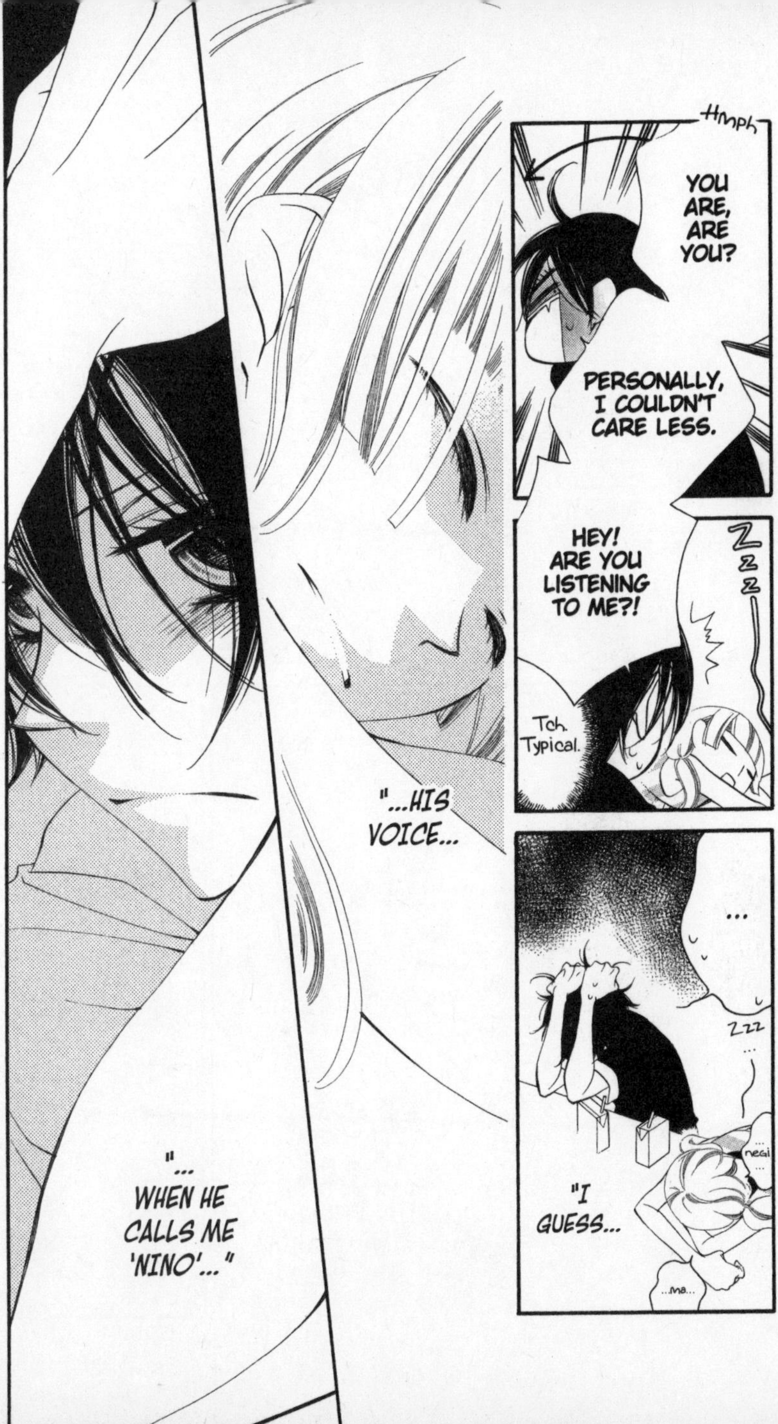
Hmph
YOU ARE, ARE YOU?
PERSONALLY, I COULDN'T CARE LESS.
HEY! ARE YOU LISTENING TO ME?!
Z Z Z
Tch. Typical.
...
Zzz
...
...negi...
"I GUESS...
...ma...
"...HIS VOICE...
"...
WHEN HE CALLS ME 'NINO'..."

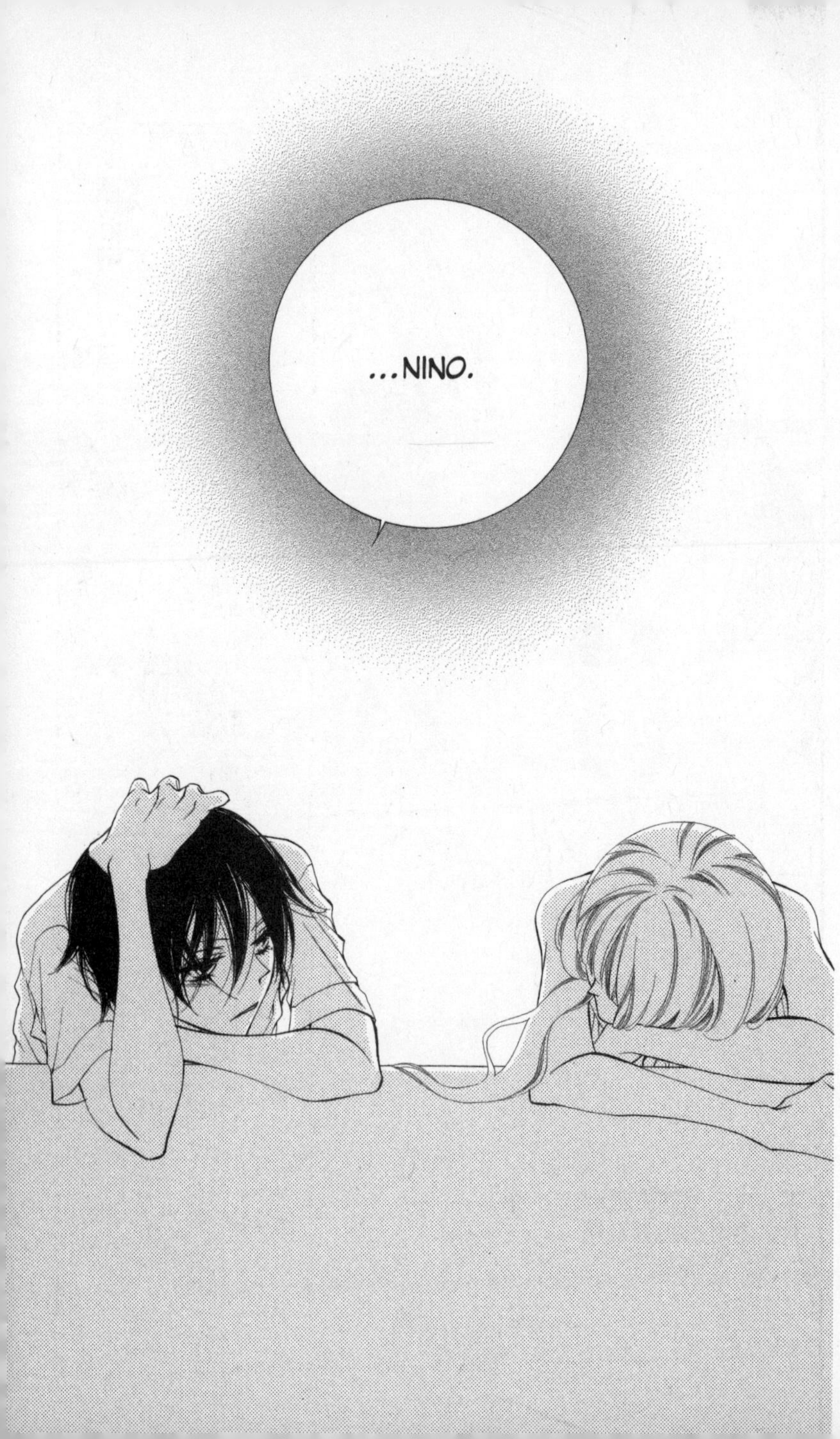
...NINO.

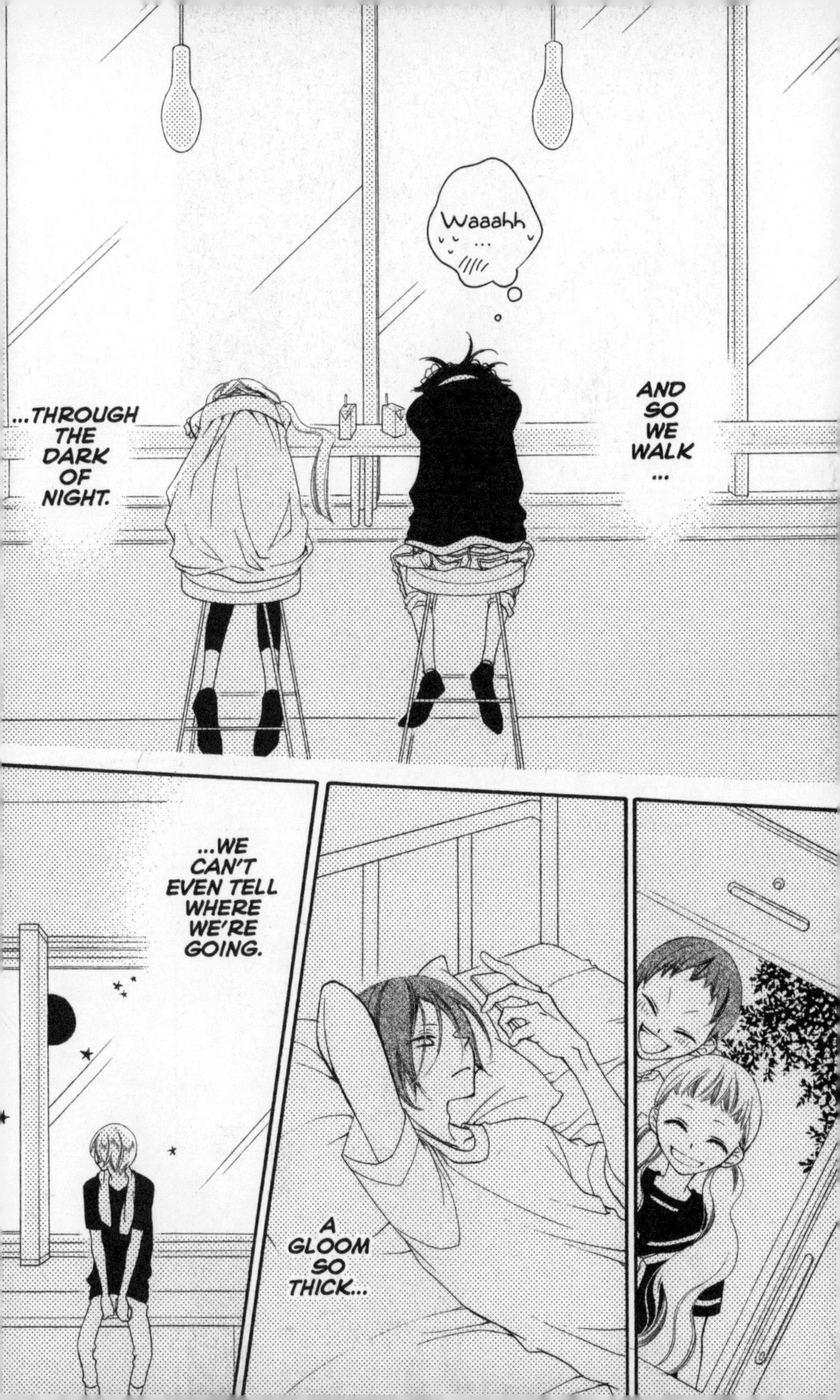
Waaahh ...
AND SO WE WALK ...
...THROUGH THE DARK OF NIGHT.
A GLOOM SO THICK...
...WE CAN'T EVEN TELL WHERE WE'RE GOING.

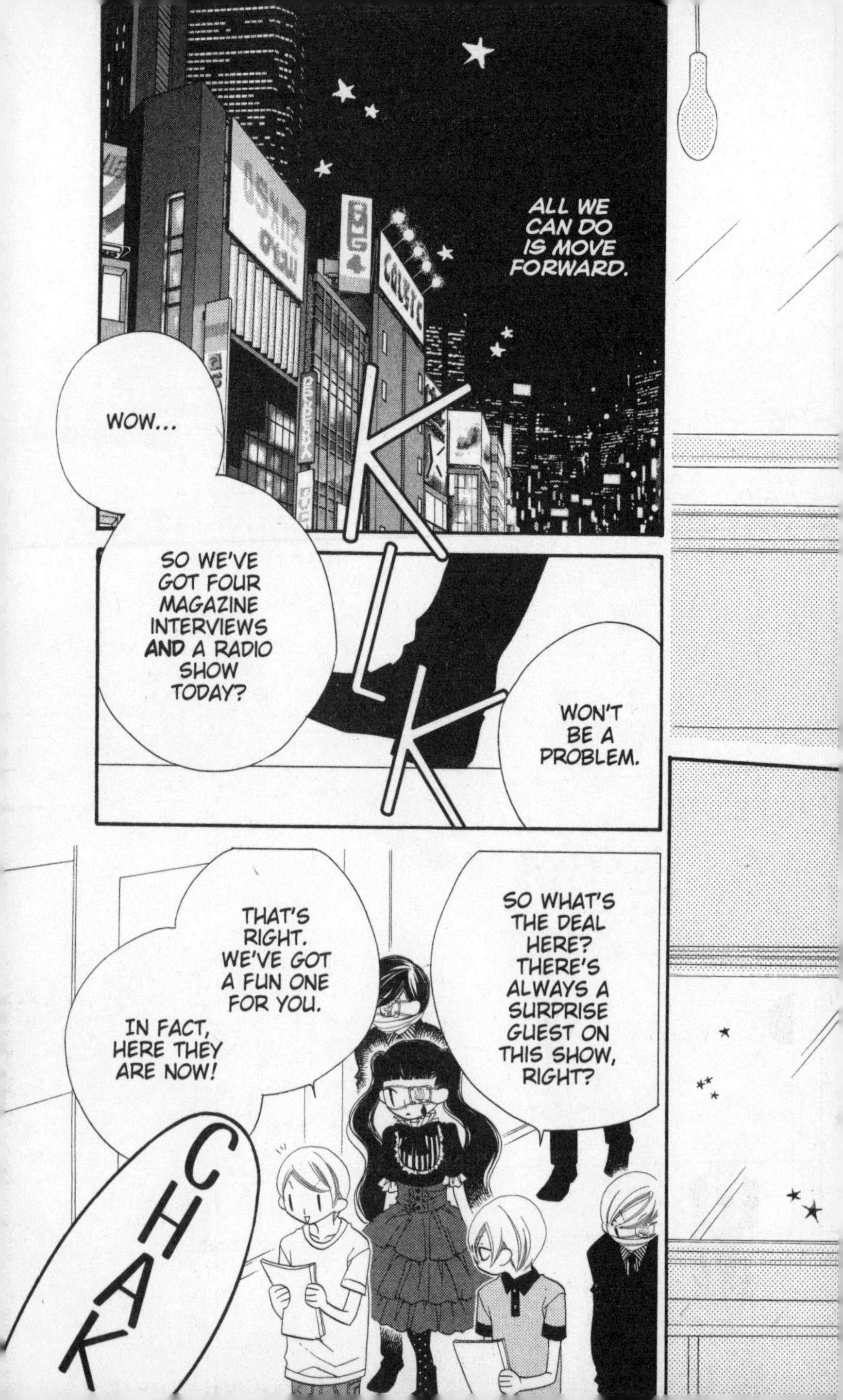
ALL WE CAN DO IS MOVE FORWARD.
WOW...
KLIK
SO WE'VE GOT FOUR MAGAZINE INTERVIEWS AND A RADIO SHOW TODAY?
WON'T BE A PROBLEM.
KLIK
SO WHAT'S THE DEAL HERE? THERE'S ALWAYS A SURPRISE GUEST ON THIS SHOW, RIGHT?
THAT'S RIGHT. WE'VE GOT A FUN ONE FOR YOU.
IN FACT, HERE THEY ARE NOW!
CHAK

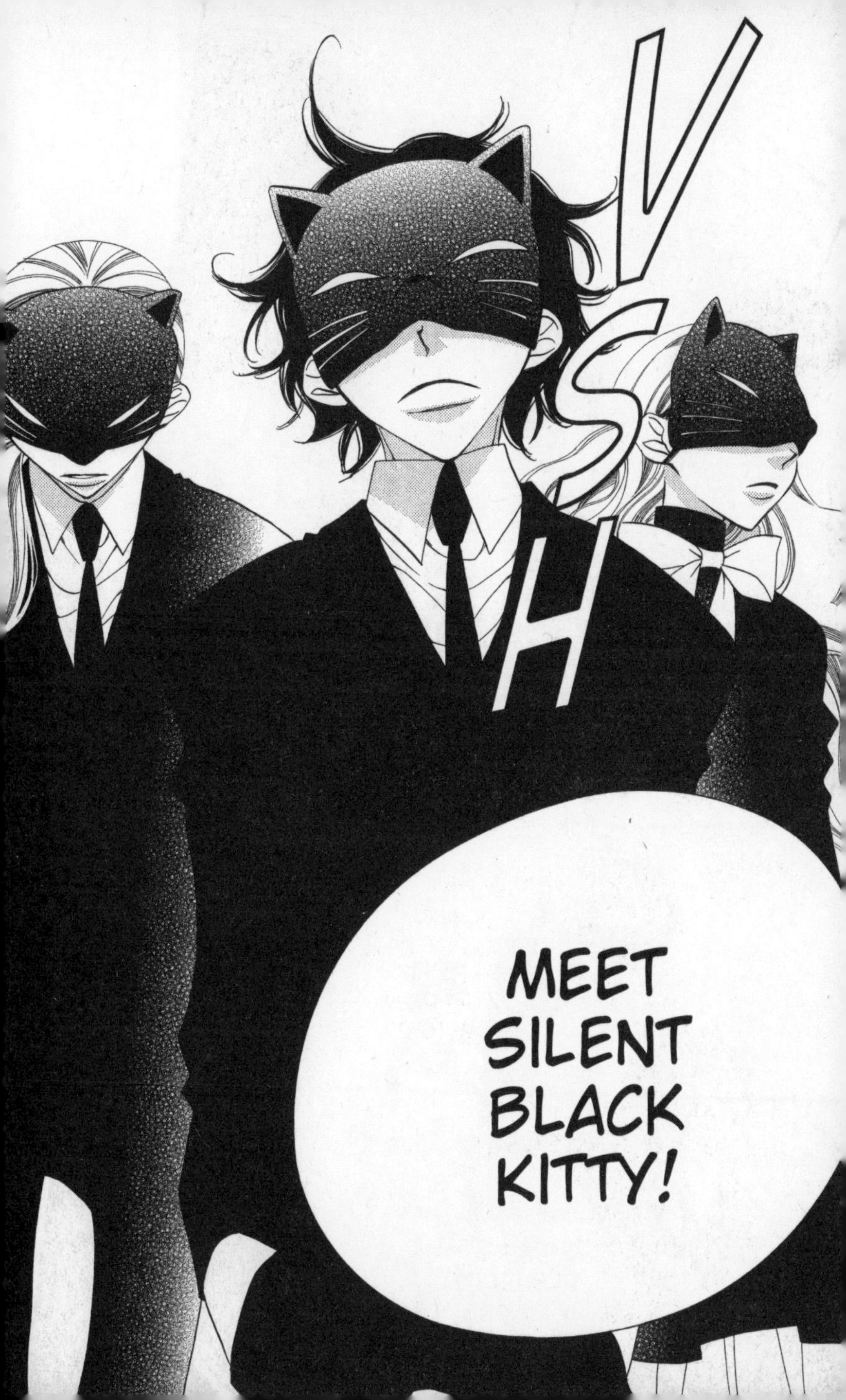
VSH
MEET SILENT BLACK KITTY!

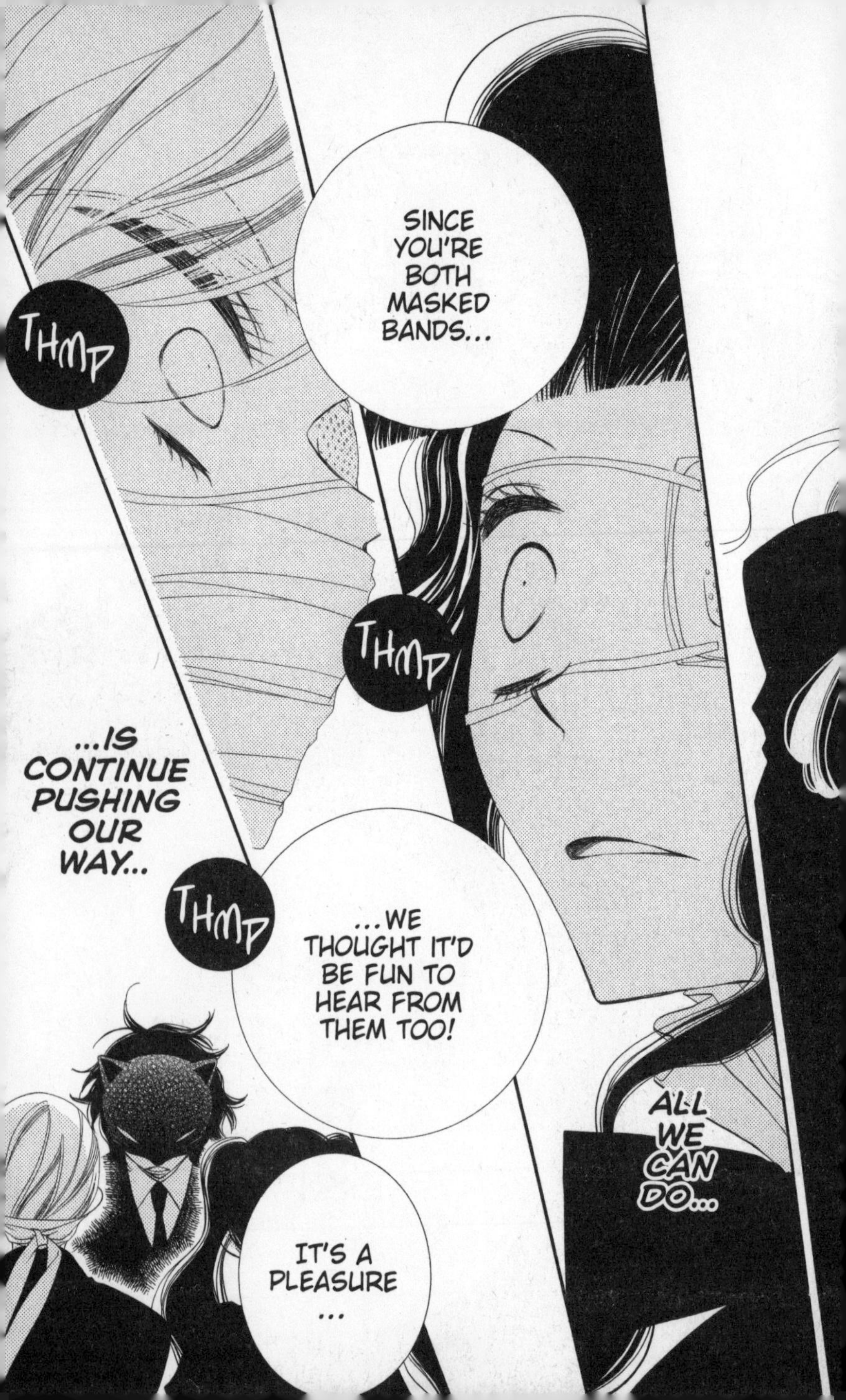
SINCE YOU'RE BOTH MASKED BANDS...
...WE THOUGHT IT'D BE FUN TO HEAR FROM THEM TOO!
IT'S A PLEASURE ...
THMP
THMP
THMP
ALL WE CAN DO...
...IS CONTINUE PUSHING OUR WAY...

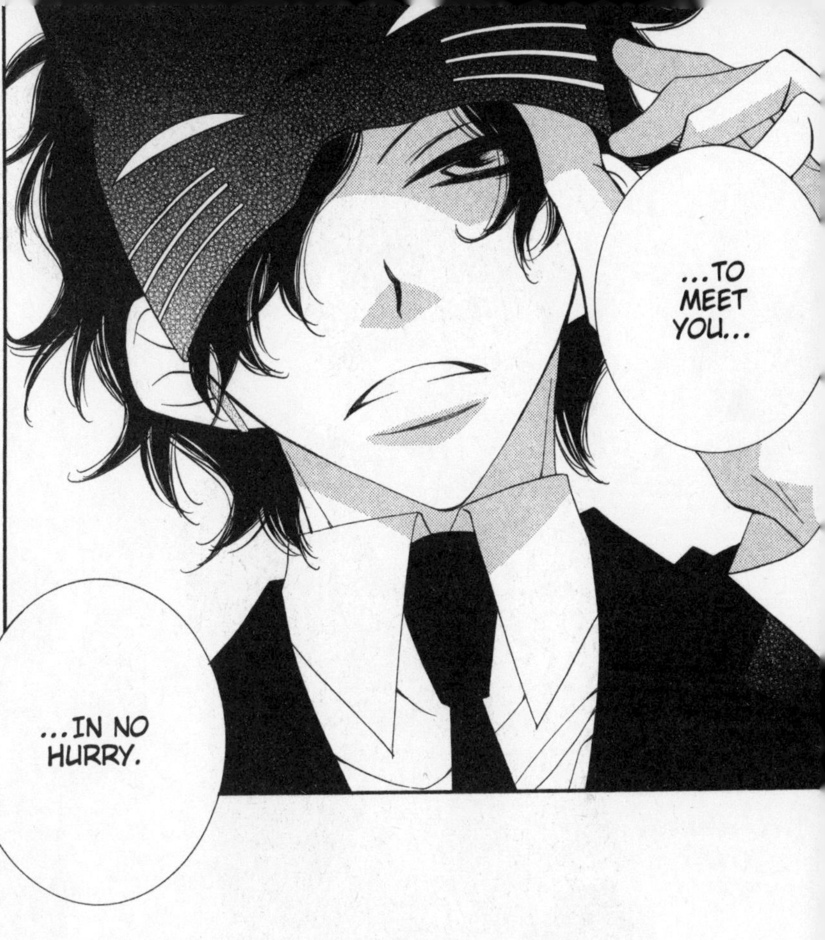
...TO MEET YOU...
...IN NO HURRY.

...FORWARD.

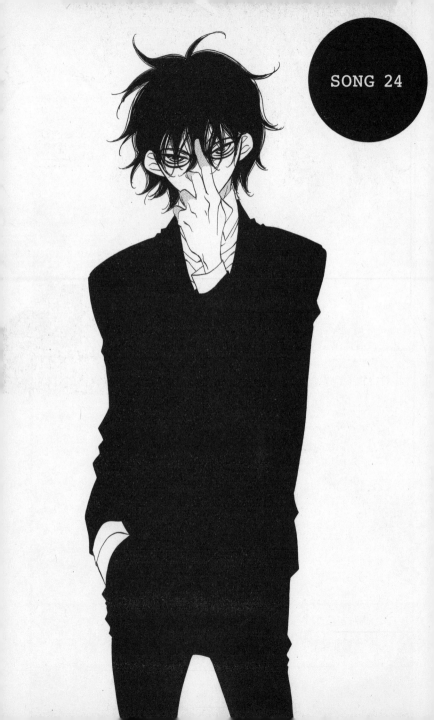

SONG 24

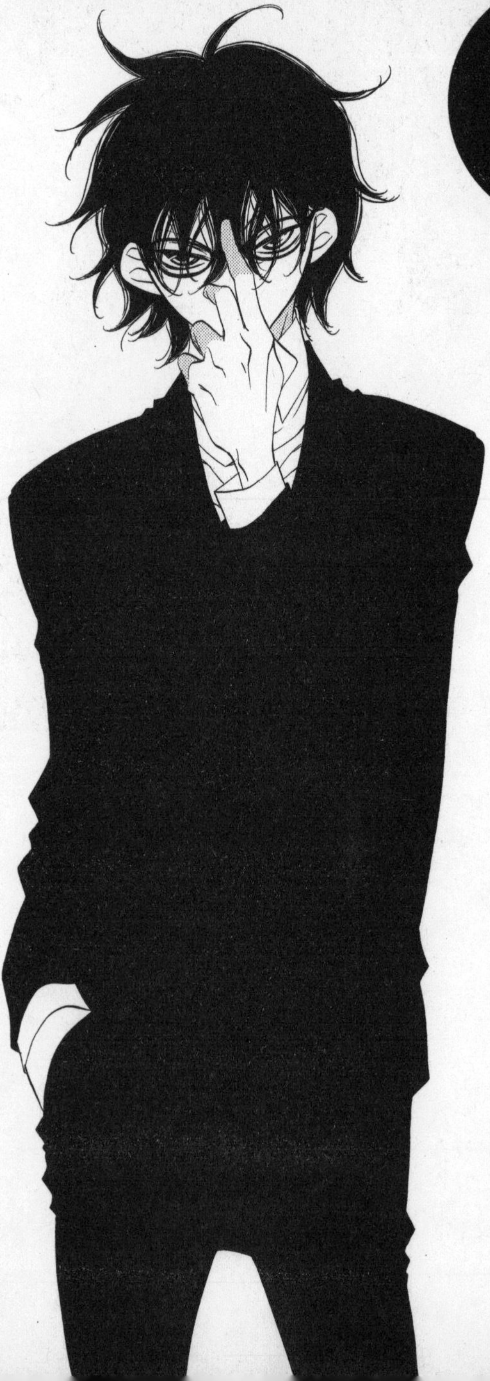

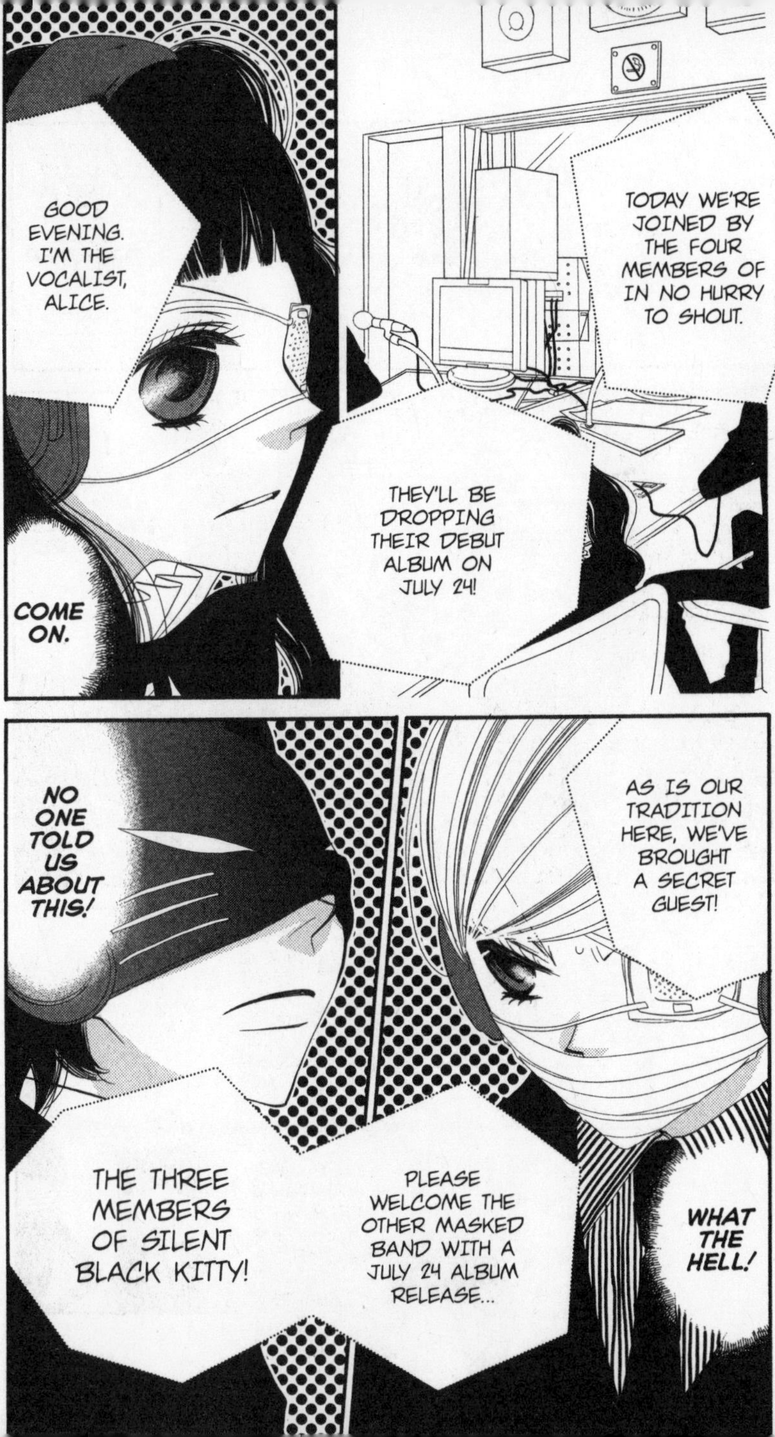
TODAY WE'RE JOINED BY THE FOUR MEMBERS OF IN NO HURRY TO SHOUT.
THEY'LL BE DROPPING THEIR DEBUT ALBUM ON JULY 24!
GOOD EVENING. I'M THE VOCALIST, ALICE.
COME ON.
AS IS OUR TRADITION HERE, WE'VE BROUGHT A SECRET GUEST!
PLEASE WELCOME THE OTHER MASKED BAND WITH A JULY 24 ALBUM RELEASE...
THE THREE MEMBERS OF SILENT BLACK KITTY!
WHAT THE HELL!
NO ONE TOLD US ABOUT THIS!

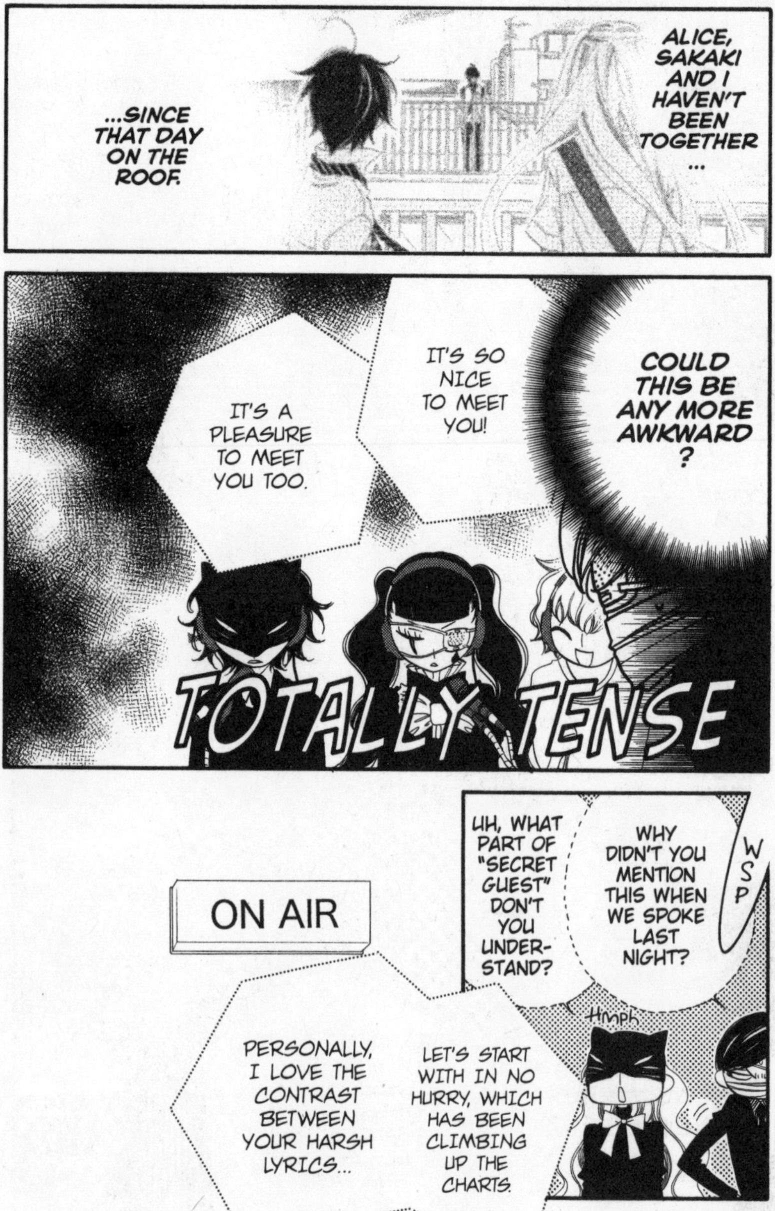
ALICE, SAKAKI AND I HAVEN'T BEEN TOGETHER ...
...SINCE THAT DAY ON THE ROOF.
COULD THIS BE ANY MORE AWKWARD?
IT'S SO NICE TO MEET YOU!
IT'S A PLEASURE TO MEET YOU TOO.
TOTALLY TENSE
WSP
WHY DIDN'T YOU MENTION THIS WHEN WE SPOKE LAST NIGHT?
UH, WHAT PART OF "SECRET GUEST" DON'T YOU UNDER-STAND?
Hmph
ON AIR
LET'S START WITH IN NO HURRY, WHICH HAS BEEN CLIMBING UP THE CHARTS.
PERSONALLY, I LOVE THE CONTRAST BETWEEN YOUR HARSH LYRICS...

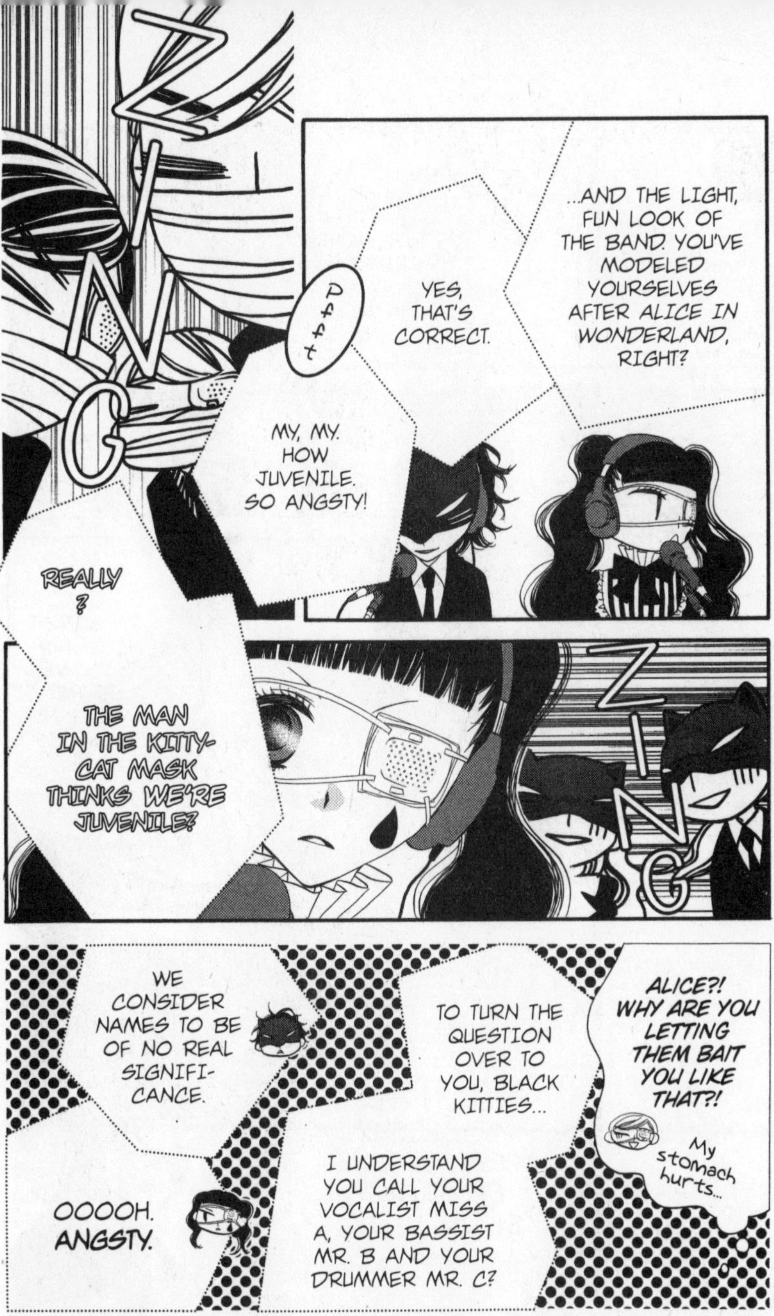
...AND THE LIGHT, FUN LOOK OF THE BAND. YOU'VE MODELED YOURSELVES AFTER ALICE IN WONDERLAND, RIGHT?
YES, THAT'S CORRECT.
Pfft
MY, MY. HOW JUVENILE. SO ANGSTY!
ZING
REALLY?
ZING
THE MAN IN THE KITTY-CAT MASK THINKS WE'RE JUVENILE?
ALICE?! WHY ARE YOU LETTING THEM BAIT YOU LIKE THAT?!
My stomach hurts...
TO TURN THE QUESTION OVER TO YOU, BLACK KITTIES...
I UNDERSTAND YOU CALL YOUR VOCALIST MISS A, YOUR BASSIST MR. B AND YOUR DRUMMER MR. C?
WE CONSIDER NAMES TO BE OF NO REAL SIGNIFI-CANCE.
OOOOH. ANGSTY.

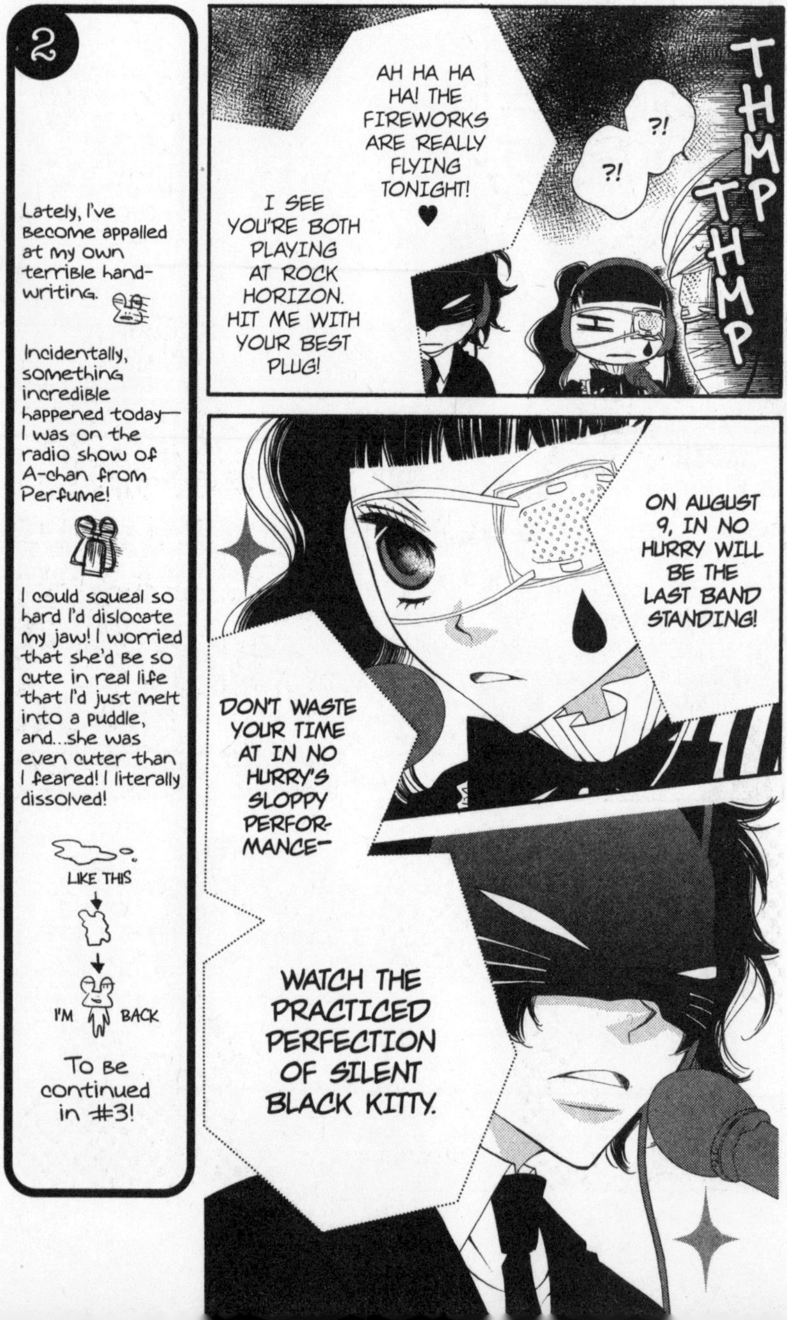
THMP THMP
?!
?!
AH HA HA HA! THE FIREWORKS ARE REALLY FLYING TONIGHT! ♥
I SEE YOU'RE BOTH PLAYING AT ROCK HORIZON. HIT ME WITH YOUR BEST PLUG!
ON AUGUST 9, IN NO HURRY WILL BE THE LAST BAND STANDING!
DON'T WASTE YOUR TIME AT IN NO HURRY'S SLOPPY PERFOR-MANCE—
WATCH THE PRACTICED PERFECTION OF SILENT BLACK KITTY.

2

Lately, I've become appalled at my own terrible hand-writing.

Incidentally, something incredible happened today—I was on the radio show of A-chan from Perfume!

I could squeal so hard I'd dislocate my jaw! I worried that she'd be so cute in real life that I'd just melt into a puddle, and...she was even cuter than I feared! I literally dissolved!

LIKE THIS

I'M BACK

To be continued in #3!

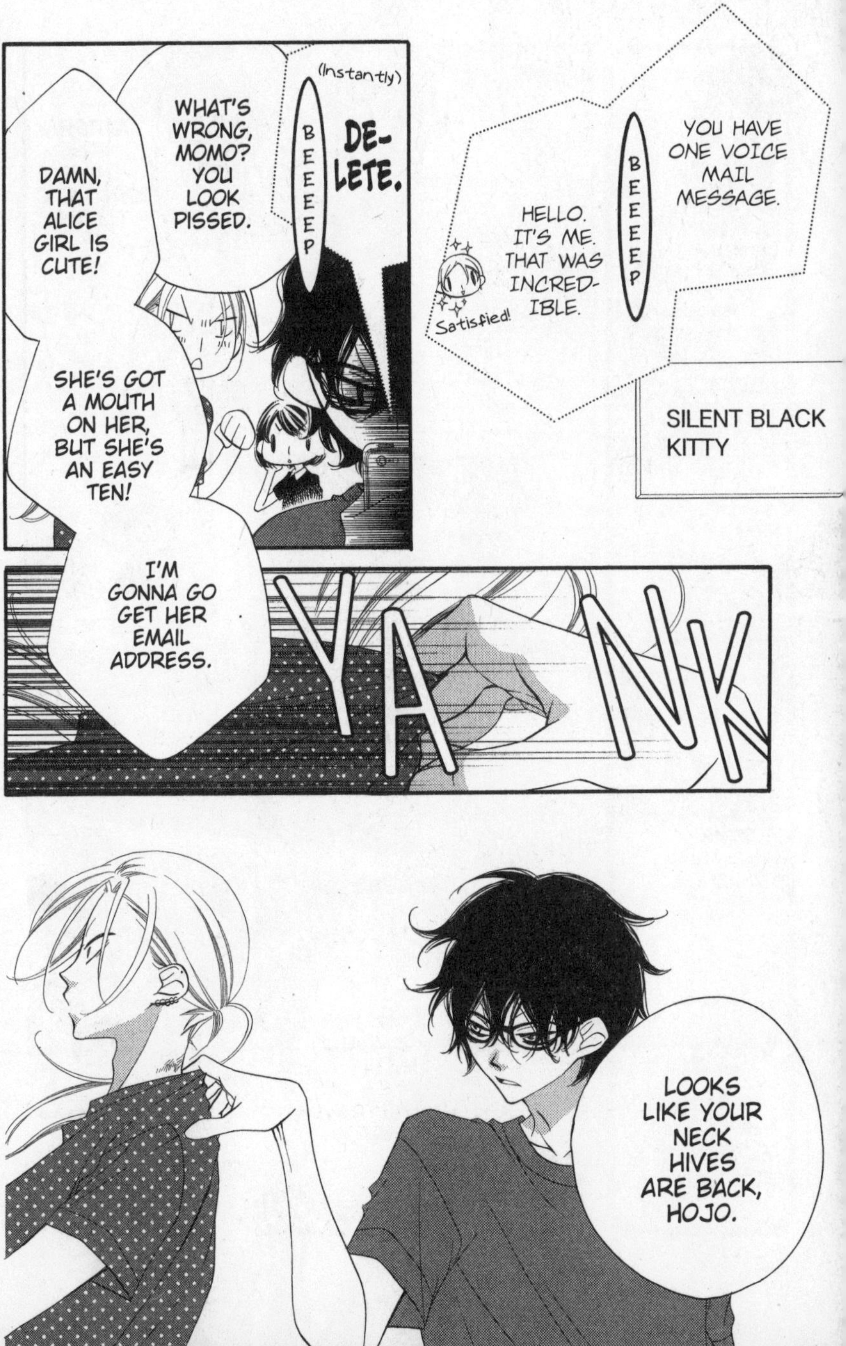
YOU HAVE ONE VOICE MAIL MESSAGE.
BEEEEP
HELLO. IT'S ME. THAT WAS INCRED-IBLE.
Satisfied!
SILENT BLACK KITTY
(Instantly)
BEEEEP
DE-LETE.
WHAT'S WRONG, MOMO? YOU LOOK PISSED.
DAMN, THAT ALICE GIRL IS CUTE!
SHE'S GOT A MOUTH ON HER, BUT SHE'S AN EASY TEN!
I'M GONNA GO GET HER EMAIL ADDRESS.
YANK
LOOKS LIKE YOUR NECK HIVES ARE BACK, HOJO.

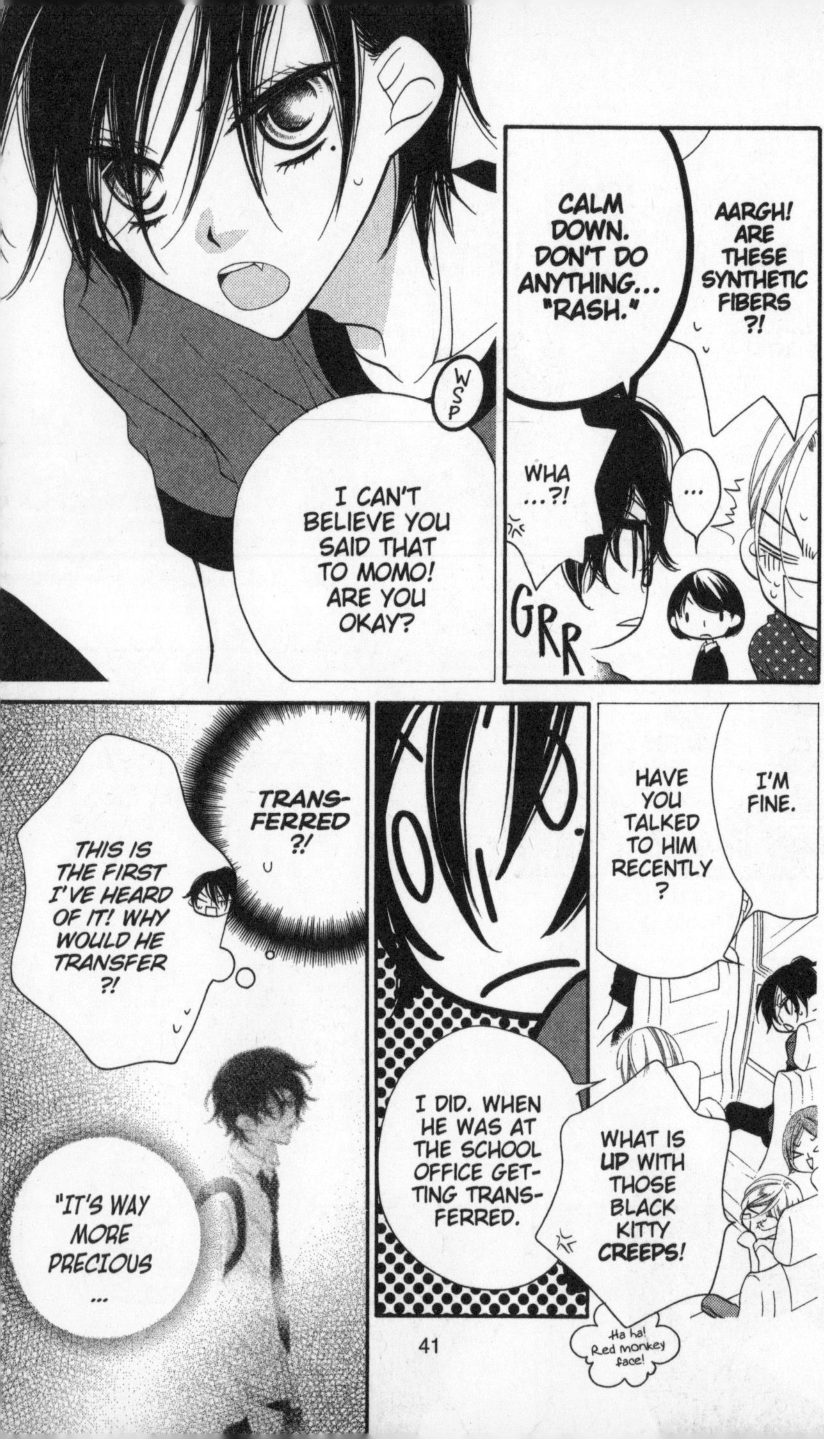
AARGH! ARE THESE SYNTHETIC FIBERS ?!
CALM DOWN. DON'T DO ANYTHING... "RASH."
WHA ...?!
...
GRR
WSP
I CAN'T BELIEVE YOU SAID THAT TO MOMO! ARE YOU OKAY?
I'M FINE.
HAVE YOU TALKED TO HIM RECENTLY ?
WHAT IS UP WITH THOSE BLACK KITTY CREEPS!
Ha ha! Red monkey face!
I DID. WHEN HE WAS AT THE SCHOOL OFFICE GETTING TRANSFERRED.
TRANSFERRED ?!
THIS IS THE FIRST I'VE HEARD OF IT! WHY WOULD HE TRANSFER ?!
"IT'S WAY MORE PRECIOUS ...

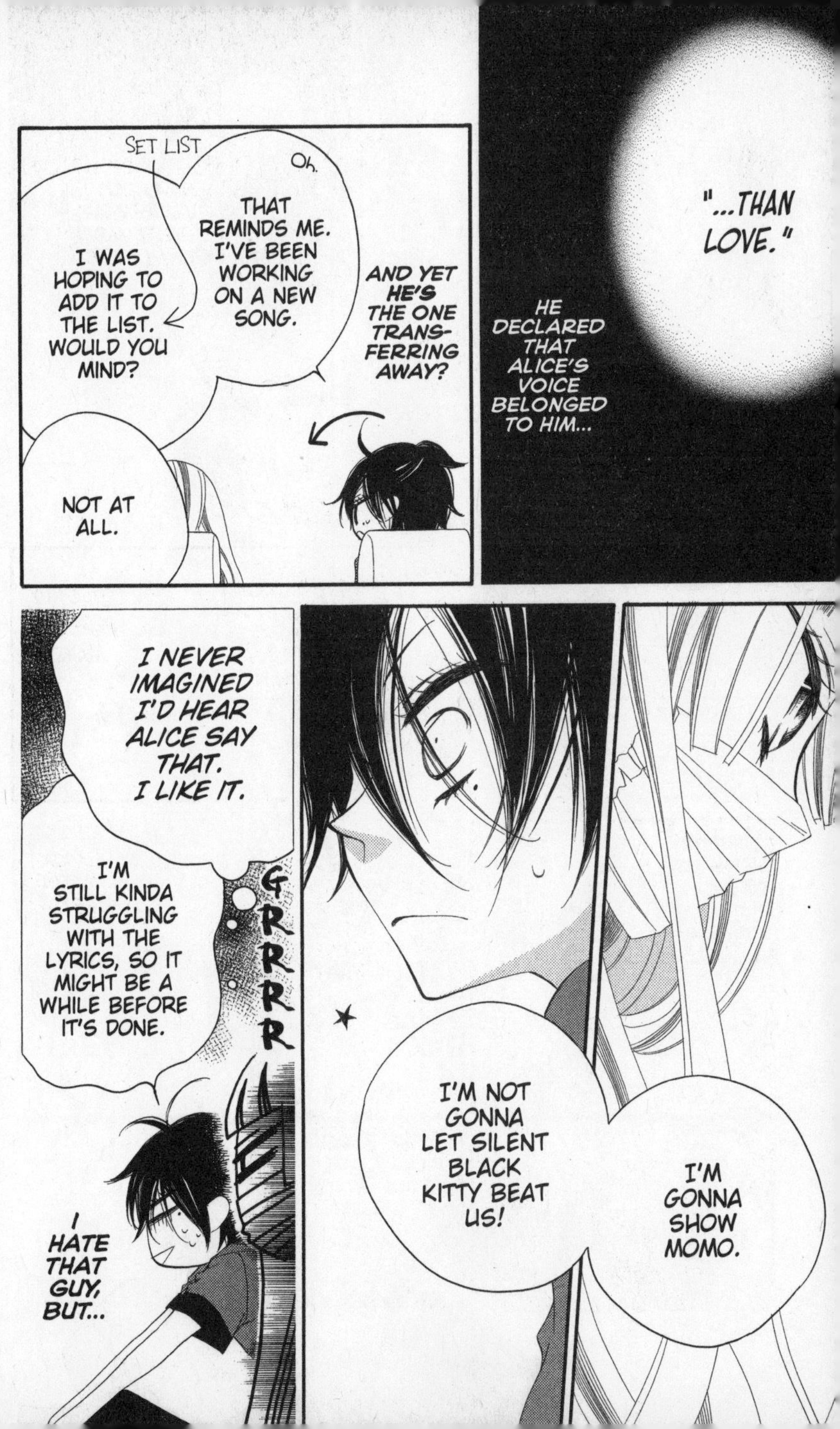
"...THAN LOVE."
HE DECLARED THAT ALICE'S VOICE BELONGED TO HIM...
AND YET HE'S THE ONE TRANSFERRING AWAY?
Oh.
THAT REMINDS ME. I'VE BEEN WORKING ON A NEW SONG.
SET LIST
I WAS HOPING TO ADD IT TO THE LIST. WOULD YOU MIND?
NOT AT ALL.
I'M GONNA SHOW MOMO.
I'M NOT GONNA LET SILENT BLACK KITTY BEAT US!
I NEVER IMAGINED I'D HEAR ALICE SAY THAT. I LIKE IT.
I'M STILL KINDA STRUGGLING WITH THE LYRICS, SO IT MIGHT BE A WHILE BEFORE IT'S DONE.
GRRRR
I HATE THAT GUY, BUT...

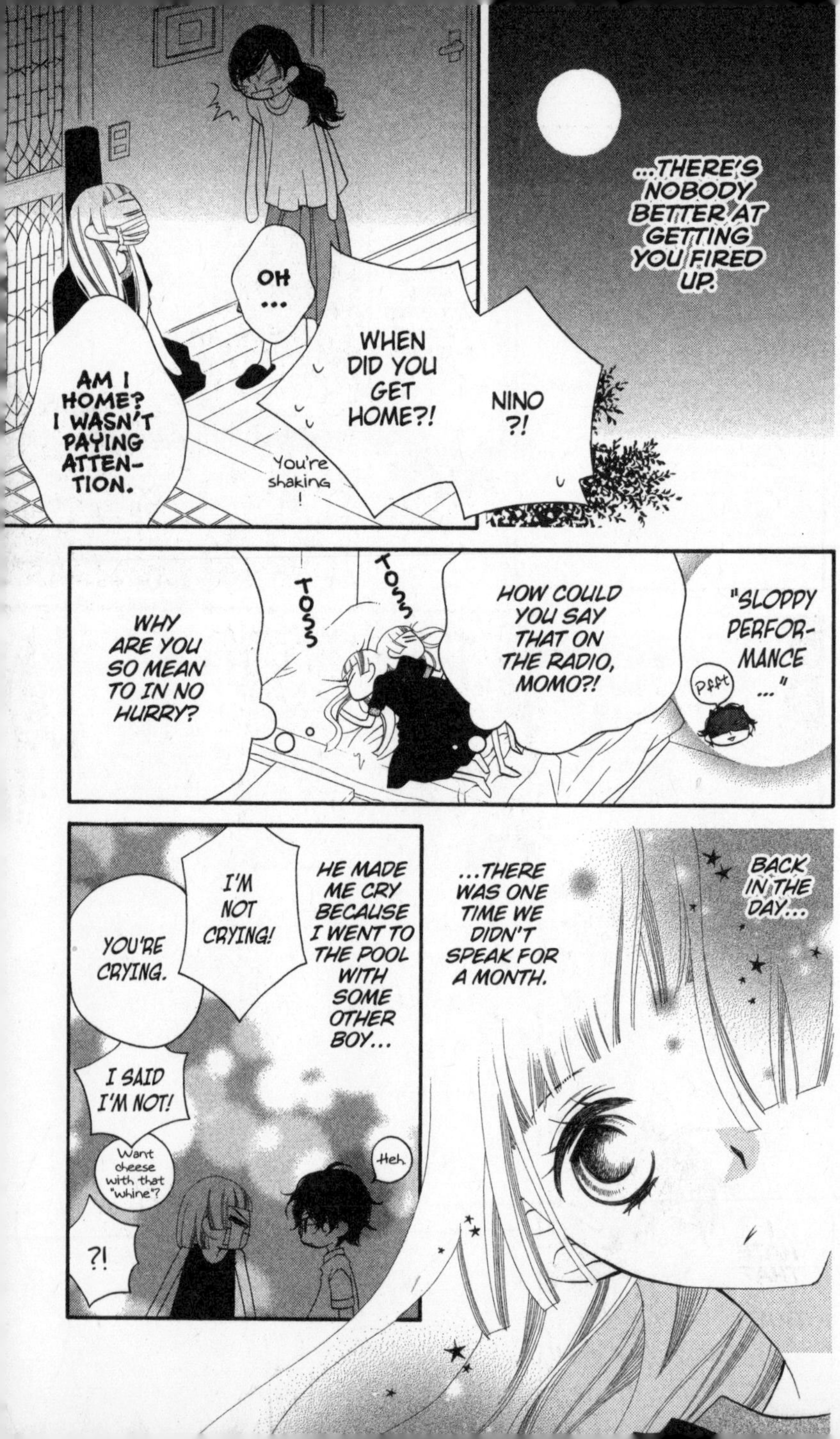
...THERE'S NOBODY BETTER AT GETTING YOU FIRED UP.
NINO ?!
WHEN DID YOU GET HOME?!
OH ...
You're shaking !
AM I HOME? I WASN'T PAYING ATTEN-TION.
"SLOPPY PERFOR-MANCE ..."
Pfft
HOW COULD YOU SAY THAT ON THE RADIO, MOMO?!
TOSS
TOSS
WHY ARE YOU SO MEAN TO IN NO HURRY?
BACK IN THE DAY...
...THERE WAS ONE TIME WE DIDN'T SPEAK FOR A MONTH.
HE MADE ME CRY BECAUSE I WENT TO THE POOL WITH SOME OTHER BOY...
I'M NOT CRYING!
YOU'RE CRYING.
I SAID I'M NOT!
Heh.
Want cheese with that "whine"?
?!

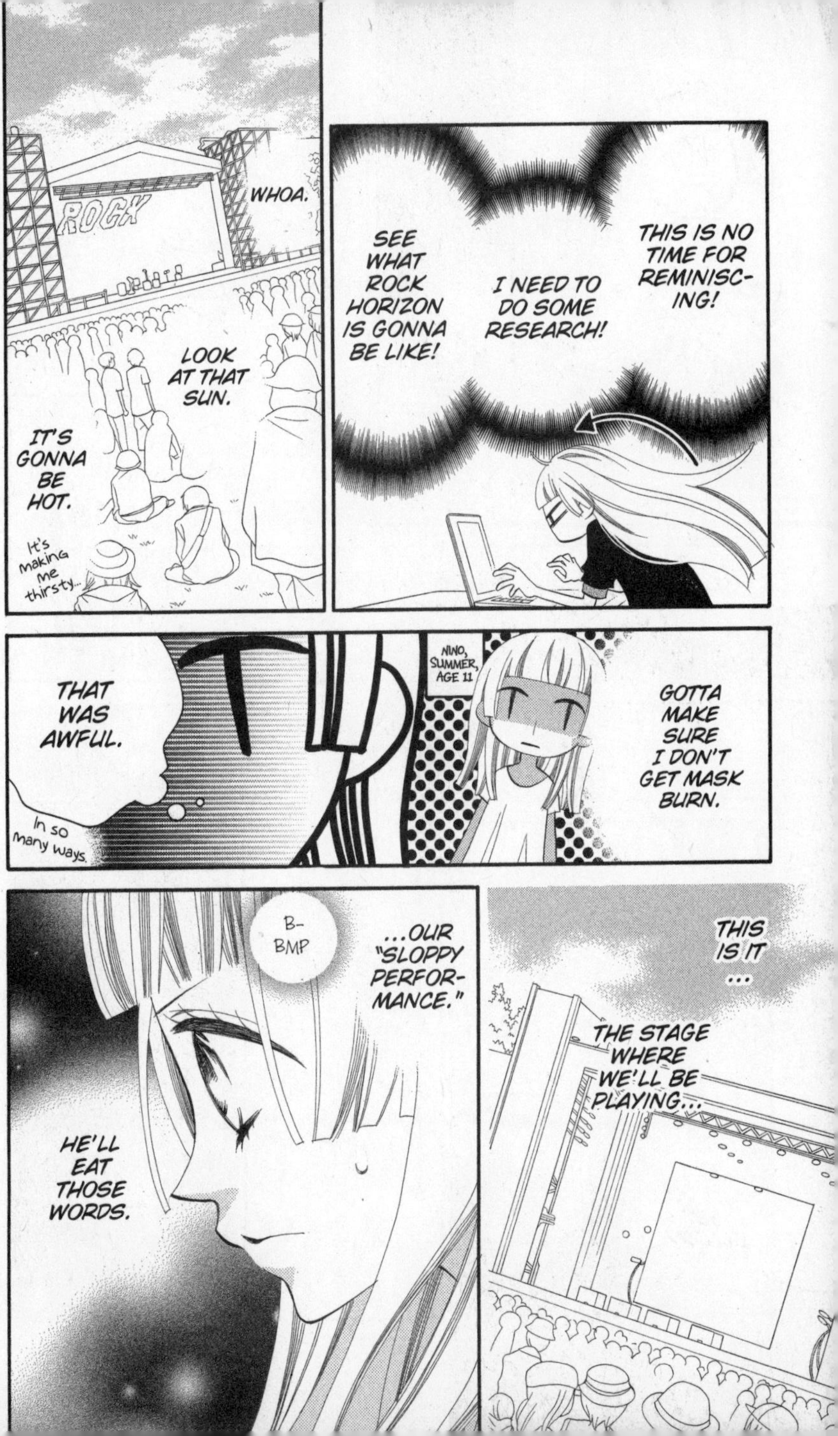
THIS IS NO TIME FOR REMINISC-ING!
I NEED TO DO SOME RESEARCH!
SEE WHAT ROCK HORIZON IS GONNA BE LIKE!
ROCK
WHOA.
LOOK AT THAT SUN.
IT'S GONNA BE HOT.
It's making me thirsty...
GOTTA MAKE SURE I DON'T GET MASK BURN.
NINO, SUMMER, AGE 11
THAT WAS AWFUL.
In so many ways.
THIS IS IT ...
THE STAGE WHERE WE'LL BE PLAYING...
...OUR "SLOPPY PERFORM-ANCE."
B-BMP
HE'LL EAT THOSE WORDS.

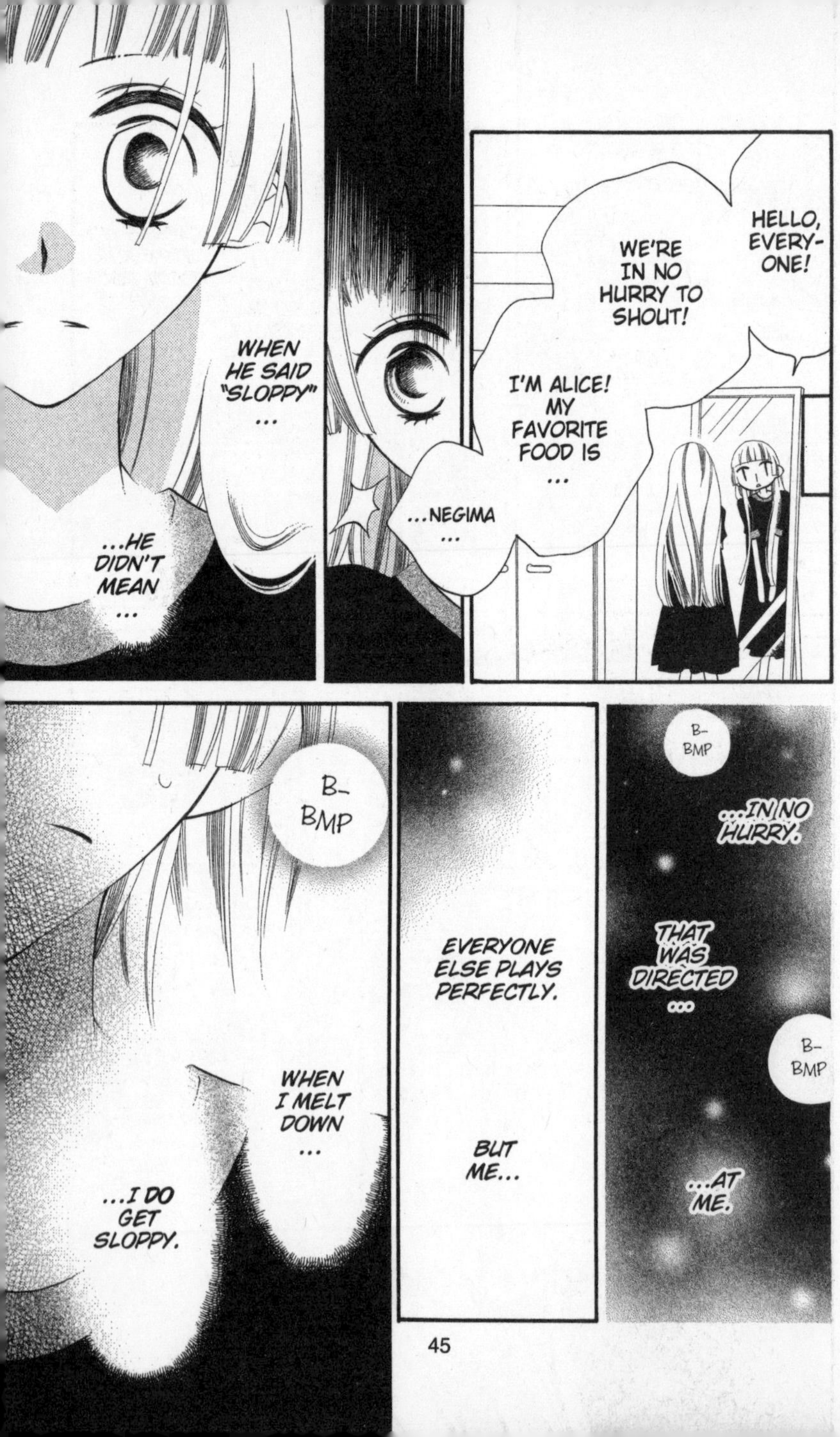
HELLO, EVERY-ONE!
WE'RE IN NO HURRY TO SHOUT!
I'M ALICE! MY FAVORITE FOOD IS ...
...NEGIMA ...
WHEN HE SAID "SLOPPY" ...
...HE DIDN'T MEAN ...
B-BMP
...IN NO HURRY.
THAT WAS DIRECTED ...
B-BMP
...AT ME.
EVERYONE ELSE PLAYS PERFECTLY.
BUT ME...
B-BMP
WHEN I MELT DOWN ...
...I DO GET SLOPPY.

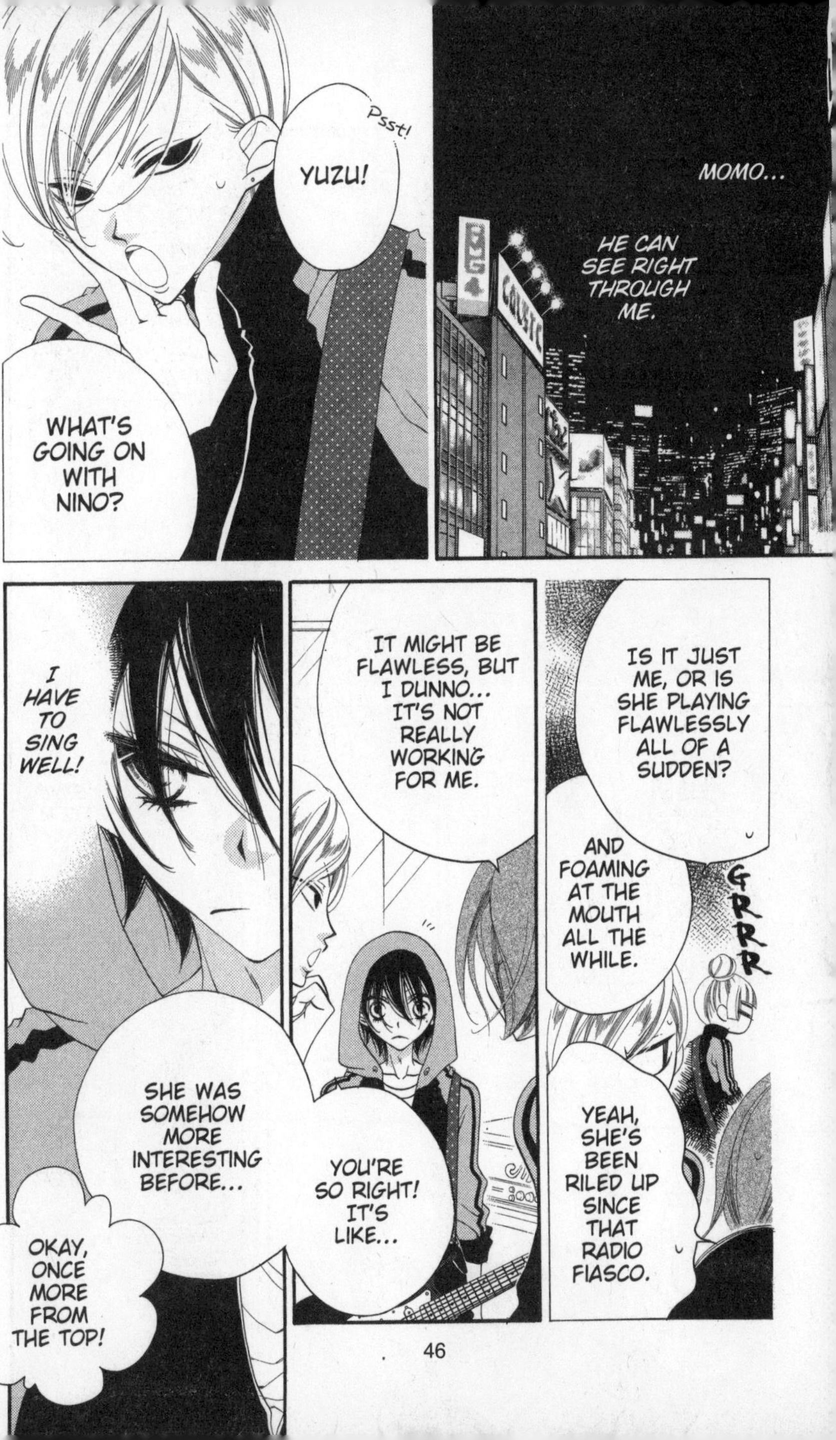
MOMO...
HE CAN SEE RIGHT THROUGH ME.
Psst!
YUZU!
WHAT'S GOING ON WITH NINO?
IS IT JUST ME, OR IS SHE PLAYING FLAWLESSLY ALL OF A SUDDEN?
AND FOAMING AT THE MOUTH ALL THE WHILE.
GRRR
YEAH, SHE'S BEEN RILED UP SINCE THAT RADIO FIASCO.
IT MIGHT BE FLAWLESS, BUT I DUNNO... IT'S NOT REALLY WORKING FOR ME.
YOU'RE SO RIGHT! IT'S LIKE...
SHE WAS SOMEHOW MORE INTERESTING BEFORE...
I HAVE TO SING WELL!
OKAY, ONCE MORE FROM THE TOP!

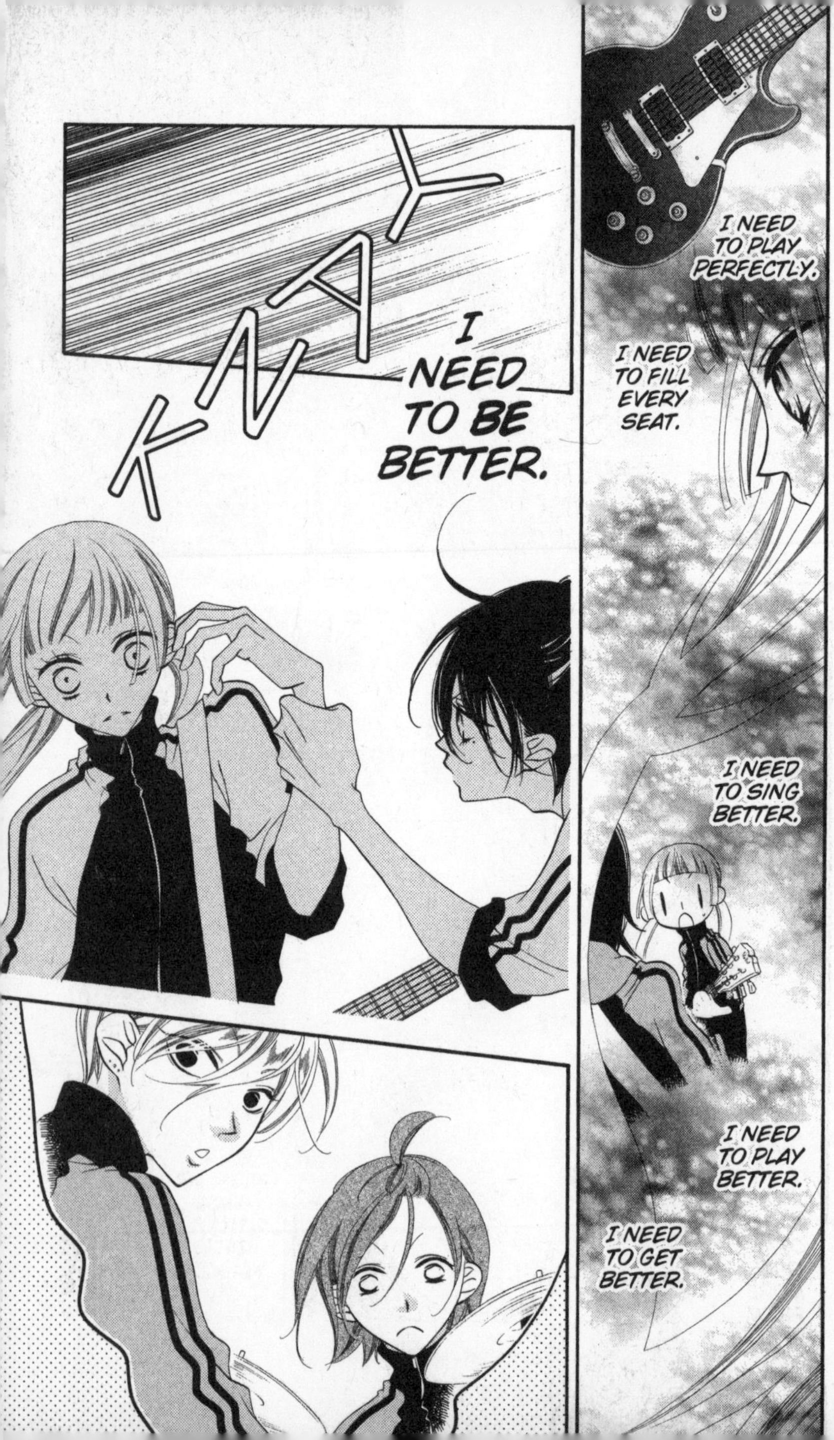
I NEED TO PLAY PERFECTLY.
I NEED TO FILL EVERY SEAT.
I NEED TO SING BETTER.
I NEED TO PLAY BETTER.
I NEED TO GET BETTER.
KNAY
I NEED TO BE BETTER.

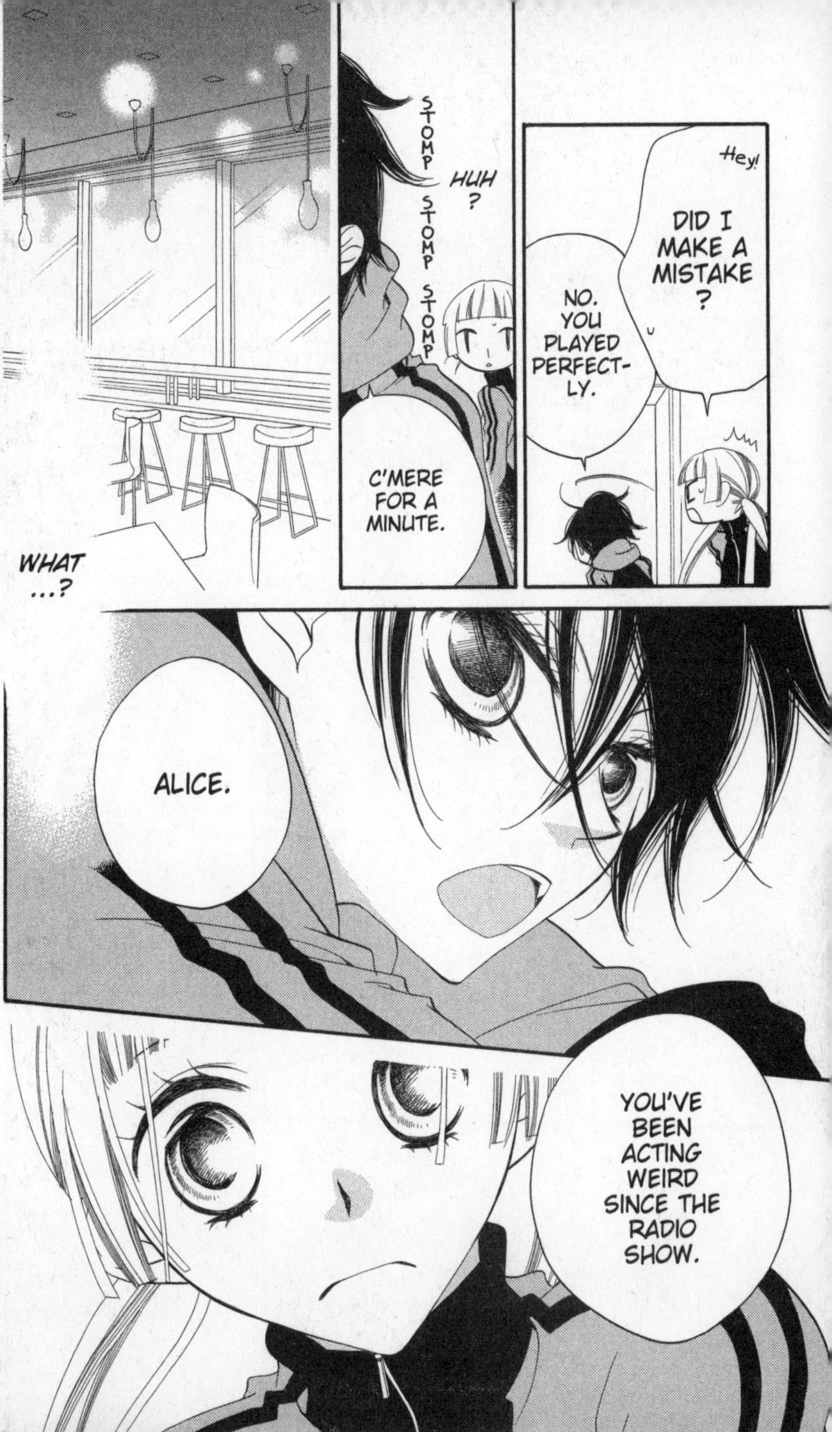
Hey!
DID I MAKE A MISTAKE?
NO. YOU PLAYED PERFECT-LY.
STOMP STOMP STOMP
HUH?
C'MERE FOR A MINUTE.
WHAT...?
ALICE.
YOU'VE BEEN ACTING WEIRD SINCE THE RADIO SHOW.

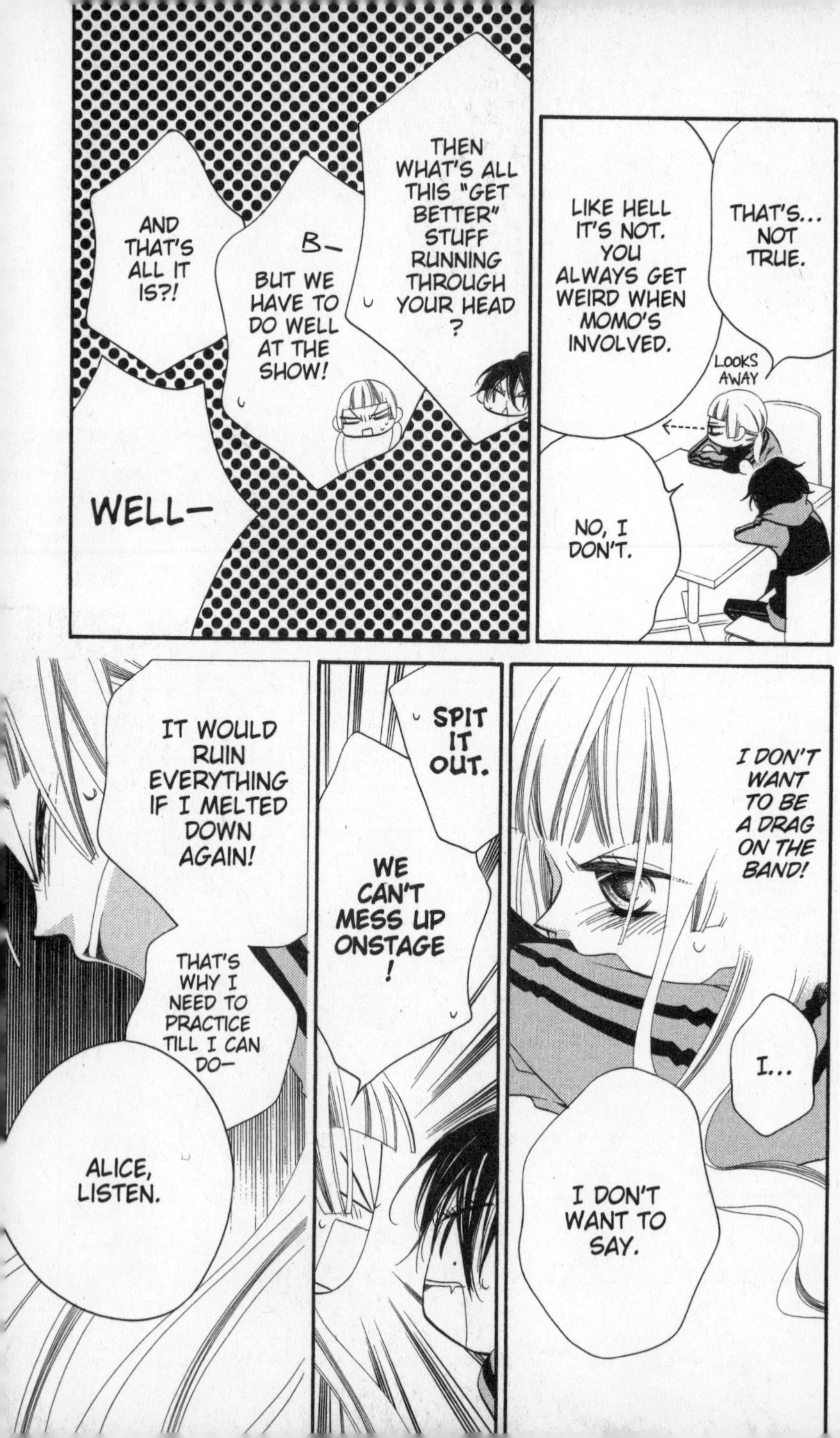
THAT'S... NOT TRUE.
LOOKS AWAY
LIKE HELL IT'S NOT. YOU ALWAYS GET WEIRD WHEN MOMO'S INVOLVED.
NO, I DON'T.
THEN WHAT'S ALL THIS "GET BETTER" STUFF RUNNING THROUGH YOUR HEAD?
B— BUT WE HAVE TO DO WELL AT THE SHOW!
AND THAT'S ALL IT IS?!
WELL—
I DON'T WANT TO BE A DRAG ON THE BAND!
I...
I DON'T WANT TO SAY.
SPIT IT OUT.
WE CAN'T MESS UP ONSTAGE!
IT WOULD RUIN EVERYTHING IF I MELTED DOWN AGAIN!
THAT'S WHY I NEED TO PRACTICE TILL I CAN DO—
ALICE, LISTEN.

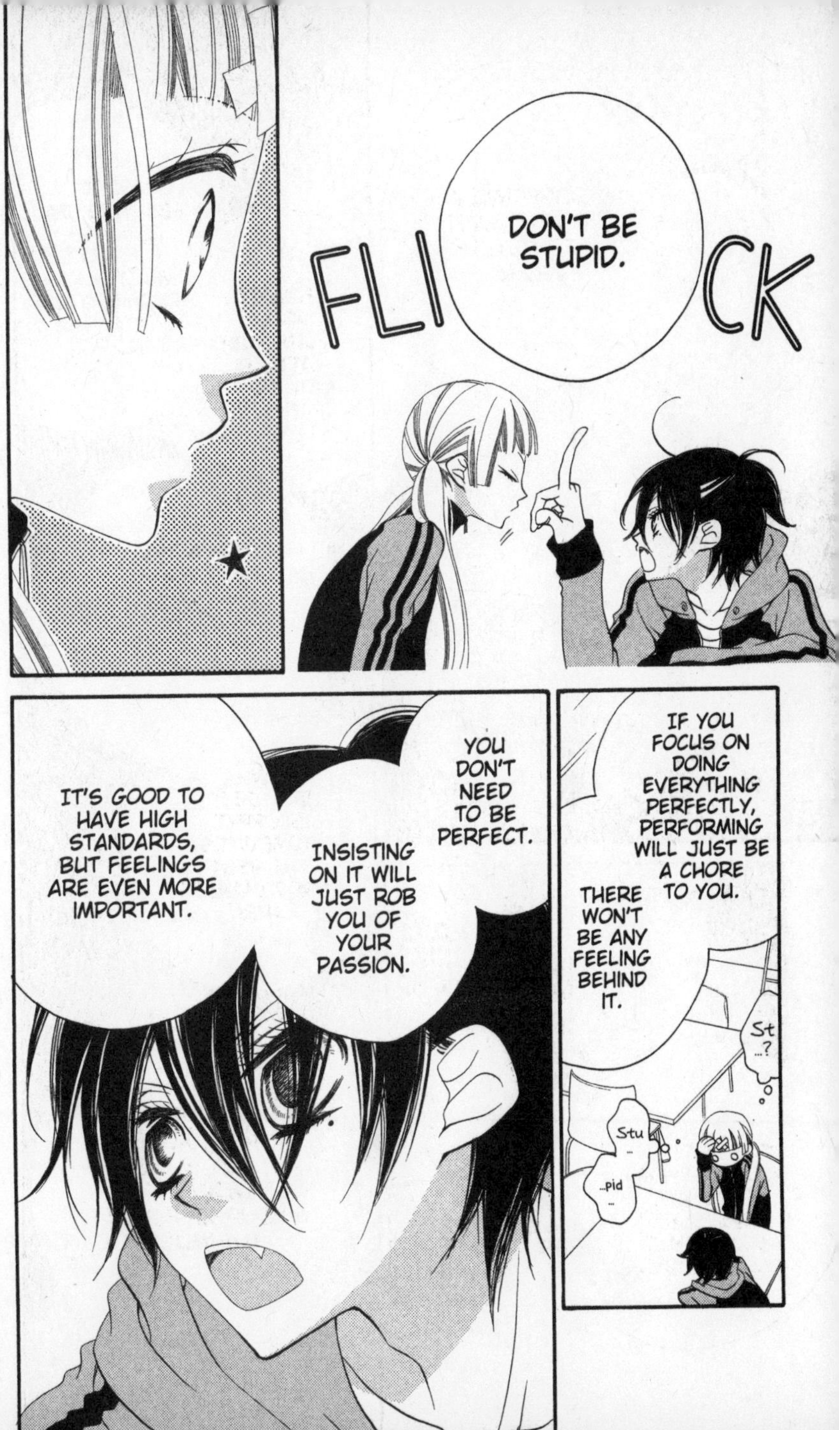
FLICK
DON'T BE STUPID.
IF YOU FOCUS ON DOING EVERYTHING PERFECTLY, PERFORMING WILL JUST BE A CHORE TO YOU.
THERE WON'T BE ANY FEELING BEHIND IT.
St ...?
Stu ...
...pid ...
YOU DON'T NEED TO BE PERFECT.
INSISTING ON IT WILL JUST ROB YOU OF YOUR PASSION.
IT'S GOOD TO HAVE HIGH STANDARDS, BUT FEELINGS ARE EVEN MORE IMPORTANT.

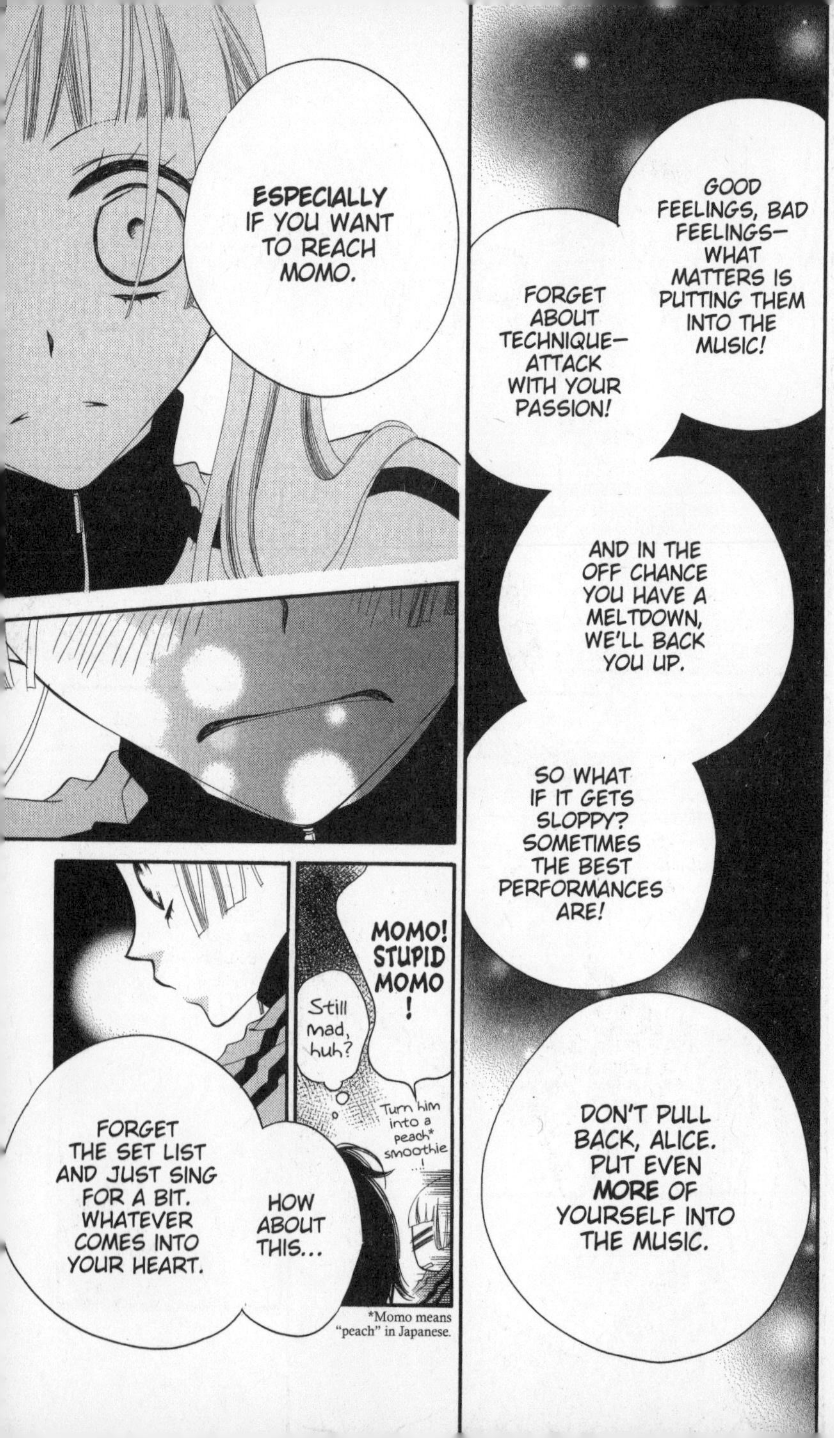
GOOD FEELINGS, BAD FEELINGS— WHAT MATTERS IS PUTTING THEM INTO THE MUSIC!
FORGET ABOUT TECHNIQUE— ATTACK WITH YOUR PASSION!
AND IN THE OFF CHANCE YOU HAVE A MELTDOWN, WE'LL BACK YOU UP.
SO WHAT IF IT GETS SLOPPY? SOMETIMES THE BEST PERFORMANCES ARE!
DON'T PULL BACK, ALICE. PUT EVEN MORE OF YOURSELF INTO THE MUSIC.
ESPECIALLY IF YOU WANT TO REACH MOMO.
MOMO! STUPID MOMO!
Still mad, huh?
Turn him into a peach* smoothie...!
HOW ABOUT THIS...
FORGET THE SET LIST AND JUST SING FOR A BIT. WHATEVER COMES INTO YOUR HEART.
*Momo means "peach" in Japanese.

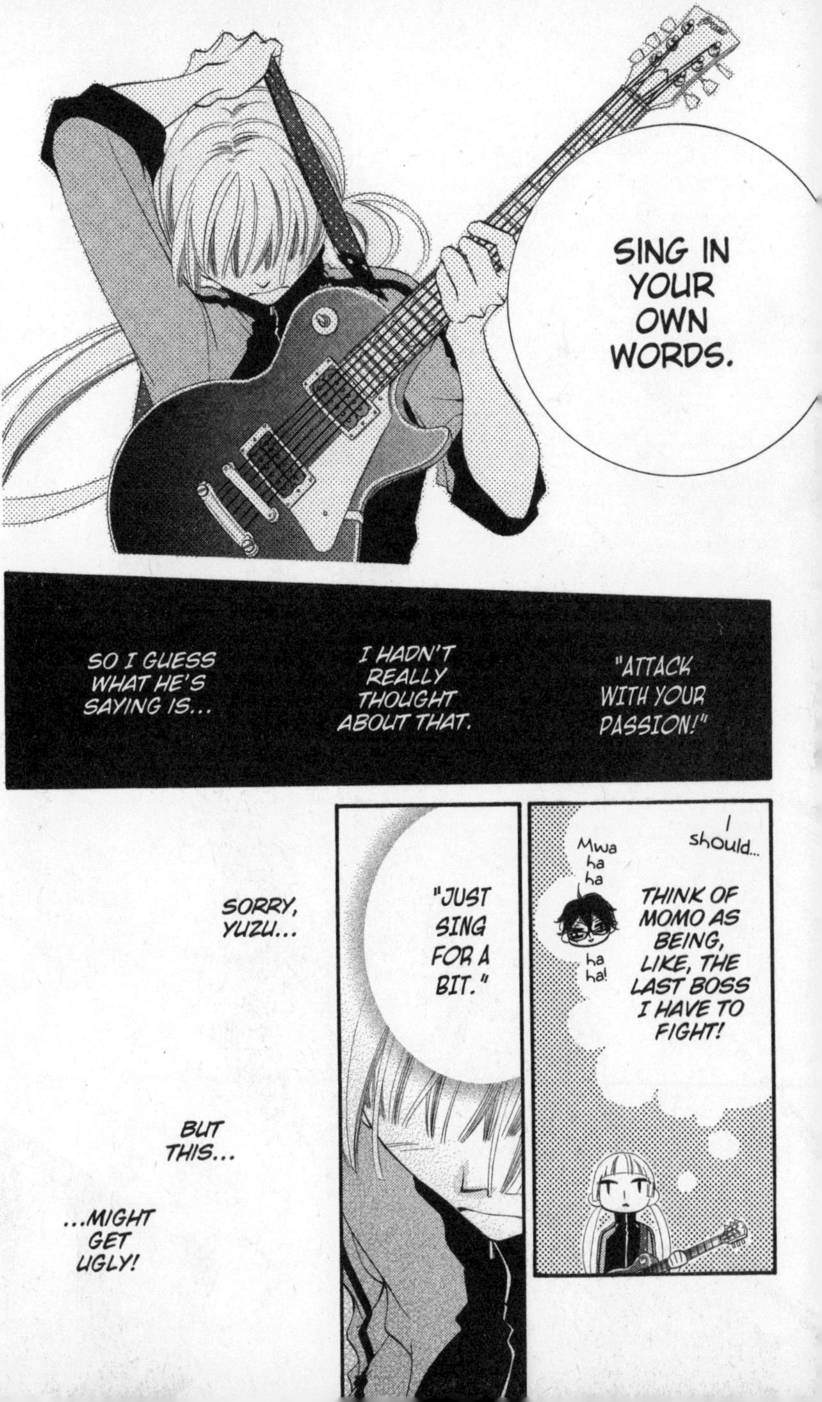
SING IN YOUR OWN WORDS.
"ATTACK WITH YOUR PASSION!"
I HADN'T REALLY THOUGHT ABOUT THAT.
SO I GUESS WHAT HE'S SAYING IS...
I should...
THINK OF MOMO AS BEING, LIKE, THE LAST BOSS I HAVE TO FIGHT!
Mwa ha ha ha ha!
"JUST SING FOR A BIT."
SORRY, YUZU...
BUT THIS...
...MIGHT GET UGLY!

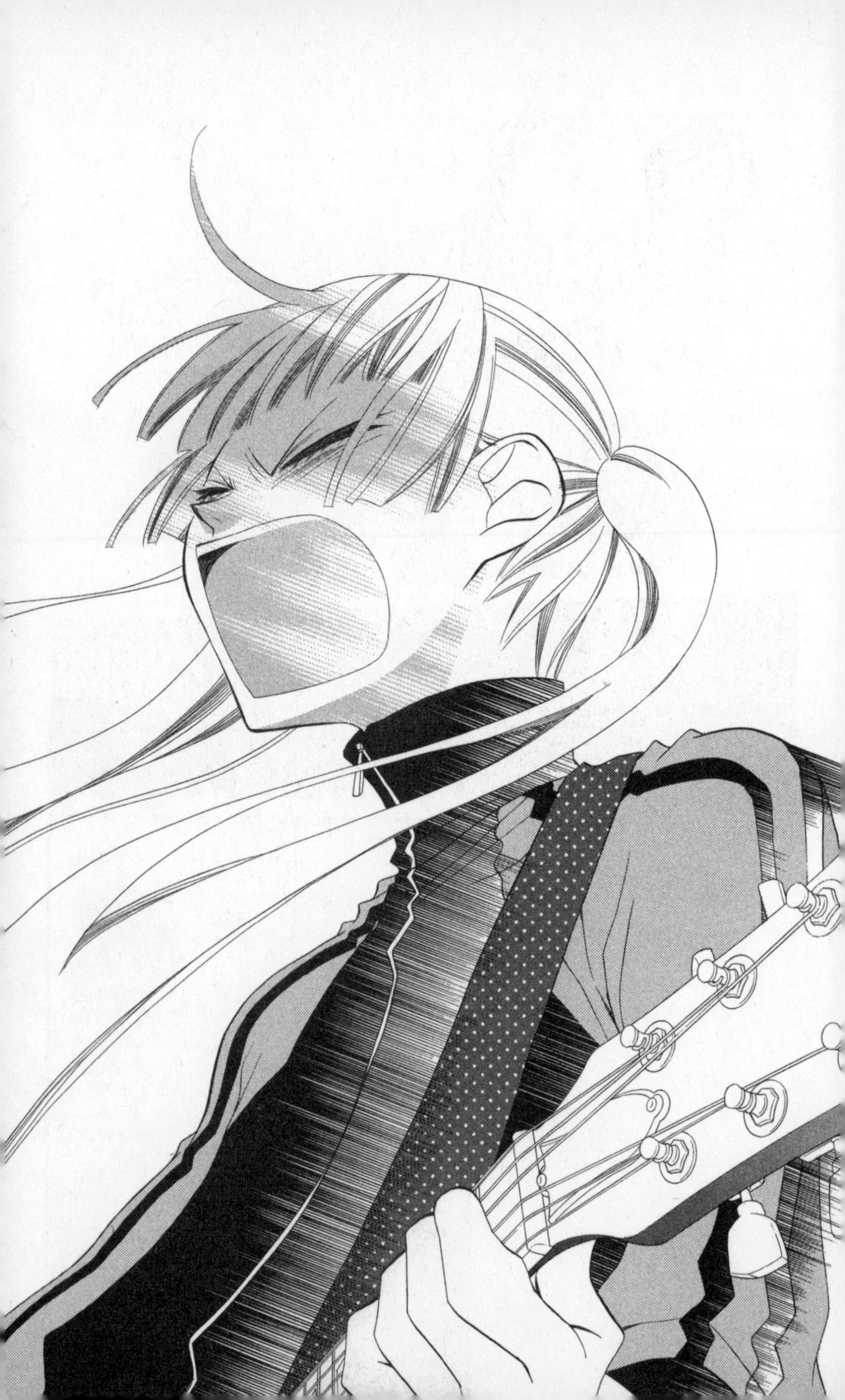

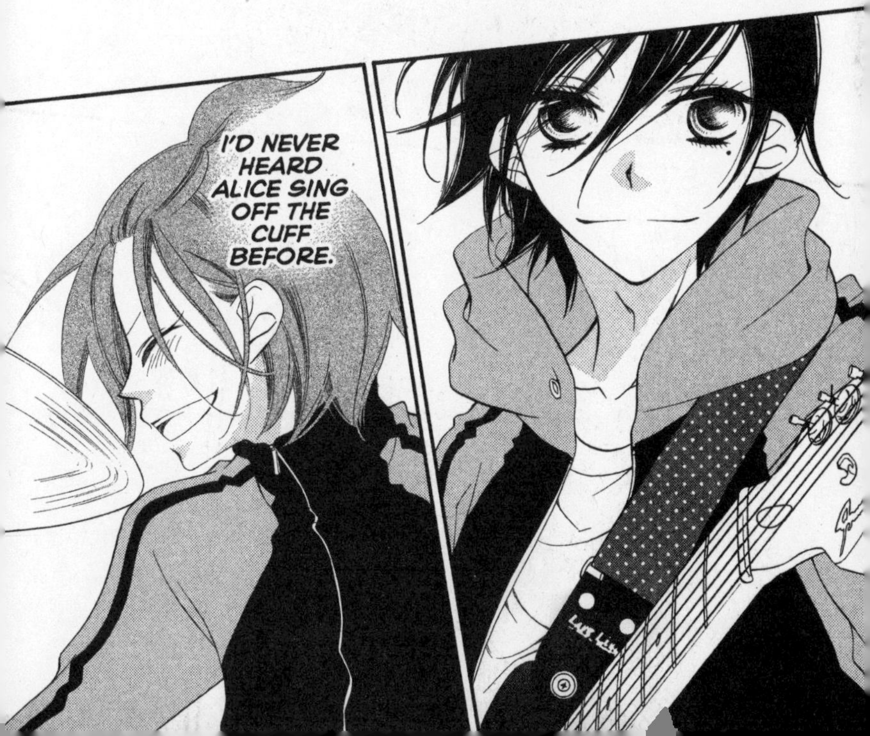
I'D NEVER HEARD ALICE SING OFF THE CUFF BEFORE.

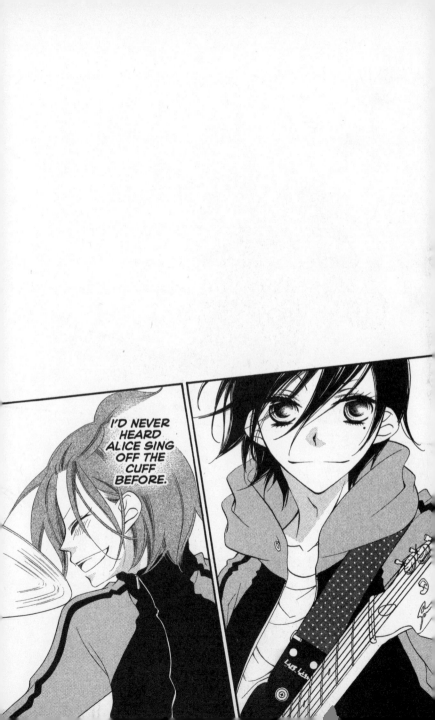

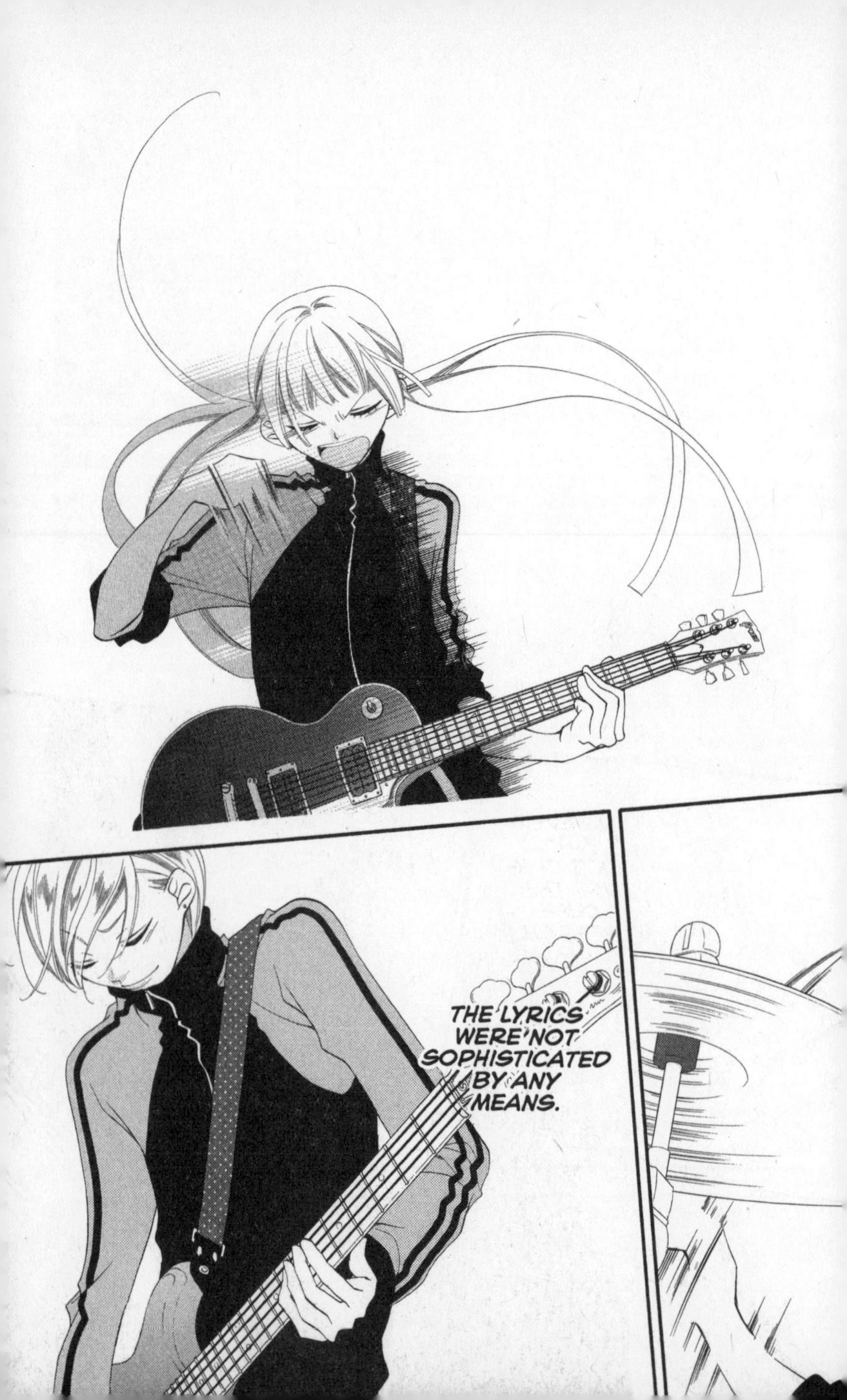
THE LYRICS WERE NOT SOPHISTICATED BY ANY MEANS.

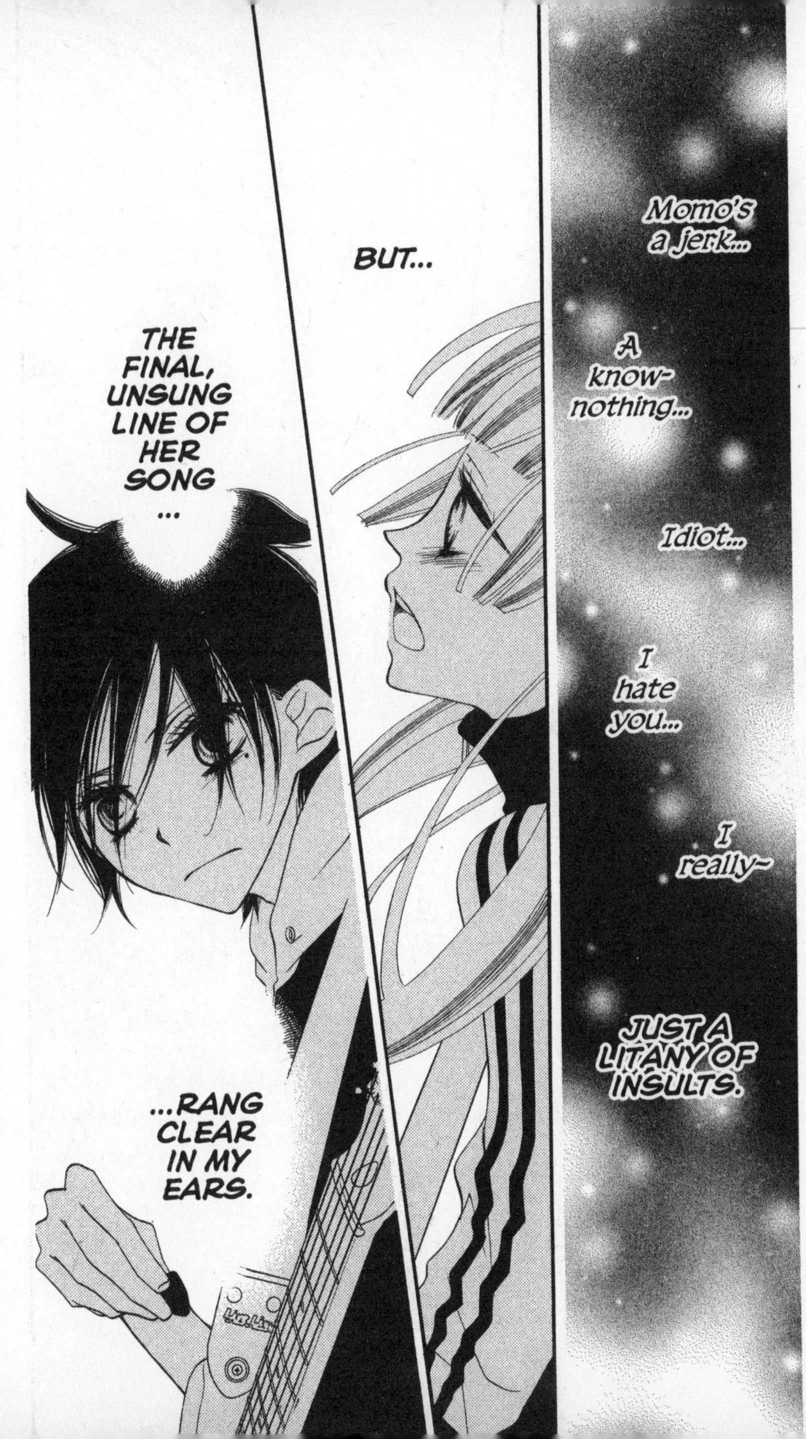
Momo's a jerk...
A know-nothing...
Idiot...
I hate you...
I really~
JUST A LITANY OF INSULTS.
BUT...
THE FINAL, UNSUNG LINE OF HER SONG ...
...RANG CLEAR IN MY EARS.

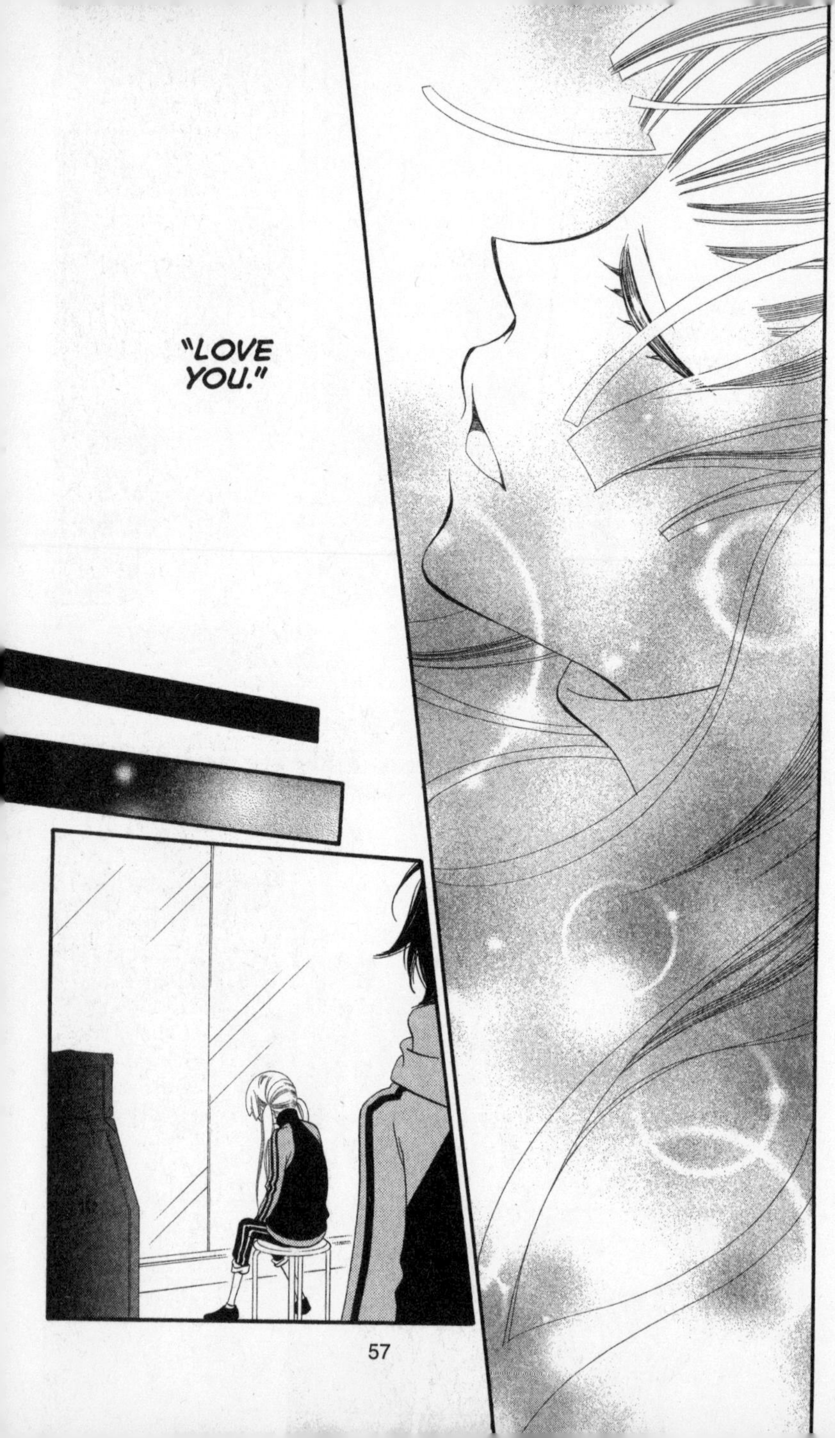
"LOVE YOU."

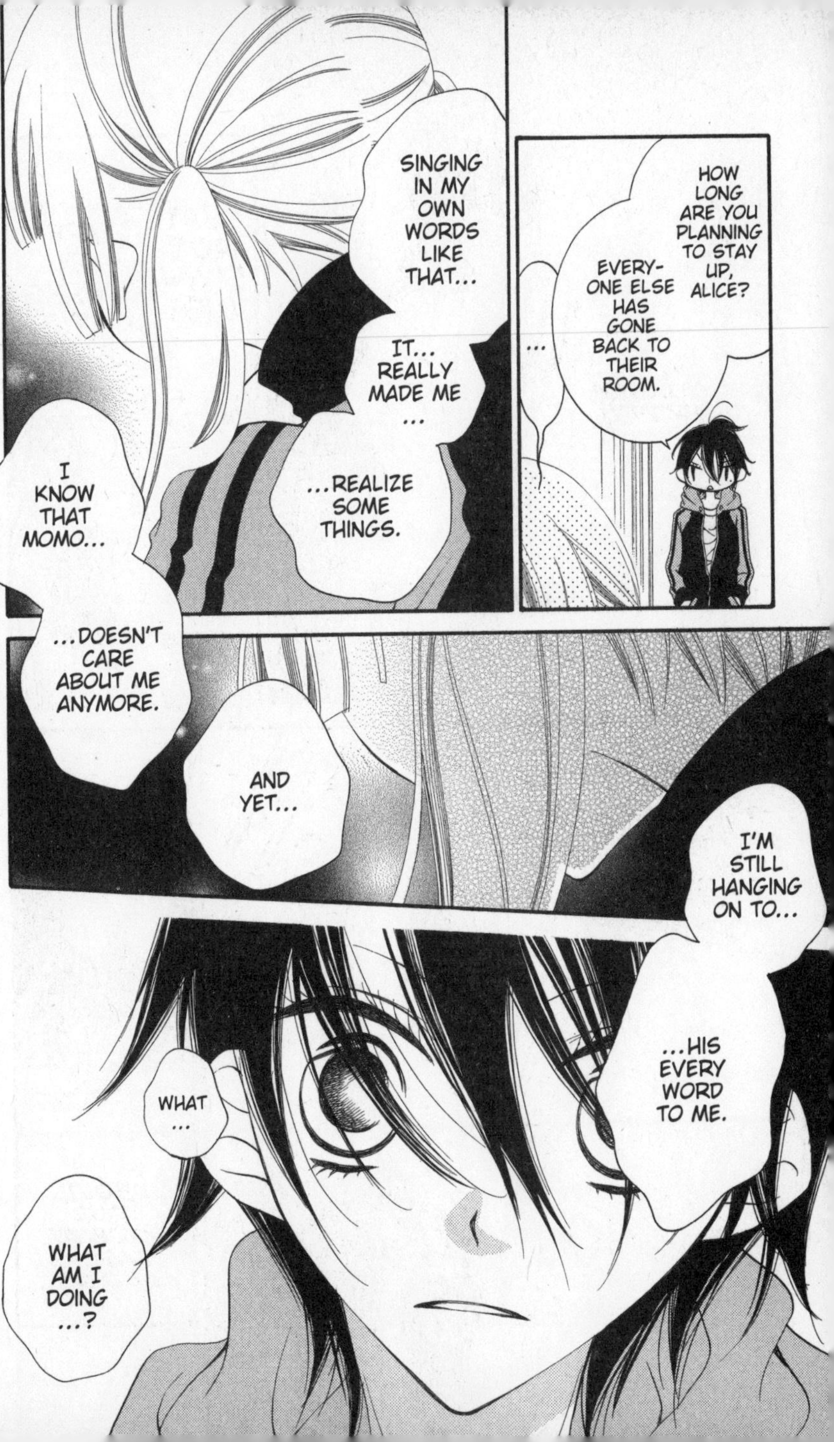
HOW LONG ARE YOU PLANNING TO STAY UP, ALICE?
EVERY-ONE ELSE HAS GONE BACK TO THEIR ROOM.
...
SINGING IN MY OWN WORDS LIKE THAT...
IT... REALLY MADE ME ...
...REALIZE SOME THINGS.
I KNOW THAT MOMO...
...DOESN'T CARE ABOUT ME ANYMORE.
AND YET...
I'M STILL HANGING ON TO...
...HIS EVERY WORD TO ME.
WHAT ...
WHAT AM I DOING ...?

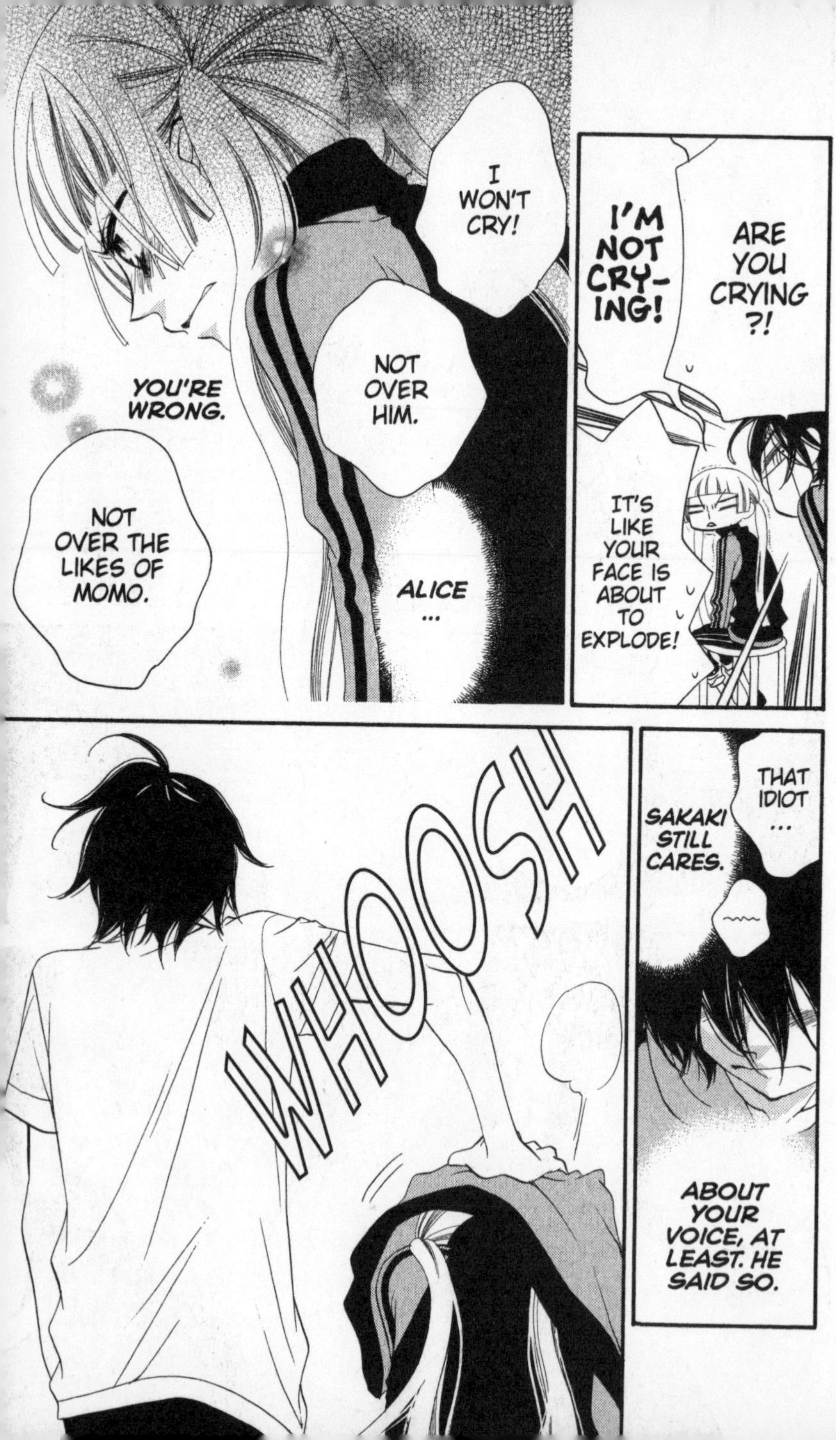
ARE YOU CRYING?!
I'M NOT CRY-ING!
IT'S LIKE YOUR FACE IS ABOUT TO EXPLODE!
I WON'T CRY!
NOT OVER HIM.
YOU'RE WRONG.
ALICE...
NOT OVER THE LIKES OF MOMO.
THAT IDIOT...
SAKAKI STILL CARES.
ABOUT YOUR VOICE, AT LEAST. HE SAID SO.
WHOOSH

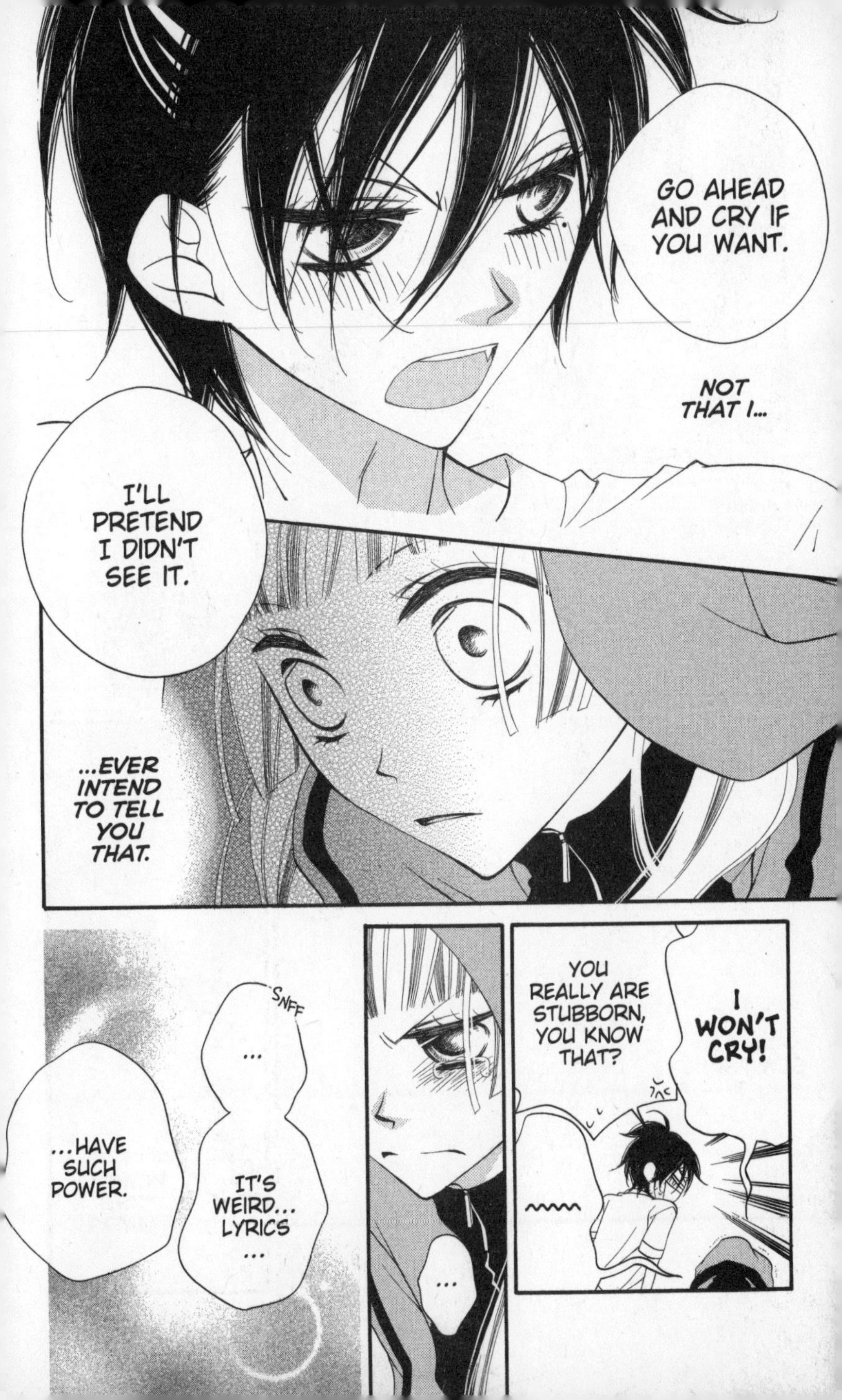
GO AHEAD AND CRY IF YOU WANT.
NOT THAT I...
I'LL PRETEND I DIDN'T SEE IT.
...EVER INTEND TO TELL YOU THAT.
I WON'T CRY!
YOU REALLY ARE STUBBORN, YOU KNOW THAT?
...
SNFF
...
IT'S WEIRD... LYRICS ...
...HAVE SUCH POWER.

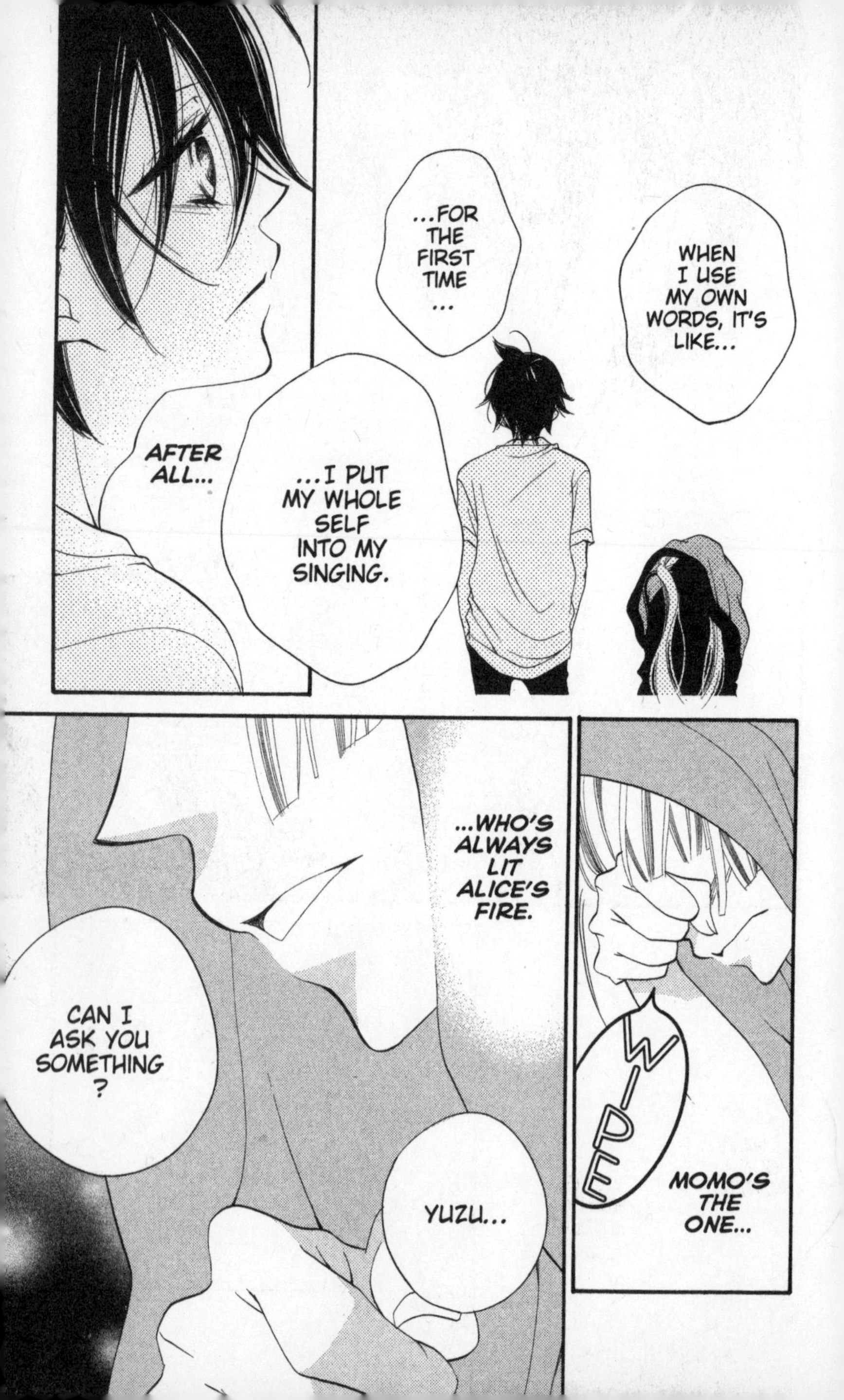
WHEN I USE MY OWN WORDS, IT'S LIKE...
...FOR THE FIRST TIME...
...I PUT MY WHOLE SELF INTO MY SINGING.
AFTER ALL...
WIPE
MOMO'S THE ONE...
...WHO'S ALWAYS LIT ALICE'S FIRE.
YUZU...
CAN I ASK YOU SOMETHING?

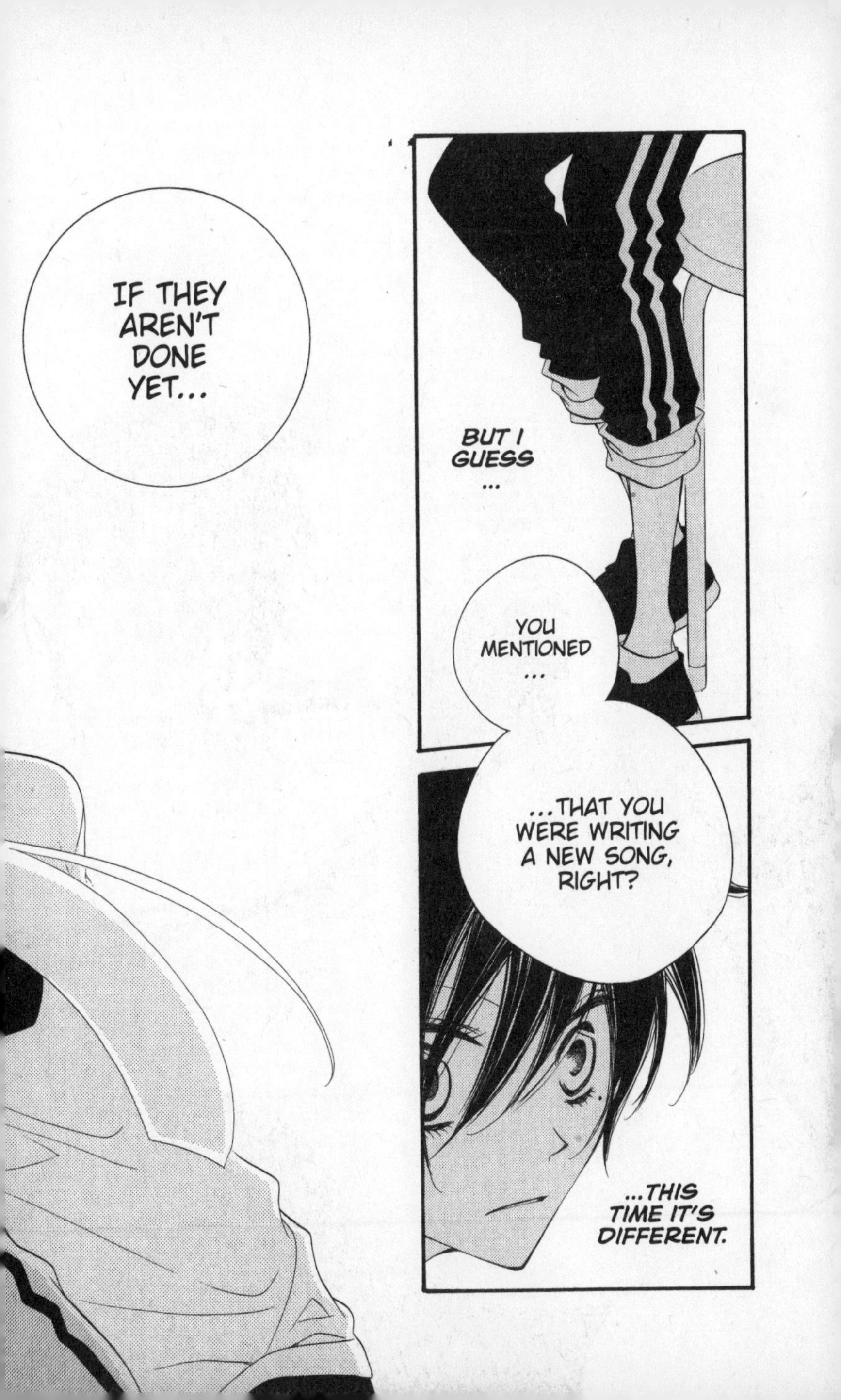
BUT I GUESS ...
YOU MENTIONED ...
...THAT YOU WERE WRITING A NEW SONG, RIGHT?
...THIS TIME IT'S DIFFERENT.
IF THEY AREN'T DONE YET...

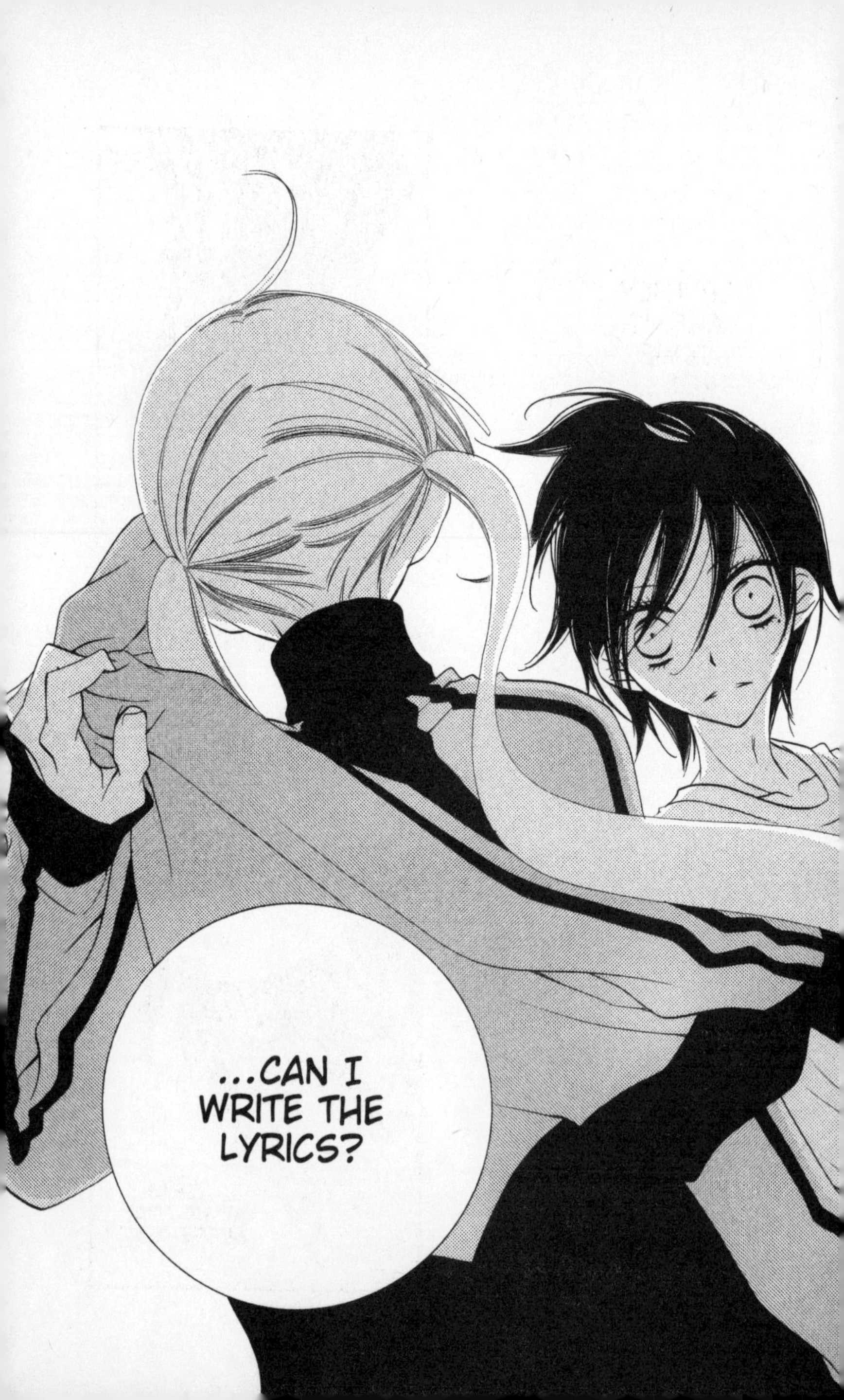
...CAN I WRITE THE LYRICS?

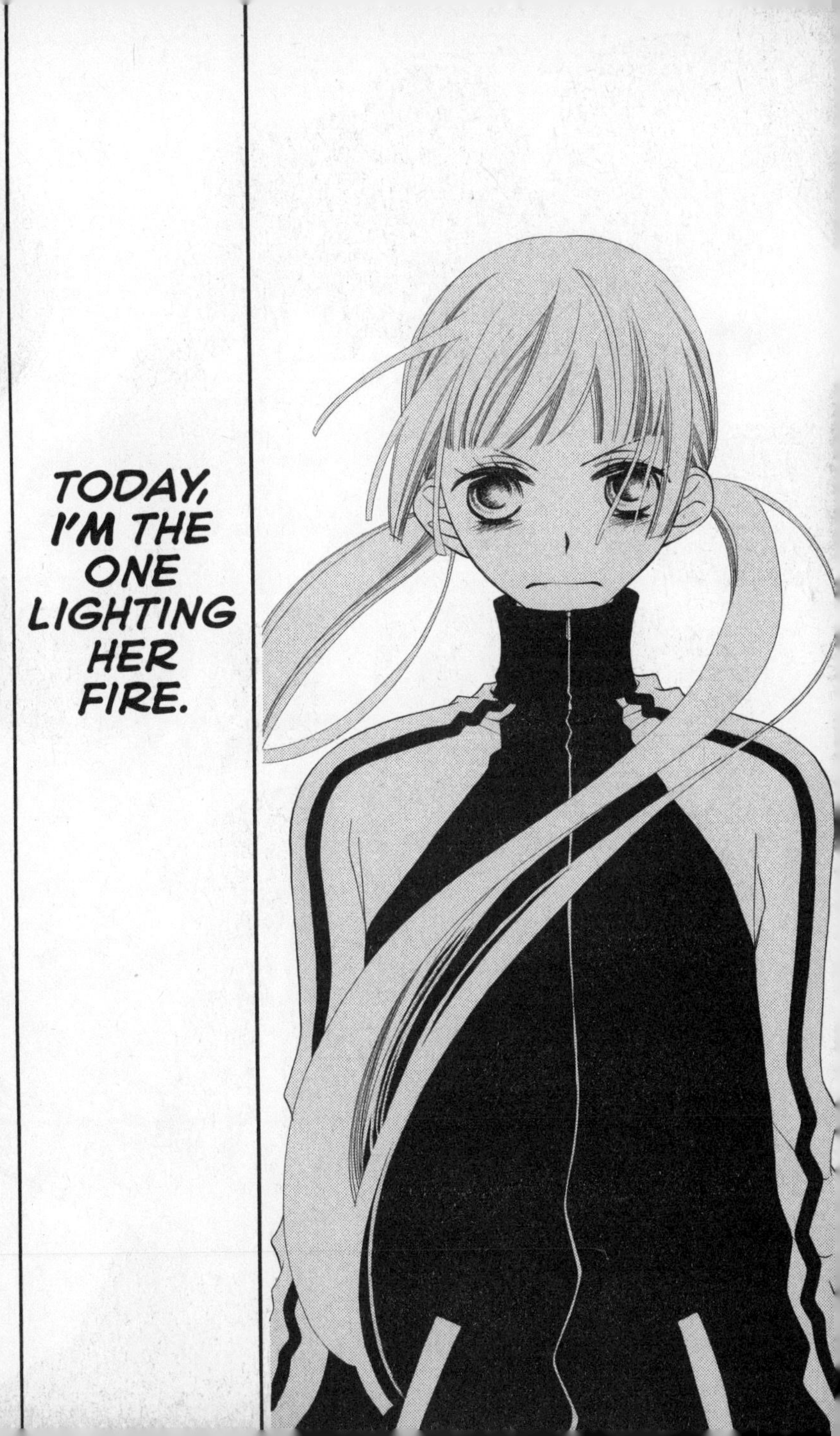
TODAY, I'M THE ONE LIGHTING HER FIRE.

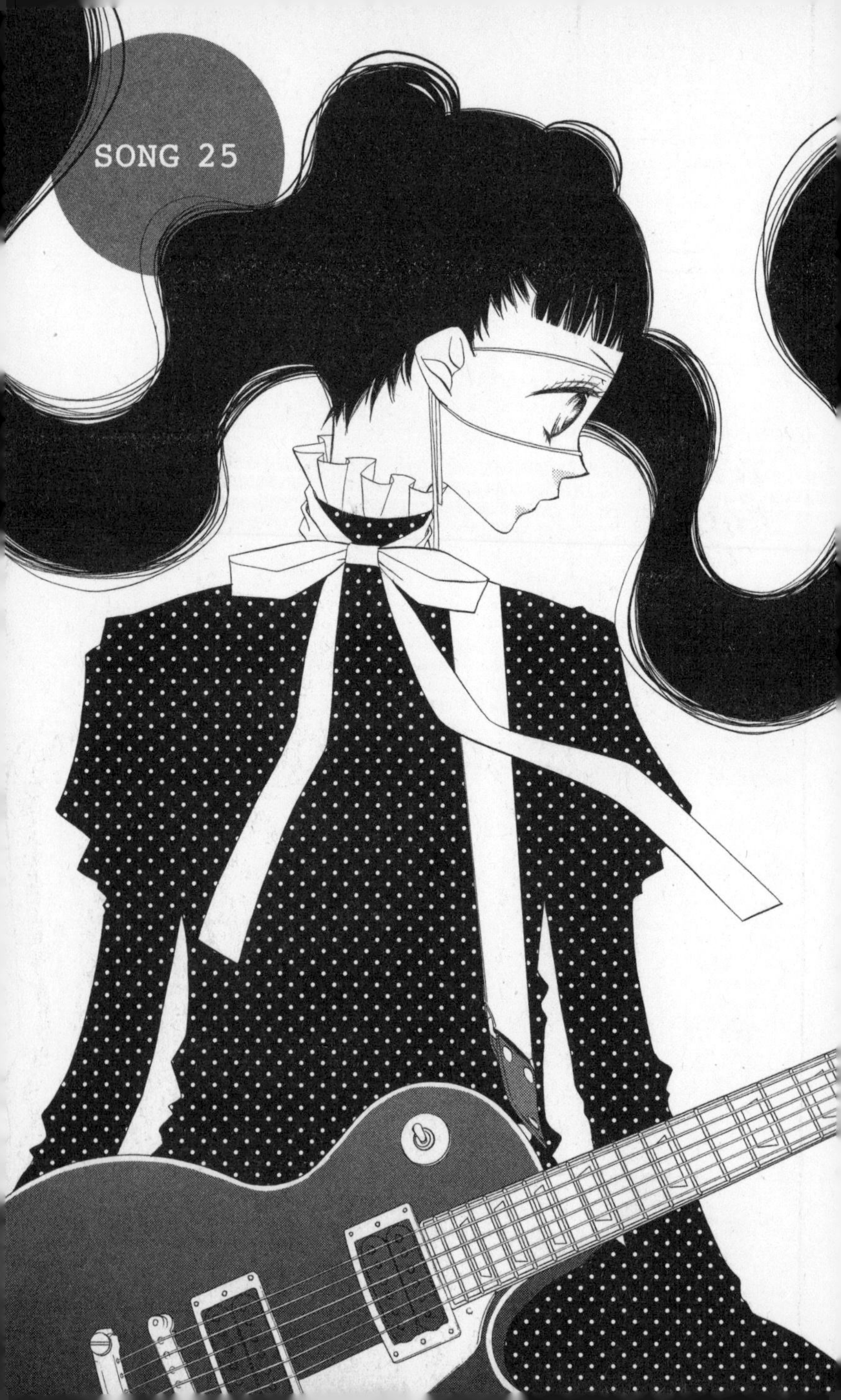
SONG 25

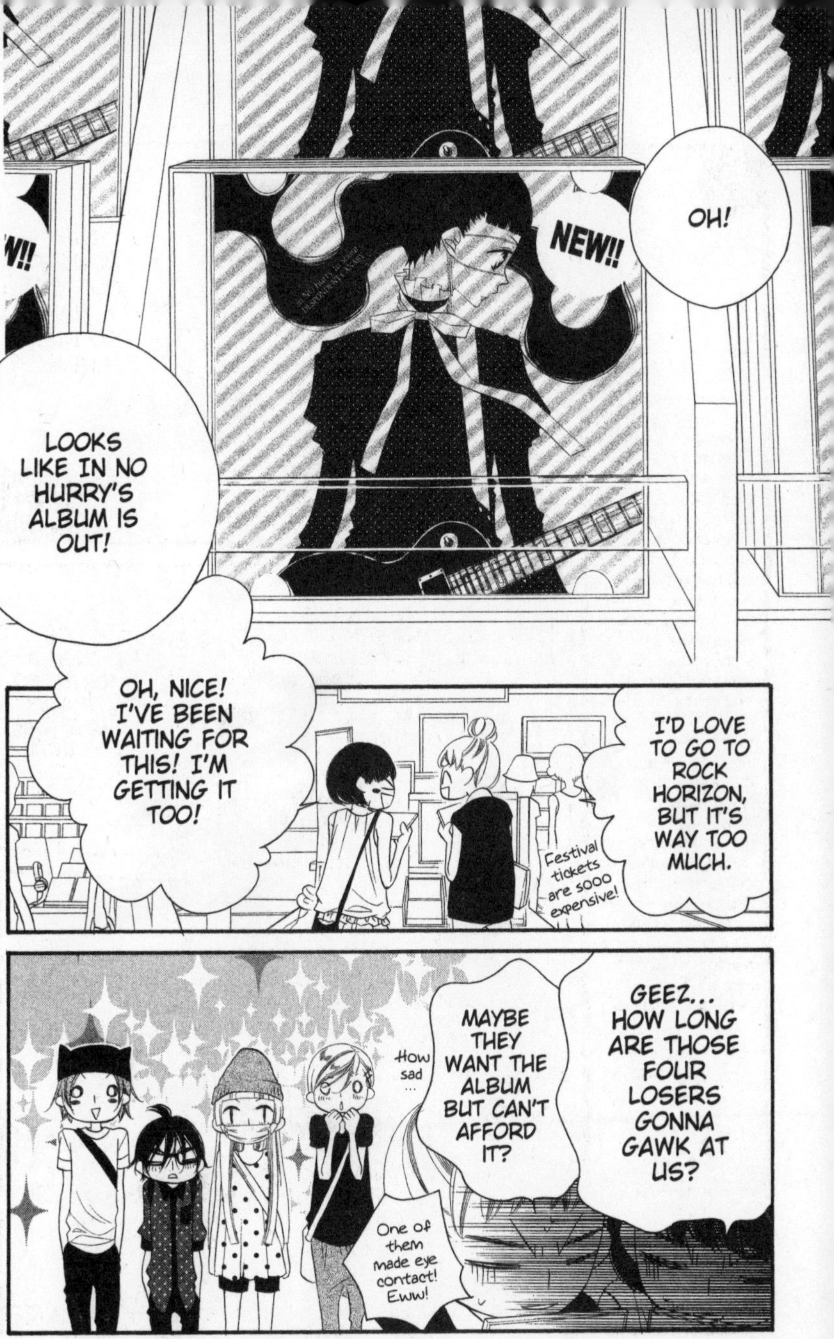
OH!
NEW!!
NEW!!
LOOKS LIKE IN NO HURRY'S ALBUM IS OUT!
I'D LOVE TO GO TO ROCK HORIZON, BUT IT'S WAY TOO MUCH.
Festival tickets are sooo expensive!
OH, NICE! I'VE BEEN WAITING FOR THIS! I'M GETTING IT TOO!
GEEZ... HOW LONG ARE THOSE FOUR LOSERS GONNA GAWK AT US?
MAYBE THEY WANT THE ALBUM BUT CAN'T AFFORD IT?
How sad...
One of them made eye contact! Eww!

3

Before I met her in person, my impression was that she was a strong and wonderful person who was always appreciative of her fans. Meeting her has only reinforced that! She's somehow so incredibly cute and cool all at once. I'm so glad that I met A-chan when I did, as I, too, have been feeling a renewed and intense sense of gratitude for all my readers lately. (I know I haven't mentioned that here.) Such perfect timing!

IT REALLY WAS!

To be continued in #4!

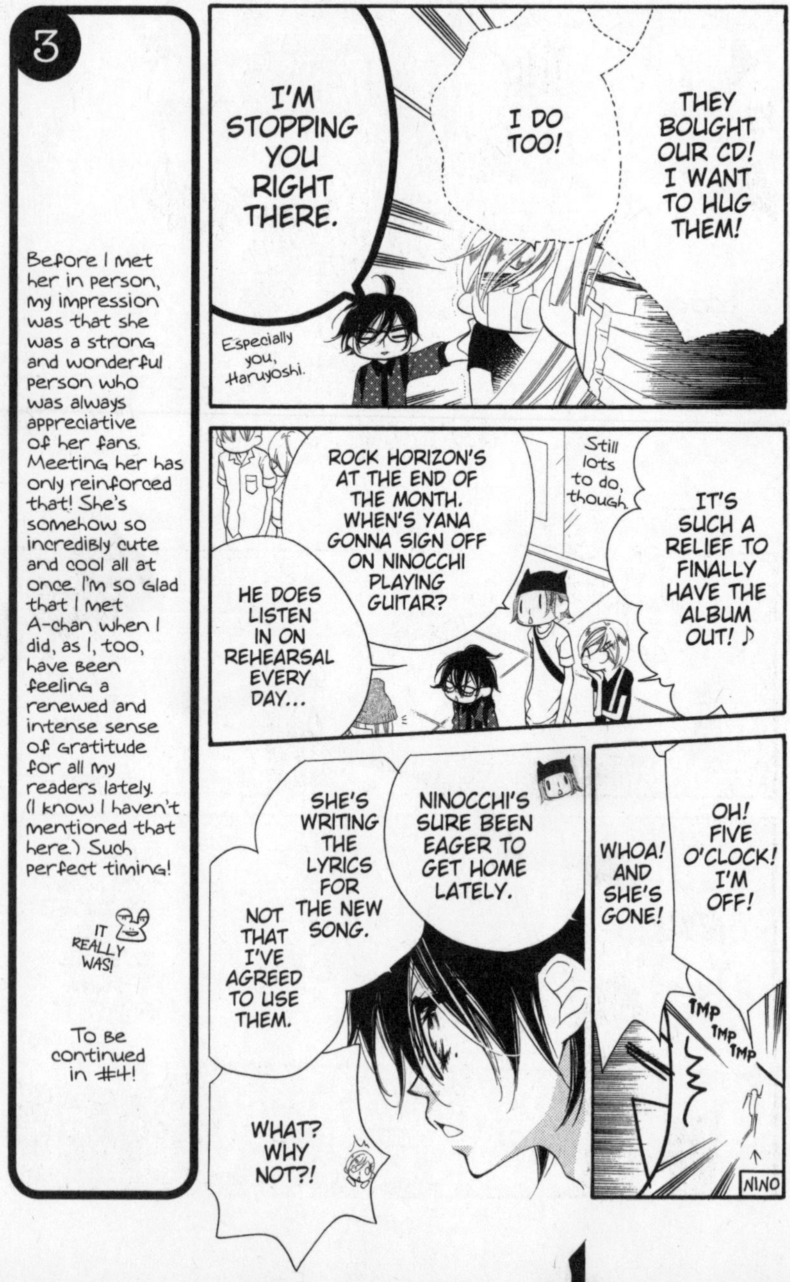
THEY BOUGHT OUR CD! I WANT TO HUG THEM!
I DO TOO!
I'M STOPPING YOU RIGHT THERE.
Especially you, Haruyoshi.
IT'S SUCH A RELIEF TO FINALLY HAVE THE ALBUM OUT! ♪
Still lots to do, though.
ROCK HORIZON'S AT THE END OF THE MONTH. WHEN'S YANA GONNA SIGN OFF ON NINOCCHI PLAYING GUITAR?
HE DOES LISTEN IN ON REHEARSAL EVERY DAY...
OH! FIVE O'CLOCK! I'M OFF!
WHOA! AND SHE'S GONE!
TMP TMP TMP
NINO
NINOCCHI'S SURE BEEN EAGER TO GET HOME LATELY.
SHE'S WRITING THE LYRICS FOR THE NEW SONG.
NOT THAT I'VE AGREED TO USE THEM.
WHAT? WHY NOT?!

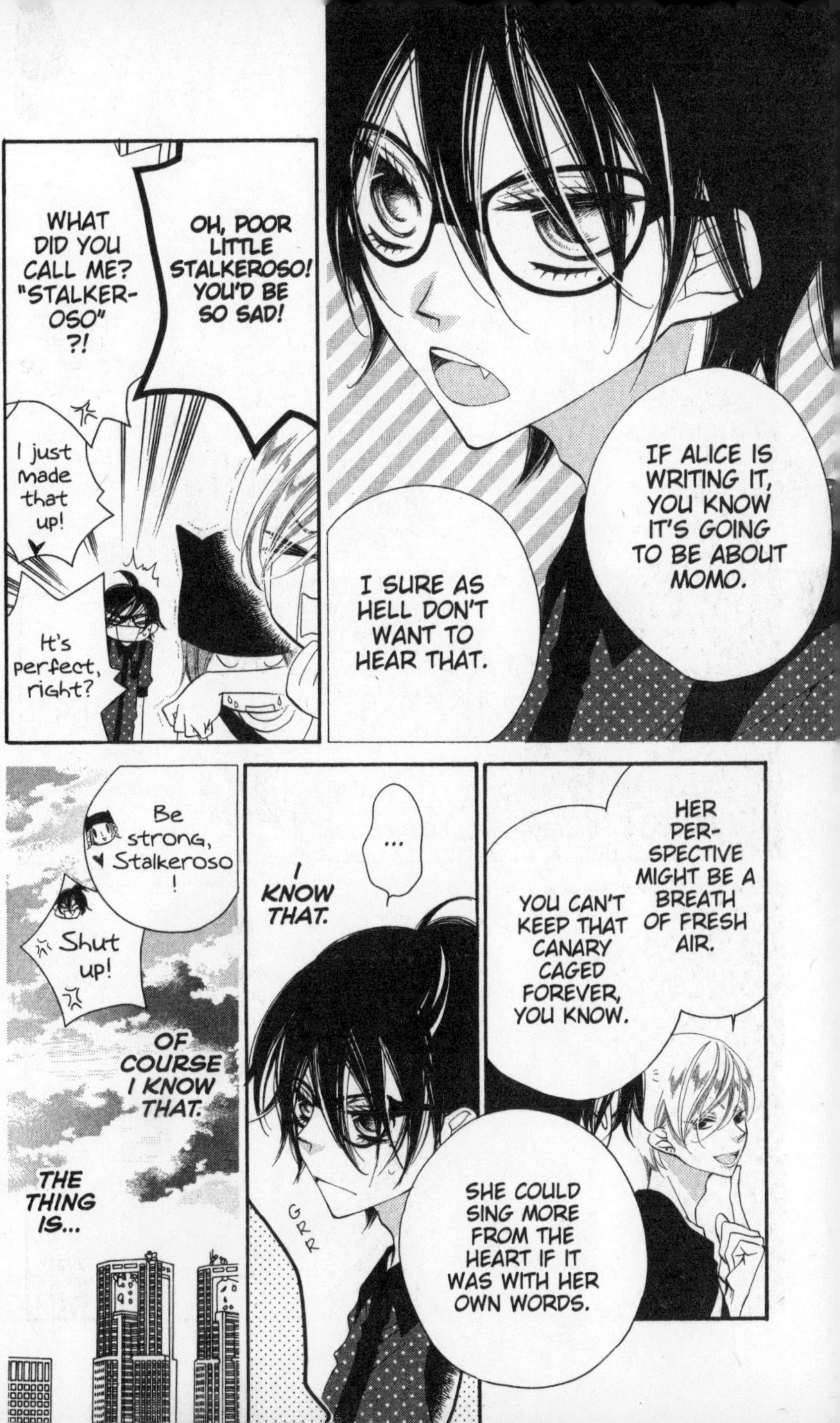
IF ALICE IS WRITING IT, YOU KNOW IT'S GOING TO BE ABOUT MOMO.
I SURE AS HELL DON'T WANT TO HEAR THAT.
OH, POOR LITTLE STALKEROSO! YOU'D BE SO SAD!
WHAT DID YOU CALL ME? "STALKER-OSO" ?!
I just made that up!
It's perfect, right?
HER PER-SPECTIVE MIGHT BE A BREATH OF FRESH AIR.
YOU CAN'T KEEP THAT CANARY CAGED FOREVER, YOU KNOW.
SHE COULD SING MORE FROM THE HEART IF IT WAS WITH HER OWN WORDS.
GRR
...
I KNOW THAT.
Be strong, Stalkeroso!
Shut up!
OF COURSE I KNOW THAT.
THE THING IS...

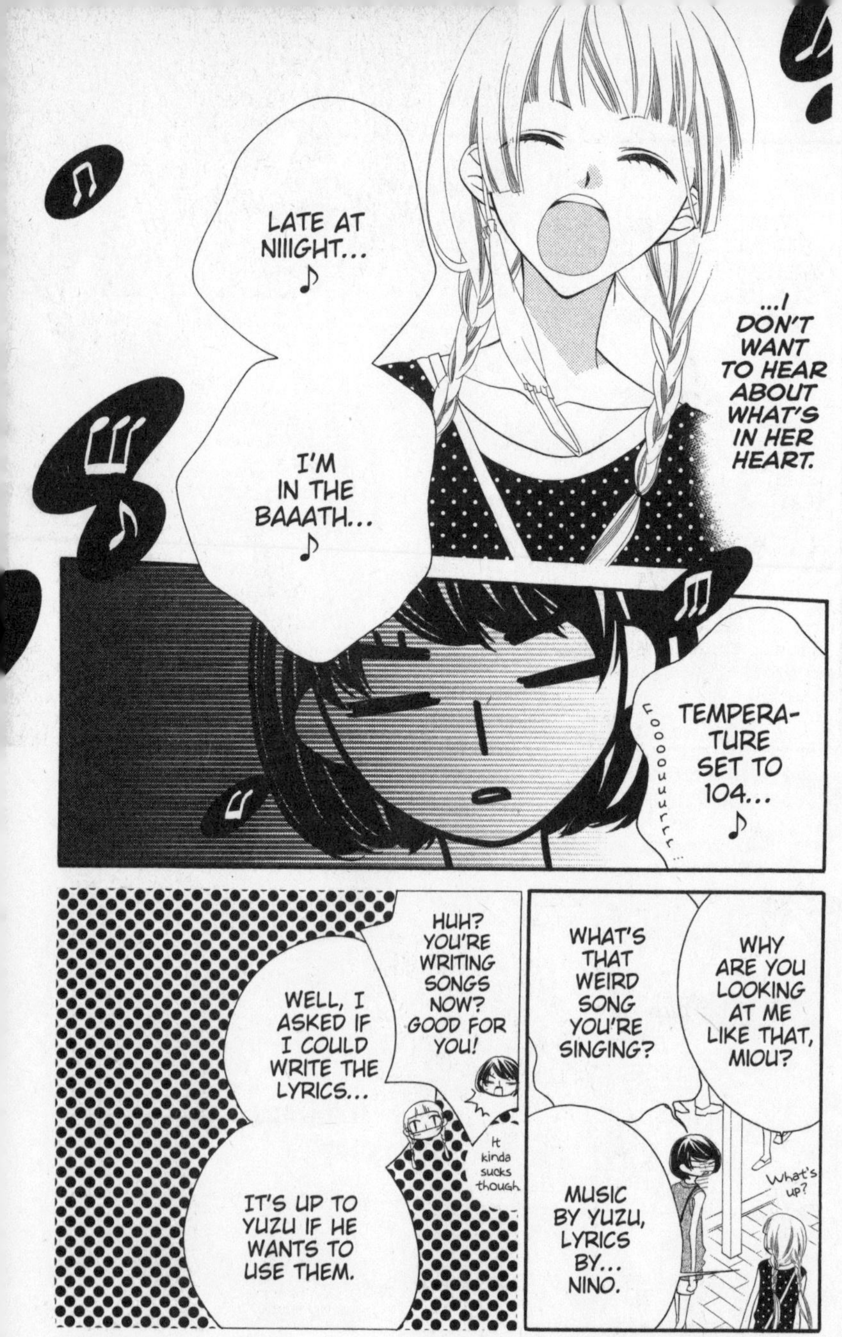
LATE AT NIIIGHT... ♪ I'M IN THE BAAATH... ♪
...I DON'T WANT TO HEAR ABOUT WHAT'S IN HER HEART.
TEMPERATURE SET TO 104... ♪
Foooouuurrr...
WHY ARE YOU LOOKING AT ME LIKE THAT, MIOU?
What's up?
WHAT'S THAT WEIRD SONG YOU'RE SINGING?
MUSIC BY YUZU, LYRICS BY... NINO.
HUH? YOU'RE WRITING SONGS NOW? GOOD FOR YOU!
WELL, I ASKED IF I COULD WRITE THE LYRICS...
It kinda sucks though
IT'S UP TO YUZU IF HE WANTS TO USE THEM.

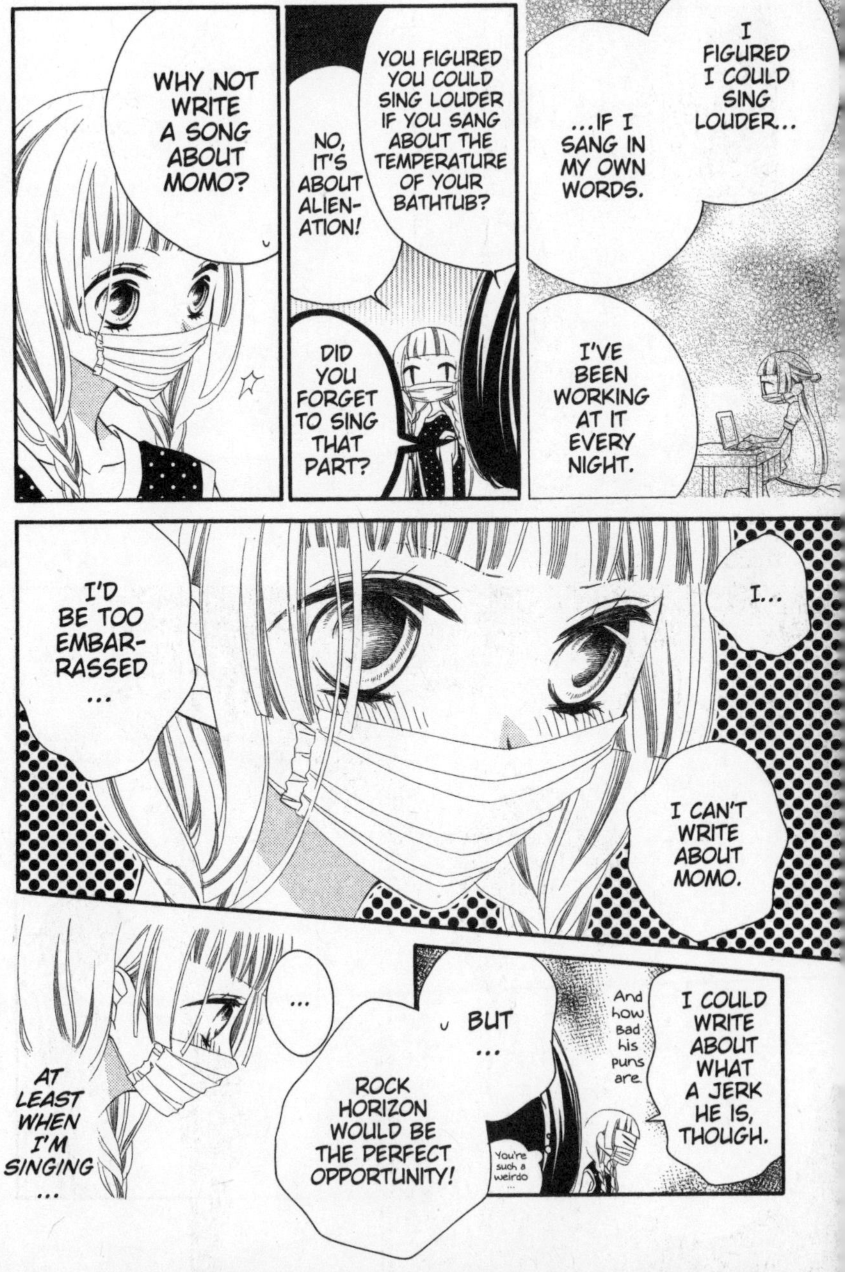
I FIGURED I COULD SING LOUDER...
...IF I SANG IN MY OWN WORDS.
I'VE BEEN WORKING AT IT EVERY NIGHT.
YOU FIGURED YOU COULD SING LOUDER IF YOU SANG ABOUT THE TEMPERATURE OF YOUR BATHTUB?
NO, IT'S ABOUT ALIEN-ATION!
DID YOU FORGET TO SING THAT PART?
WHY NOT WRITE A SONG ABOUT MOMO?
I...
I'D BE TOO EMBAR-RASSED...
I CAN'T WRITE ABOUT MOMO.
I COULD WRITE ABOUT WHAT A JERK HE IS, THOUGH.
And how bad his puns are.
You're such a weirdo...
...
BUT...
ROCK HORIZON WOULD BE THE PERFECT OPPORTUNITY!
AT LEAST WHEN I'M SINGING...

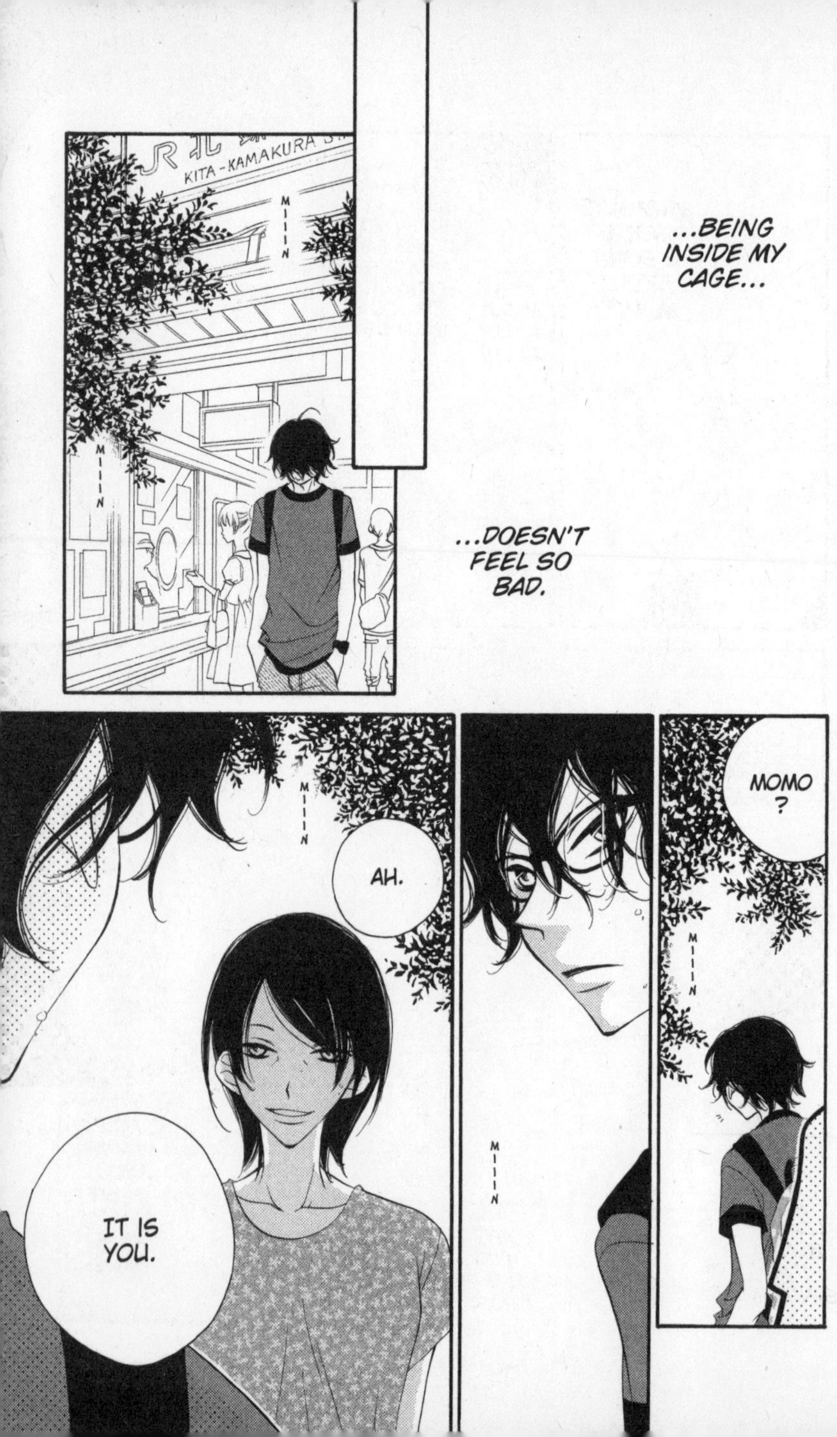
...BEING INSIDE MY CAGE...
...DOESN'T FEEL SO BAD.
KITA-KAMAKURA
MIIN
MIIN
MOMO ?
MIIN
MIIN
MIIN
AH.
IT IS YOU.

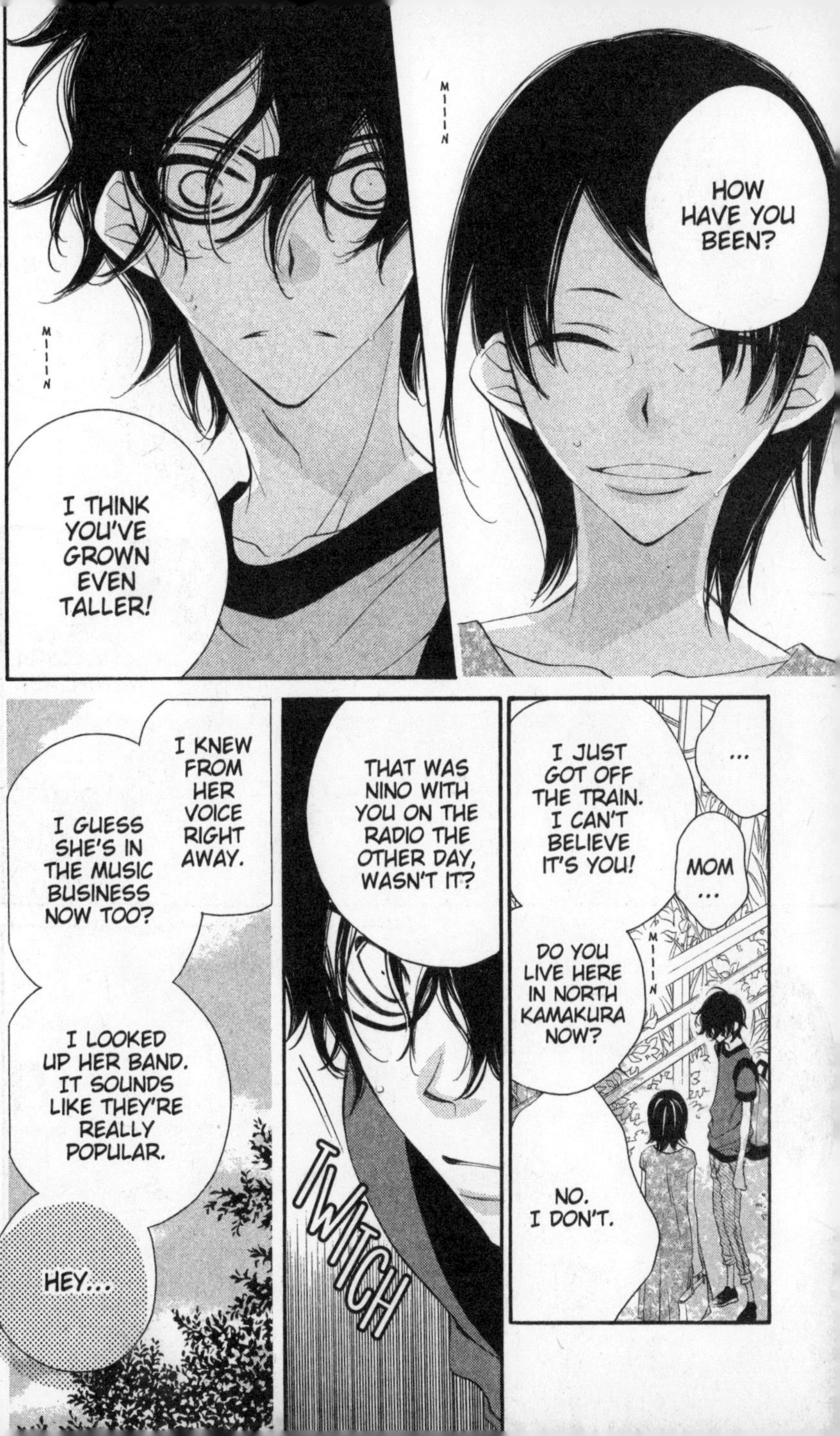
MIIN
HOW HAVE YOU BEEN?
MIIN
I THINK YOU'VE GROWN EVEN TALLER!
...
I JUST GOT OFF THE TRAIN. I CAN'T BELIEVE IT'S YOU!
MOM ...
MIIN
DO YOU LIVE HERE IN NORTH KAMAKURA NOW?
NO. I DON'T.
THAT WAS NINO WITH YOU ON THE RADIO THE OTHER DAY, WASN'T IT?
TWITCH
I KNEW FROM HER VOICE RIGHT AWAY.
I GUESS SHE'S IN THE MUSIC BUSINESS NOW TOO?
I LOOKED UP HER BAND. IT SOUNDS LIKE THEY'RE REALLY POPULAR.
HEY...

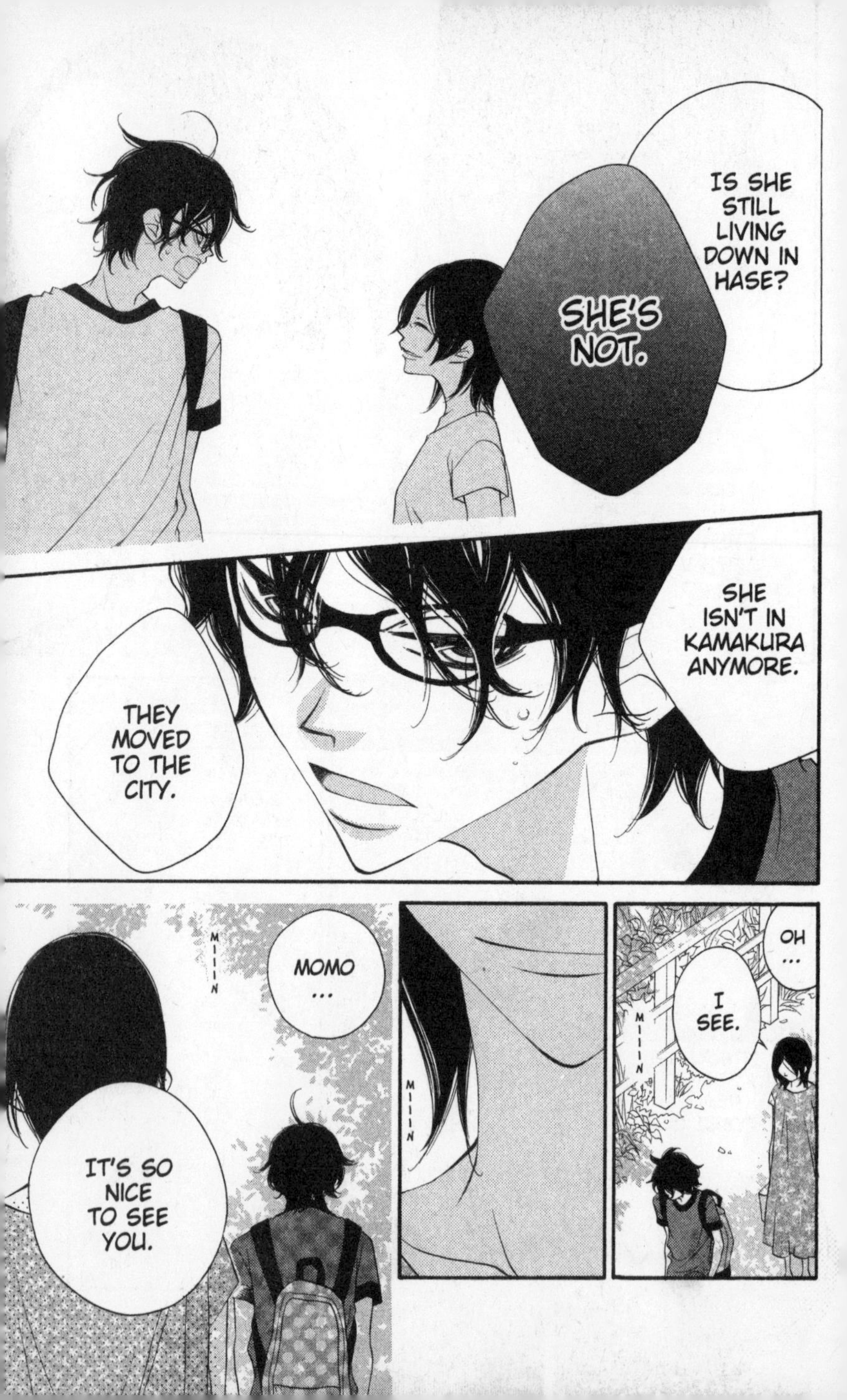
IS SHE STILL LIVING DOWN IN HASE?
SHE'S NOT.
SHE ISN'T IN KAMAKURA ANYMORE.
THEY MOVED TO THE CITY.
OH ...
I SEE.
MIIN
MIIN
MIIN
MOMO ...
IT'S SO NICE TO SEE YOU.

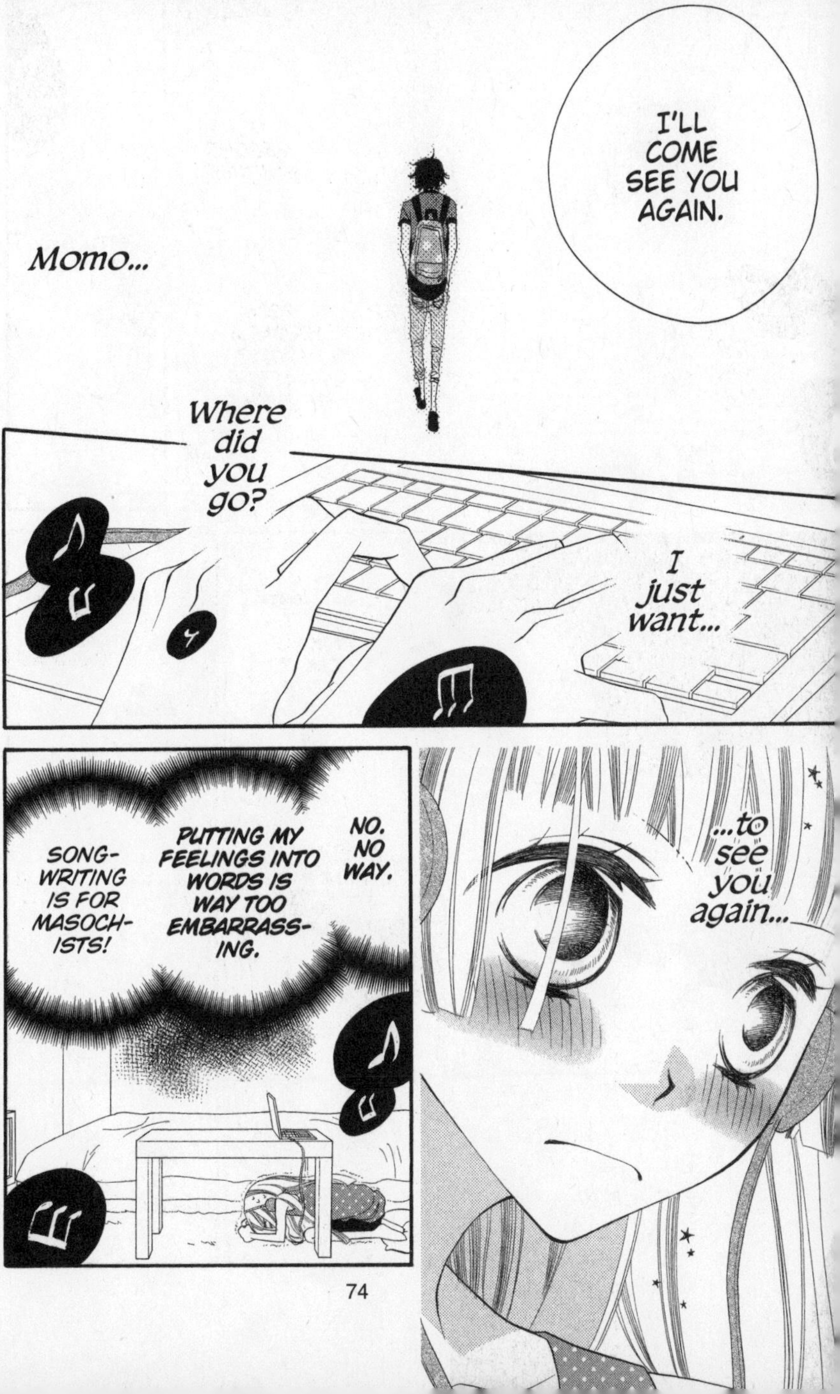
I'LL COME SEE YOU AGAIN.
Momo...
Where did you go?
I just want...
...to see you again...
NO. NO WAY.
PUTTING MY FEELINGS INTO WORDS IS WAY TOO EMBARRASSING.
SONGWRITING IS FOR MASOCHISTS!

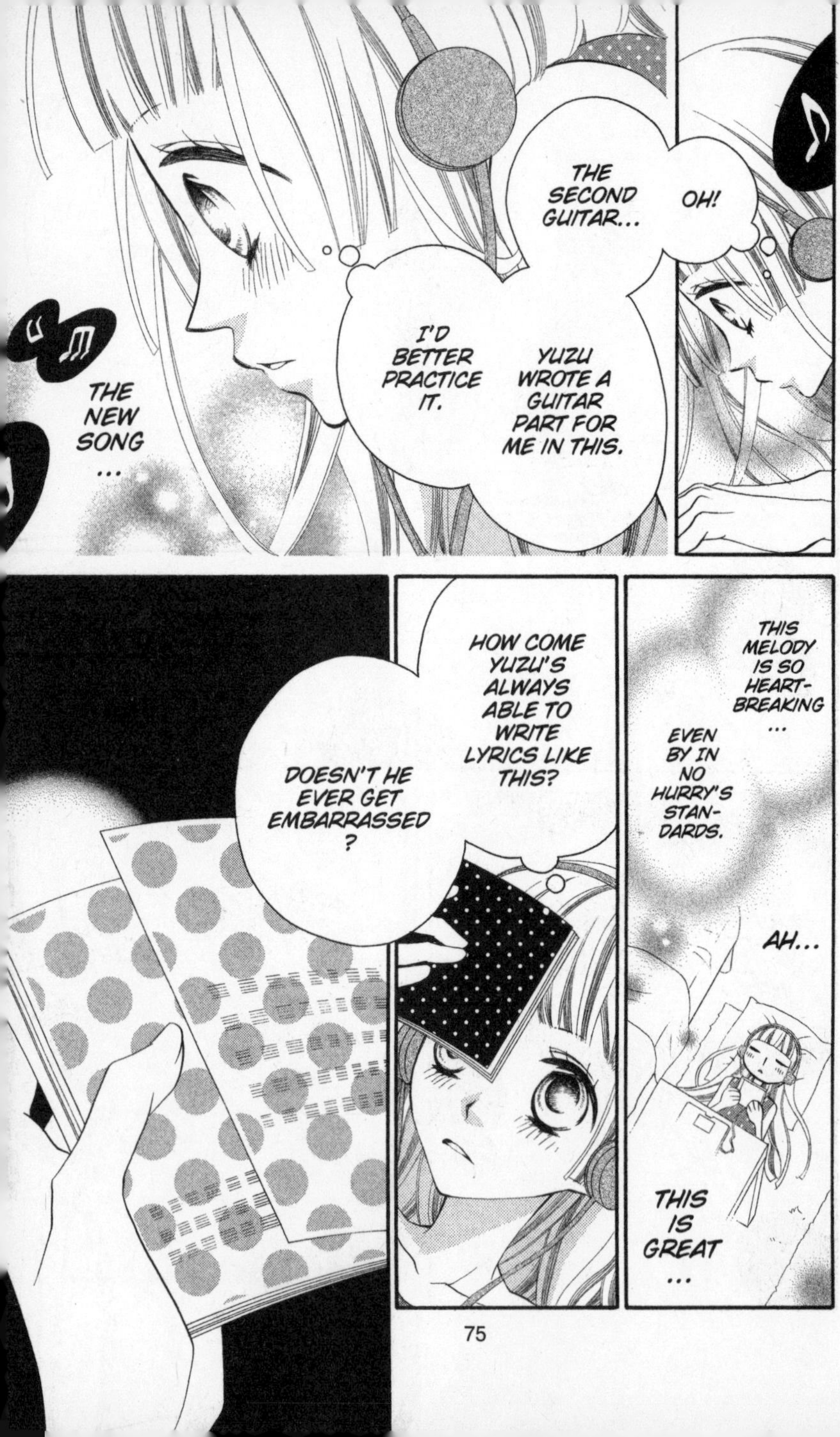
OH!
THE SECOND GUITAR...
YUZU WROTE A GUITAR PART FOR ME IN THIS.
I'D BETTER PRACTICE IT.
THE NEW SONG ...
THIS MELODY IS SO HEART-BREAKING ...
EVEN BY IN NO HURRY'S STAN-DARDS.
AH...
THIS IS GREAT ...
HOW COME YUZU'S ALWAYS ABLE TO WRITE LYRICS LIKE THIS?
DOESN'T HE EVER GET EMBARRASSED ?

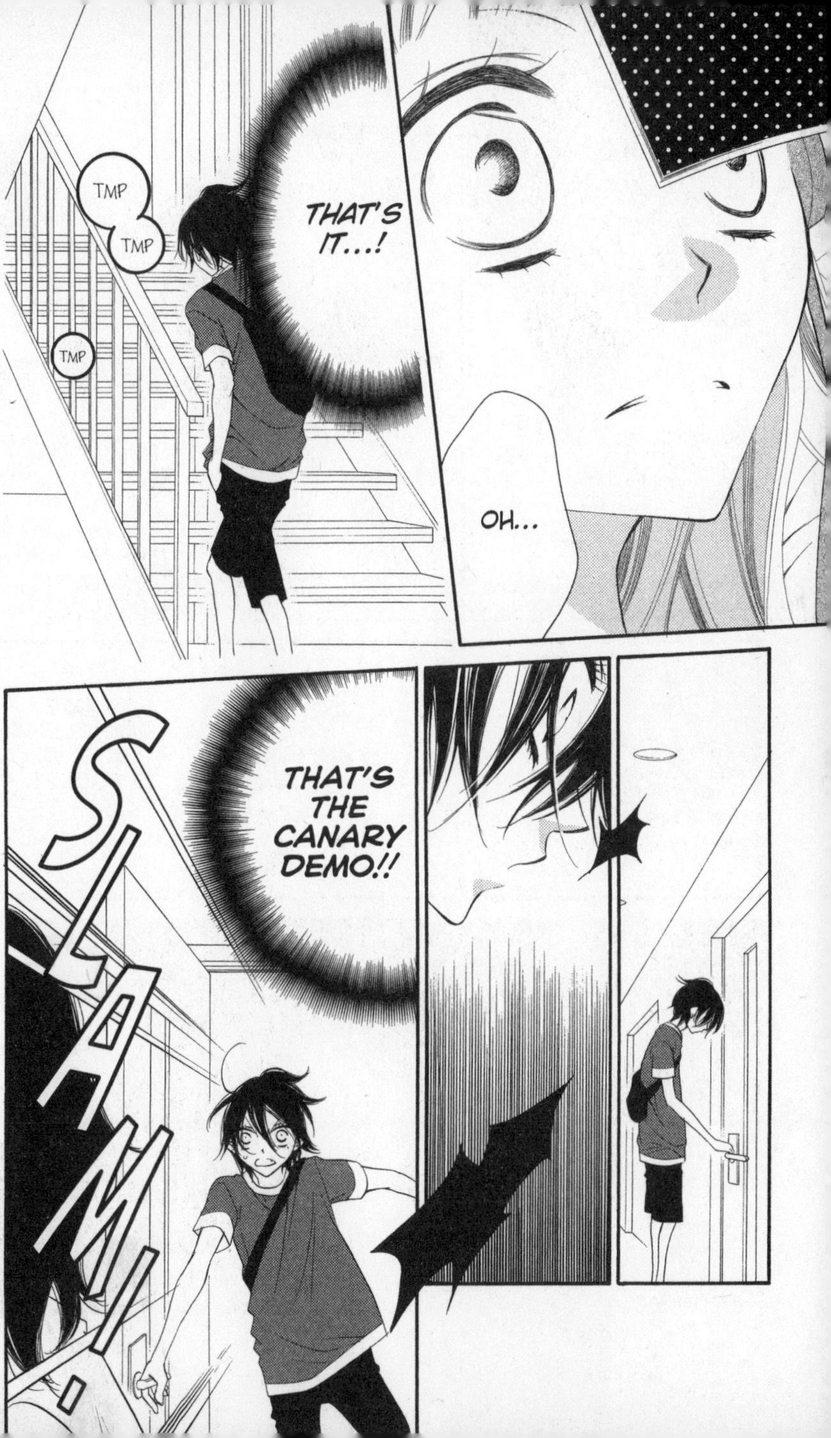
OH...
THAT'S IT...!
TMP
TMP
TMP
THAT'S THE CANARY DEMO!!
SLAM!

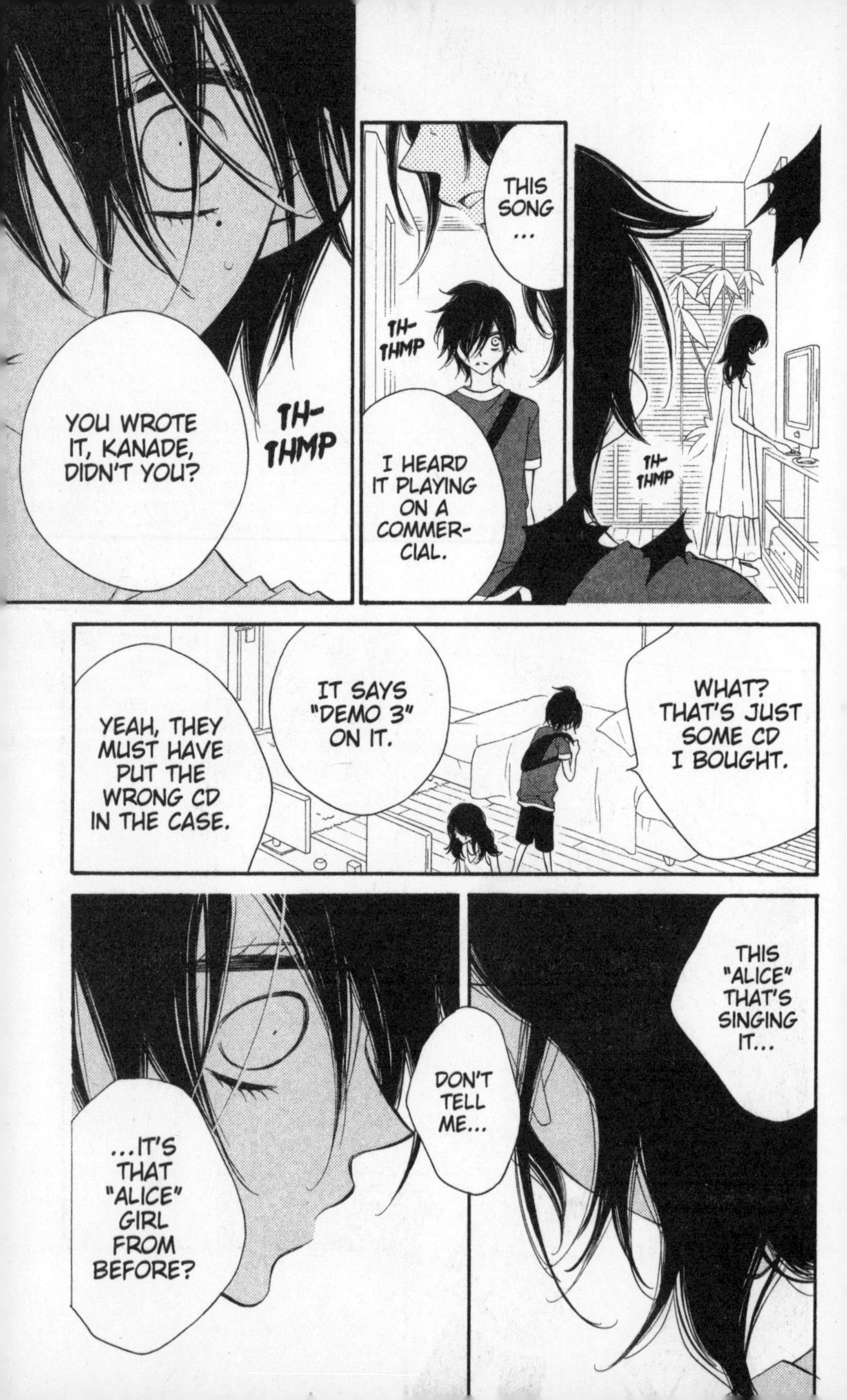
TH-THMP
THIS SONG...
TH-THMP
I HEARD IT PLAYING ON A COMMERCIAL.
YOU WROTE IT, KANADE, DIDN'T YOU?
TH-THMP
WHAT? THAT'S JUST SOME CD I BOUGHT.
IT SAYS "DEMO 3" ON IT.
YEAH, THEY MUST HAVE PUT THE WRONG CD IN THE CASE.
THIS "ALICE" THAT'S SINGING IT...
DON'T TELL ME...
...IT'S THAT "ALICE" GIRL FROM BEFORE?

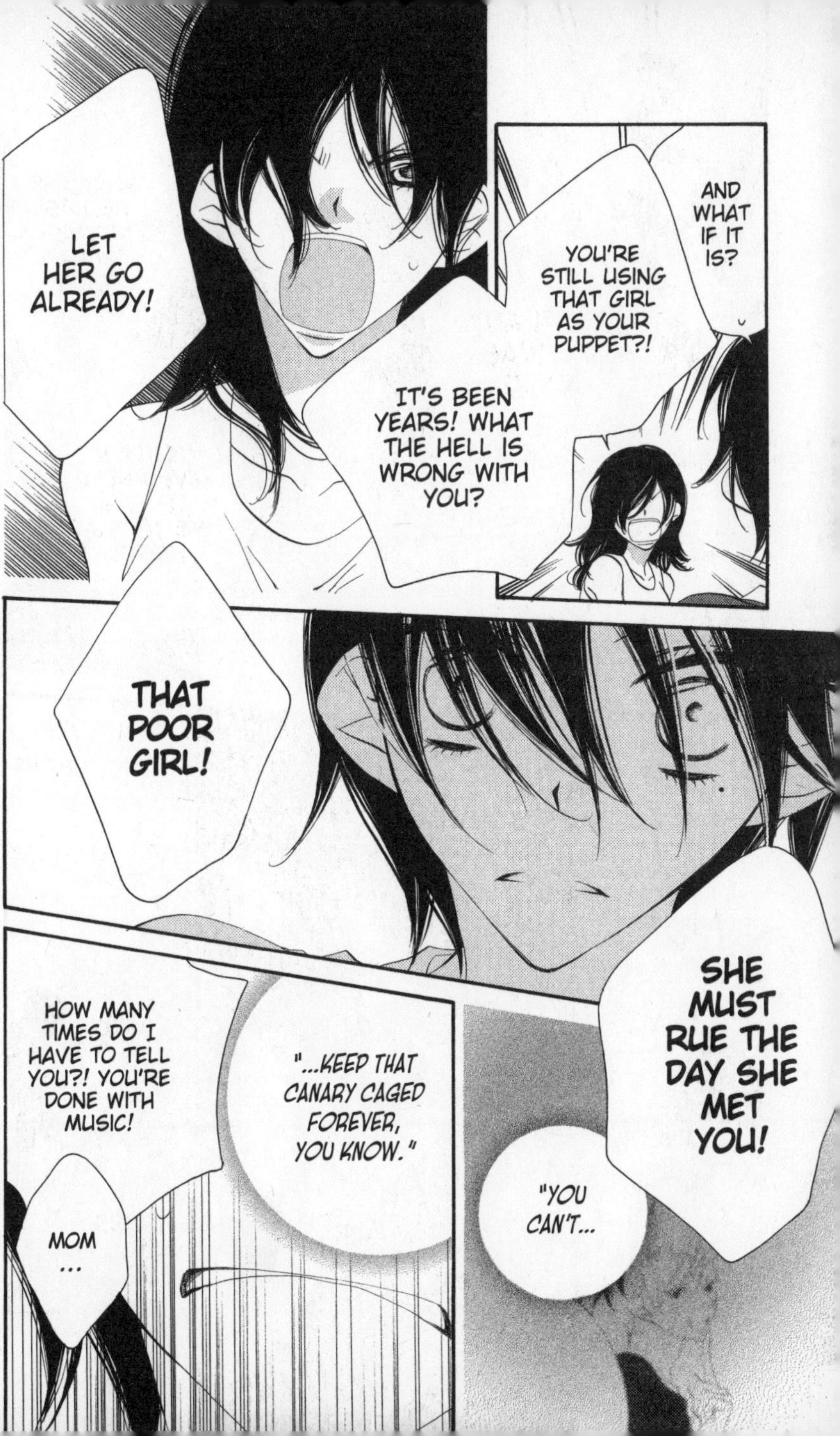
YOU'RE STILL USING THAT GIRL AS YOUR PUPPET?!
AND WHAT IF IT IS?
IT'S BEEN YEARS! WHAT THE HELL IS WRONG WITH YOU?
LET HER GO ALREADY!
THAT POOR GIRL!
SHE MUST RUE THE DAY SHE MET YOU!
"YOU CAN'T...
"...KEEP THAT CANARY CAGED FOREVER, YOU KNOW."
HOW MANY TIMES DO I HAVE TO TELL YOU?! YOU'RE DONE WITH MUSIC!
MOM ...

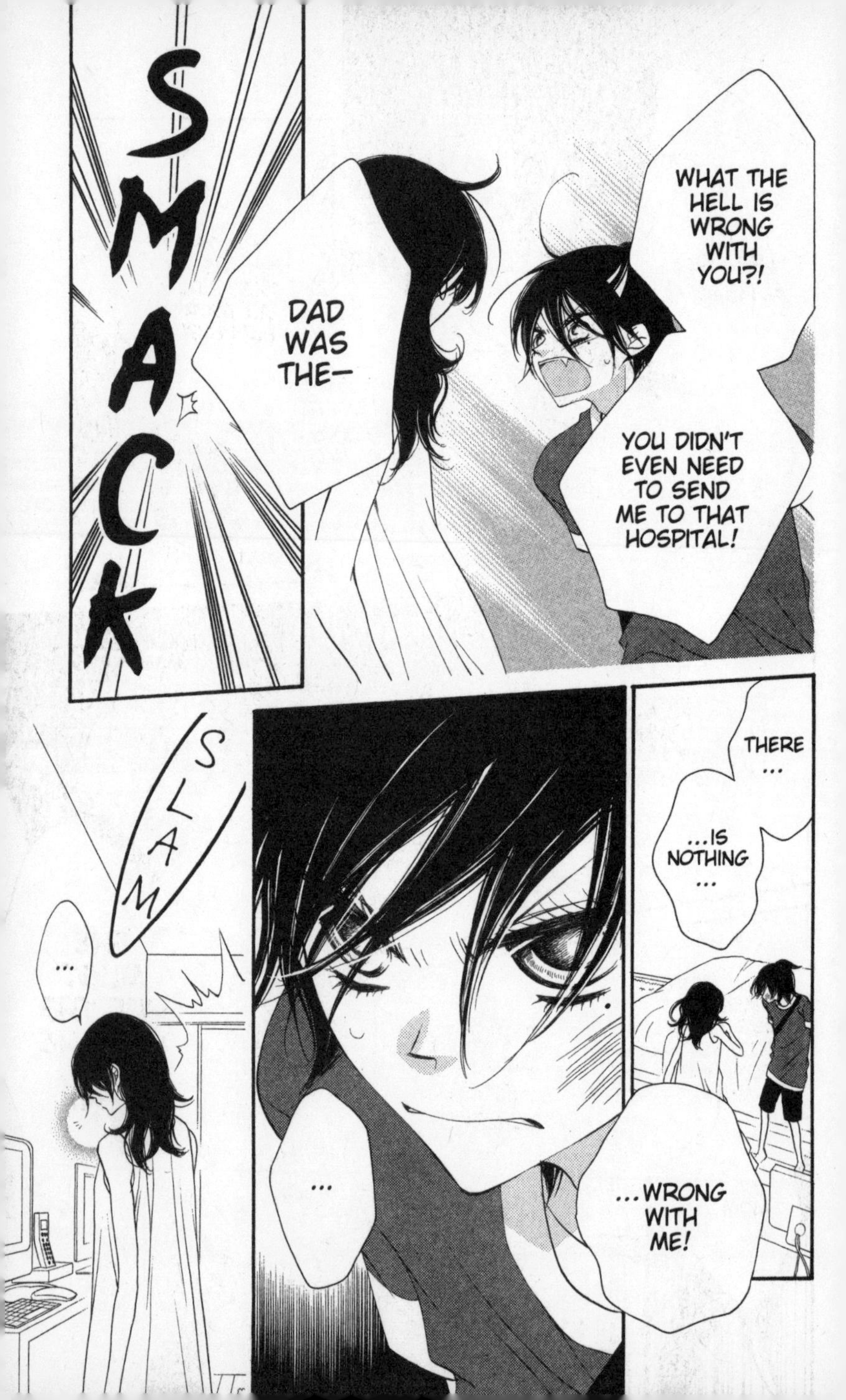
WHAT THE HELL IS WRONG WITH YOU?!
YOU DIDN'T EVEN NEED TO SEND ME TO THAT HOSPITAL!
DAD WAS THE—
SMACK
THERE ...
...IS NOTHING ...
...WRONG WITH ME!
...
SLAM
...

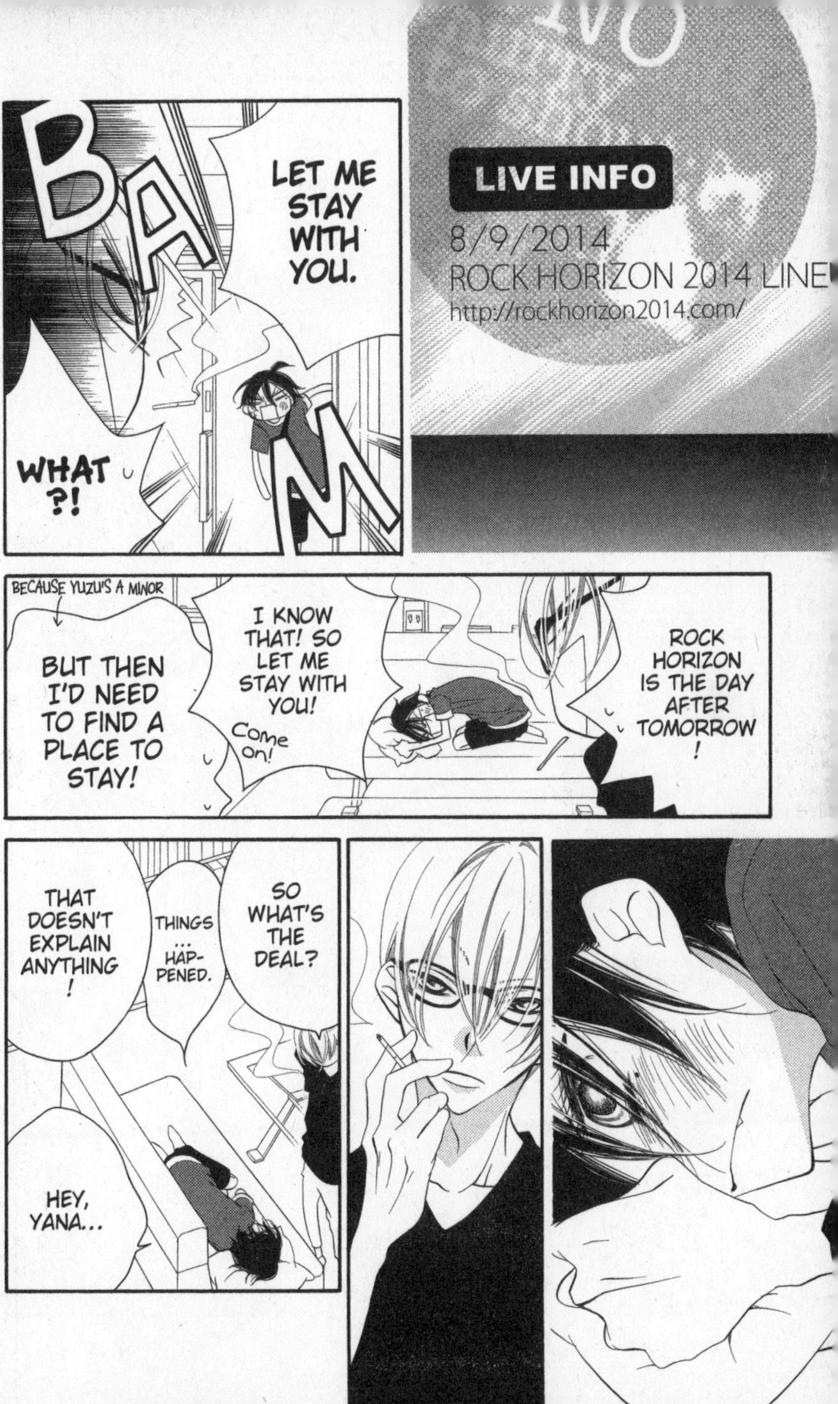
LIVE INFO
8/9/2014
ROCK HORIZON 2014 LINE
http://rockhorizon2014.com/
BAM
LET ME STAY WITH YOU.
WHAT?!
ROCK HORIZON IS THE DAY AFTER TOMORROW!
I KNOW THAT! SO LET ME STAY WITH YOU!
Come on!
BECAUSE YUZU'S A MINOR
BUT THEN I'D NEED TO FIND A PLACE TO STAY!
SO WHAT'S THE DEAL?
THINGS... HAP-PENED.
THAT DOESN'T EXPLAIN ANYTHING!
HEY, YANA...

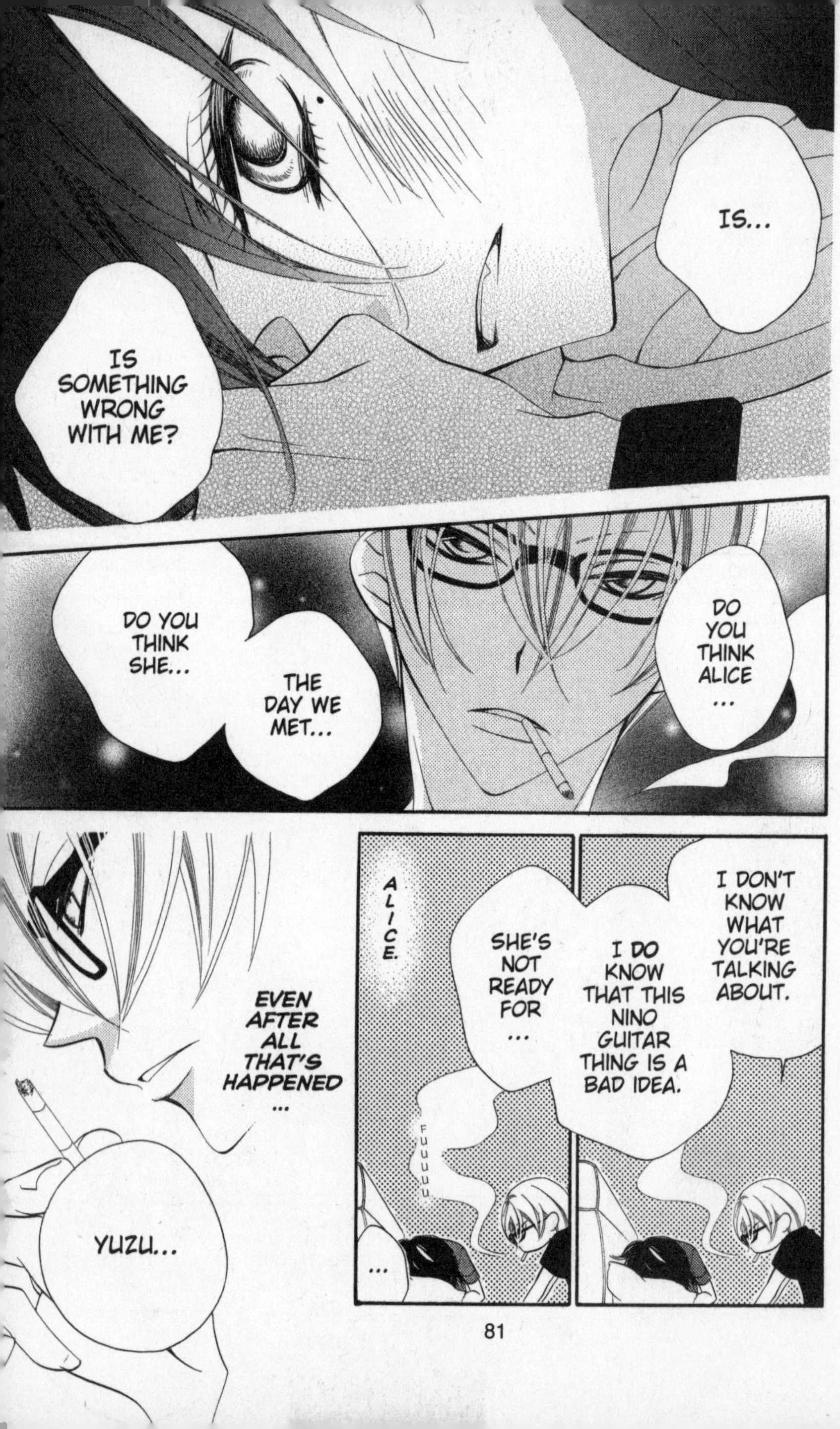
IS...
IS SOMETHING WRONG WITH ME?
DO YOU THINK ALICE ...
THE DAY WE MET...
DO YOU THINK SHE...
I DON'T KNOW WHAT YOU'RE TALKING ABOUT.
I DO KNOW THAT THIS NINO GUITAR THING IS A BAD IDEA.
SHE'S NOT READY FOR ...
ALICE.
Fuuuuu
...
EVEN AFTER ALL THAT'S HAPPENED ...
YUZU...

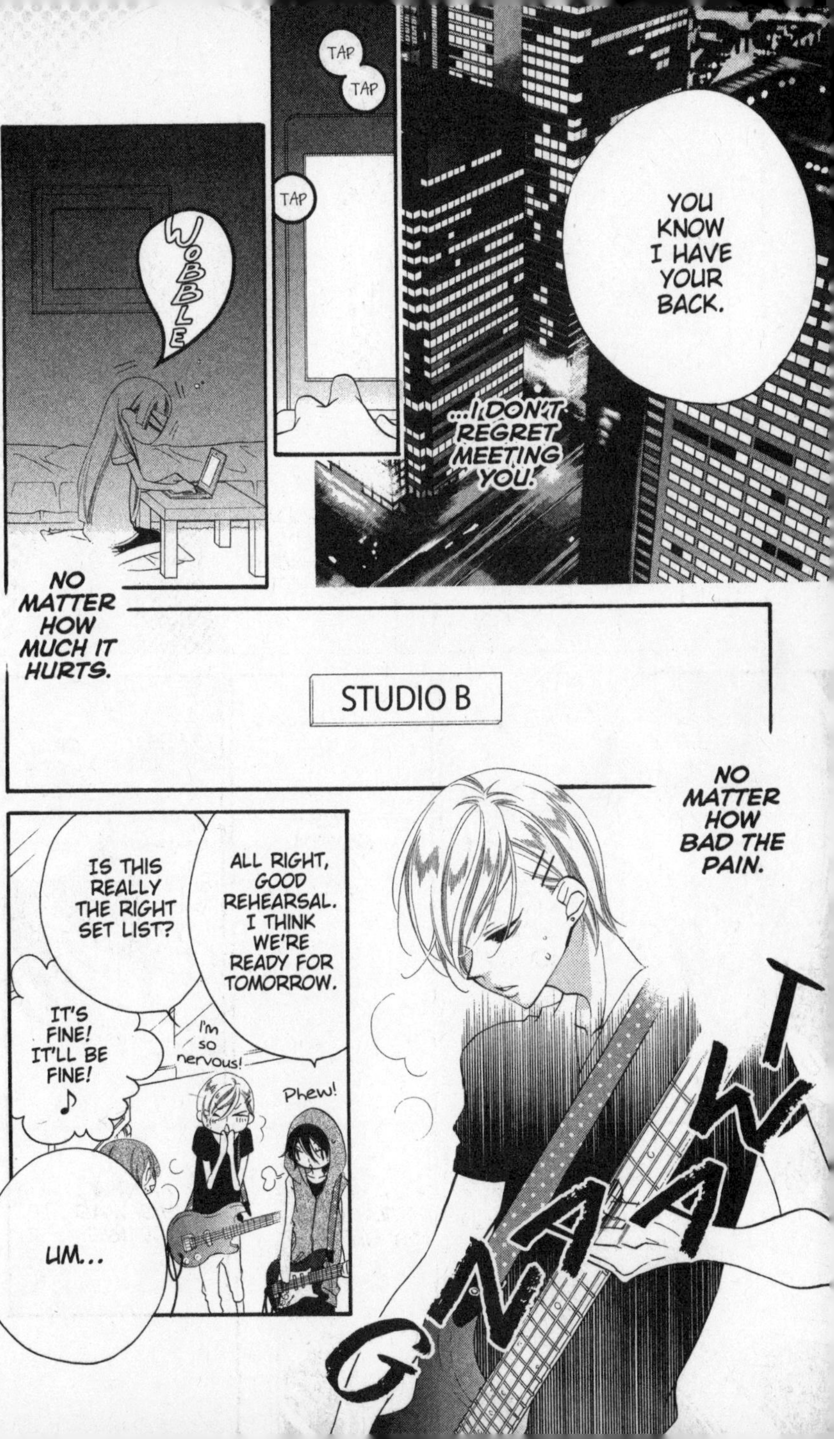
YOU KNOW I HAVE YOUR BACK.
...I DON'T REGRET MEETING YOU.
TAP
TAP
TAP
WOBBLE
NO MATTER HOW MUCH IT HURTS.
STUDIO B
NO MATTER HOW BAD THE PAIN.
ALL RIGHT, GOOD REHEARSAL. I THINK WE'RE READY FOR TOMORROW.
IS THIS REALLY THE RIGHT SET LIST?
Phew!
I'm so nervous!
IT'S FINE! IT'LL BE FINE! ♪
UM...

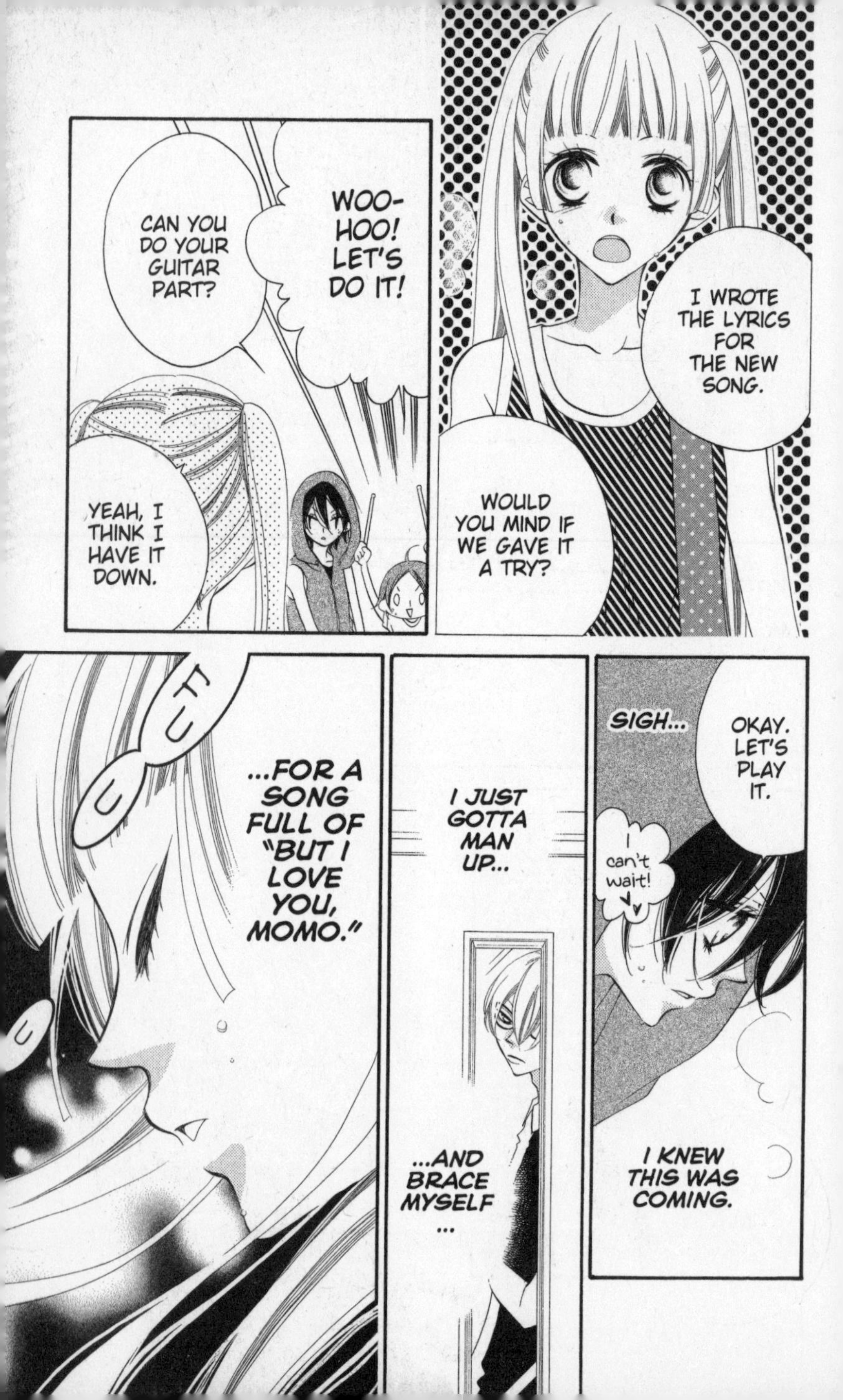
I WROTE THE LYRICS FOR THE NEW SONG.
WOULD YOU MIND IF WE GAVE IT A TRY?
WOO-HOO! LET'S DO IT!
CAN YOU DO YOUR GUITAR PART?
YEAH, I THINK I HAVE IT DOWN.
OKAY. LET'S PLAY IT.
SIGH...
I can't wait!
I KNEW THIS WAS COMING.
I JUST GOTTA MAN UP...
...AND BRACE MYSELF ...
FUUU
...FOR A SONG FULL OF "BUT I LOVE YOU, MOMO."

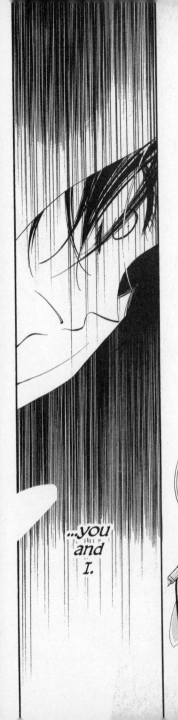

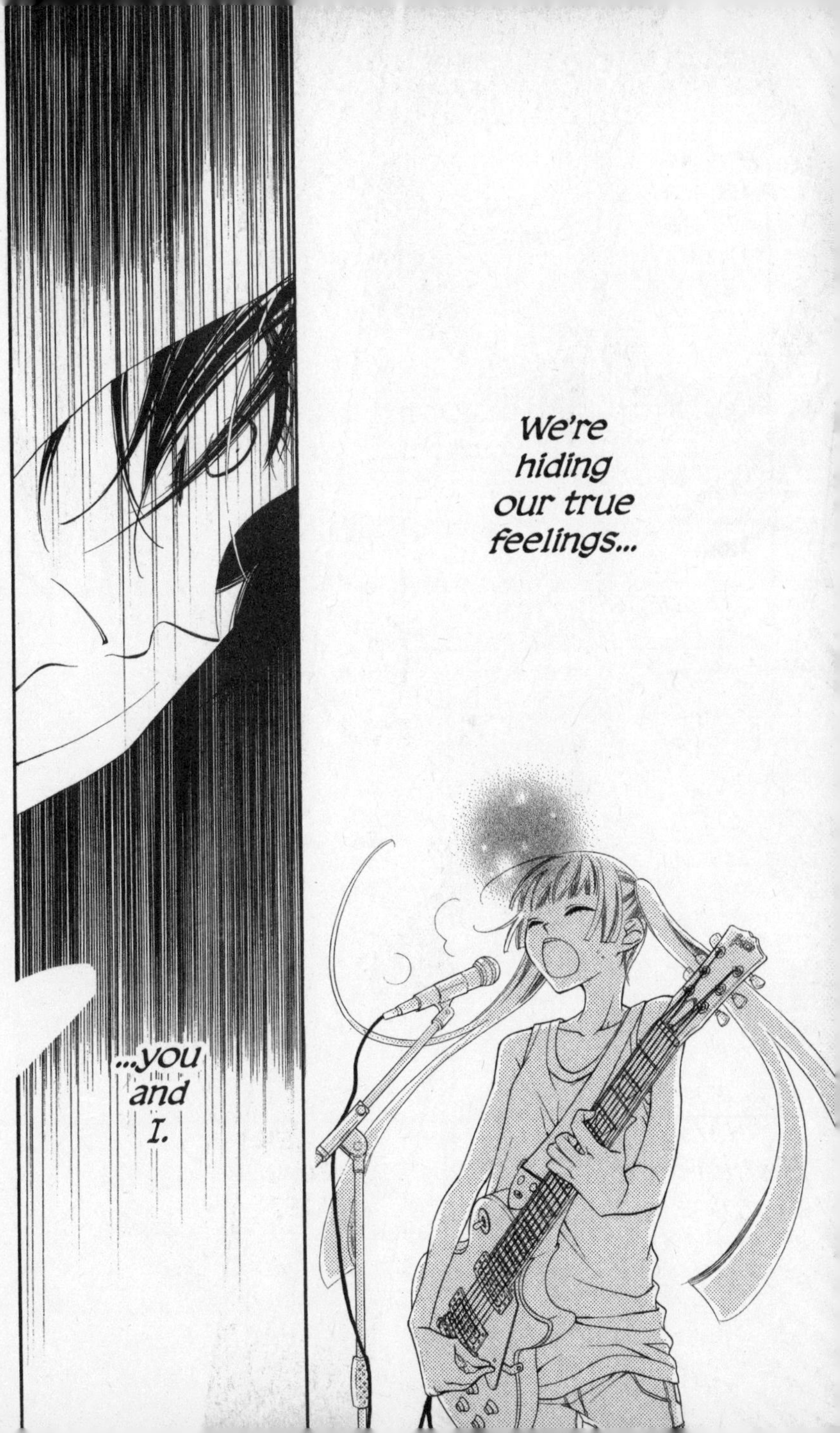

We're
hiding
our true
feelings...

...you
and
I.

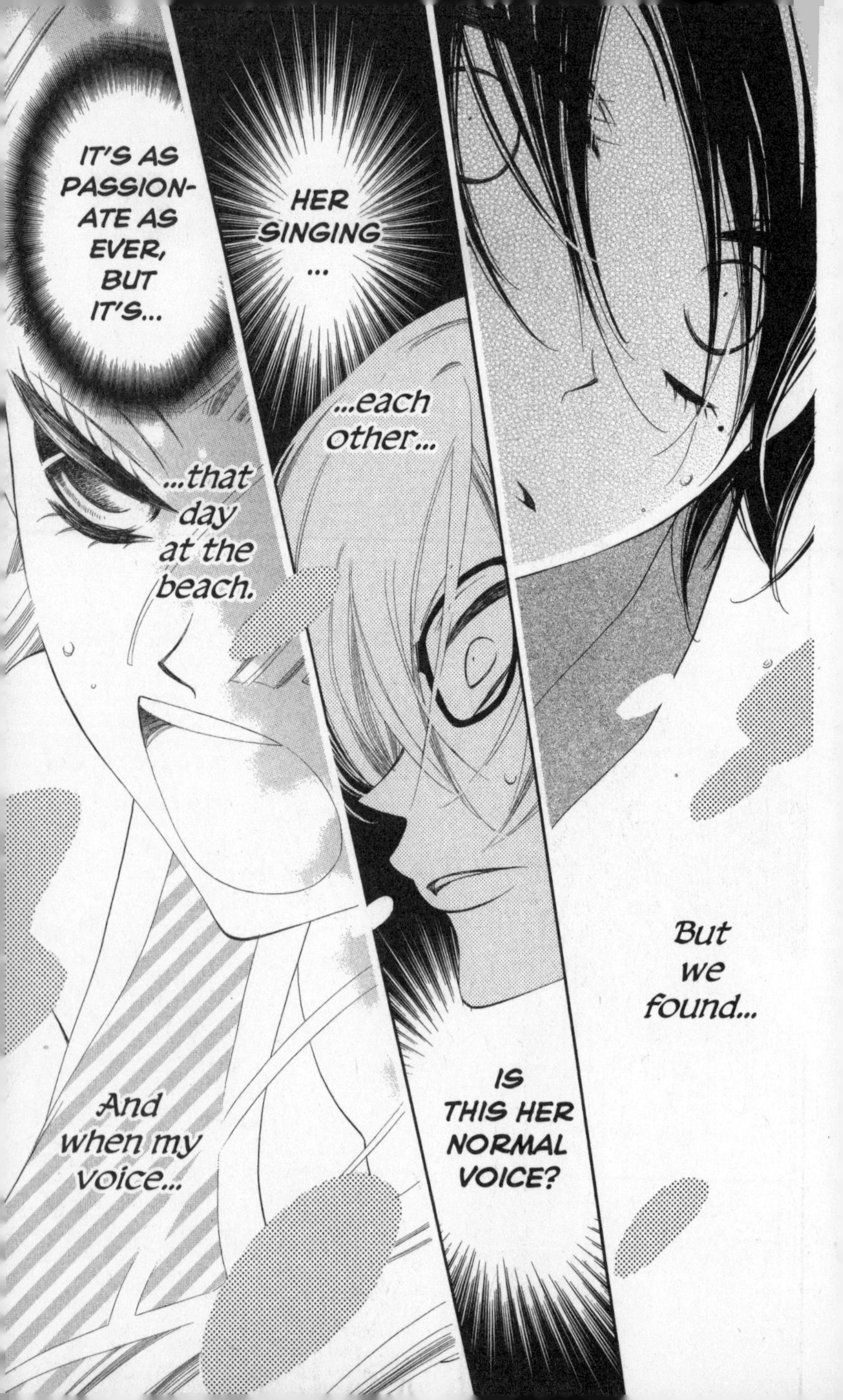
But we found...
HER SINGING...
...each other...
IS THIS HER NORMAL VOICE?
IT'S AS PASSION-ATE AS EVER, BUT IT'S...
...that day at the beach.
And when my voice...

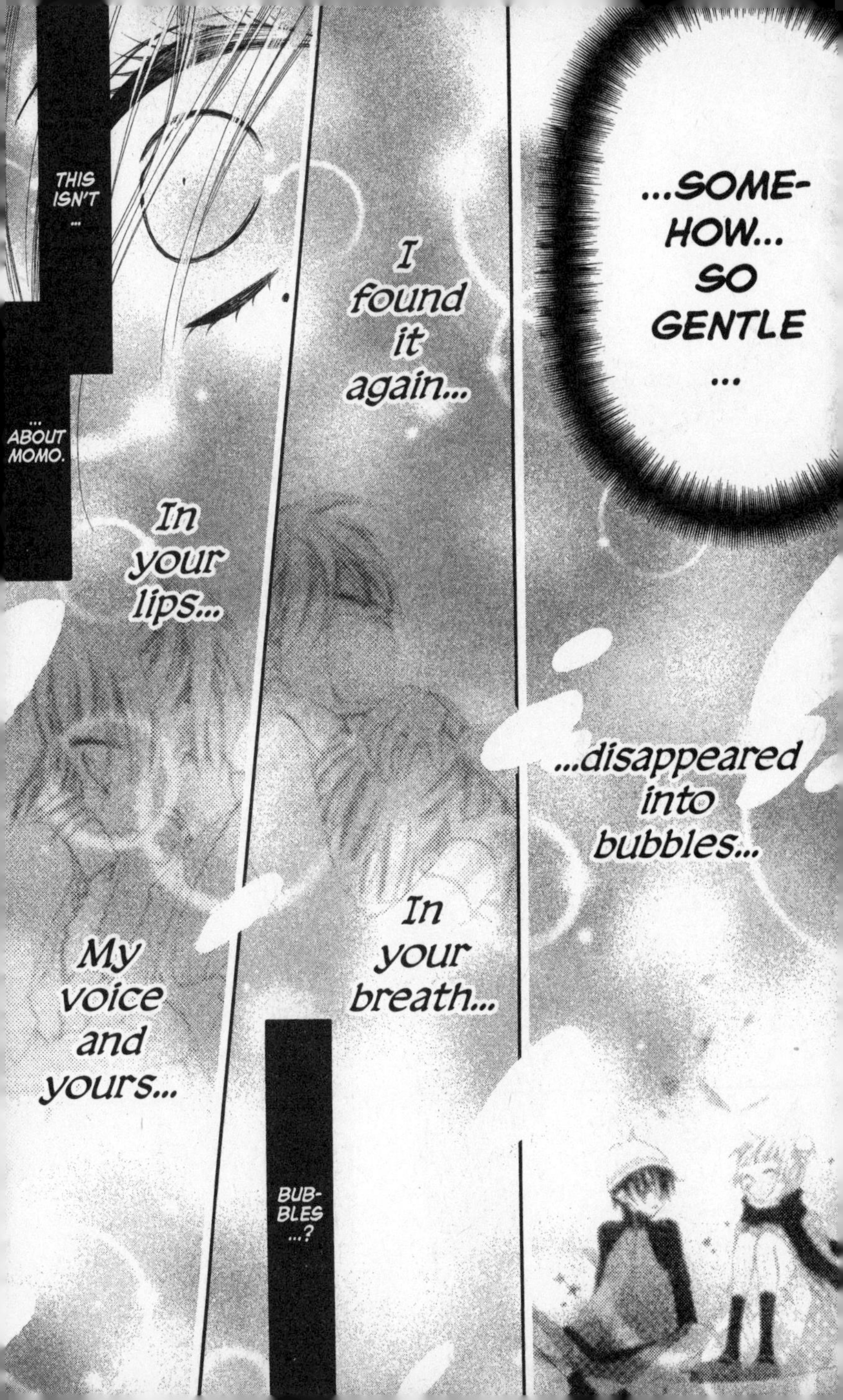
...SOME-HOW... SO GENTLE ...
...disappeared into bubbles...
I found it again...
In your breath...
BUB-BLES ...?
THIS ISN'T ...
... ABOUT MOMO.
In your lips...
My voice and yours...

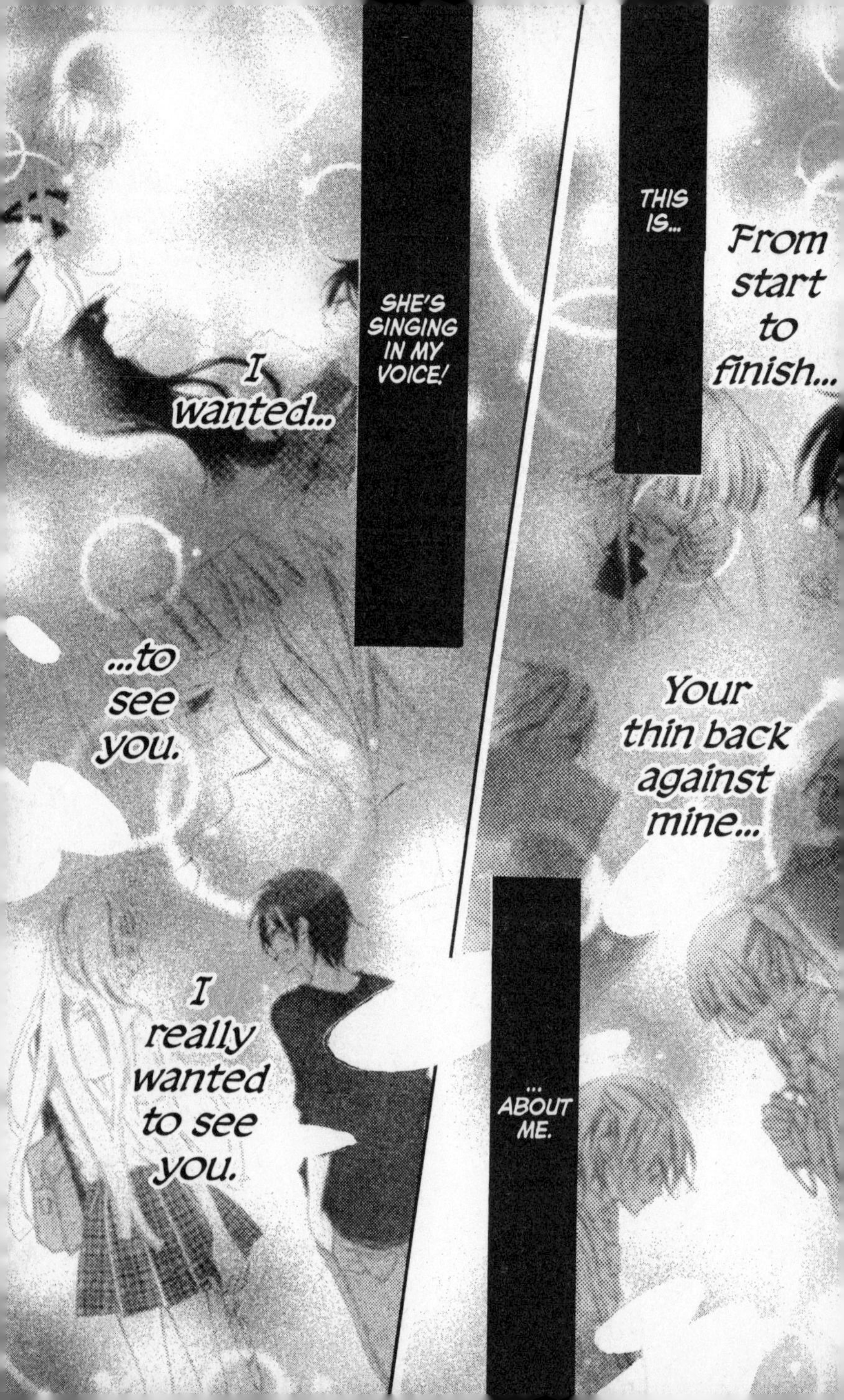
THIS IS...
From start to finish...
Your thin back against mine...
...ABOUT ME.
SHE'S SINGING IN MY VOICE!
I wanted...
...to see you.
I really wanted to see you.

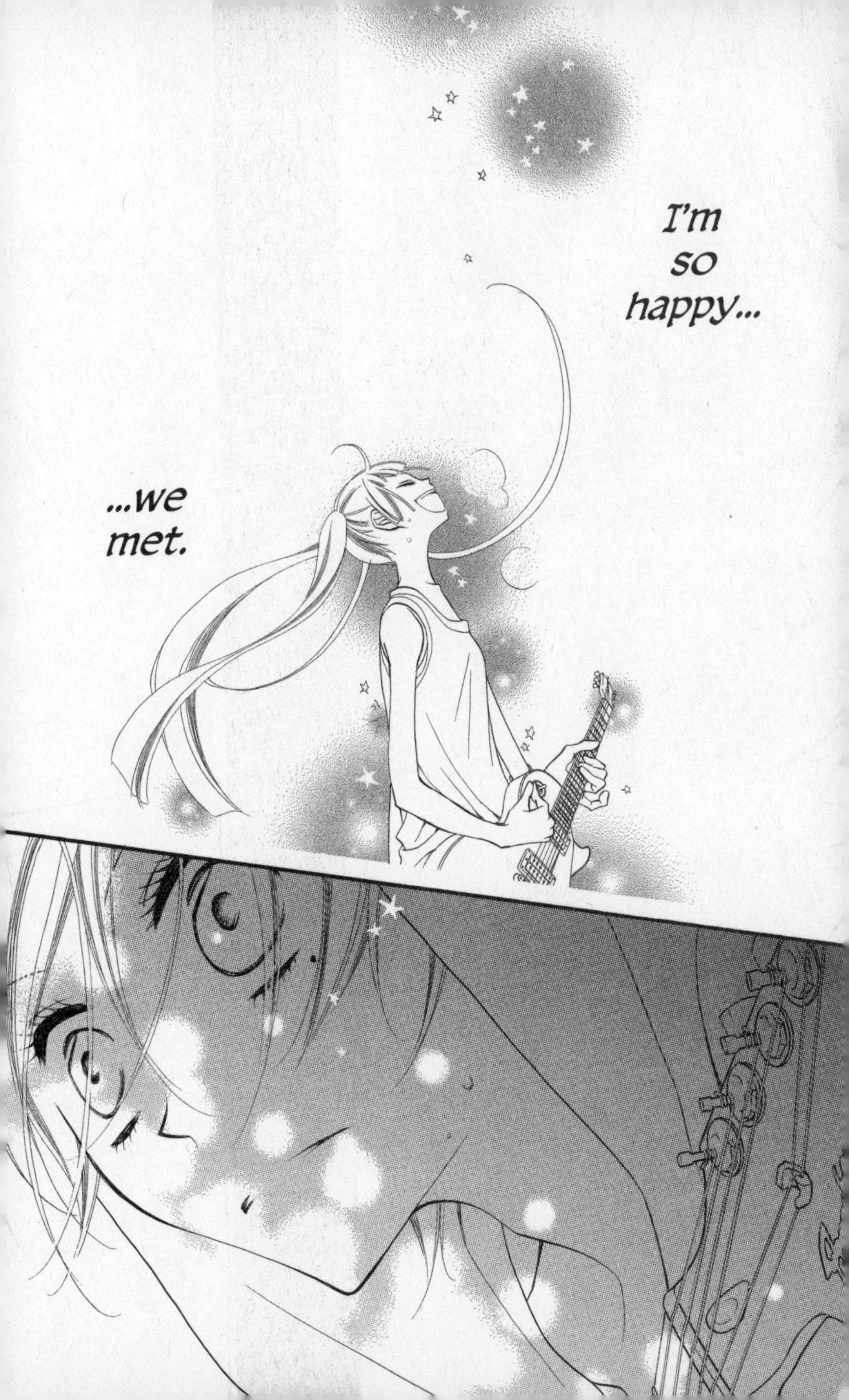
I'm so happy...
...we met.

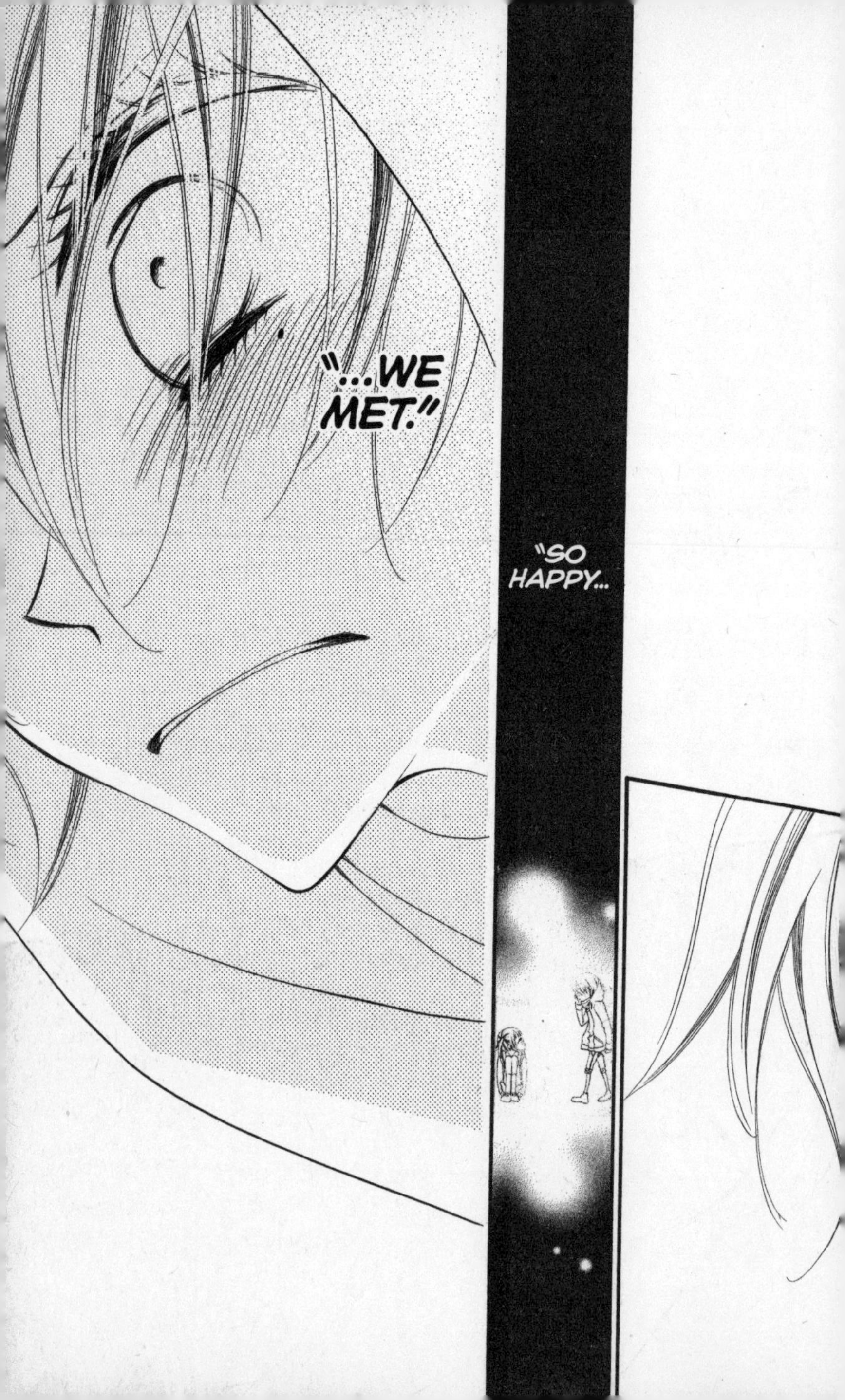
"SO HAPPY...
"...WE MET."

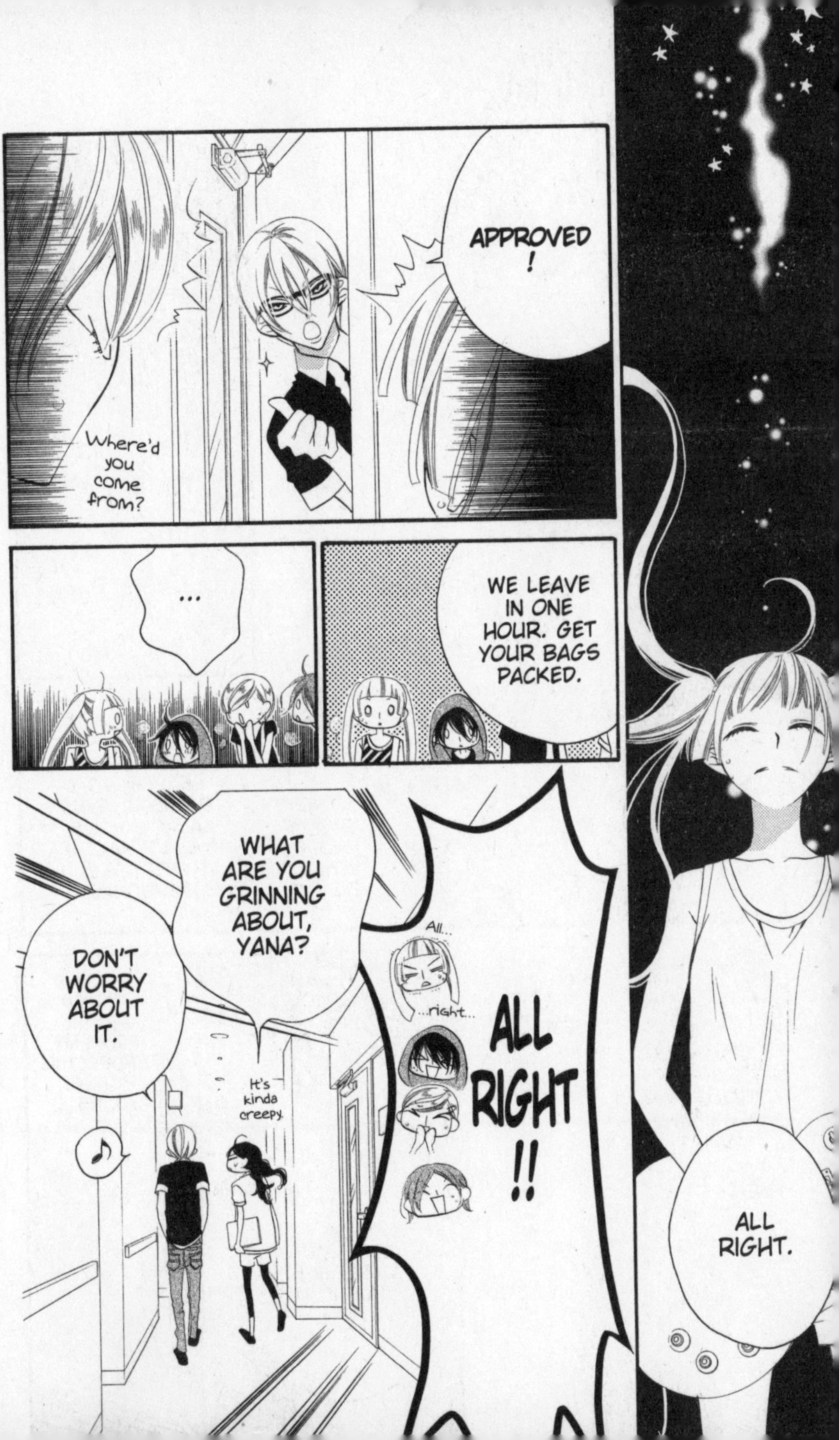
ALL RIGHT.
APPROVED!
Where'd you come from?
WE LEAVE IN ONE HOUR. GET YOUR BAGS PACKED.
...
ALL RIGHT!!
All...
...right...
WHAT ARE YOU GRINNING ABOUT, YANA?
It's kinda creepy.
DON'T WORRY ABOUT IT.
♪

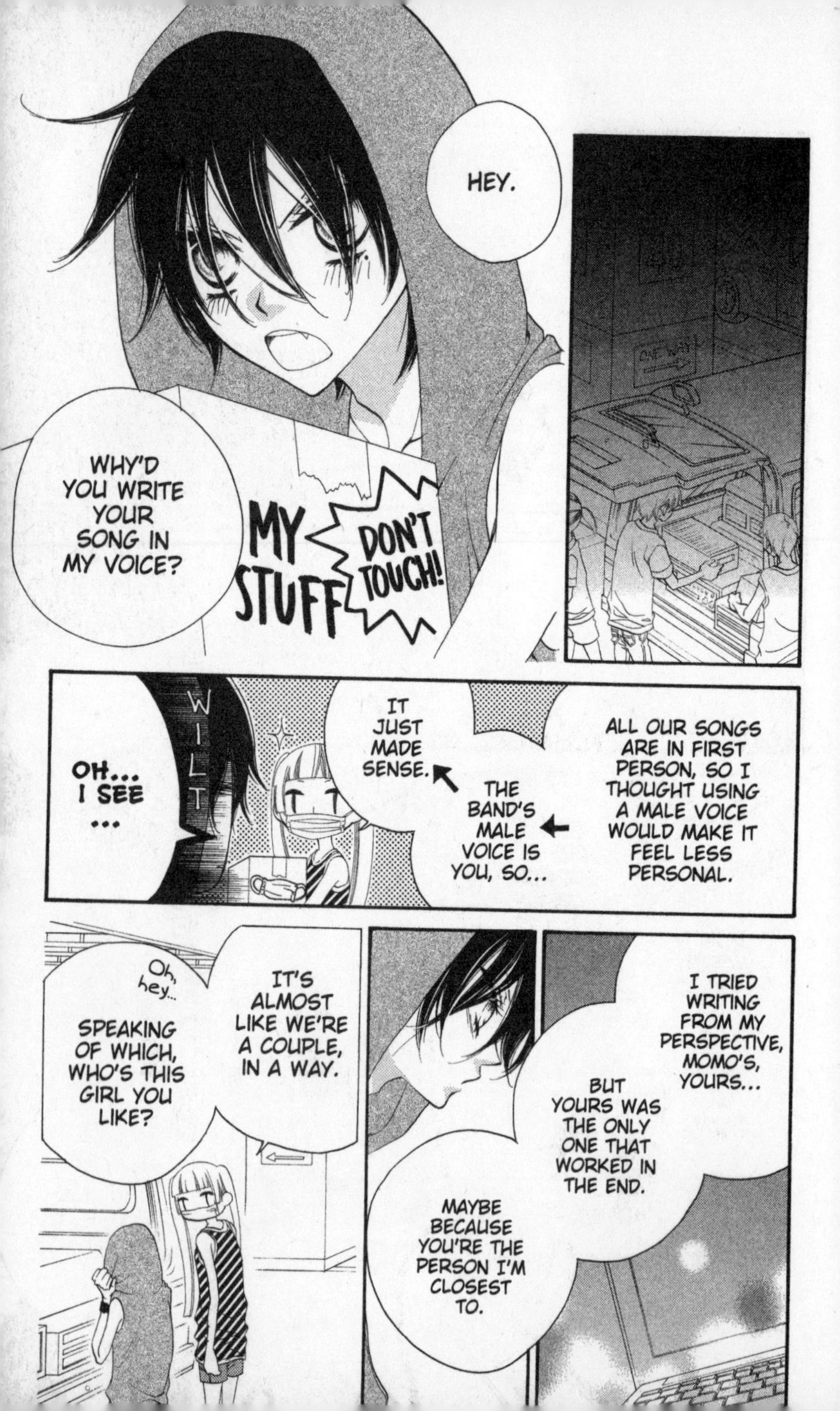
HEY.
DON'T TOUCH!
MY STUFF
WHY'D YOU WRITE YOUR SONG IN MY VOICE?
ALL OUR SONGS ARE IN FIRST PERSON, SO I THOUGHT USING A MALE VOICE WOULD MAKE IT FEEL LESS PERSONAL.
THE BAND'S MALE VOICE IS YOU, SO...
IT JUST MADE SENSE.
WILT
OH... I SEE...
I TRIED WRITING FROM MY PERSPECTIVE, MOMO'S, YOURS...
BUT YOURS WAS THE ONLY ONE THAT WORKED IN THE END.
MAYBE BECAUSE YOU'RE THE PERSON I'M CLOSEST TO.
IT'S ALMOST LIKE WE'RE A COUPLE, IN A WAY.
Oh, hey...
SPEAKING OF WHICH, WHO'S THIS GIRL YOU LIKE?

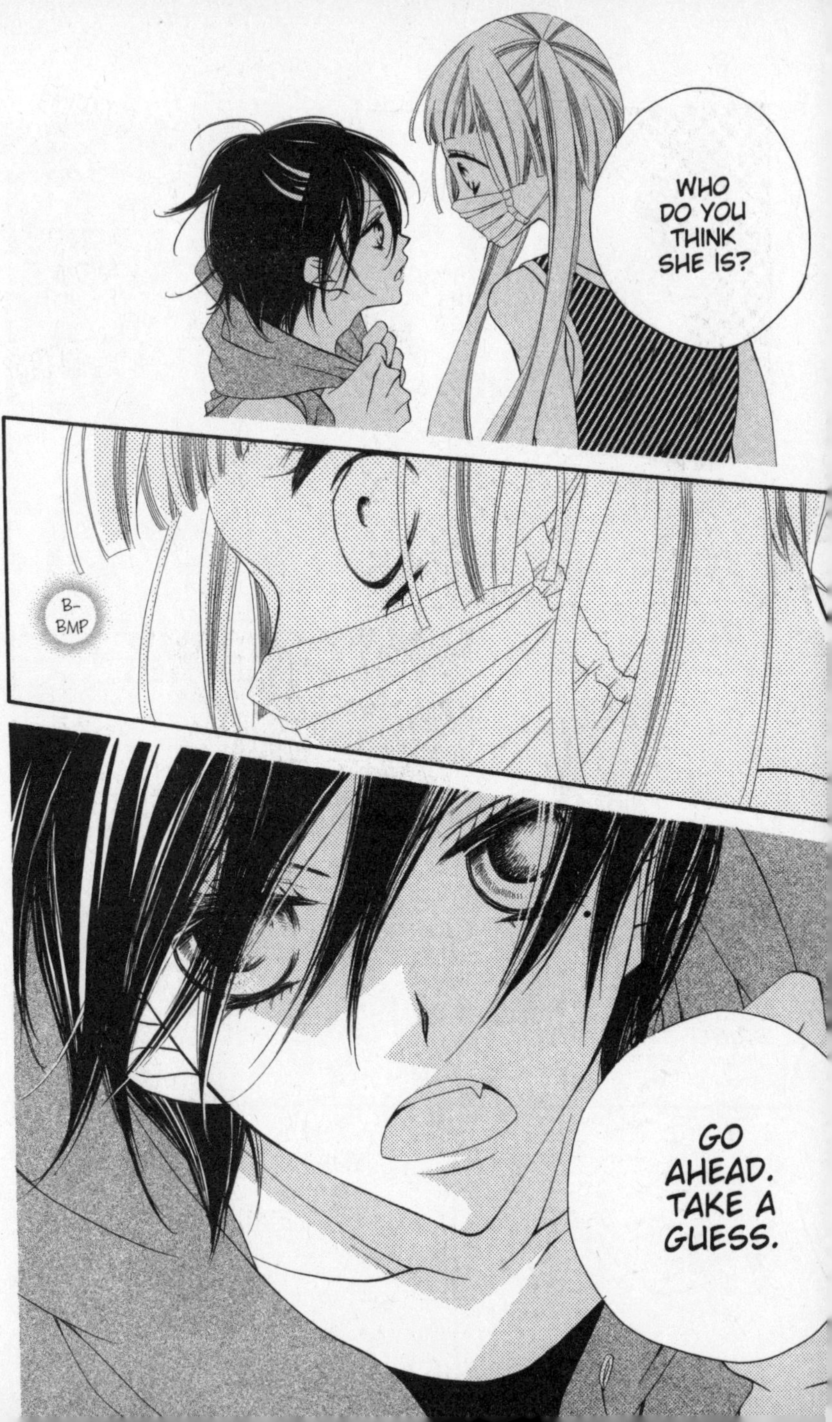
WHO DO YOU THINK SHE IS?
B-BMP
GO AHEAD. TAKE A GUESS.

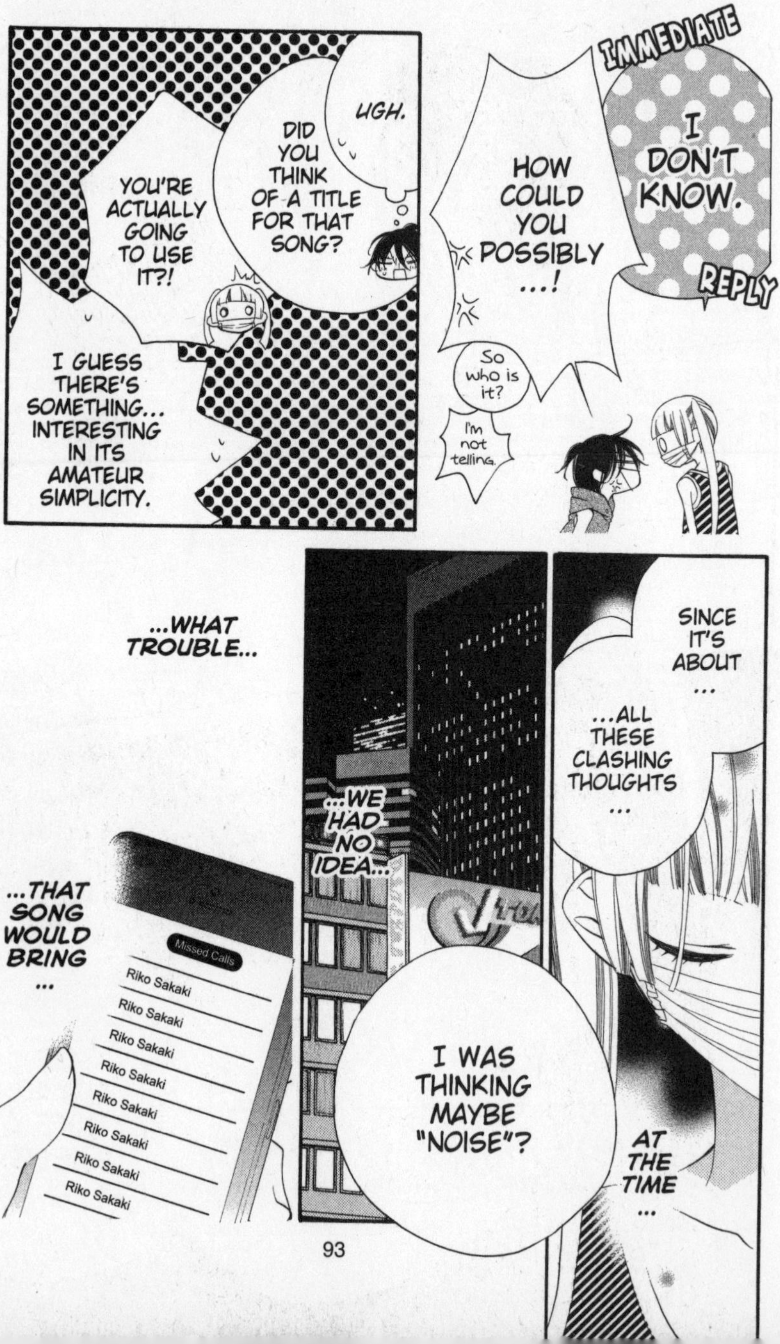
IMMEDIATE REPLY
I DON'T KNOW.
HOW COULD YOU POSSIBLY...!
So who is it?
I'm not telling.
UGH.
DID YOU THINK OF A TITLE FOR THAT SONG?
YOU'RE ACTUALLY GOING TO USE IT?!
I GUESS THERE'S SOMETHING... INTERESTING IN ITS AMATEUR SIMPLICITY.
SINCE IT'S ABOUT...
...ALL THESE CLASHING THOUGHTS...
I WAS THINKING MAYBE "NOISE"?
AT THE TIME...
...WE HAD NO IDEA...
...WHAT TROUBLE...
...THAT SONG WOULD BRING...
Missed Calls
Riko Sakaki
Riko Sakaki
Riko Sakaki
Riko Sakaki
Riko Sakaki
Riko Sakaki
Riko Sakaki
Riko Sakaki

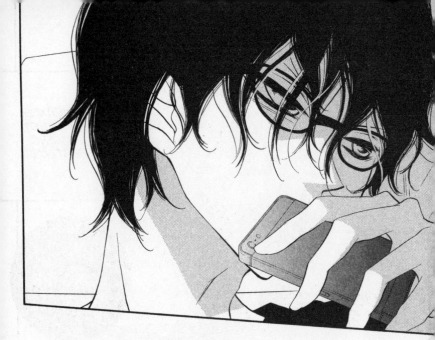

...AT OUR FIRST EVER CONCERT.

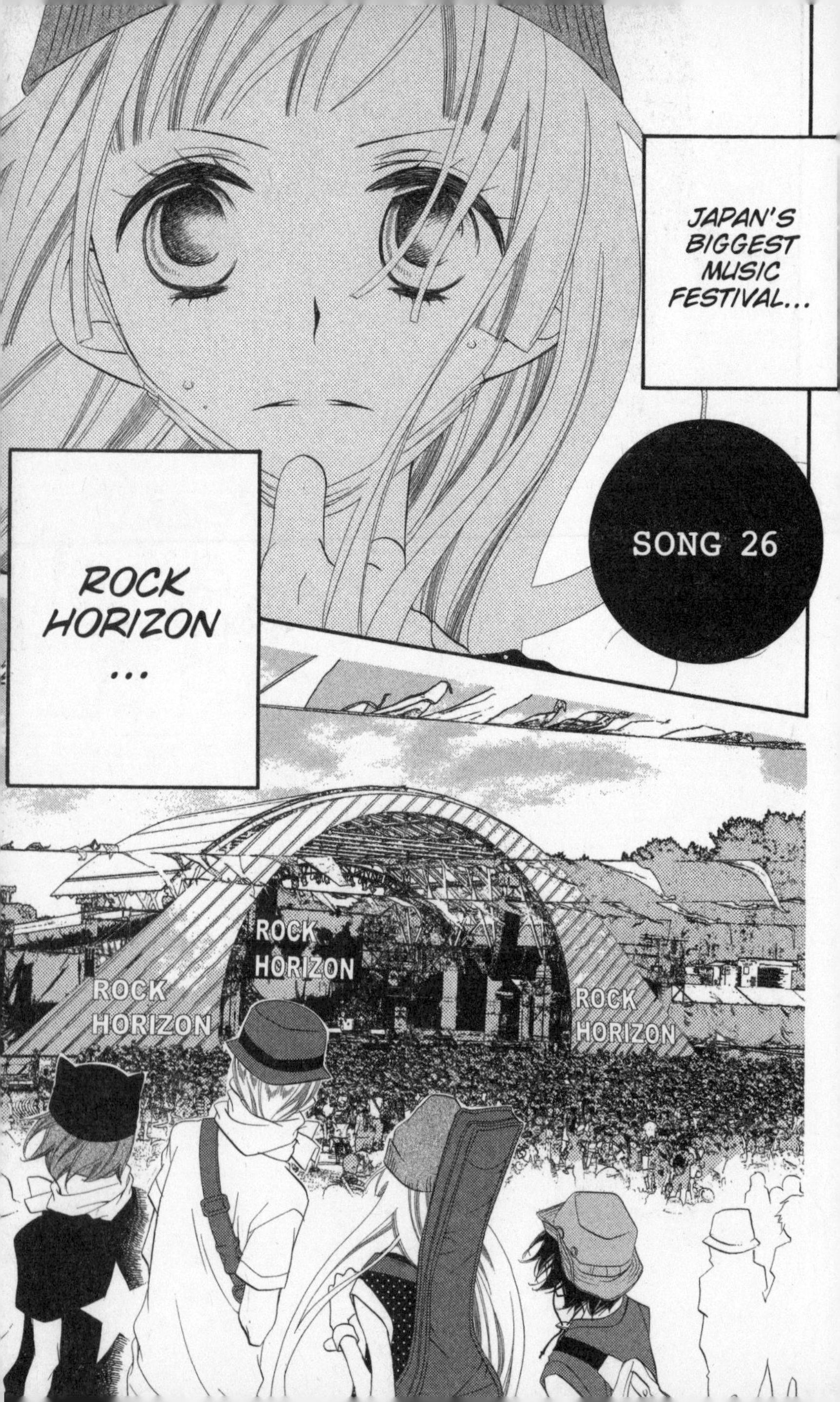
JAPAN'S BIGGEST MUSIC FESTIVAL...
SONG 26
ROCK HORIZON ...
ROCK HORIZON
ROCK HORIZON
ROCK HORIZON

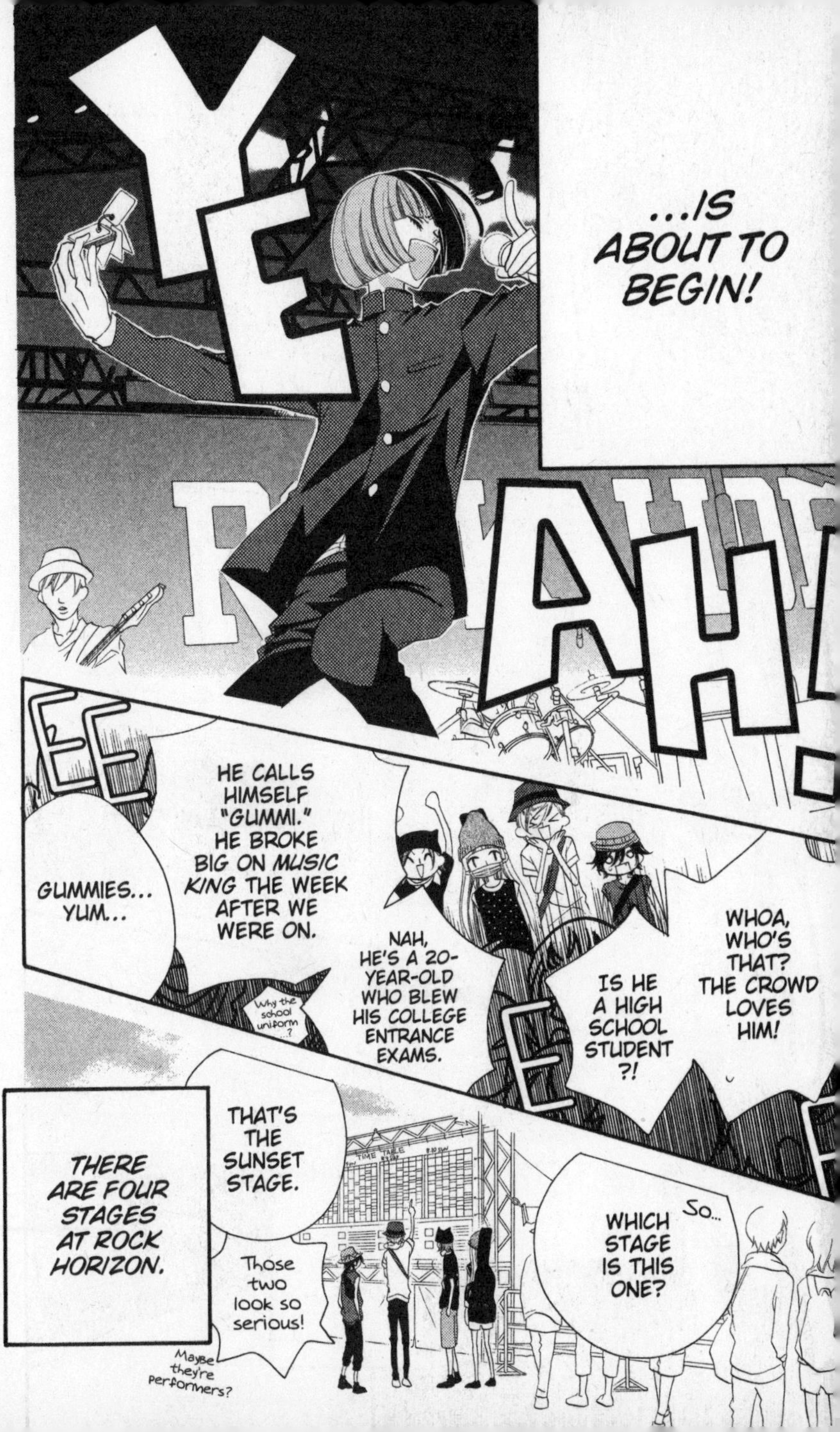
...IS ABOUT TO BEGIN!
YEAH!
WHOA, WHO'S THAT? THE CROWD LOVES HIM!
IS HE A HIGH SCHOOL STUDENT?!
NAH, HE'S A 20-YEAR-OLD WHO BLEW HIS COLLEGE ENTRANCE EXAMS.
Why the school uniform...?
HE CALLS HIMSELF "GUMMI." HE BROKE BIG ON *MUSIC KING* THE WEEK AFTER WE WERE ON.
GUMMIES... YUM...
So...
WHICH STAGE IS THIS ONE?
THAT'S THE SUNSET STAGE.
TIME TABLE
Those two look so serious!
Maybe they're performers?
THERE ARE FOUR STAGES AT ROCK HORIZON.

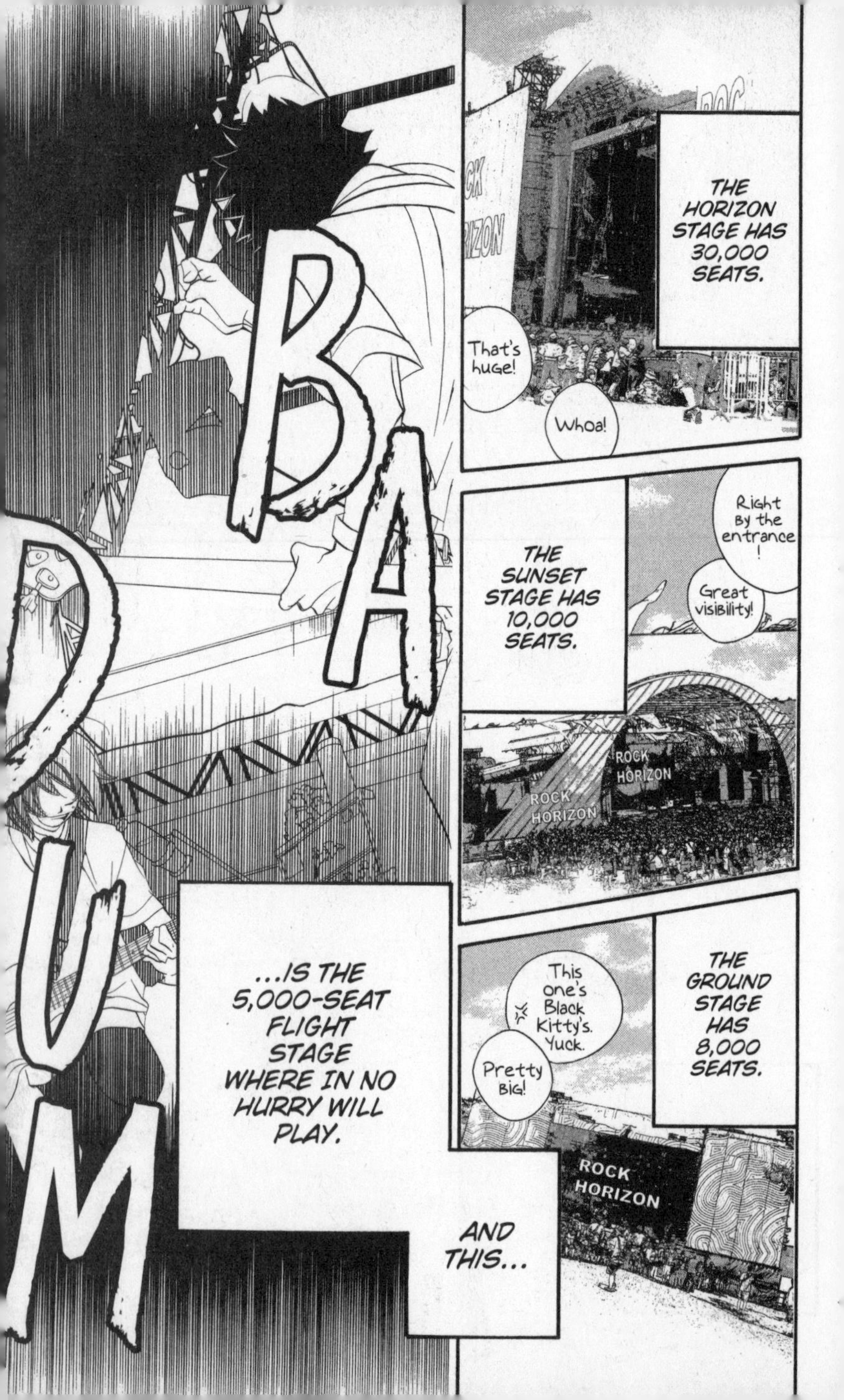
THE HORIZON STAGE HAS 30,000 SEATS.
That's huge!
Whoa!
ROCK HORIZON
Right by the entrance!
THE SUNSET STAGE HAS 10,000 SEATS.
Great visibility!
ROCK HORIZON
ROCK HORIZON
THE GROUND STAGE HAS 8,000 SEATS.
This one's Black Kitty's. Yuck.
Pretty big!
ROCK HORIZON
AND THIS...
...IS THE 5,000-SEAT FLIGHT STAGE WHERE IN NO HURRY WILL PLAY.
BA
DUM

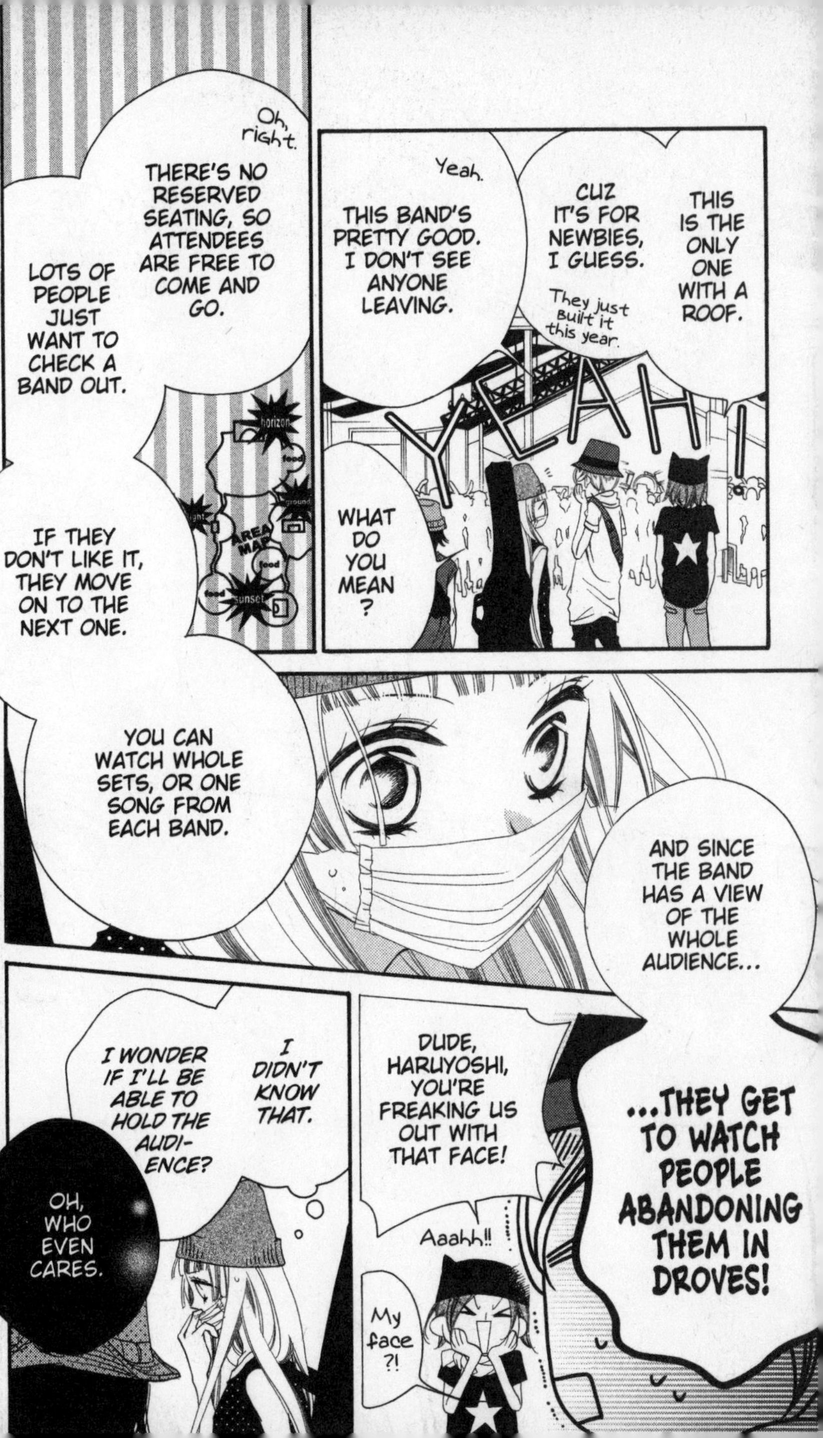
THIS IS THE ONLY ONE WITH A ROOF.
CUZ IT'S FOR NEWBIES, I GUESS.
They just built it this year.
Yeah.
THIS BAND'S PRETTY GOOD. I DON'T SEE ANYONE LEAVING.
YEAH!
WHAT DO YOU MEAN?
Oh, right.
THERE'S NO RESERVED SEATING, SO ATTENDEES ARE FREE TO COME AND GO.
LOTS OF PEOPLE JUST WANT TO CHECK A BAND OUT.
horizon
food
ground
AREA MAP
food
food
sunset
IF THEY DON'T LIKE IT, THEY MOVE ON TO THE NEXT ONE.
YOU CAN WATCH WHOLE SETS, OR ONE SONG FROM EACH BAND.
AND SINCE THE BAND HAS A VIEW OF THE WHOLE AUDIENCE...
...THEY GET TO WATCH PEOPLE ABANDONING THEM IN DROVES!
DUDE, HARUYOSHI, YOU'RE FREAKING US OUT WITH THAT FACE!
Aaahh!!
My face?!
I DIDN'T KNOW THAT.
I WONDER IF I'LL BE ABLE TO HOLD THE AUDI-ENCE?
OH, WHO EVEN CARES.

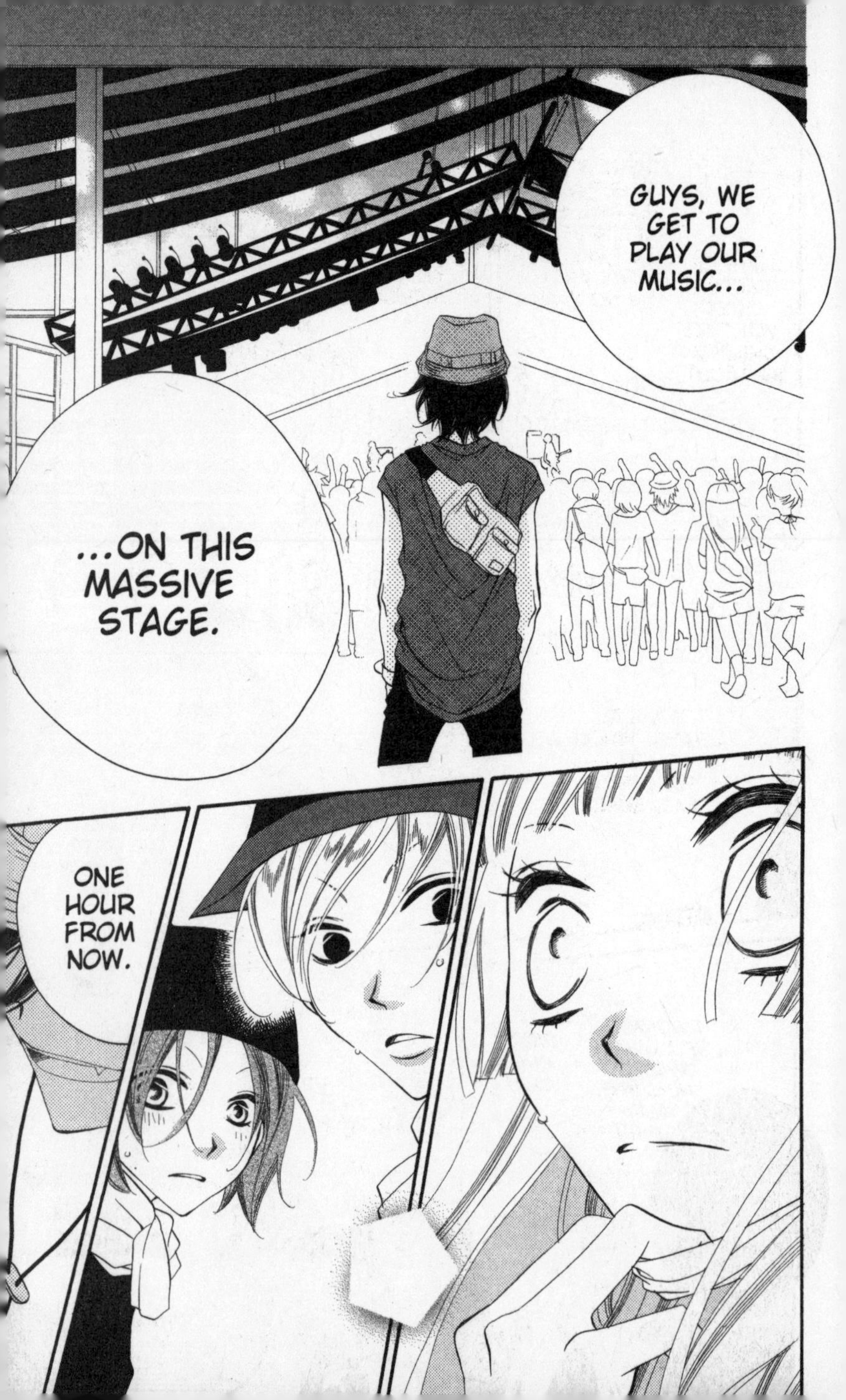
GUYS, WE GET TO PLAY OUR MUSIC...
...ON THIS MASSIVE STAGE.
ONE HOUR FROM NOW.

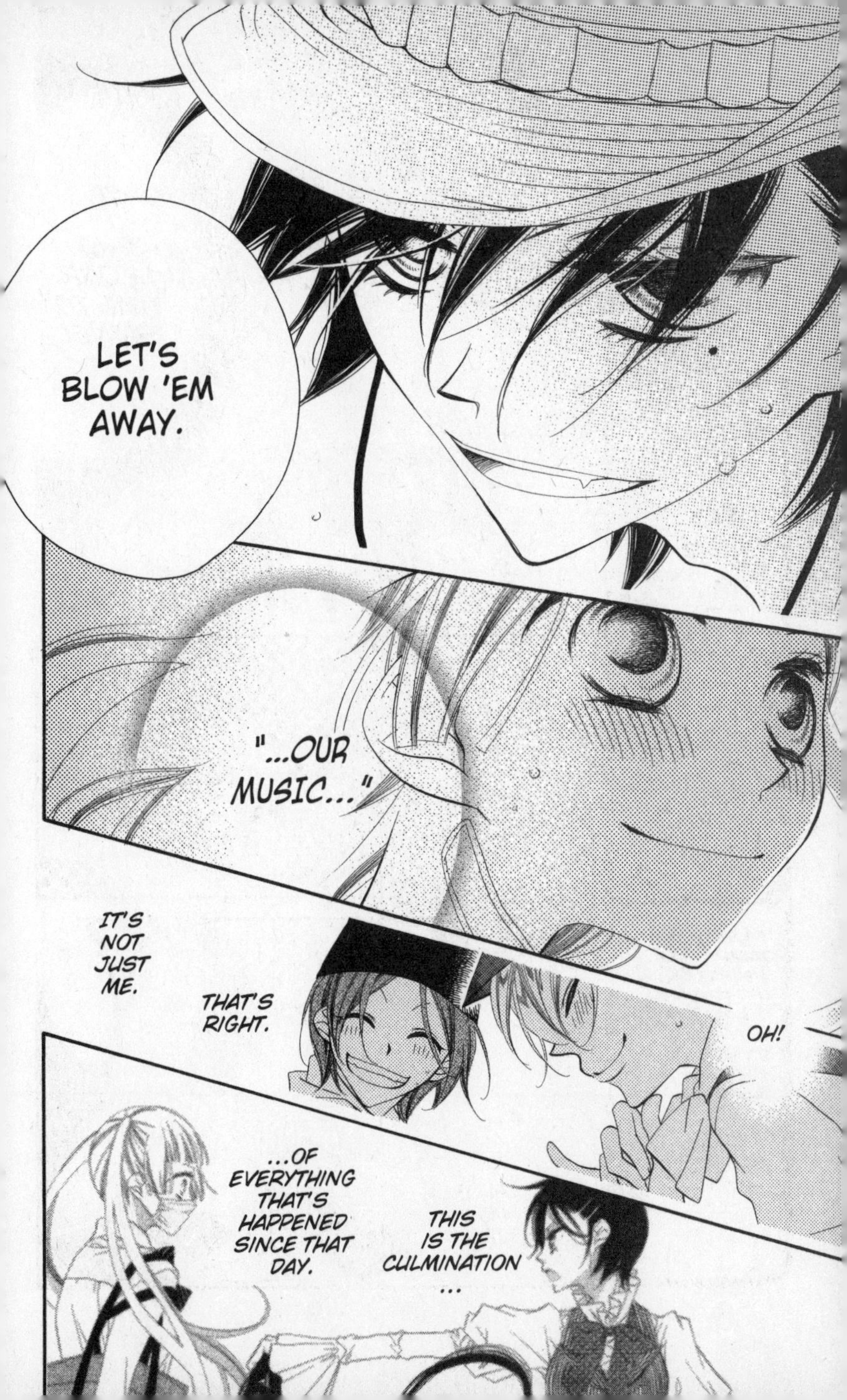
LET'S BLOW 'EM AWAY.
"...OUR MUSIC..."
OH!
THAT'S RIGHT.
IT'S NOT JUST ME.
THIS IS THE CULMINATION ...
...OF EVERYTHING THAT'S HAPPENED SINCE THAT DAY.

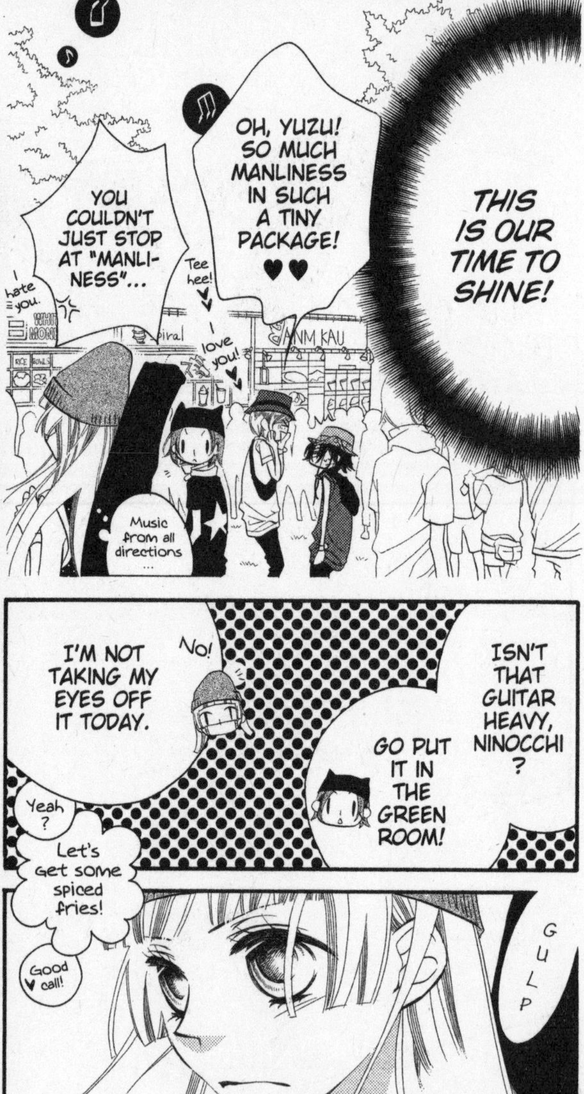
THIS IS OUR TIME TO SHINE!
OH, YUZU! SO MUCH MANLINESS IN SUCH A TINY PACKAGE! ♥♥
Tee hee!
I love you!
YOU COULDN'T JUST STOP AT "MANLI-NESS"...
I hate you.
Music from all directions ...
ISN'T THAT GUITAR HEAVY, NINOCCHI?
GO PUT IT IN THE GREEN ROOM!
No!
I'M NOT TAKING MY EYES OFF IT TODAY.
Yeah?
Let's get some spiced fries!
Good call!
GULP
MOMO ...
HE'S HERE TOO.

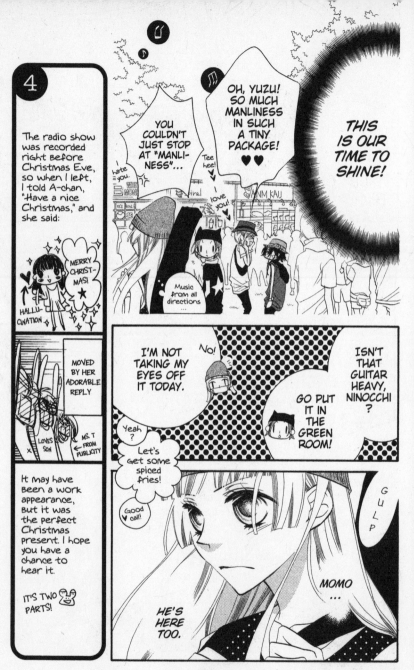

4

The radio show was recorded right before Christmas Eve, so when I left, I told A-chan, "Have a nice Christmas," and she said:

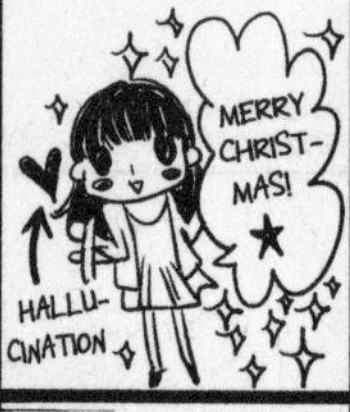
MERRY CHRIST-MAS! ★
HALLU-CINATION

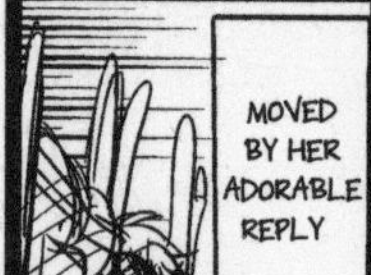
MOVED BY HER ADORABLE REPLY
LOVES SON
MS. T FROM PUBLICITY

It may have been a work appearance, but it was the perfect Christmas present. I hope you have a chance to hear it.

IT'S TWO PARTS!

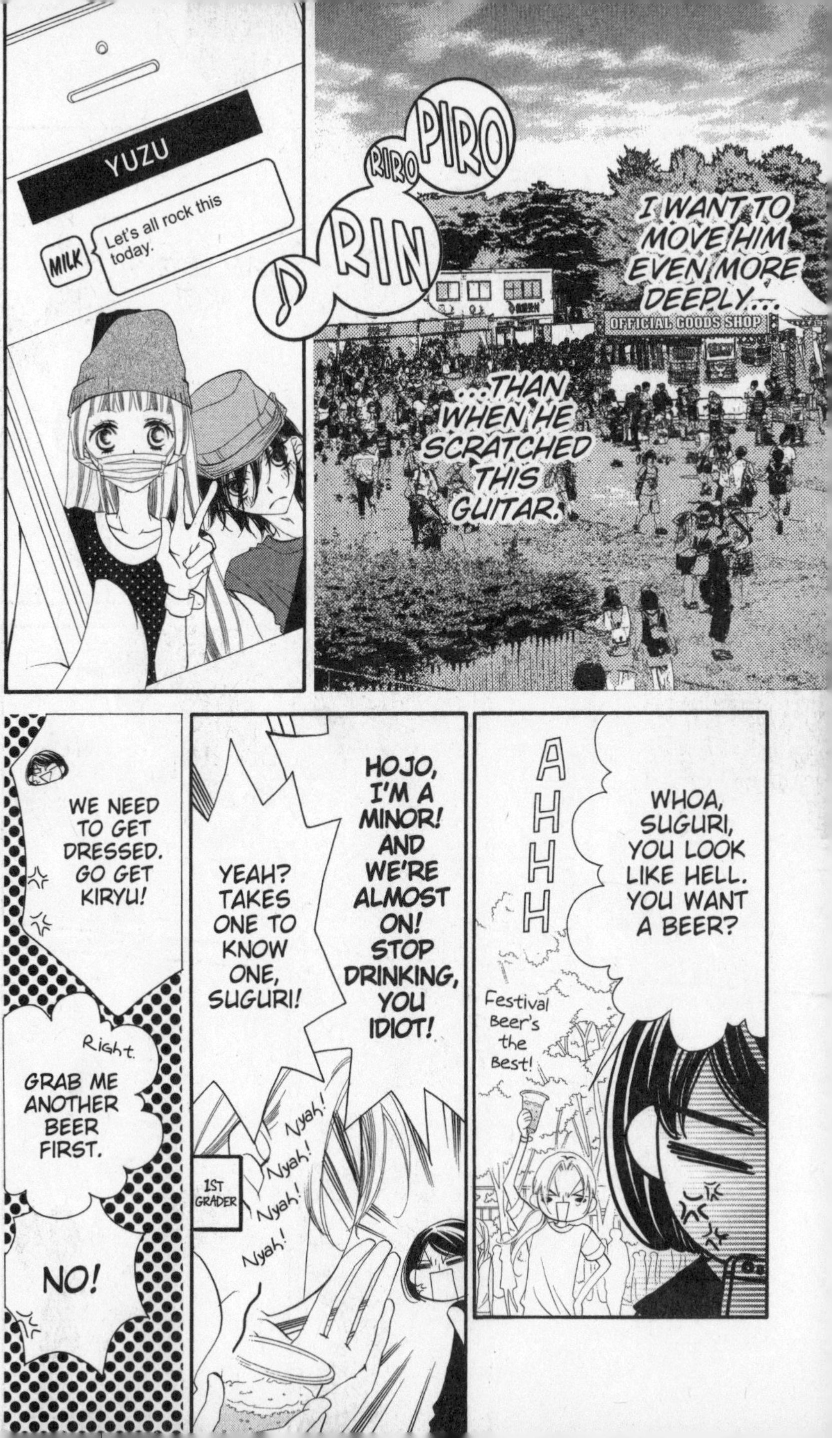
PIRO
RIRO
RIN
I WANT TO MOVE HIM EVEN MORE DEEPLY...
OFFICIAL GOODS SHOP
...THAN WHEN HE SCRATCHED THIS GUITAR.
YUZU
MILK
Let's all rock this today.
AHHH
WHOA, SUGURI, YOU LOOK LIKE HELL. YOU WANT A BEER?
Festival Beer's the Best!
HOJO, I'M A MINOR! AND WE'RE ALMOST ON! STOP DRINKING, YOU IDIOT!
YEAH? TAKES ONE TO KNOW ONE, SUGURI!
1ST GRADER
Nyah!
Nyah!
Nyah!
Nyah!
WE NEED TO GET DRESSED. GO GET KIRYU!
Right.
GRAB ME ANOTHER BEER FIRST.
NO!

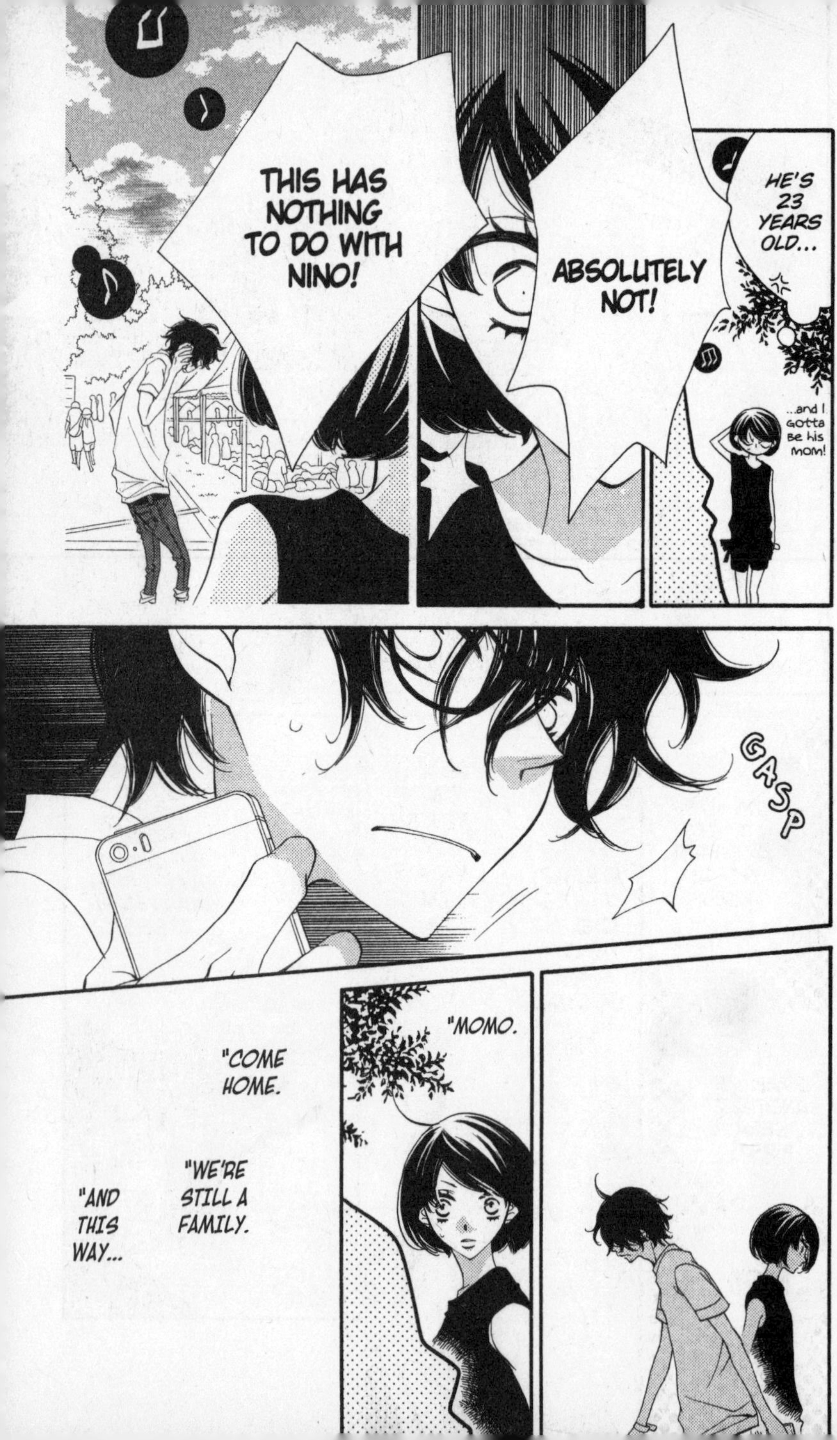
HE'S 23 YEARS OLD...
...and I gotta be his mom!
ABSOLUTELY NOT!
THIS HAS NOTHING TO DO WITH NINO!
GASP
"MOMO.
"COME HOME.
"WE'RE STILL A FAMILY.
"AND THIS WAY...

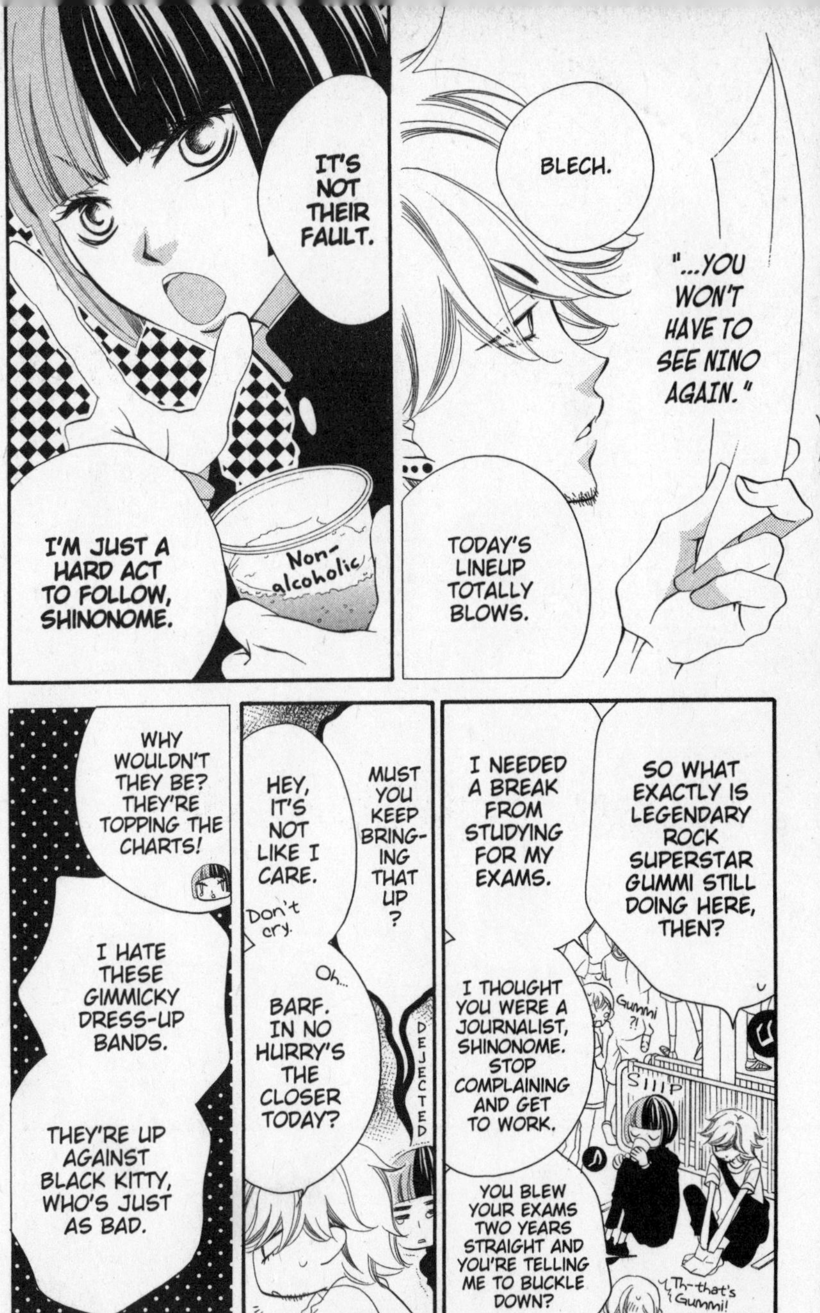
BLECH.
"...YOU WON'T HAVE TO SEE NINO AGAIN."
TODAY'S LINEUP TOTALLY BLOWS.
IT'S NOT THEIR FAULT.
I'M JUST A HARD ACT TO FOLLOW, SHINONOME.
Non-alcoholic
SO WHAT EXACTLY IS LEGENDARY ROCK SUPERSTAR GUMMI STILL DOING HERE, THEN?
I NEEDED A BREAK FROM STUDYING FOR MY EXAMS.
Gummi ?!
I THOUGHT YOU WERE A JOURNALIST, SHINONOME. STOP COMPLAINING AND GET TO WORK.
SIIIP
YOU BLEW YOUR EXAMS TWO YEARS STRAIGHT AND YOU'RE TELLING ME TO BUCKLE DOWN?
Th-that's Gummi!
MUST YOU KEEP BRINGING THAT UP?
HEY, IT'S NOT LIKE I CARE.
Don't cry.
Oh...
DEJECTED
BARF. IN NO HURRY'S THE CLOSER TODAY?
WHY WOULDN'T THEY BE? THEY'RE TOPPING THE CHARTS!
I HATE THESE GIMMICKY DRESS-UP BANDS.
THEY'RE UP AGAINST BLACK KITTY, WHO'S JUST AS BAD.

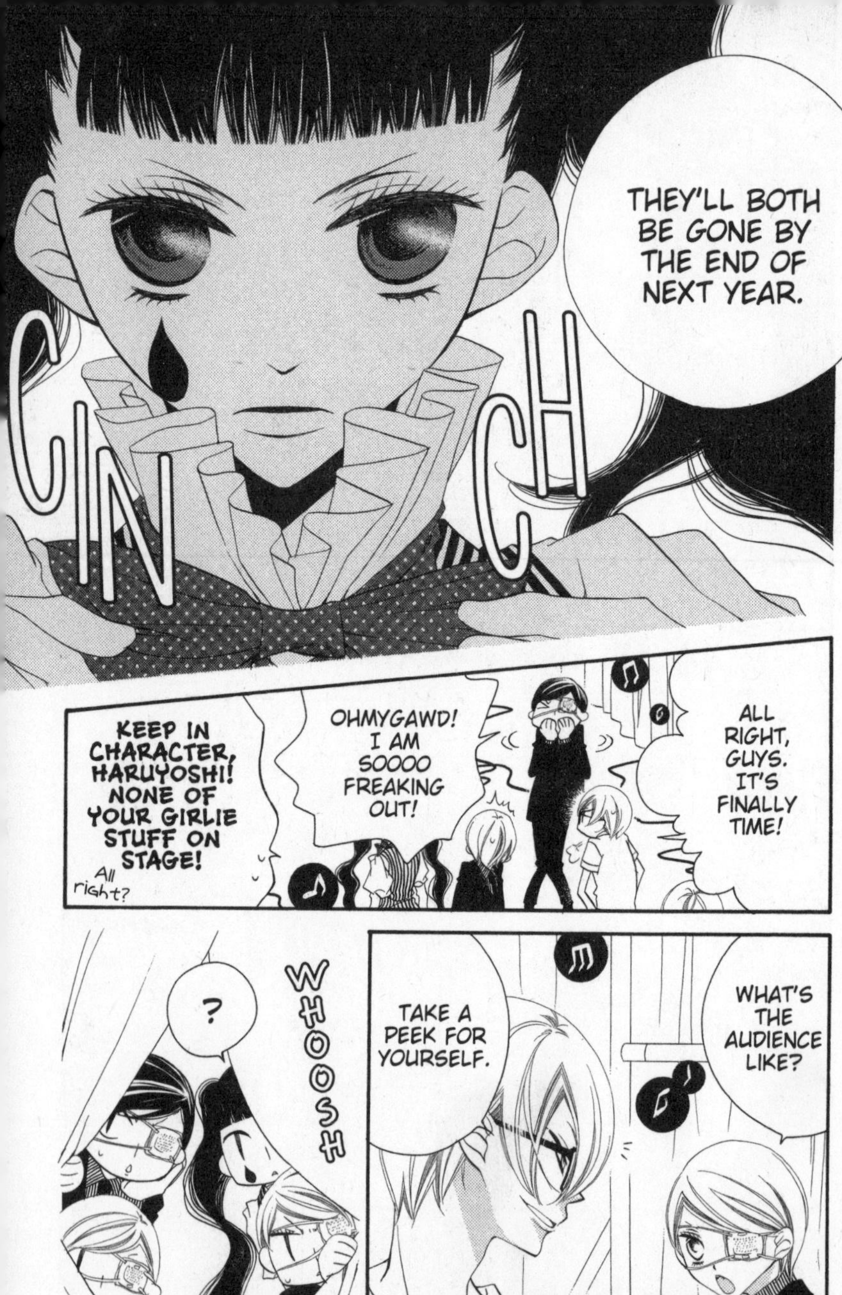
THEY'LL BOTH BE GONE BY THE END OF NEXT YEAR.
CINCH
ALL RIGHT, GUYS. IT'S FINALLY TIME!
OHMYGAWD! I AM SOOOO FREAKING OUT!
KEEP IN CHARACTER, HARUYOSHI! NONE OF YOUR GIRLIE STUFF ON STAGE!
All right?
WHAT'S THE AUDIENCE LIKE?
TAKE A PEEK FOR YOURSELF.
WHOOSH
?

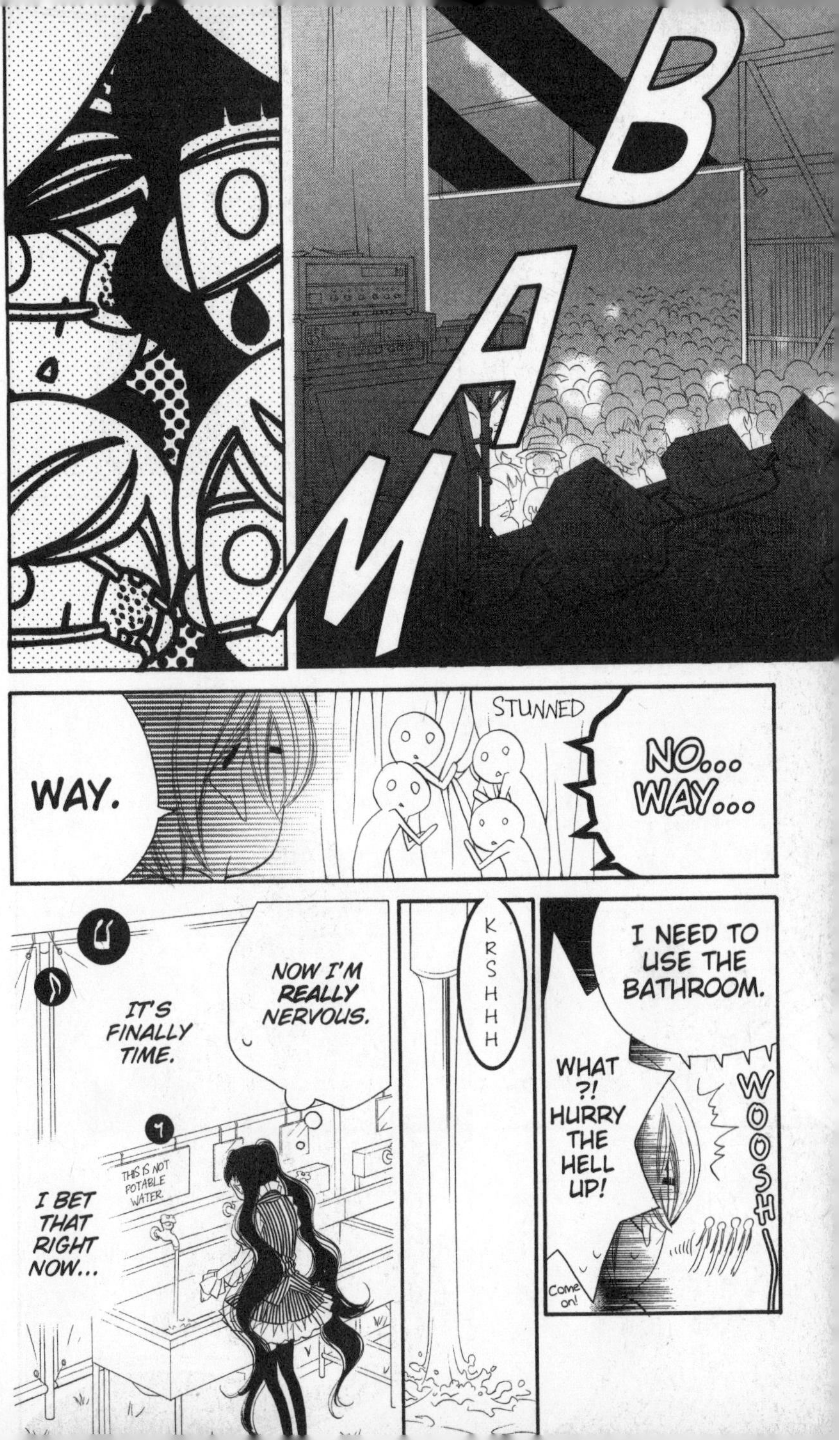
BAM
NO... WAY...
STUNNED
WAY.
I NEED TO USE THE BATHROOM.
WHAT?! HURRY THE HELL UP!
WOOSH
Come on!
KRSHHH
NOW I'M REALLY NERVOUS.
IT'S FINALLY TIME.
THIS IS NOT POTABLE WATER.
I BET THAT RIGHT NOW...

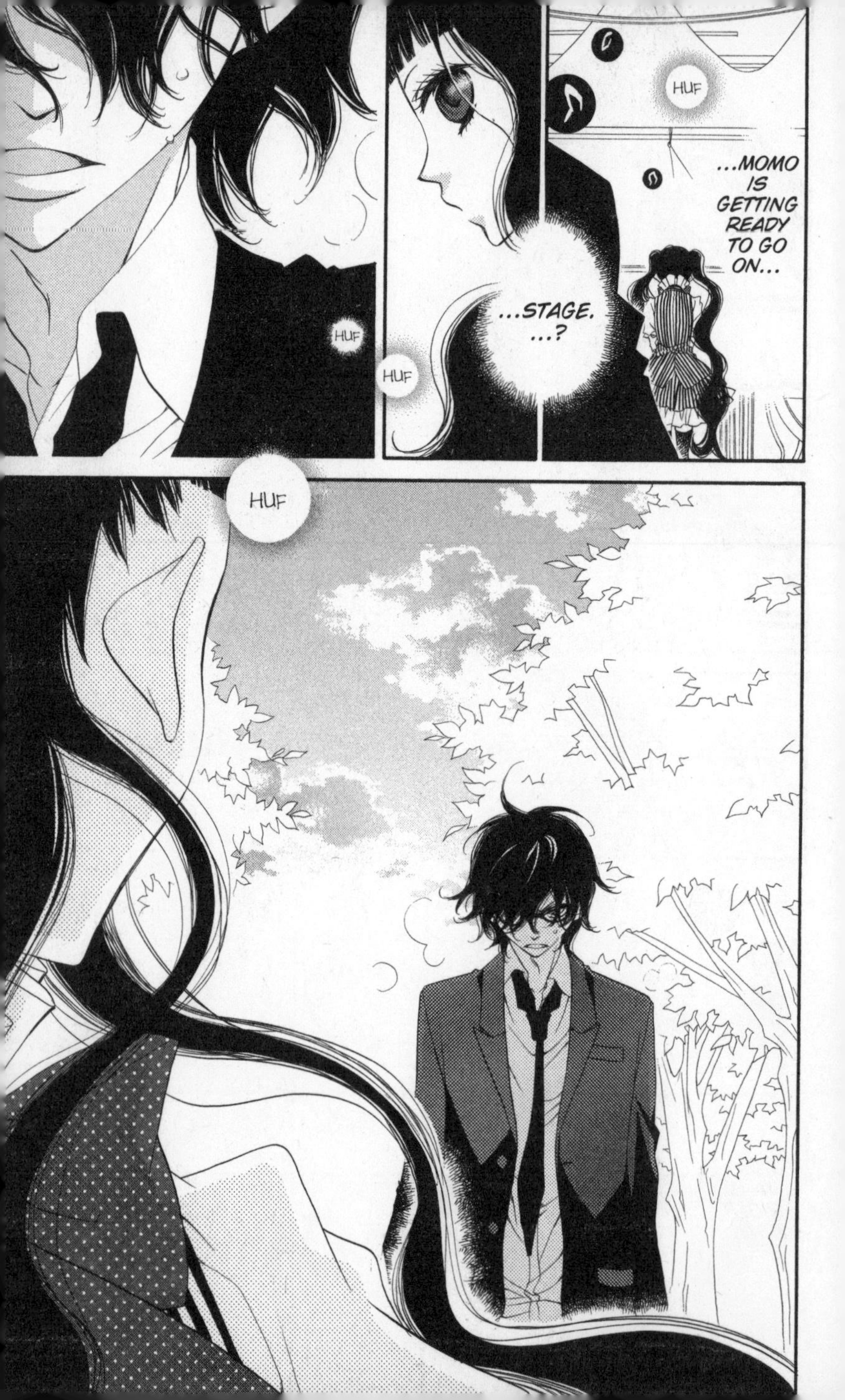
HUF
...MOMO IS GETTING READY TO GO ON...
...STAGE.
...?
HUF
HUF
HUF

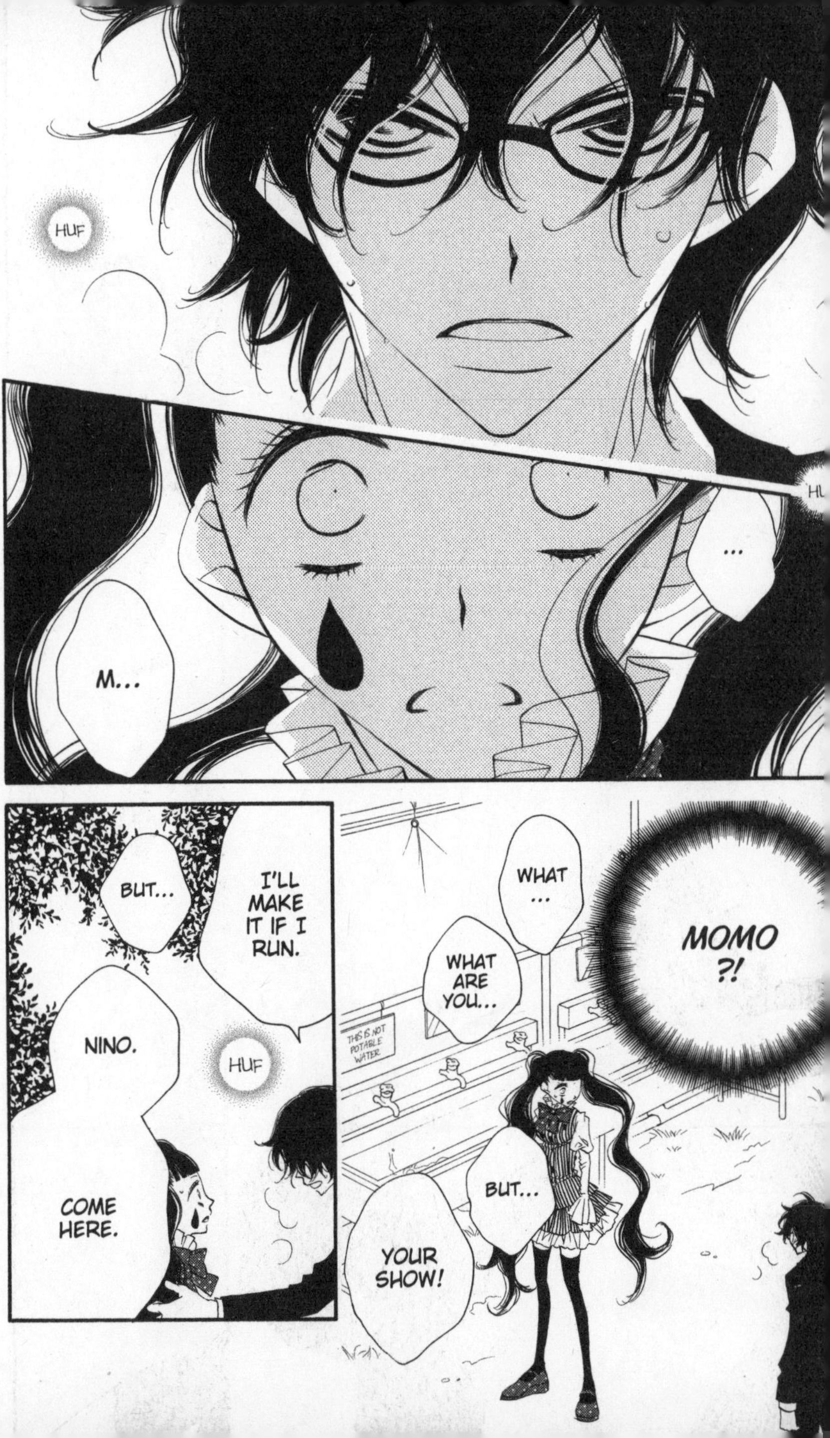
HUF
...
M...
MOMO ?!
WHAT ...
WHAT ARE YOU...
THIS IS NOT POTABLE WATER
BUT...
YOUR SHOW!
I'LL MAKE IT IF I RUN.
BUT...
HUF
NINO.
COME HERE.

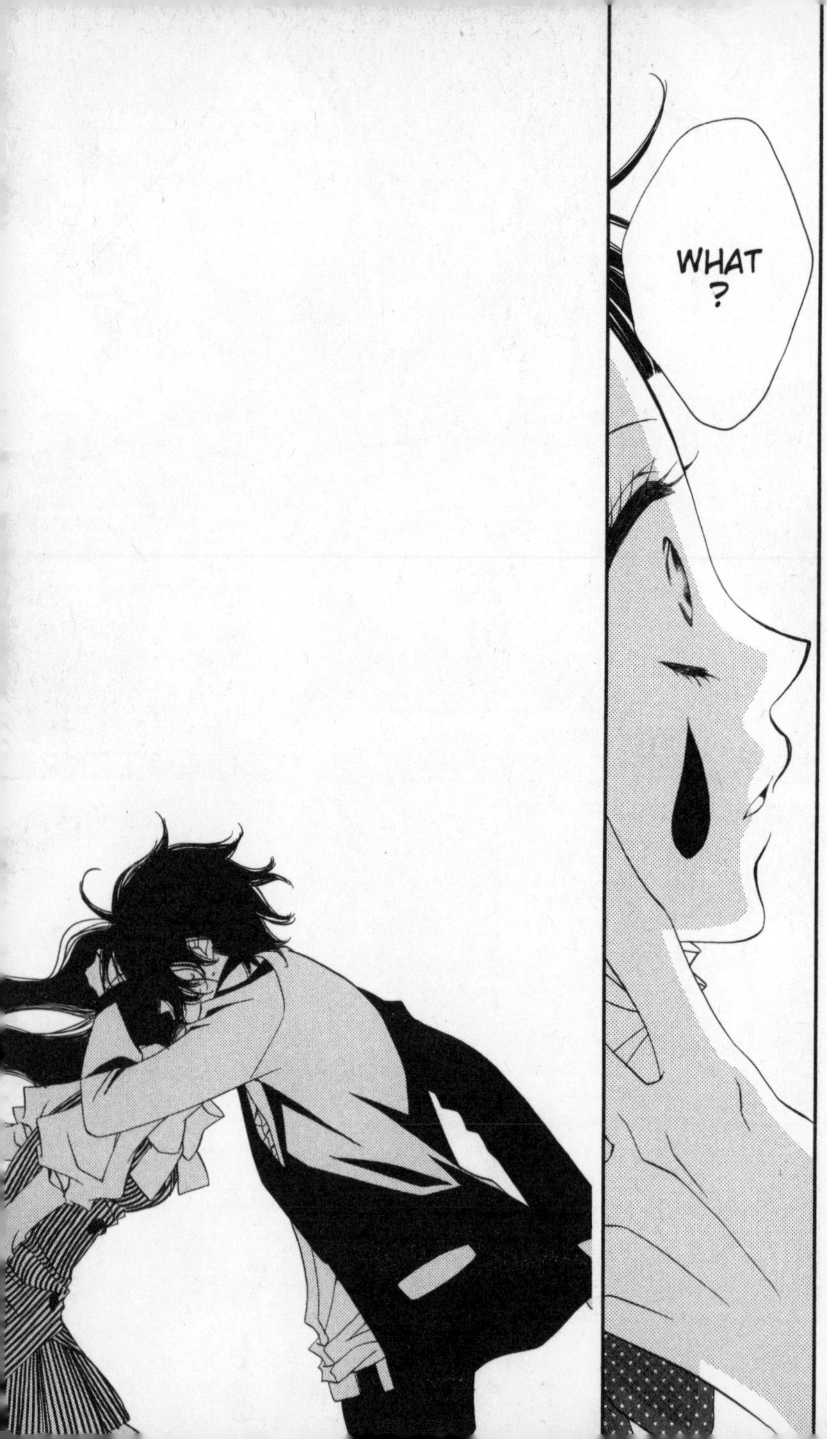
WHAT?

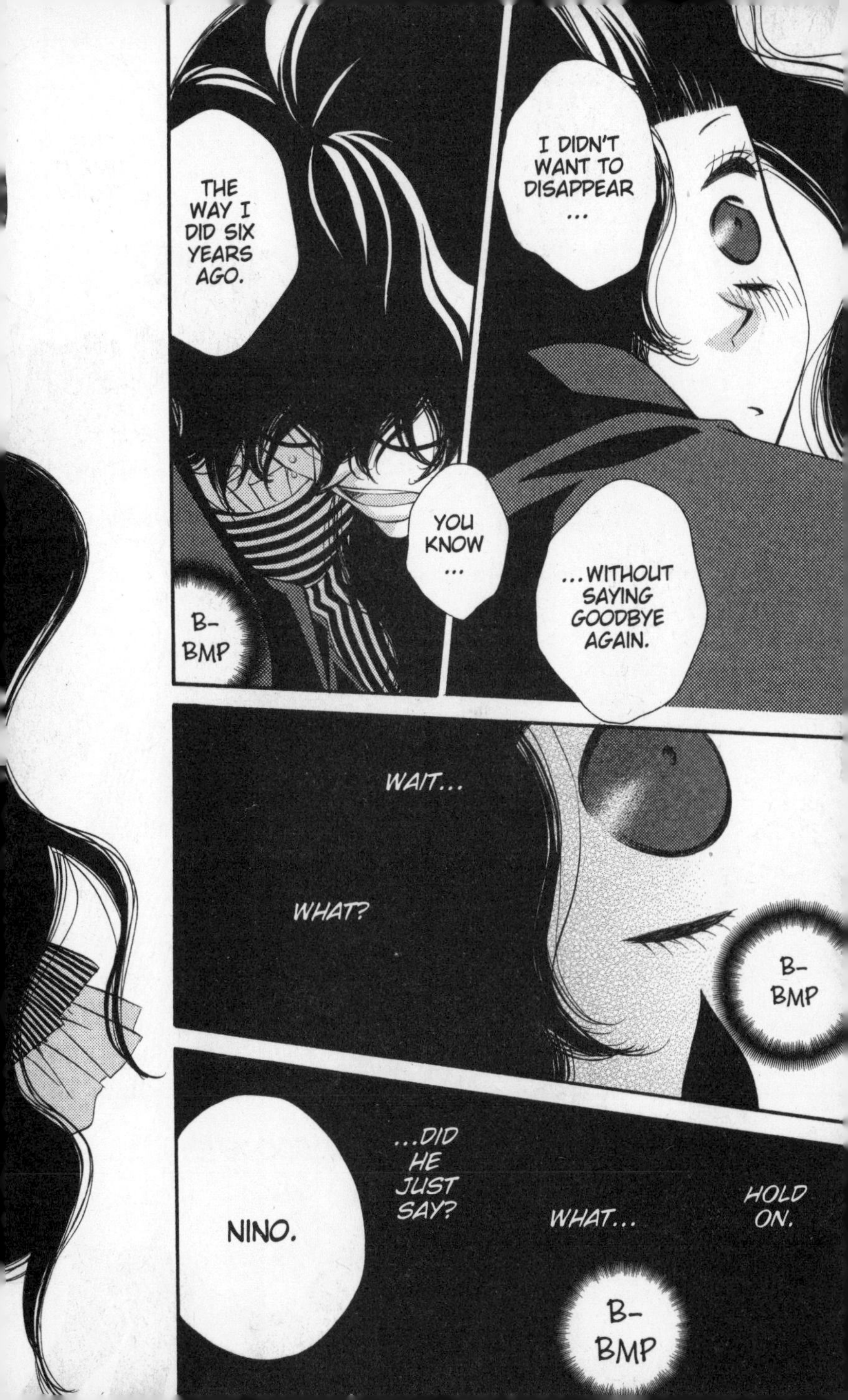

I DIDN'T WANT TO DISAPPEAR ...
...WITHOUT SAYING GOODBYE AGAIN.
THE WAY I DID SIX YEARS AGO.
YOU KNOW ...
B-BMP
B-BMP
WAIT...
WHAT?
HOLD ON.
WHAT...
...DID HE JUST SAY?
NINO.
B-BMP

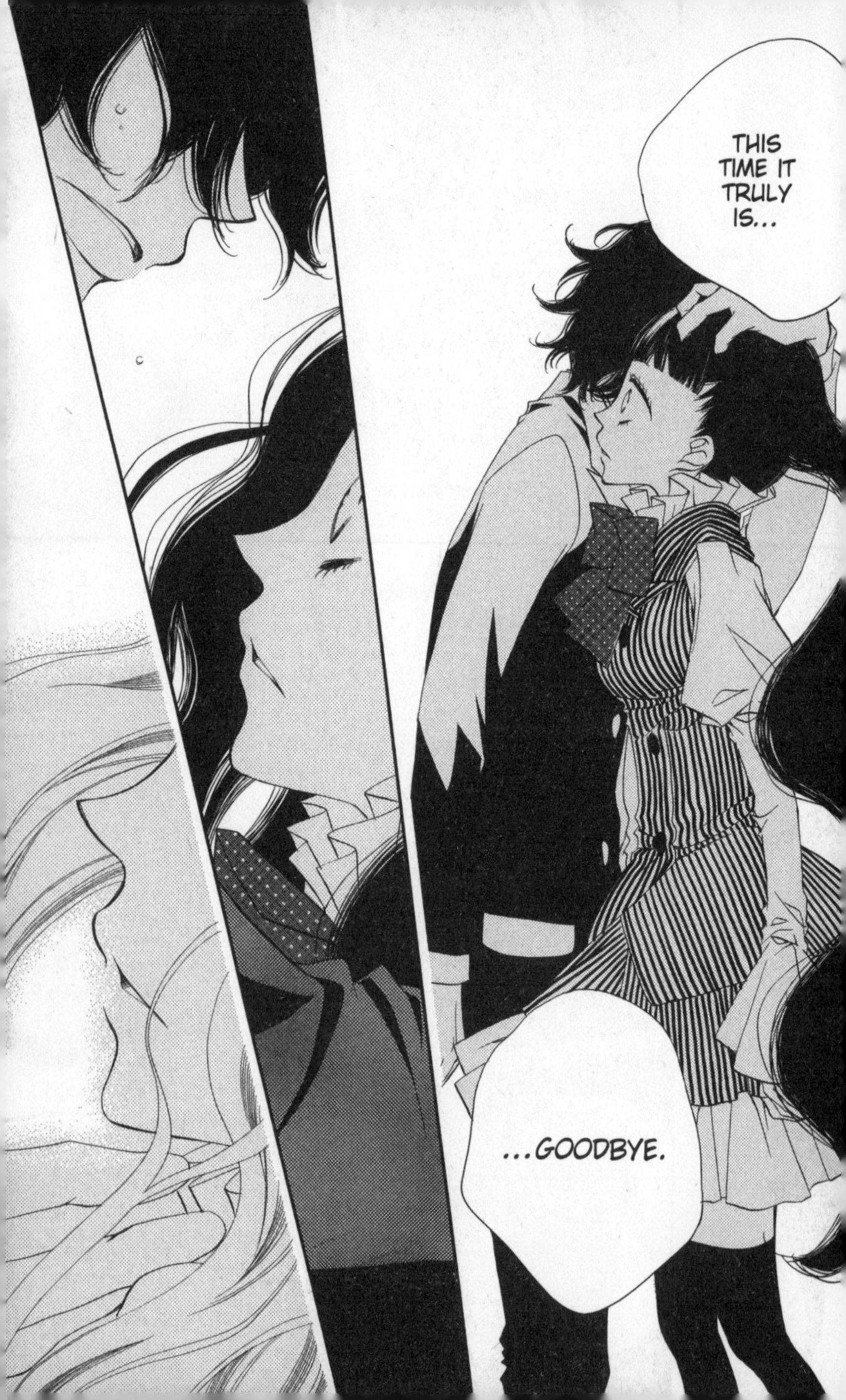
THIS TIME IT TRULY IS...
...GOODBYE.

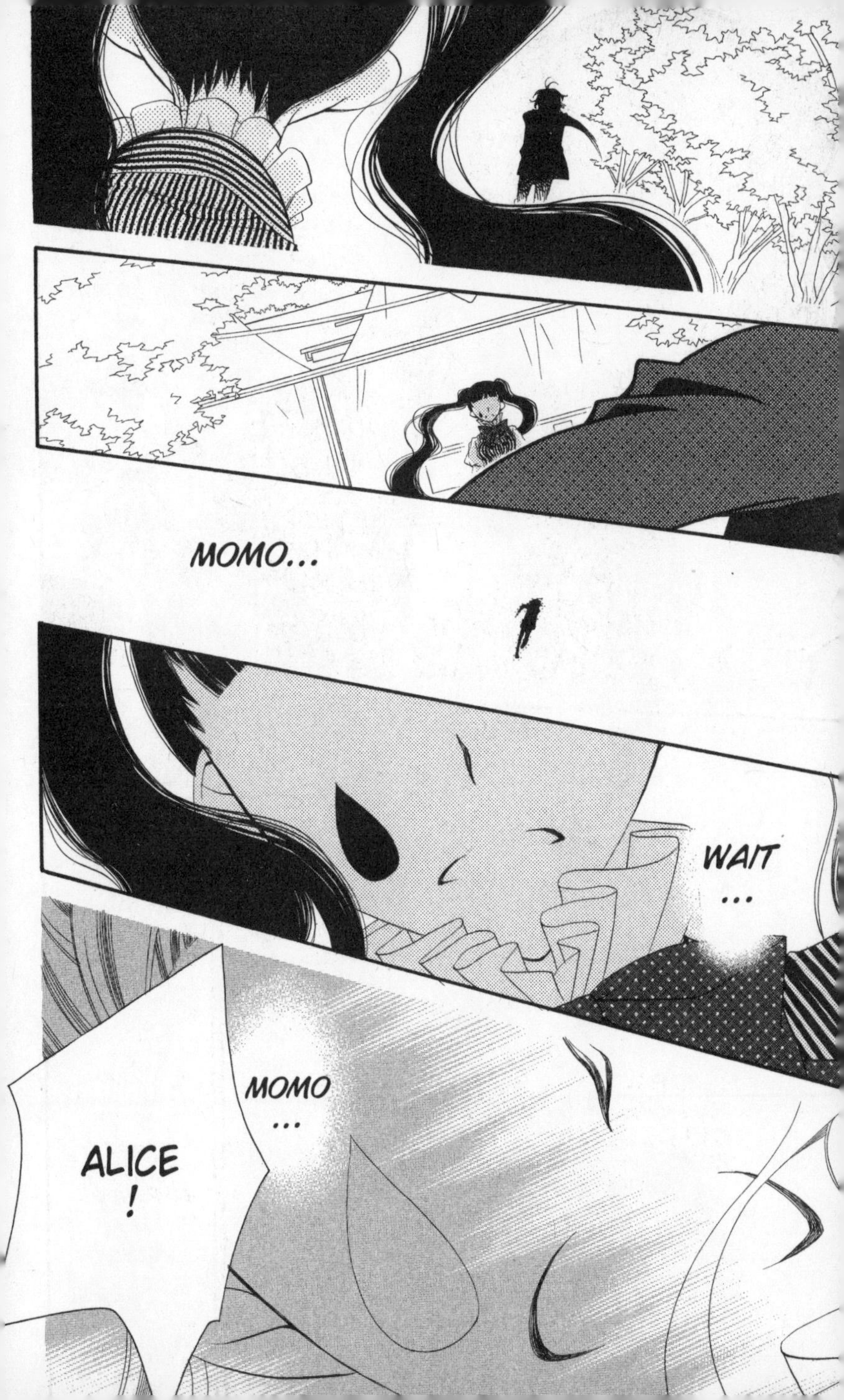
MOMO...
WAIT ...
MOMO ...
ALICE !

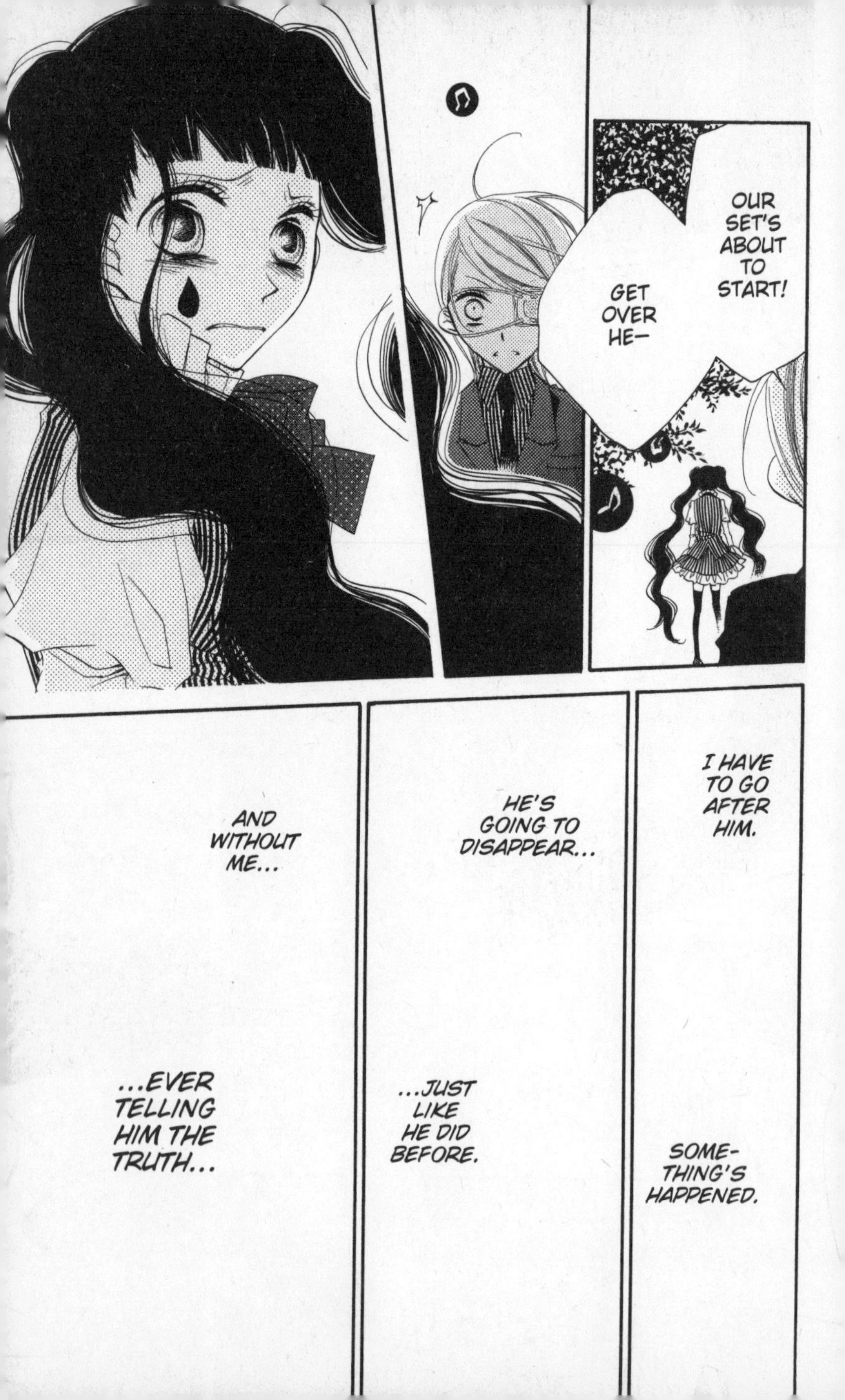
OUR SET'S ABOUT TO START!
GET OVER HE—
I HAVE TO GO AFTER HIM.
SOME-THING'S HAPPENED.
HE'S GOING TO DISAPPEAR...
...JUST LIKE HE DID BEFORE.
AND WITHOUT ME...
...EVER TELLING HIM THE TRUTH...

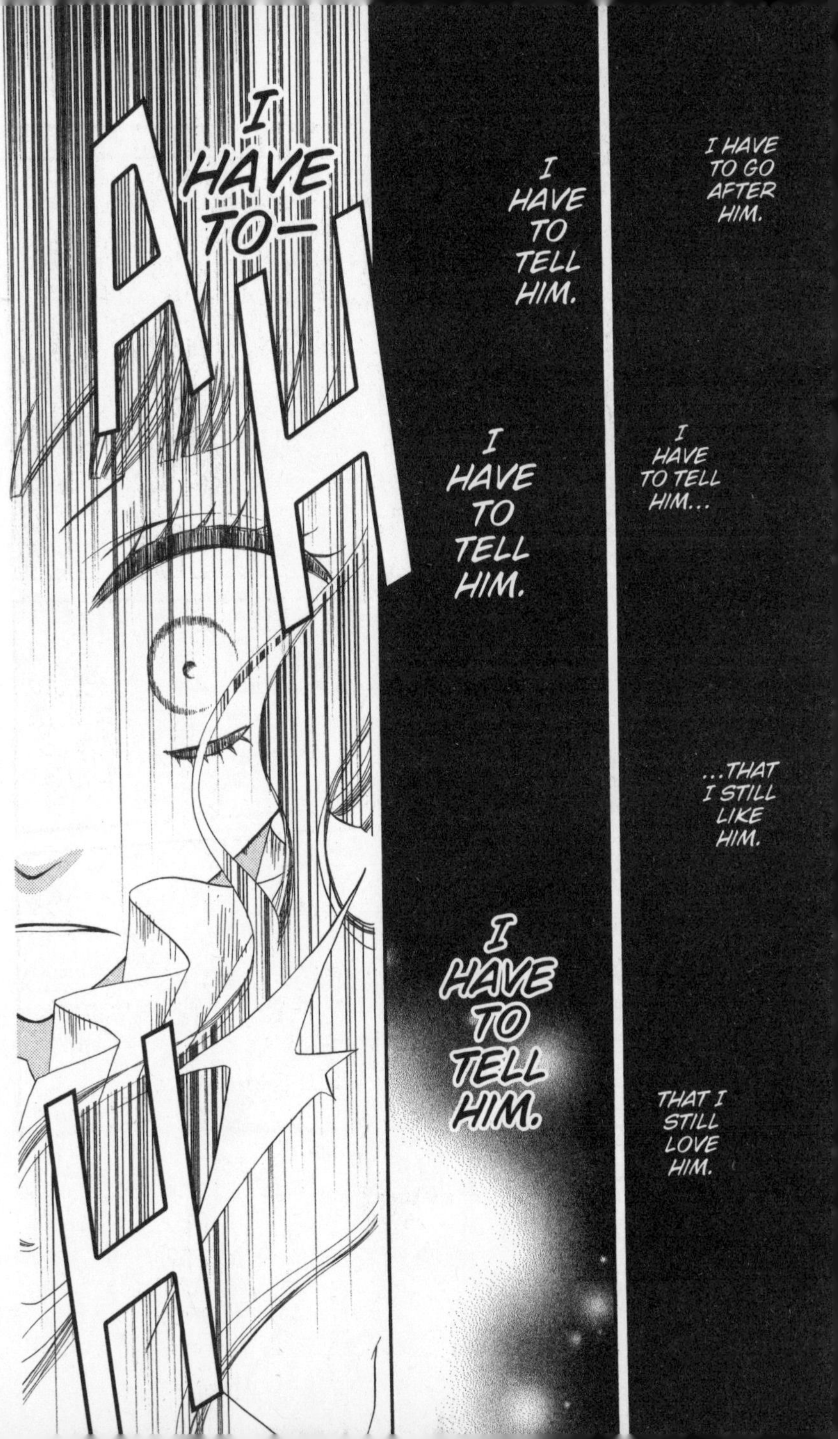
I HAVE TO GO AFTER HIM.
I HAVE TO TELL HIM...
...THAT I STILL LIKE HIM.
THAT I STILL LOVE HIM.
I HAVE TO TELL HIM.
I HAVE TO TELL HIM.
I HAVE TO TELL HIM.
I HAVE TO—
AHHH

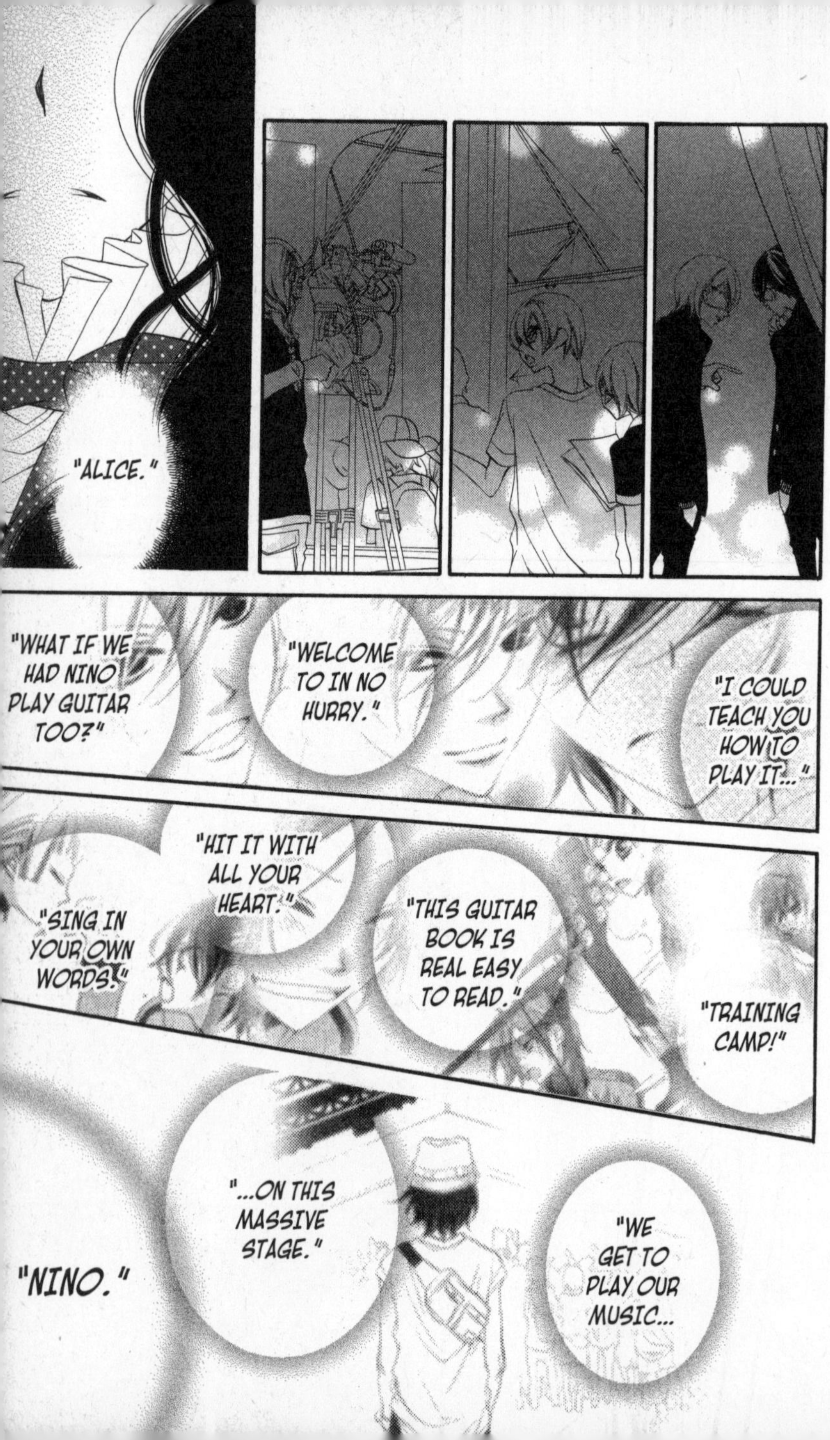
"ALICE."
"I COULD TEACH YOU HOW TO PLAY IT..."
"WELCOME TO IN NO HURRY."
"WHAT IF WE HAD NINO PLAY GUITAR TOO?"
"TRAINING CAMP!"
"THIS GUITAR BOOK IS REAL EASY TO READ."
"HIT IT WITH ALL YOUR HEART."
"SING IN YOUR OWN WORDS."
"WE GET TO PLAY OUR MUSIC...
...ON THIS MASSIVE STAGE."
"NINO."

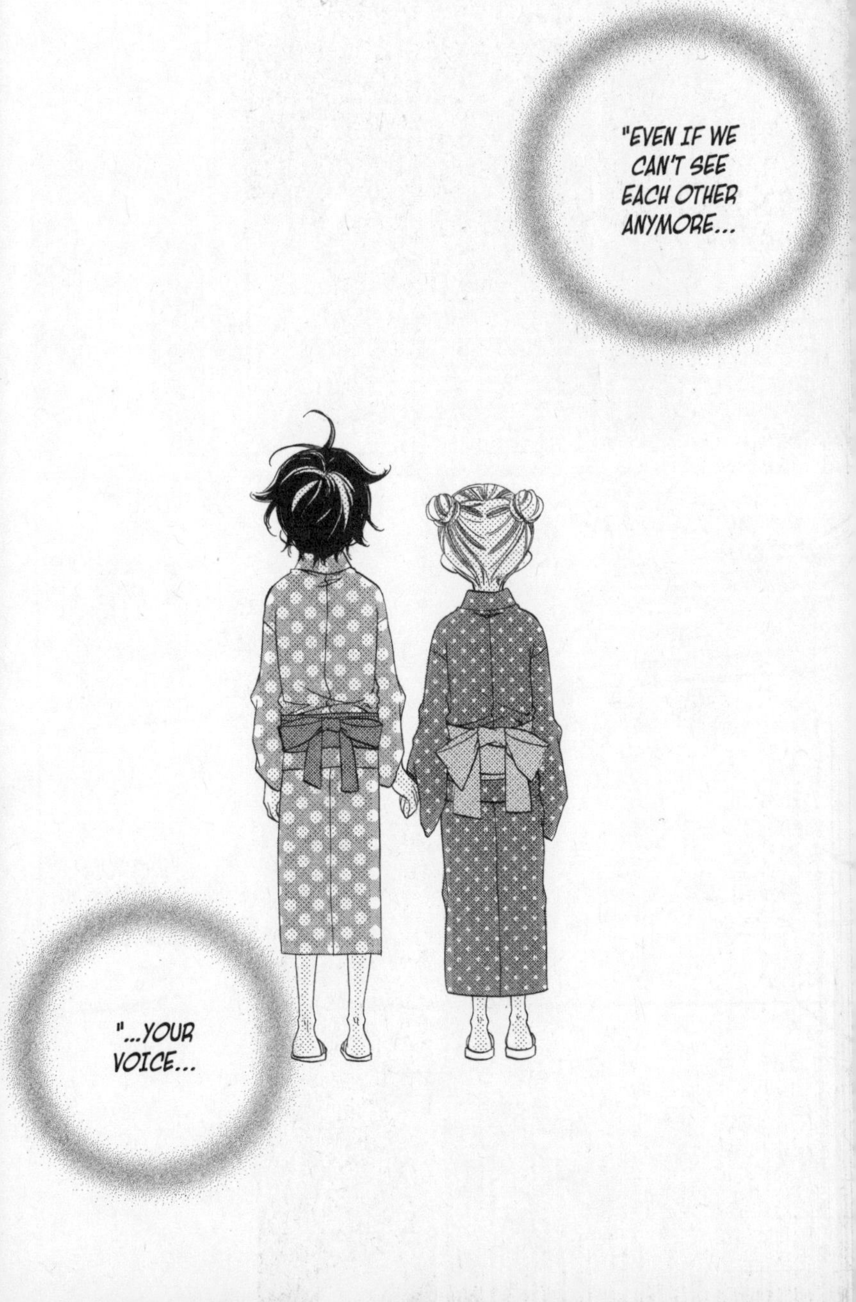
"EVEN IF WE CAN'T SEE EACH OTHER ANYMORE...
"...YOUR VOICE...

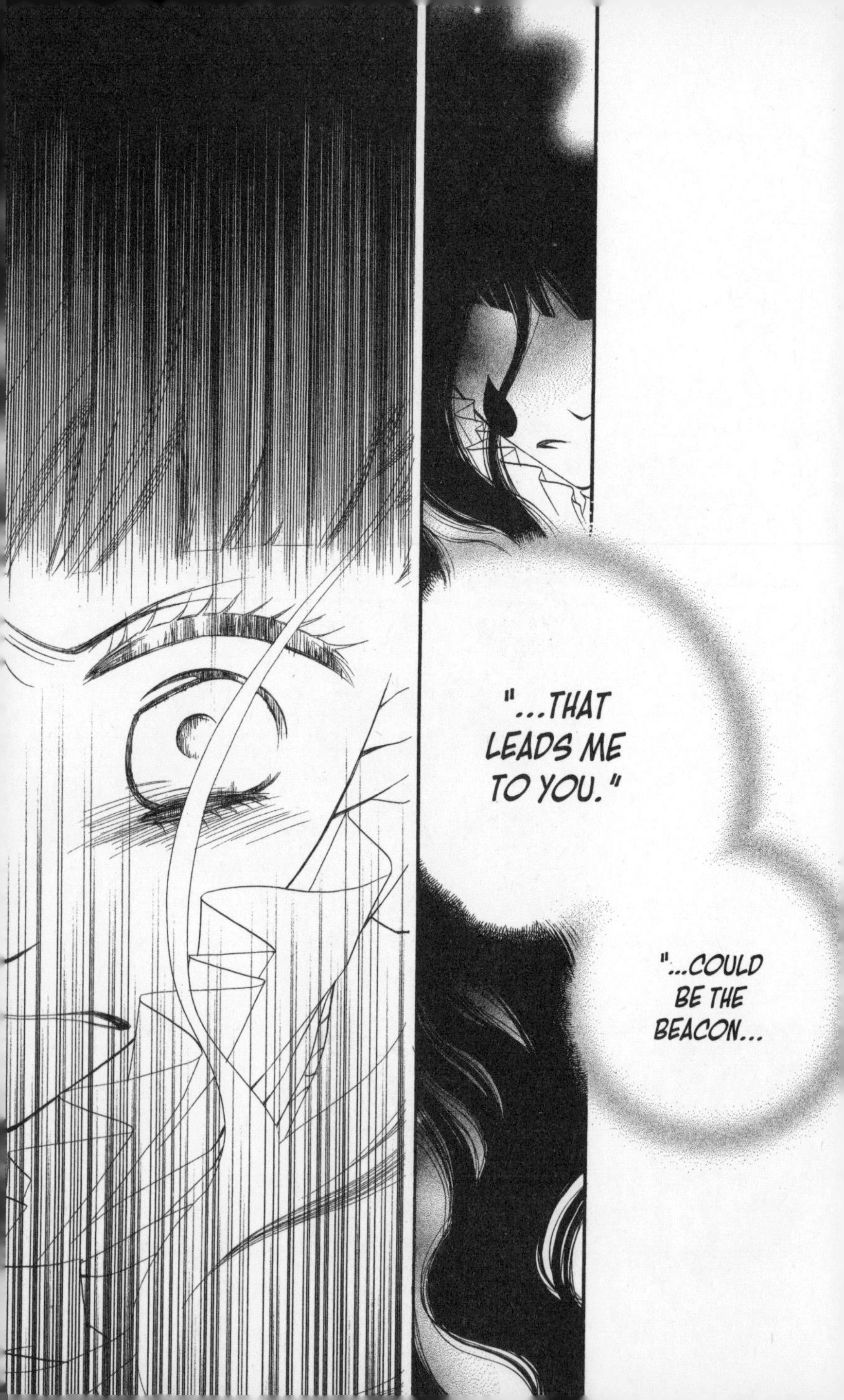
"...COULD BE THE BEACON...
"...THAT LEADS ME TO YOU."

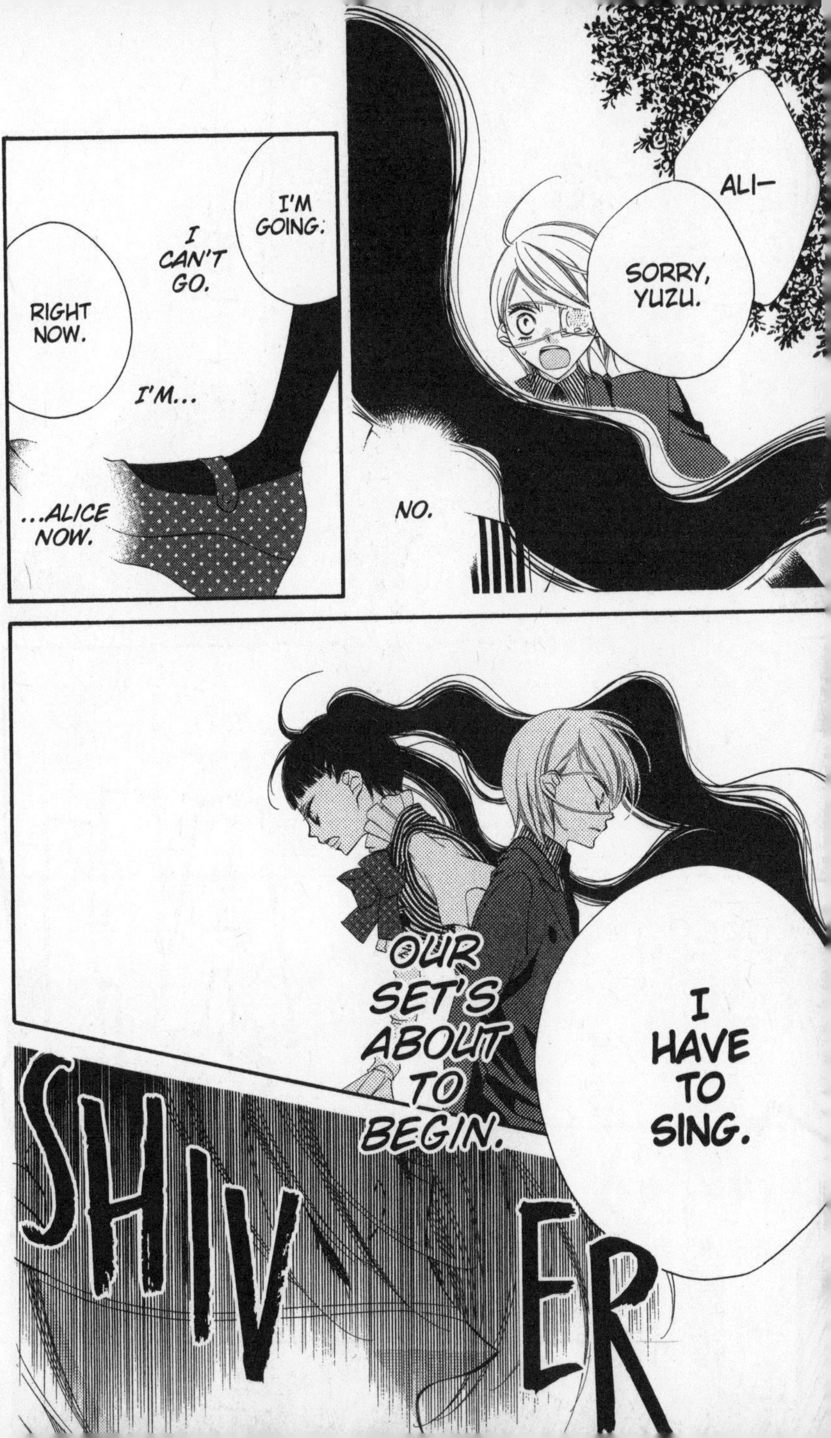
ALI—
SORRY, YUZU.
NO.
I'M GOING.
I CAN'T GO.
RIGHT NOW.
I'M...
...ALICE NOW.
I HAVE TO SING.
OUR SET'S ABOUT TO BEGIN.
SHIVER

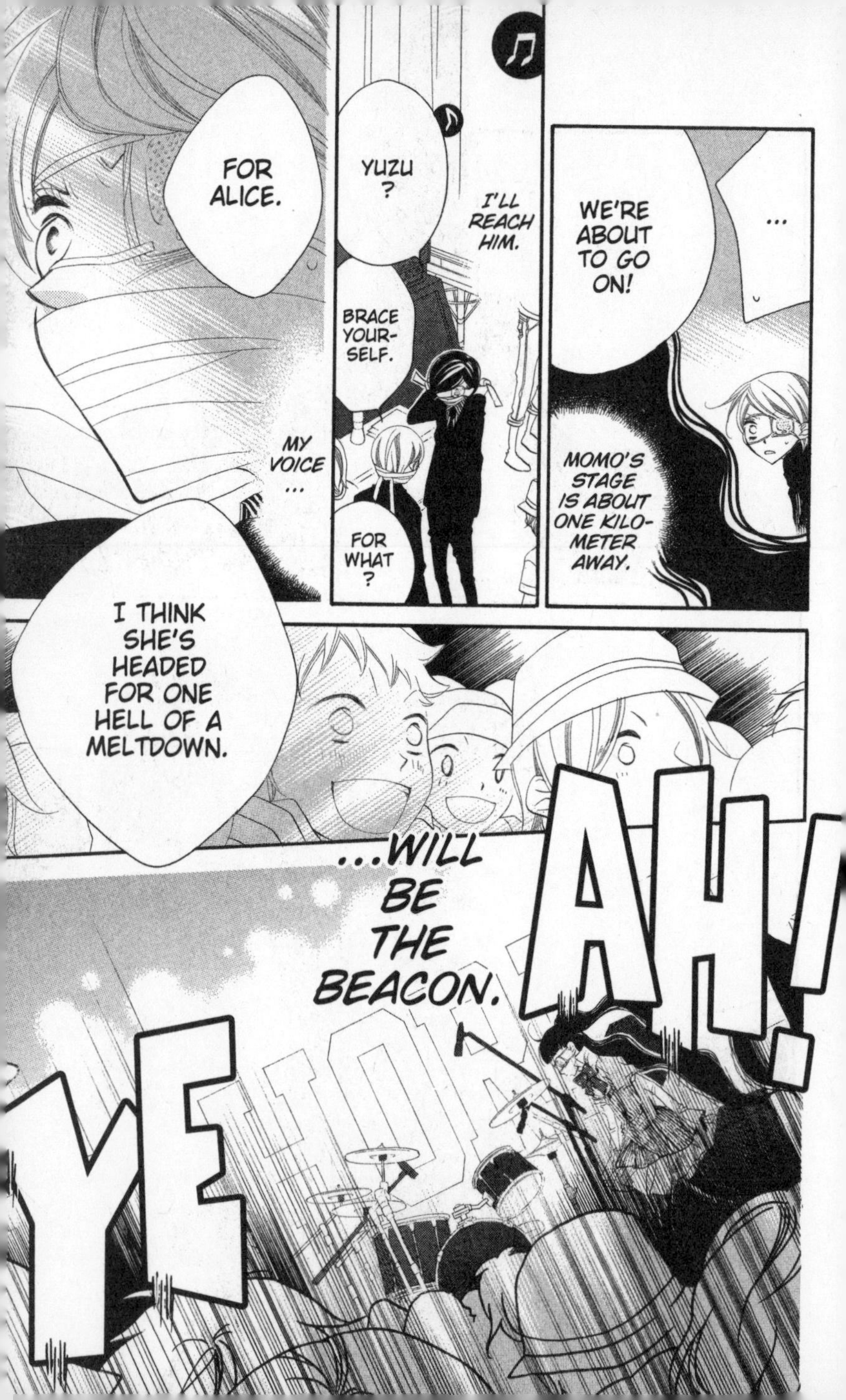
...
WE'RE ABOUT TO GO ON!
MOMO'S STAGE IS ABOUT ONE KILOMETER AWAY.
YUZU?
I'LL REACH HIM.
BRACE YOURSELF.
FOR WHAT?
MY VOICE...
FOR ALICE.
I THINK SHE'S HEADED FOR ONE HELL OF A MELTDOWN.
...WILL BE THE BEACON.
YE
AH!

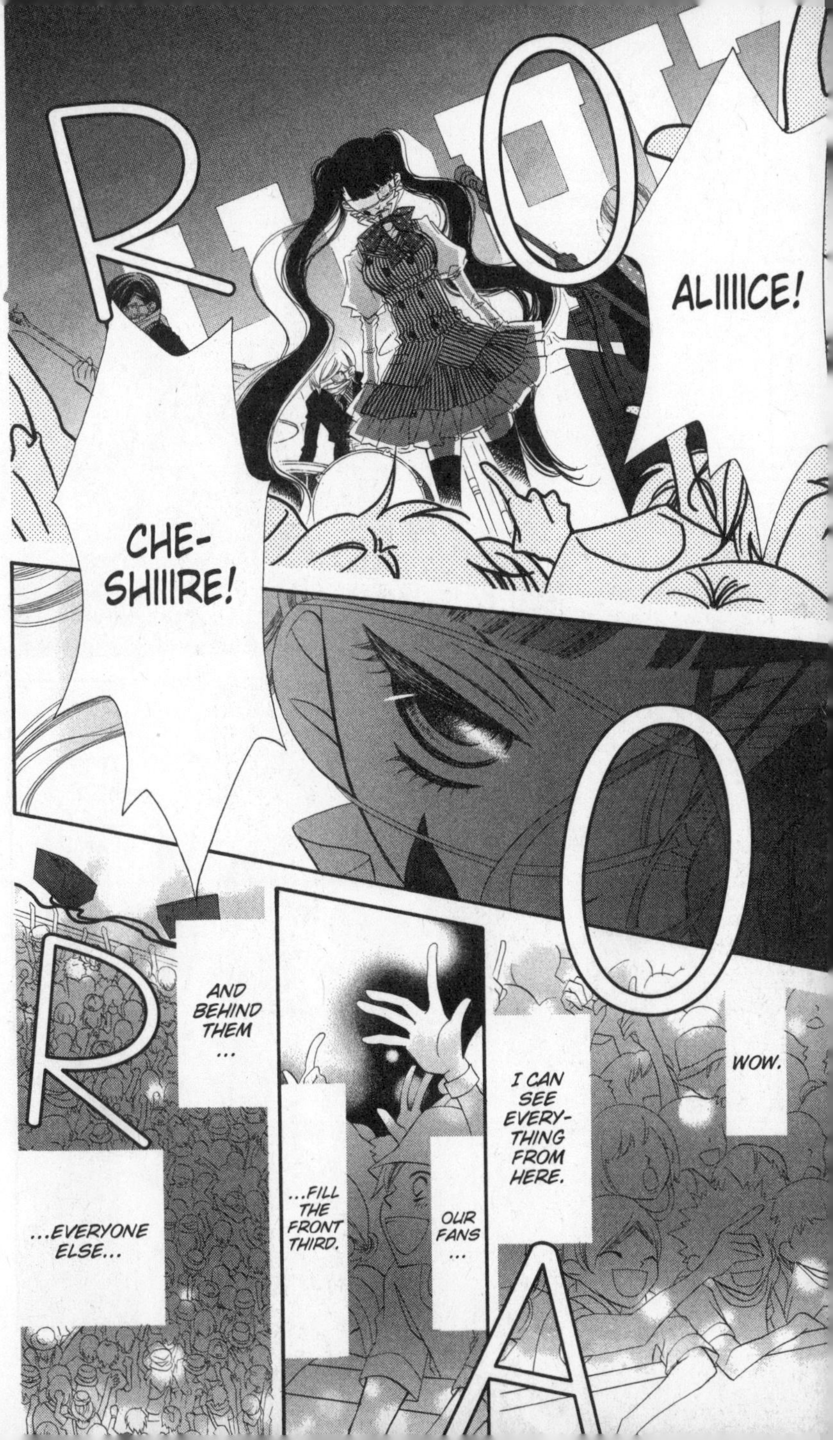
ALIIIICE!
CHE-SHIIIRE!
ROAR
WOW.
I CAN SEE EVERYTHING FROM HERE.
OUR FANS...
...FILL THE FRONT THIRD.
AND BEHIND THEM...
...EVERYONE ELSE...

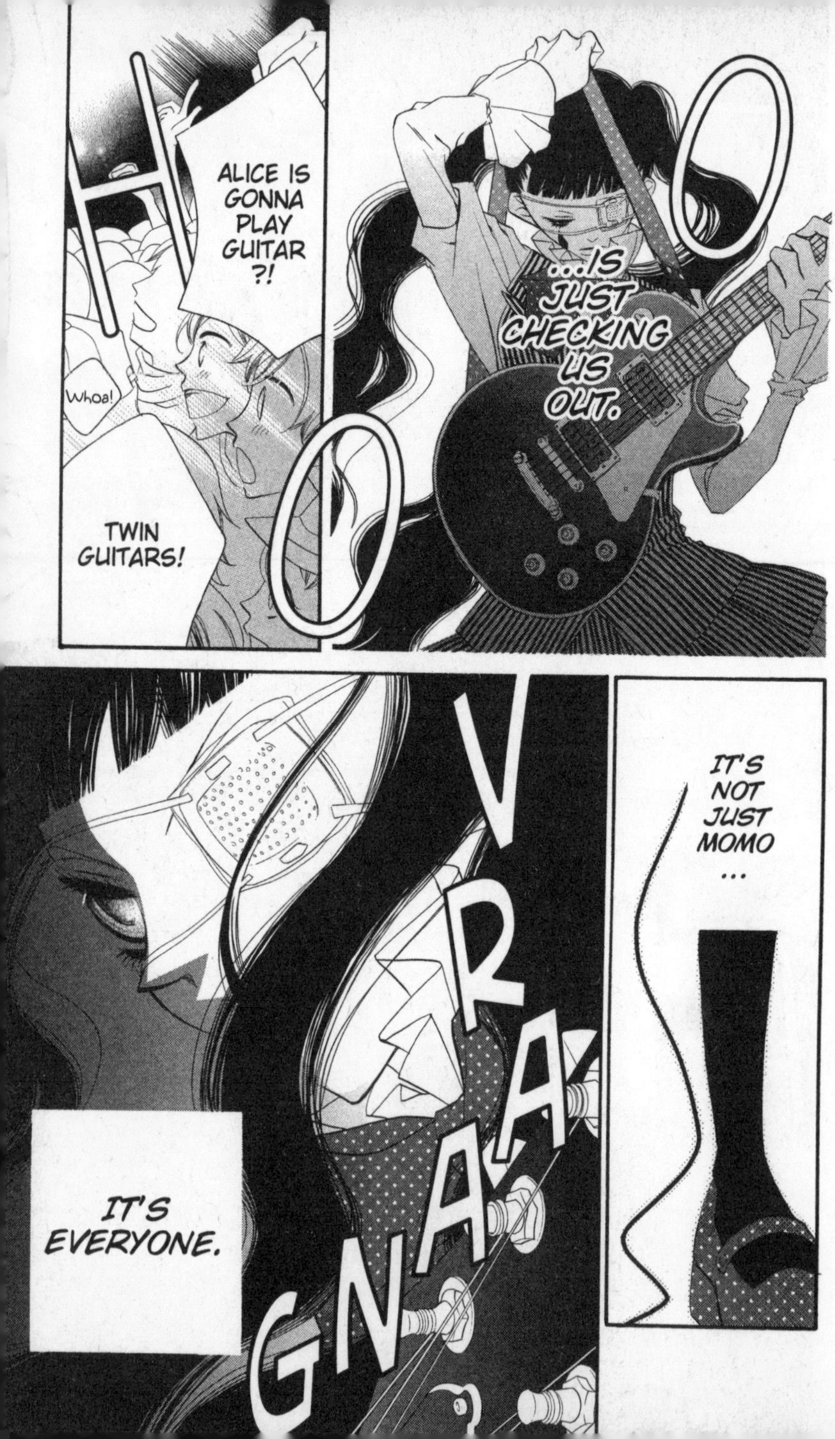
...IS JUST CHECKING US OUT.
HOO
ALICE IS GONNA PLAY GUITAR?!
Whoa!
TWIN GUITARS!
IT'S NOT JUST MOMO...
VRAAANG
IT'S EVERYONE.

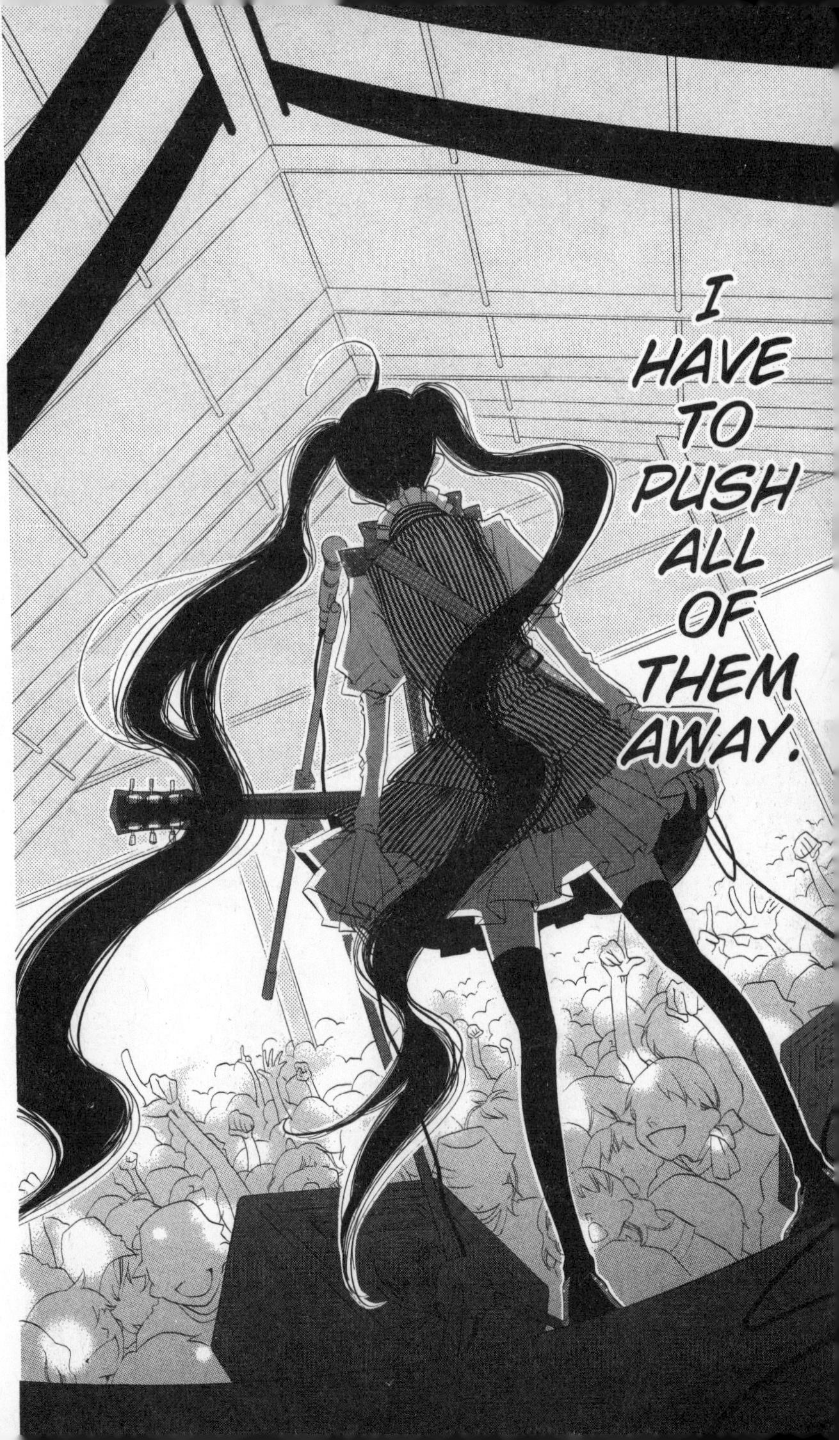
I HAVE TO PUSH ALL OF THEM AWAY.

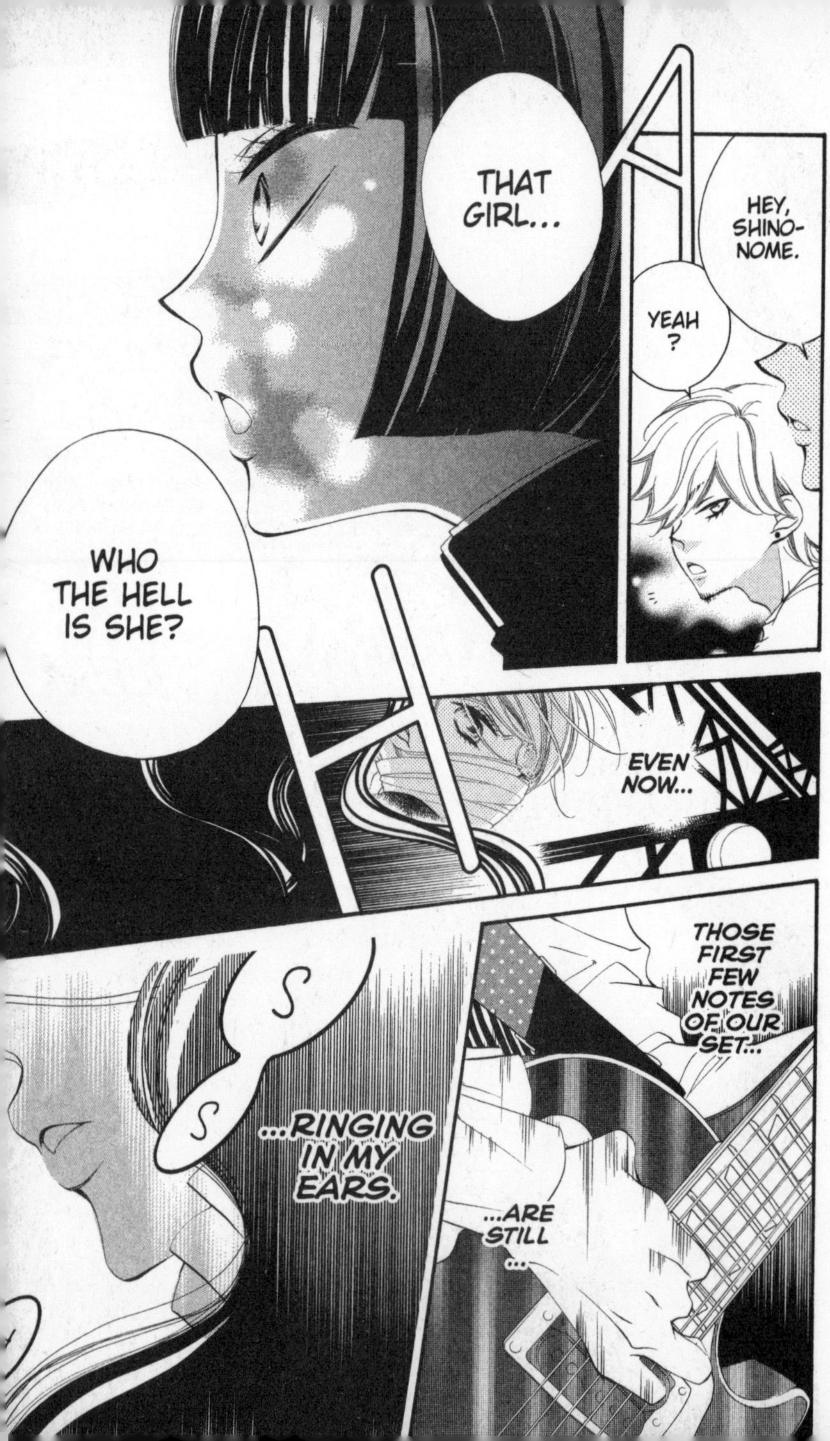
HEY, SHINO-NOME.
YEAH?
THAT GIRL...
WHO THE HELL IS SHE?
EVEN NOW...
THOSE FIRST FEW NOTES OF OUR SET...
...ARE STILL ...
...RINGING IN MY EARS.

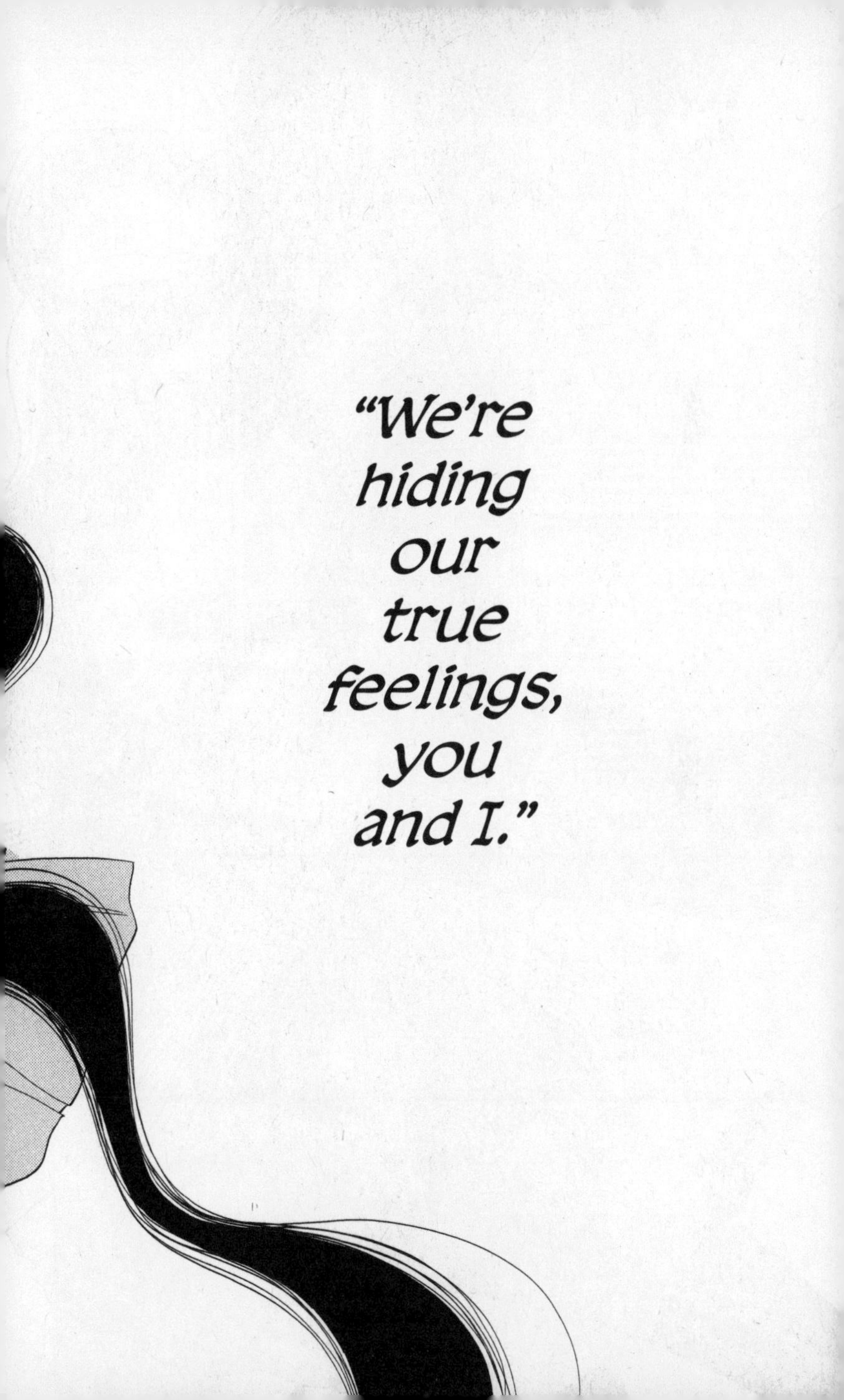
"We're hiding our true feelings, you and I."

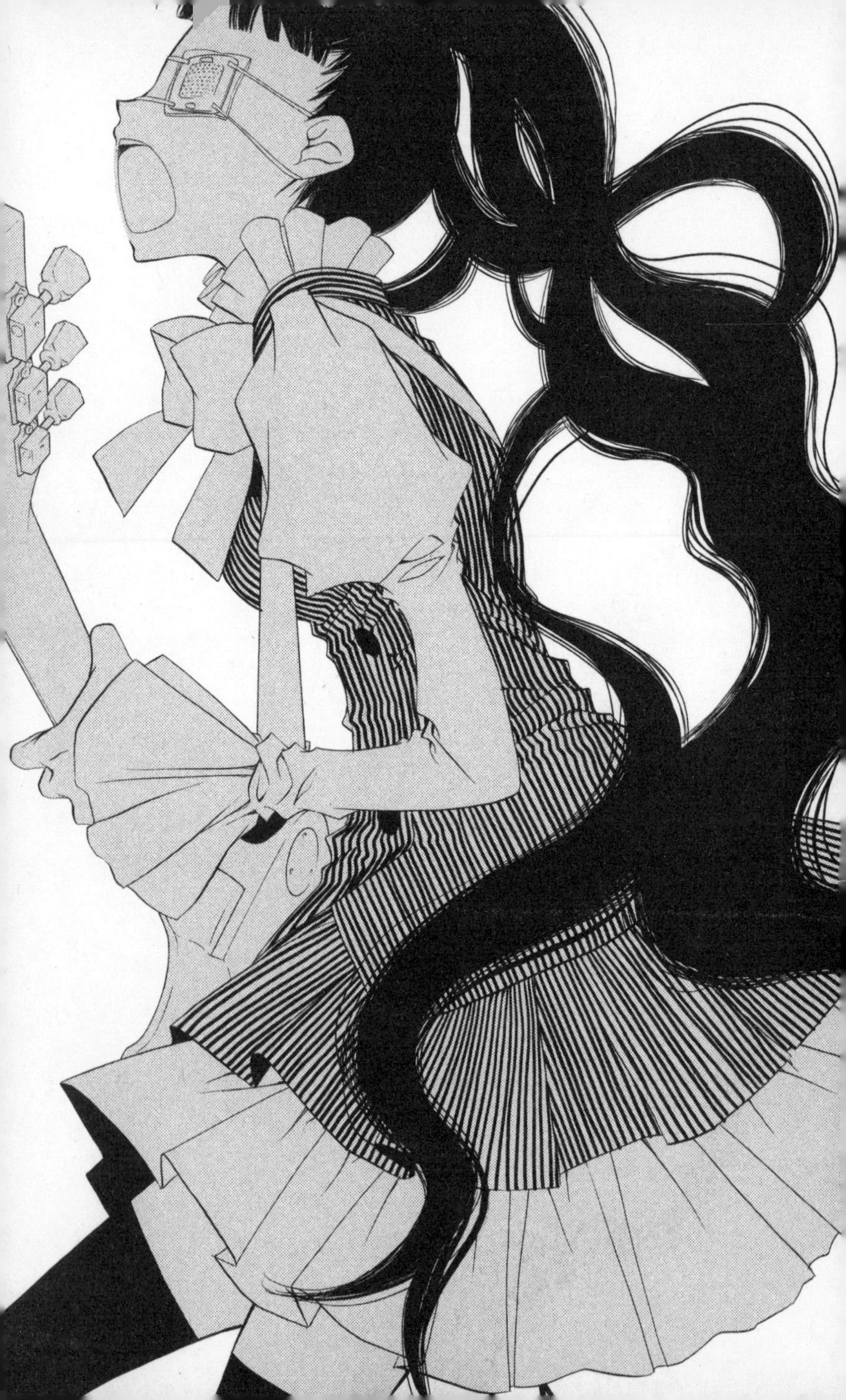

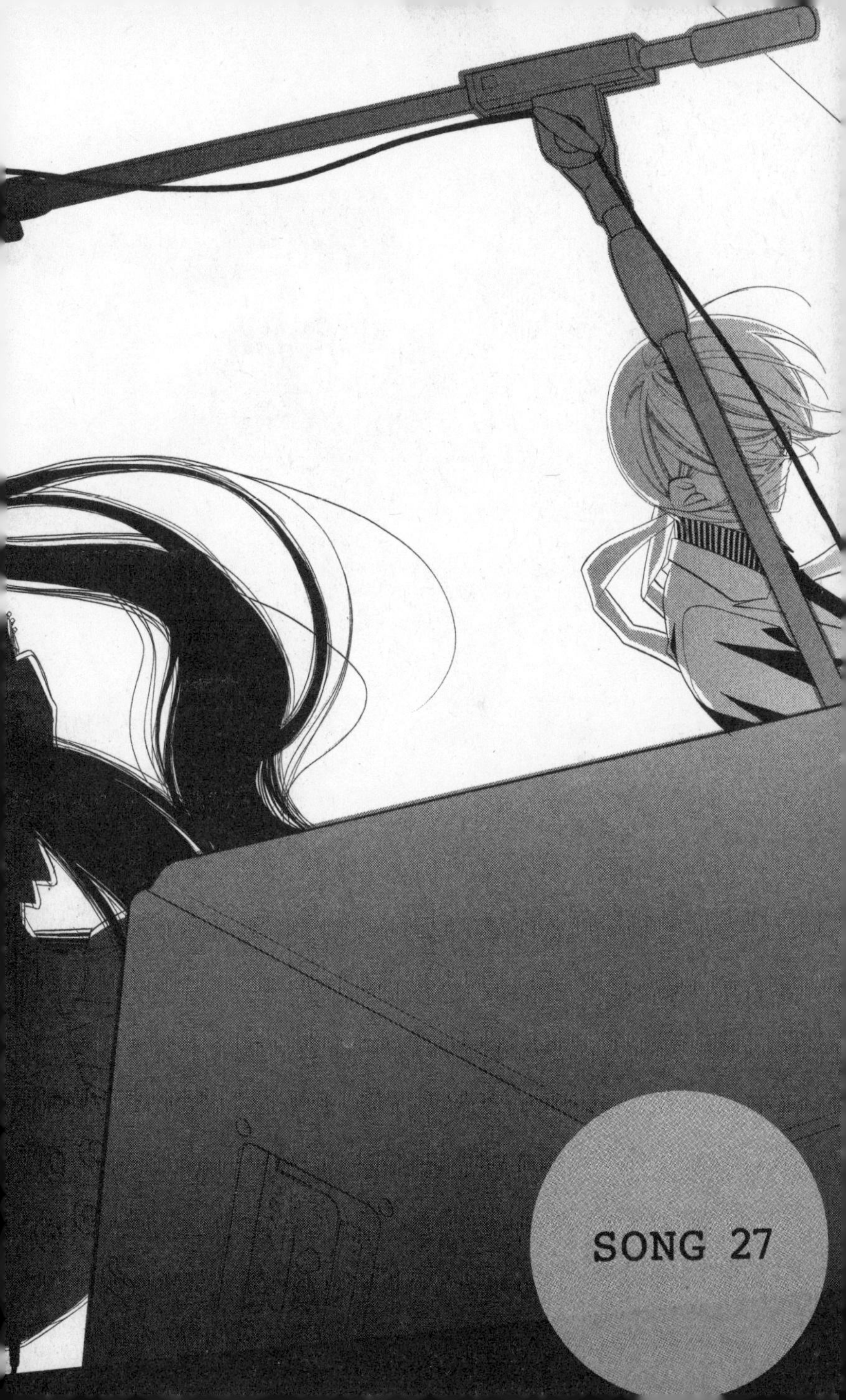
SONG 27

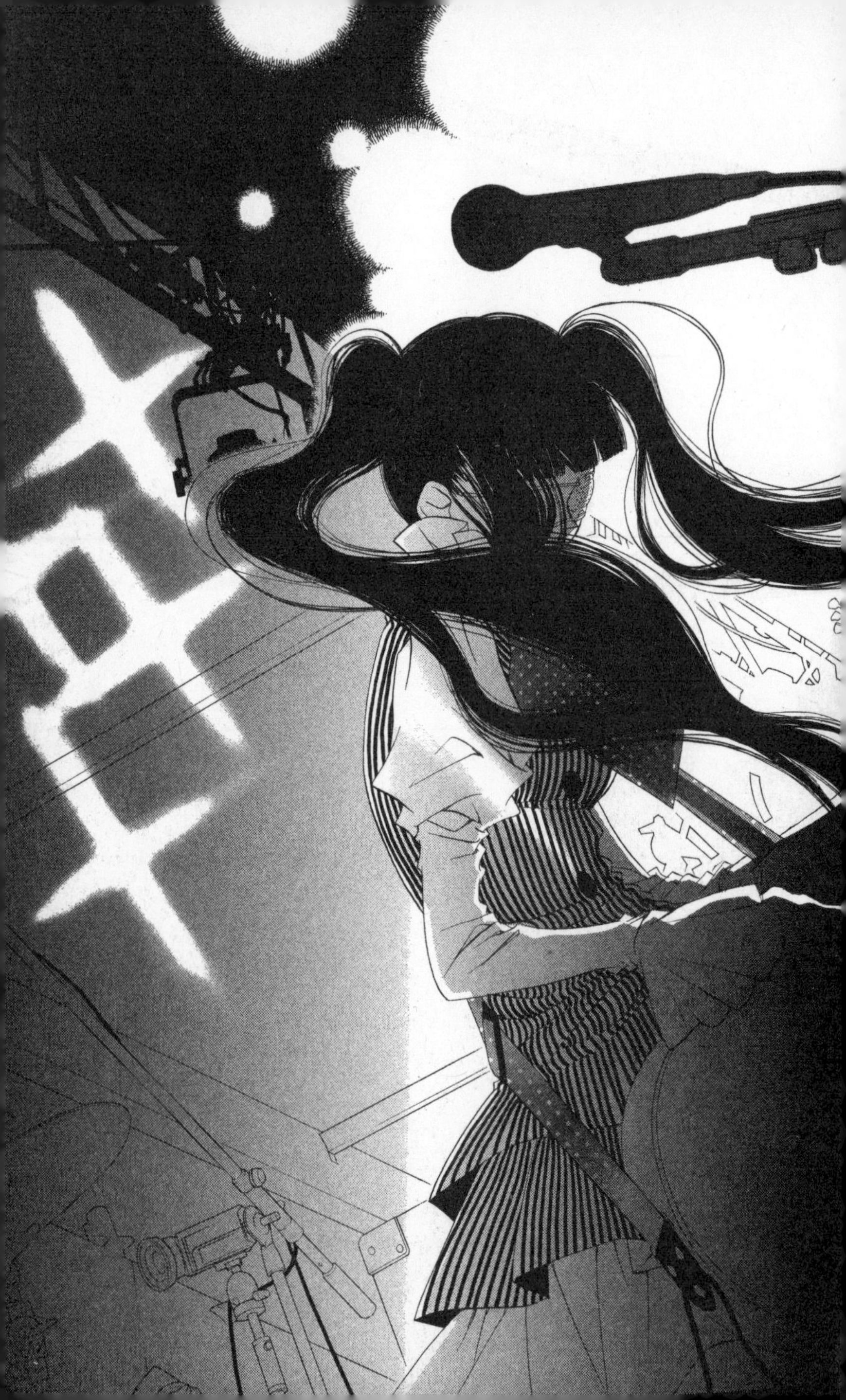

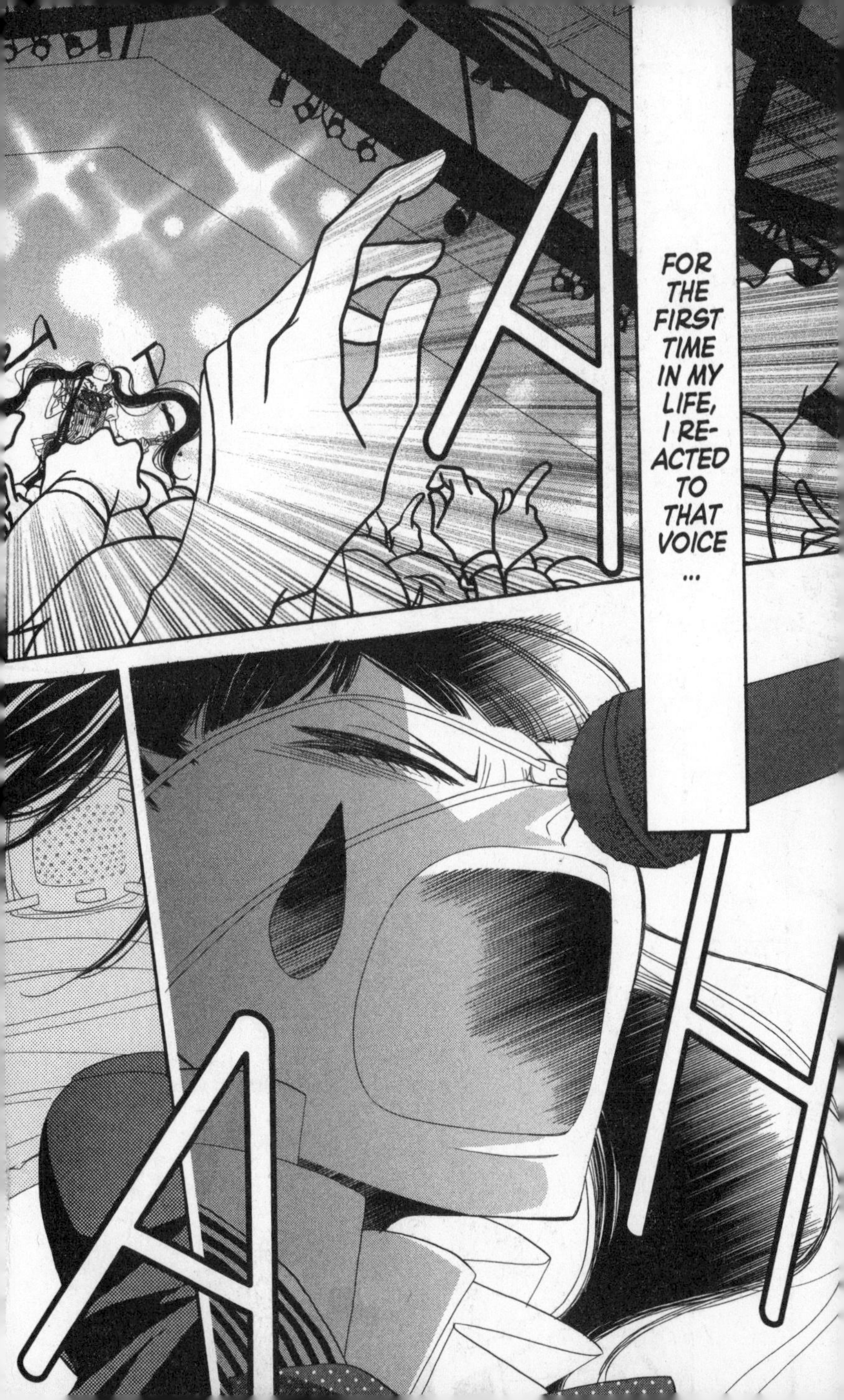
FOR THE FIRST TIME IN MY LIFE, I RE-ACTED TO THAT VOICE ...
A
AH

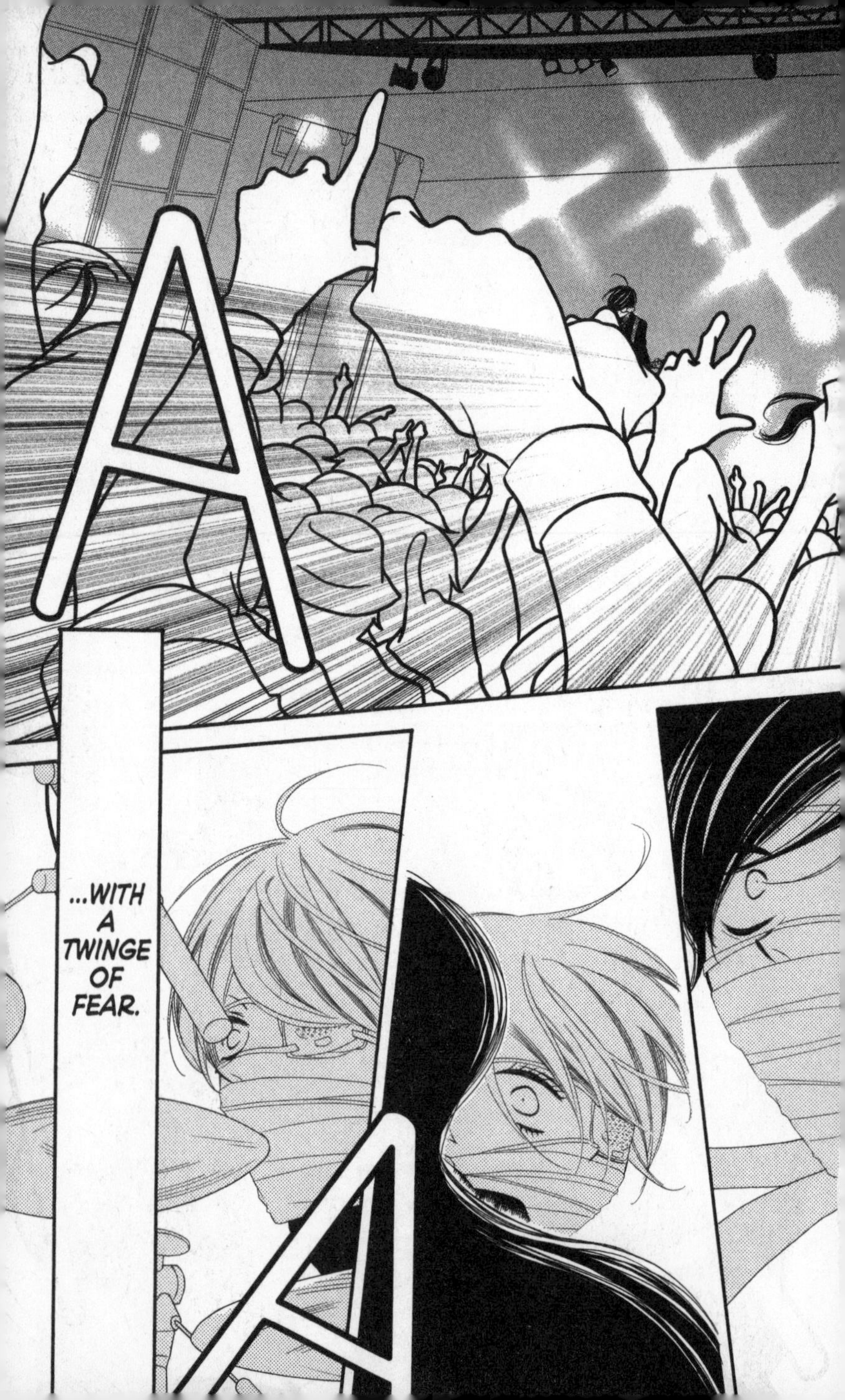
...WITH A TWINGE OF FEAR.

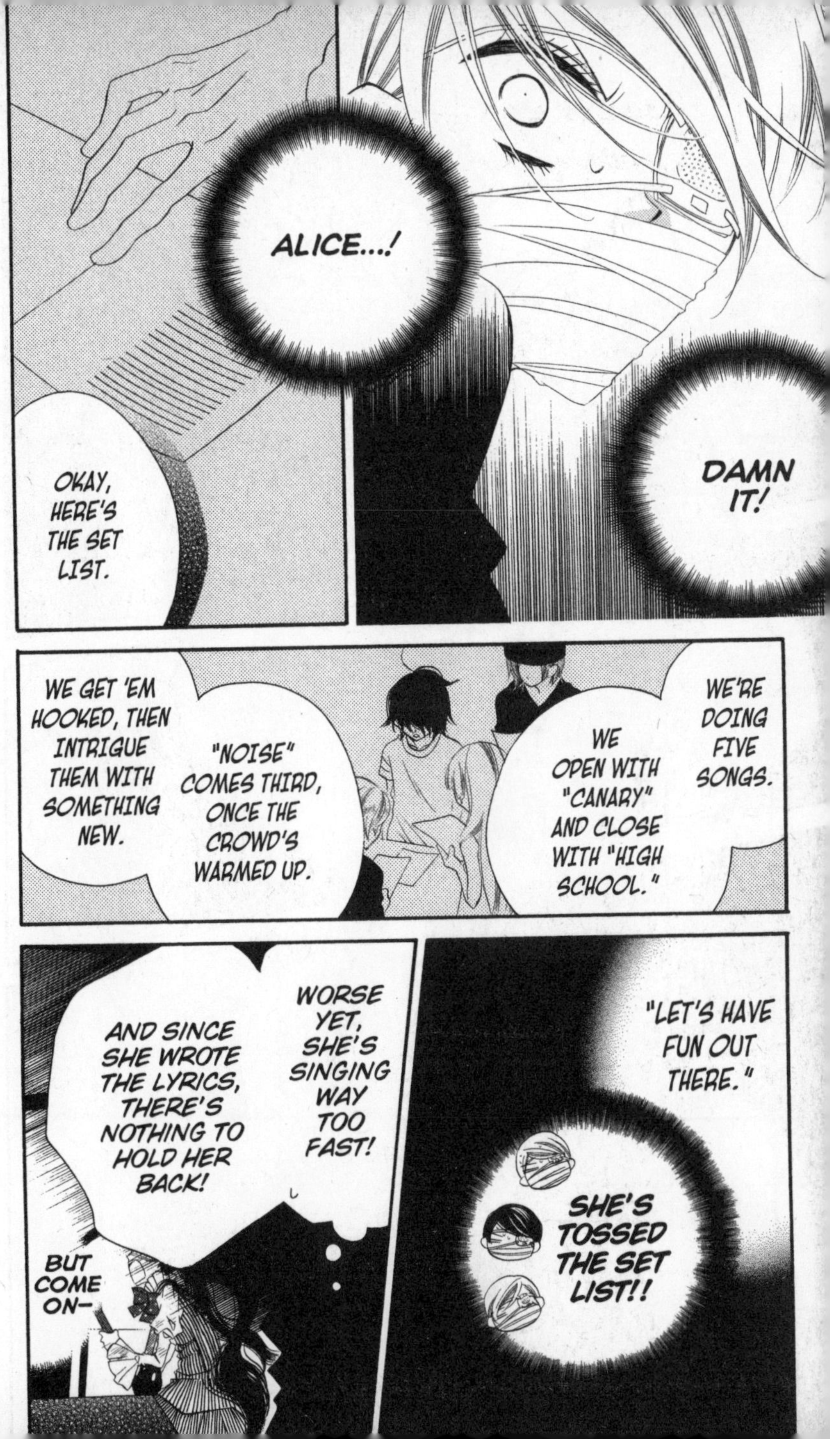
ALICE...!
DAMN IT!
OKAY, HERE'S THE SET LIST.
WE'RE DOING FIVE SONGS.
WE OPEN WITH "CANARY" AND CLOSE WITH "HIGH SCHOOL."
"NOISE" COMES THIRD, ONCE THE CROWD'S WARMED UP.
WE GET 'EM HOOKED, THEN INTRIGUE THEM WITH SOMETHING NEW.
"LET'S HAVE FUN OUT THERE."
SHE'S TOSSED THE SET LIST!!
WORSE YET, SHE'S SINGING WAY TOO FAST!
AND SINCE SHE WROTE THE LYRICS, THERE'S NOTHING TO HOLD HER BACK!
BUT COME ON–

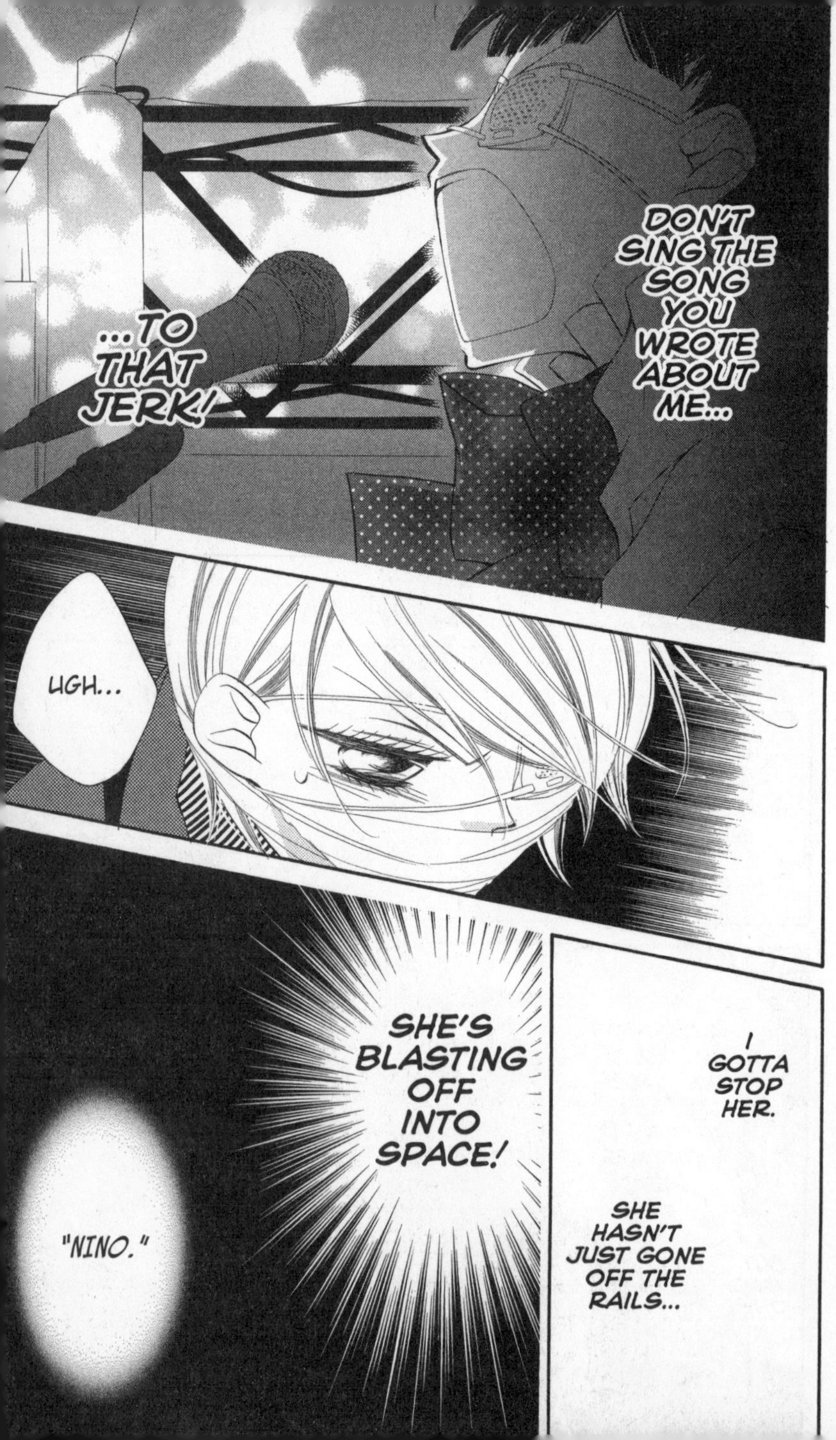
DON'T SING THE SONG YOU WROTE ABOUT ME...
...TO THAT JERK!
UGH...
I GOTTA STOP HER.
SHE HASN'T JUST GONE OFF THE RAILS...
SHE'S BLASTING OFF INTO SPACE!
"NINO."

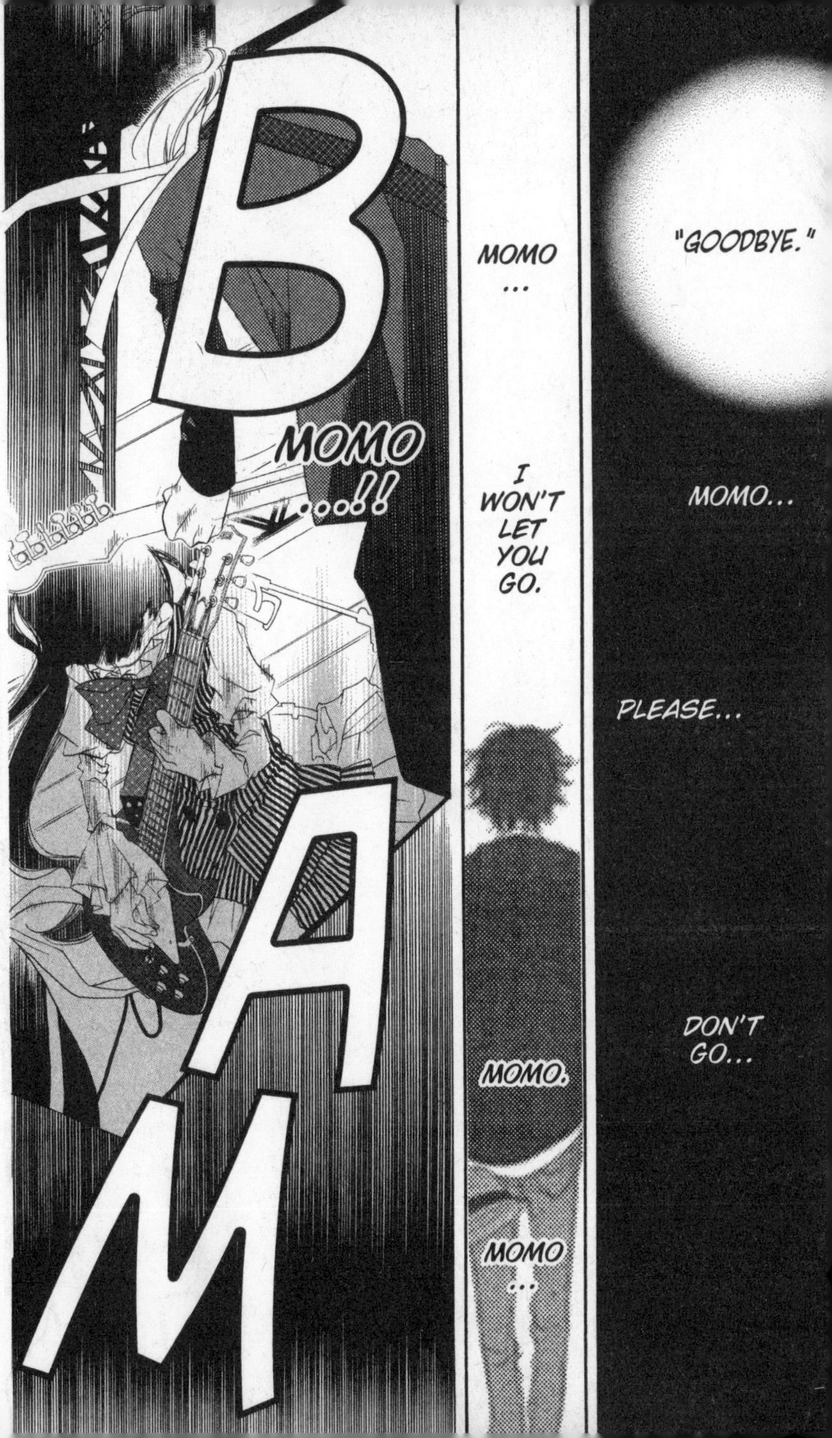
"GOODBYE."
MOMO...
PLEASE...
DON'T GO...
MOMO ...
I WON'T LET YOU GO.
MOMO.
MOMO ...
B
MOMO ...!!
A
M

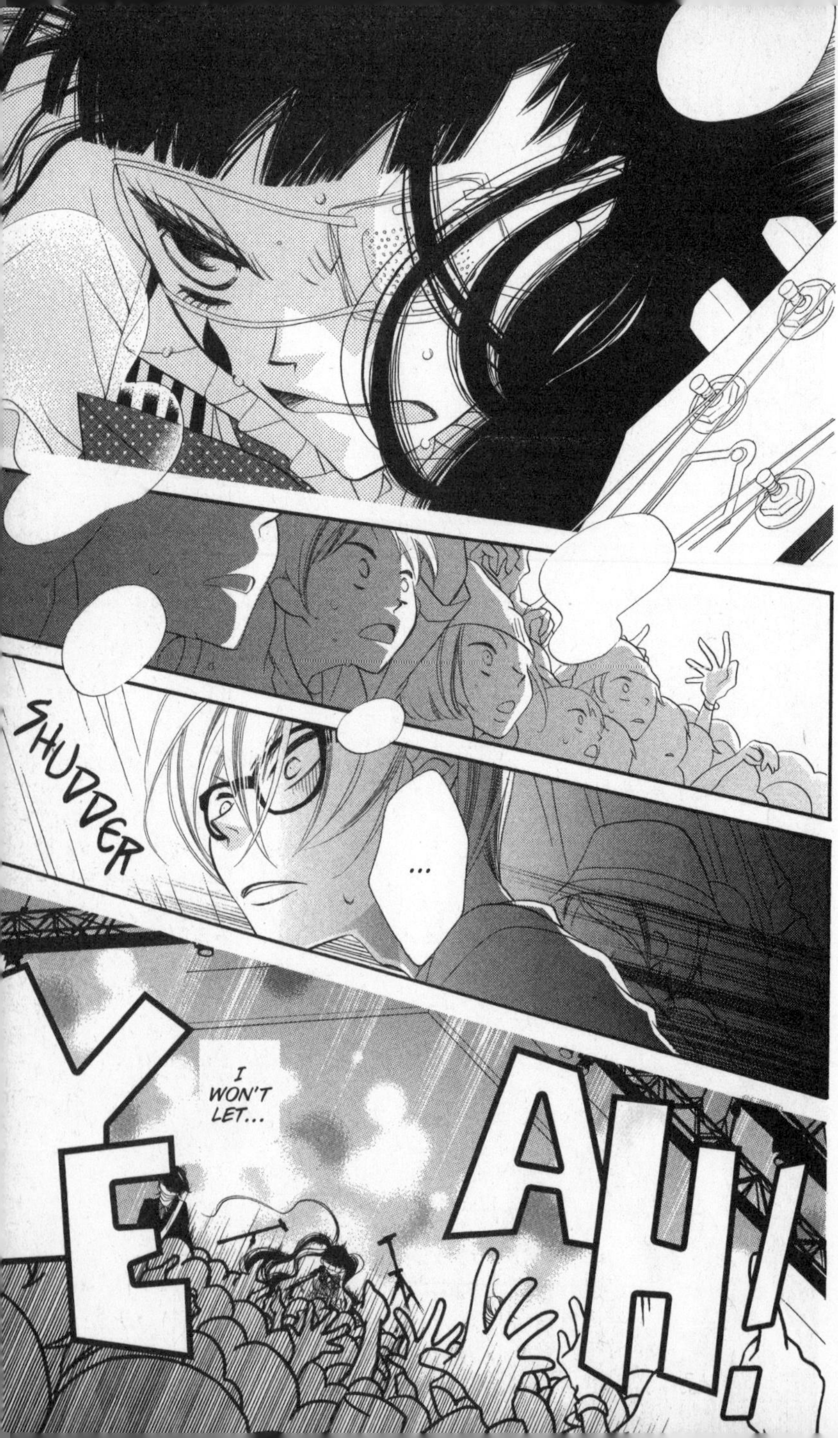
SHUDDER
...
I WON'T LET...
EAH!!

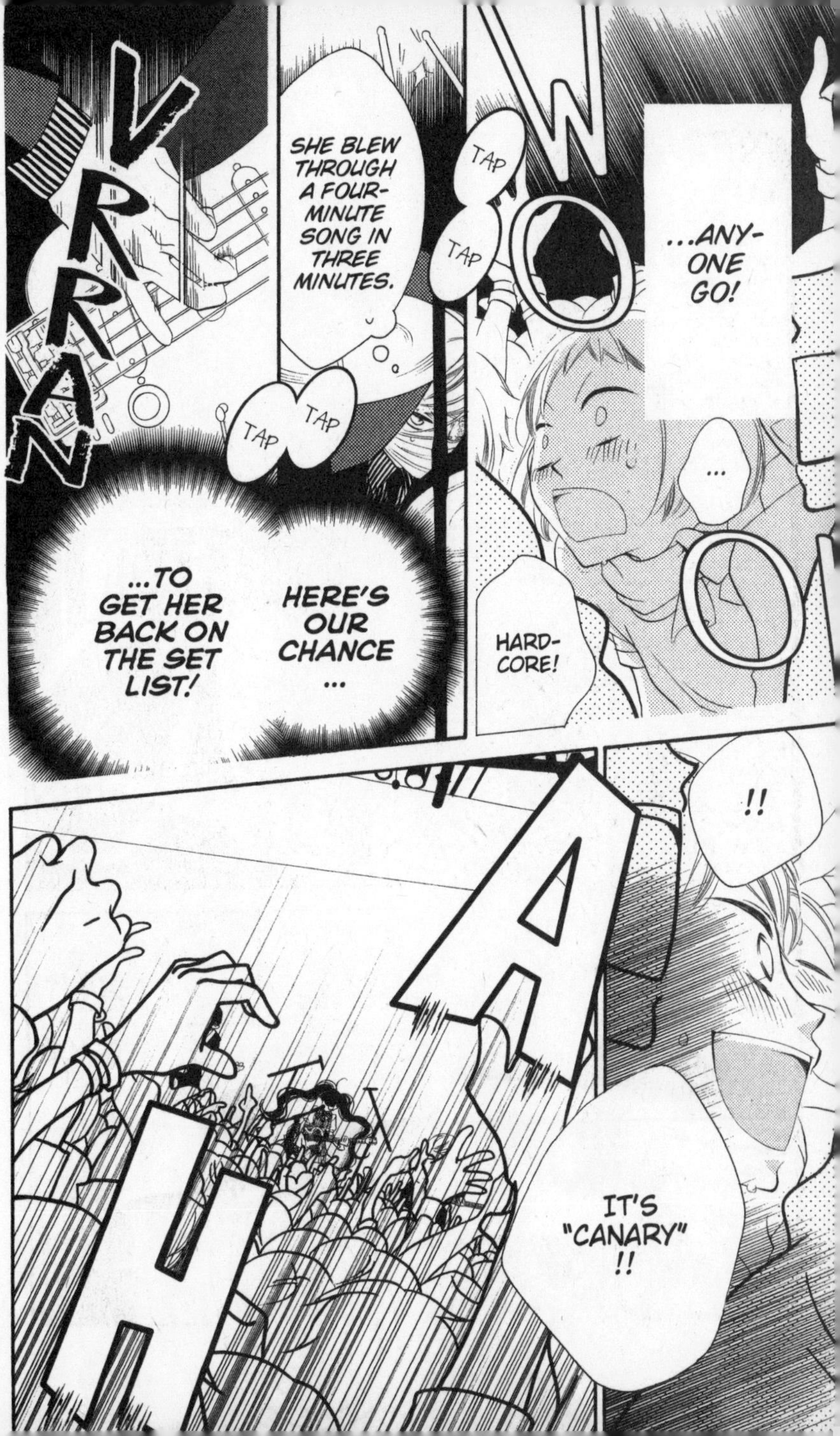
...ANY-ONE GO!
...
HARD-CORE!
SHE BLEW THROUGH A FOUR-MINUTE SONG IN THREE MINUTES.
TAP
TAP
TAP
TAP
HERE'S OUR CHANCE ...
...TO GET HER BACK ON THE SET LIST!
!!
IT'S "CANARY" !!

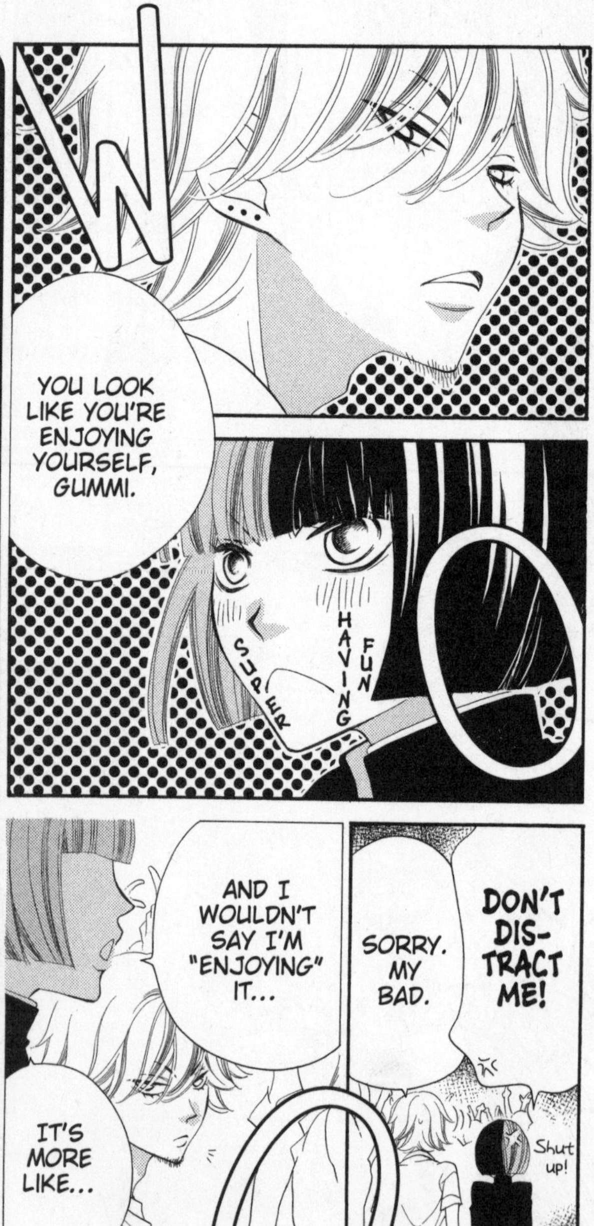
W
YOU LOOK LIKE YOU'RE ENJOYING YOURSELF, GUMMI.
O
SUPER HAVING FUN
DON'T DIS-TRACT ME!
SORRY. MY BAD.
Shut up!
AND I WOULDN'T SAY I'M "ENJOYING" IT...
IT'S MORE LIKE...
O

5

Shortly after I submitted the manuscript for chapter 26, my cat Sora made the journey to heaven. Since chapter 26 was the first part of the rock festival arc, I never would have been able to draw it without the materials we gathered at Rock in Japan. Luckily, I was able to go, because at that time, Sora was at the healthiest point of a three-month illness. So in a way, it was thanks to Sora that I was able to create this chapter. It's still painful for me to look through chapters 23 to 26 of this volume, but at the same time, they're dear to me because I remember how Sora was still with me when I wrote them. So in a strange way, this has become a very important volume to me.

SEE YOU LATER, SORA.

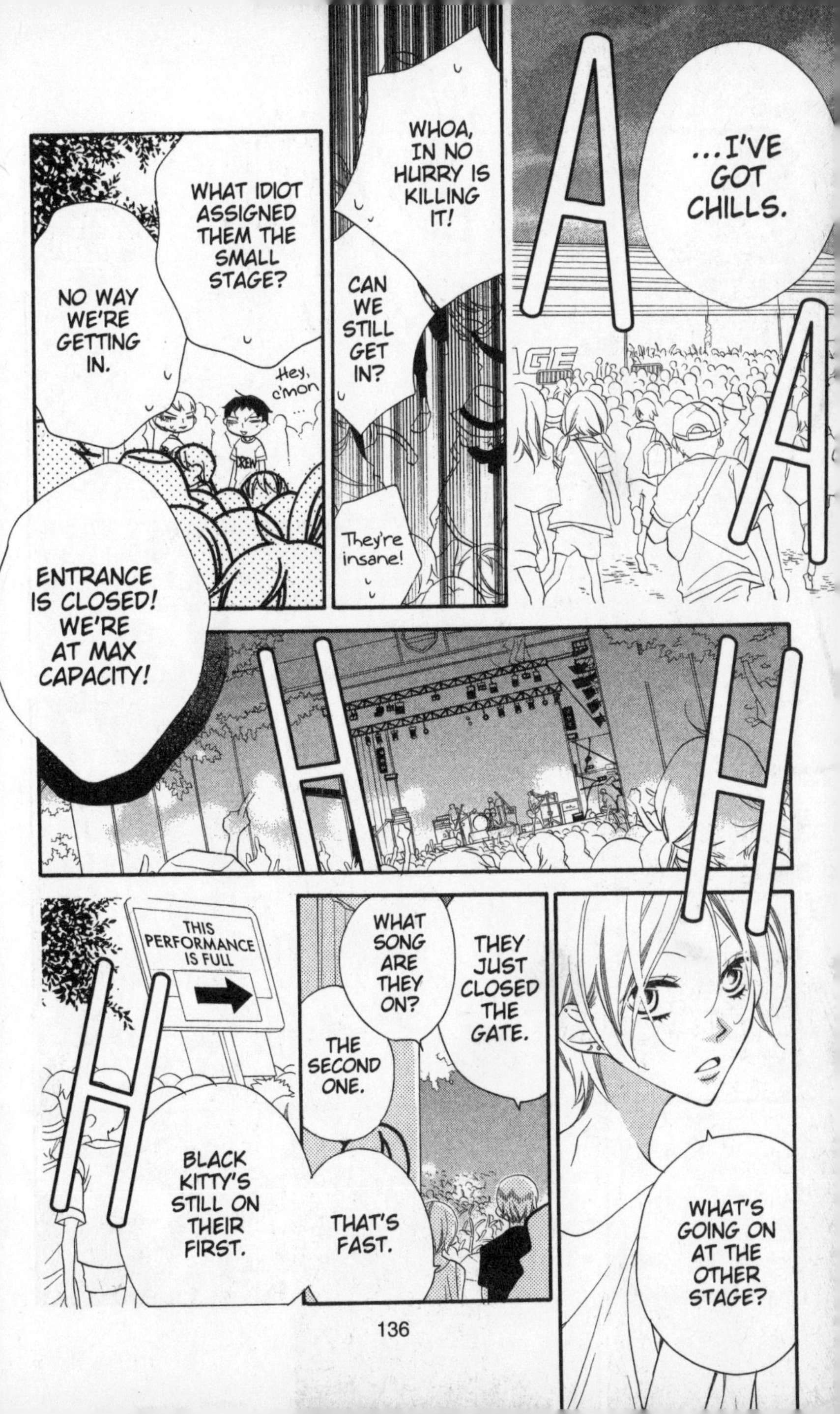
AA
...I'VE GOT CHILLS.
WHOA, IN NO HURRY IS KILLING IT!
CAN WE STILL GET IN?
They're insane!
WHAT IDIOT ASSIGNED THEM THE SMALL STAGE?
Hey, c'mon...
NO WAY WE'RE GETTING IN.
ENTRANCE IS CLOSED! WE'RE AT MAX CAPACITY!
HHH
WHAT'S GOING ON AT THE OTHER STAGE?
THEY JUST CLOSED THE GATE.
WHAT SONG ARE THEY ON?
THE SECOND ONE.
THAT'S FAST.
THIS PERFORMANCE IS FULL
H
BLACK KITTY'S STILL ON THEIR FIRST.

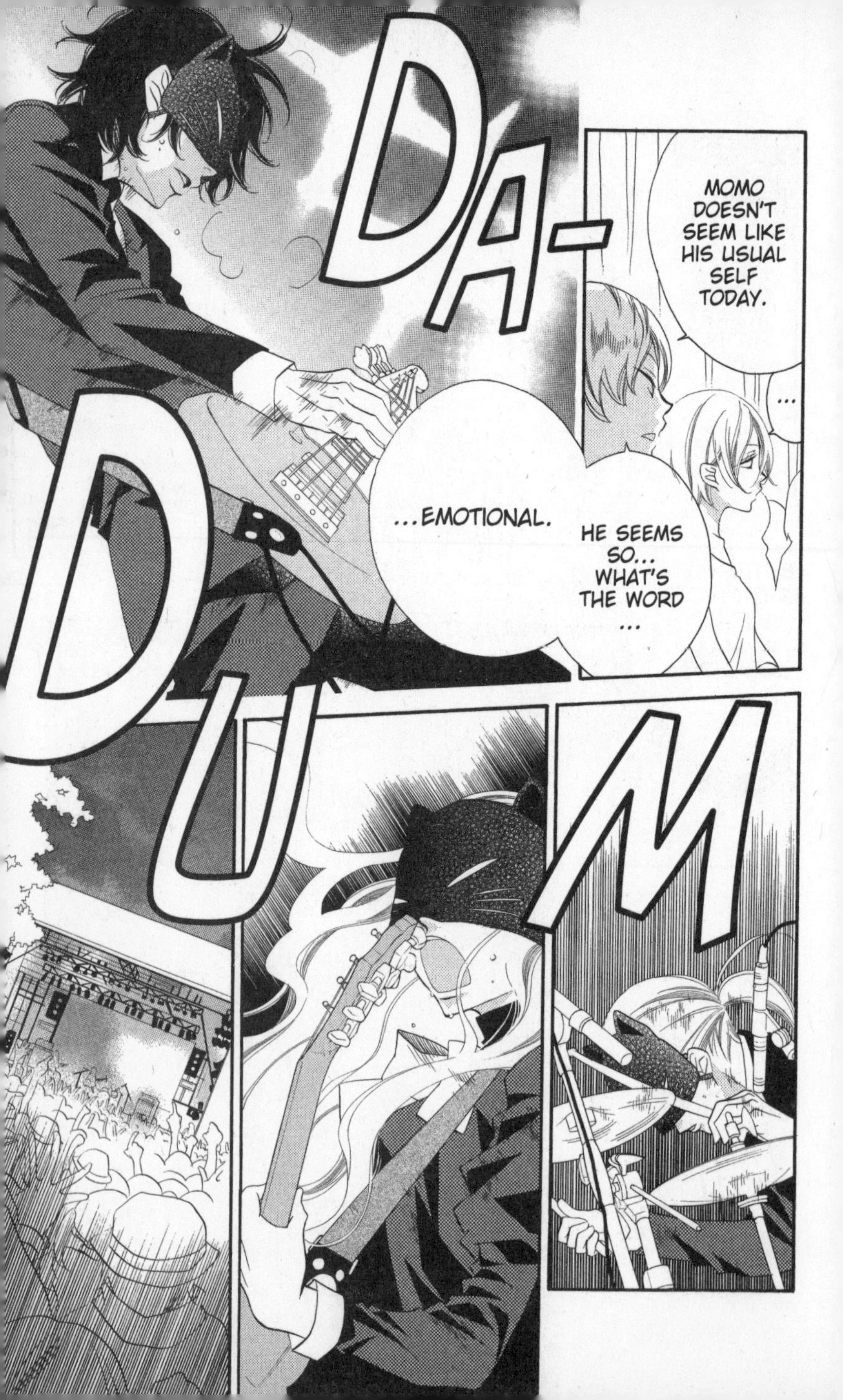
MOMO DOESN'T SEEM LIKE HIS USUAL SELF TODAY.
...
HE SEEMS SO... WHAT'S THE WORD ...
...EMOTIONAL.
DA-DUM

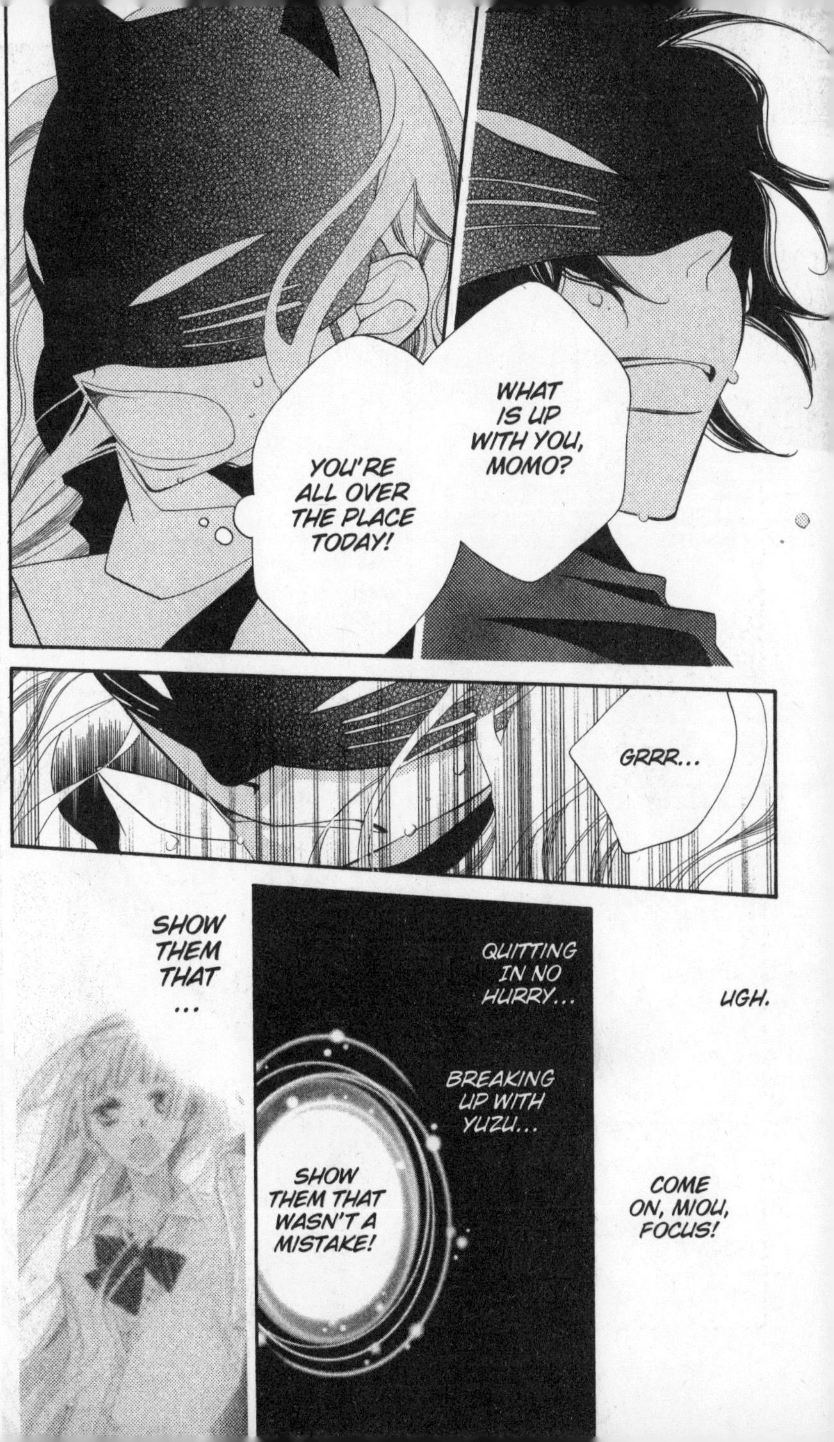
WHAT IS UP WITH YOU, MOMO?
YOU'RE ALL OVER THE PLACE TODAY!
GRRR...
UGH.
QUITTING IN NO HURRY...
BREAKING UP WITH YUZU...
SHOW THEM THAT ...
SHOW THEM THAT WASN'T A MISTAKE!
COME ON, MIOU, FOCUS!

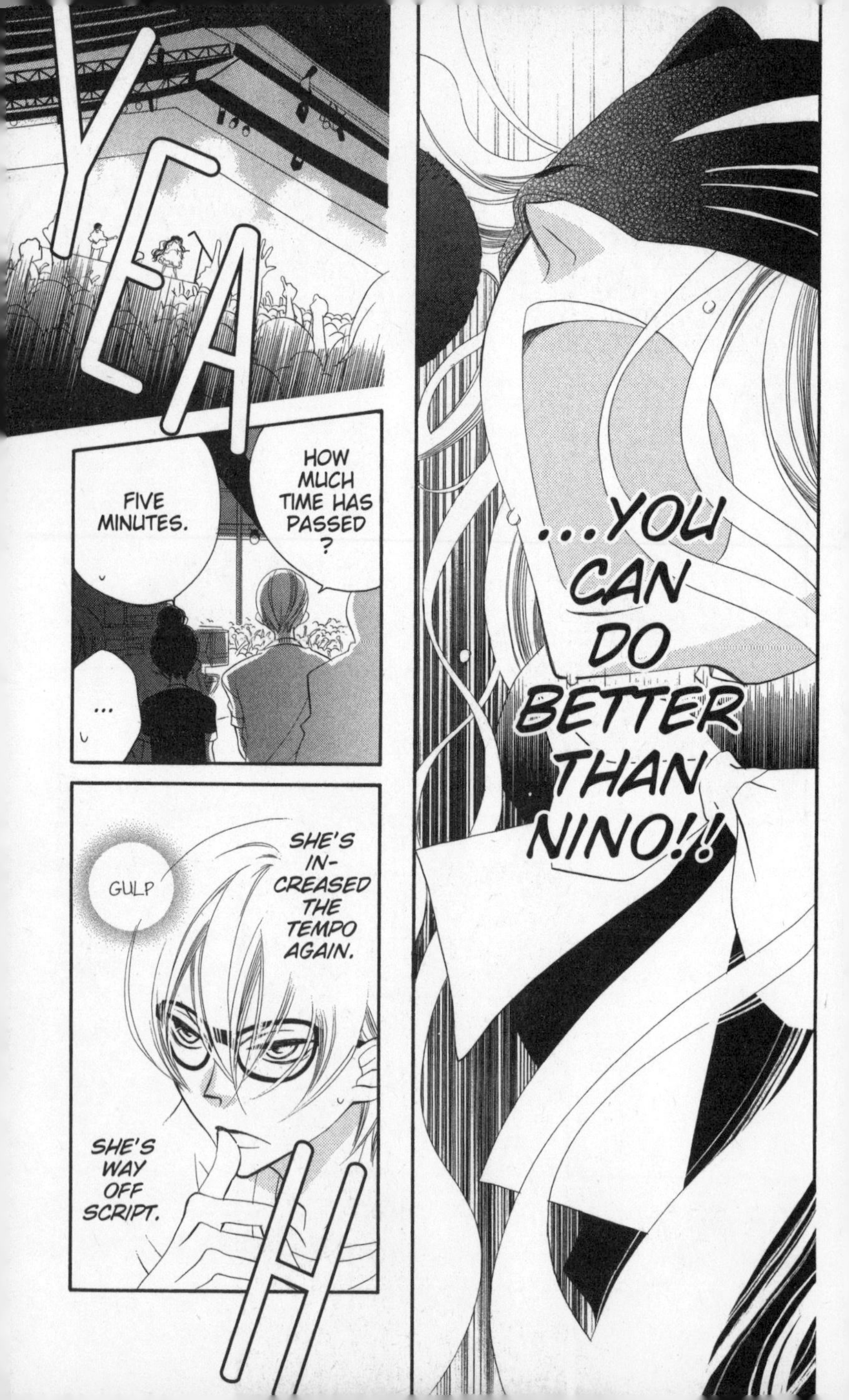
...YOU CAN DO BETTER THAN NINO!!
YEA
HOW MUCH TIME HAS PASSED?
FIVE MINUTES.
...
SHE'S IN-CREASED THE TEMPO AGAIN.
GULP
SHE'S WAY OFF SCRIPT.
H

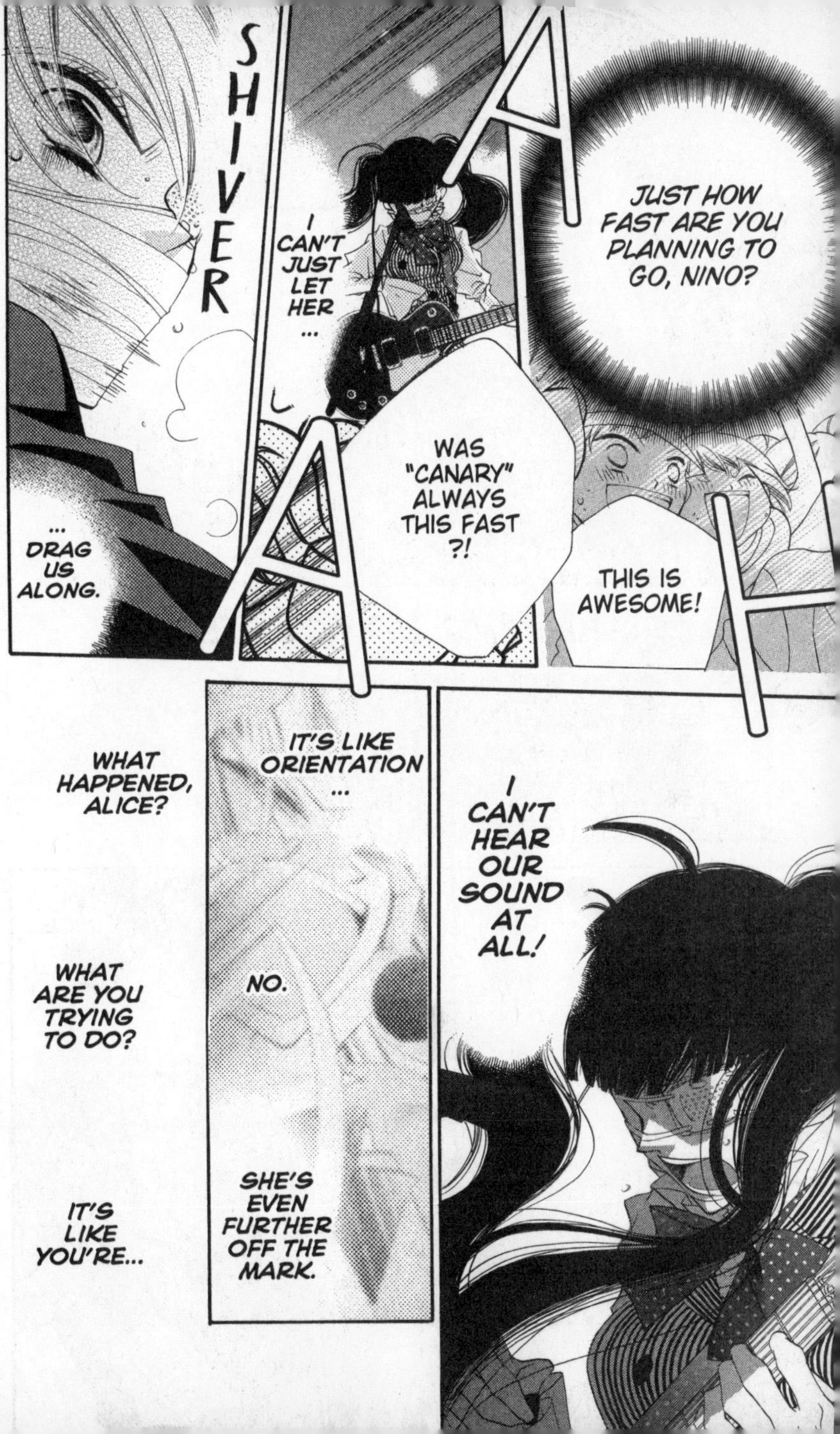
AAAH
JUST HOW FAST ARE YOU PLANNING TO GO, NINO?
THIS IS AWESOME!
I CAN'T JUST LET HER...
WAS "CANARY" ALWAYS THIS FAST?!
SHIVER
...DRAG US ALONG.
I CAN'T HEAR OUR SOUND AT ALL!
IT'S LIKE ORIENTATION...
NO.
SHE'S EVEN FURTHER OFF THE MARK.
WHAT HAPPENED, ALICE?
WHAT ARE YOU TRYING TO DO?
IT'S LIKE YOU'RE...

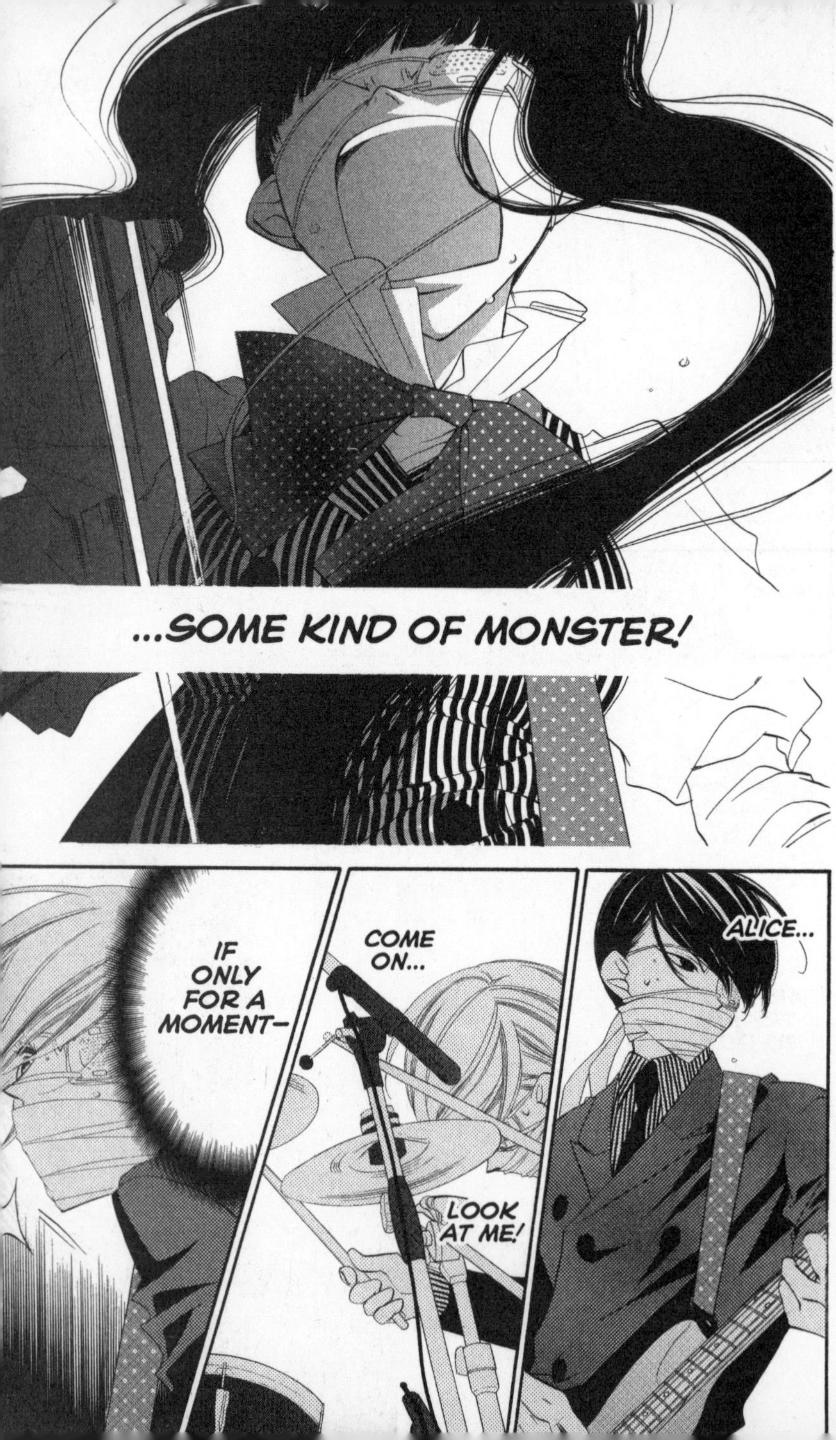
...SOME KIND OF MONSTER!
ALICE...
COME ON...
LOOK AT ME!
IF ONLY FOR A MOMENT—

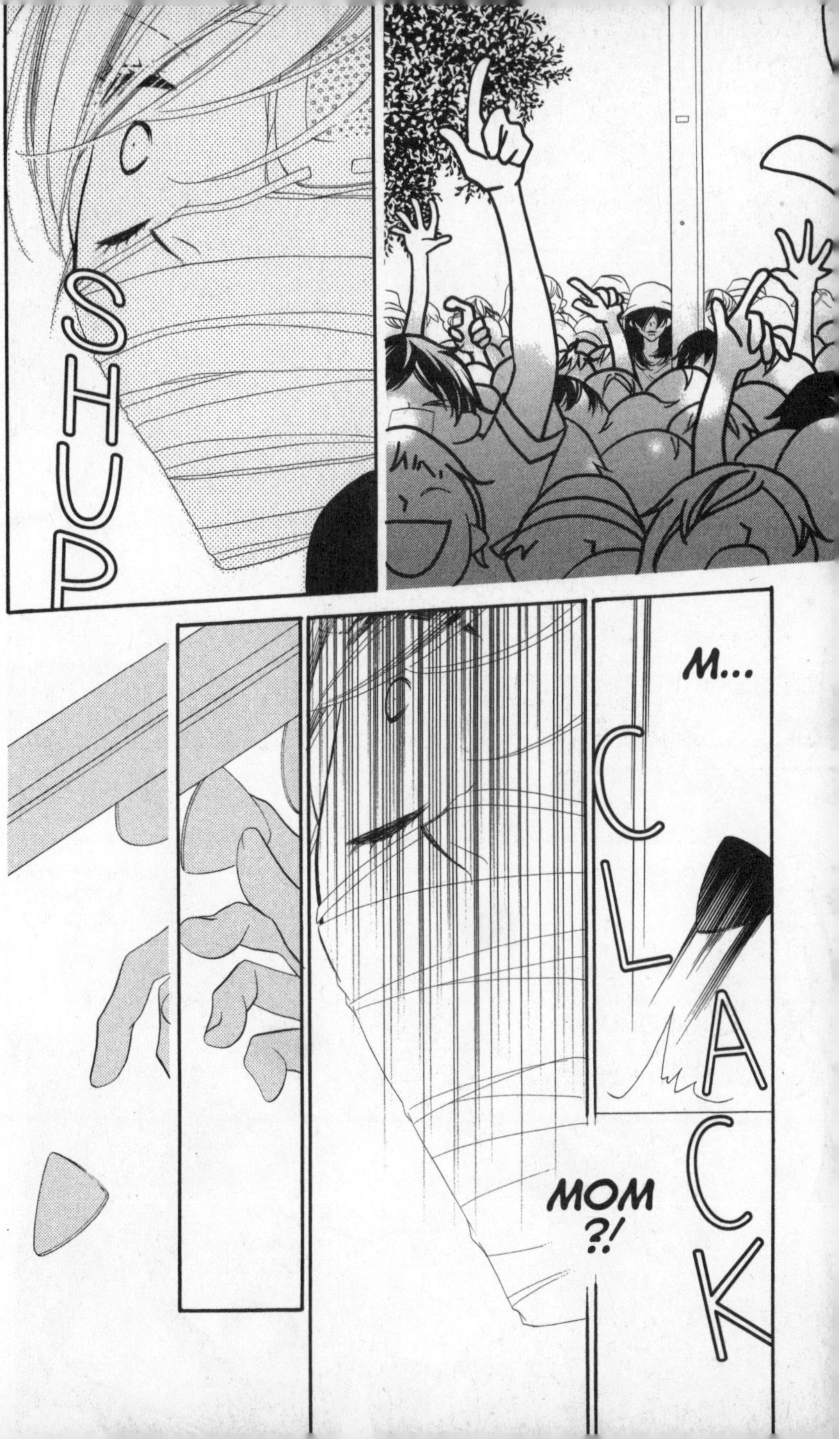
SHUP
M...
CLACK
MOM ?!

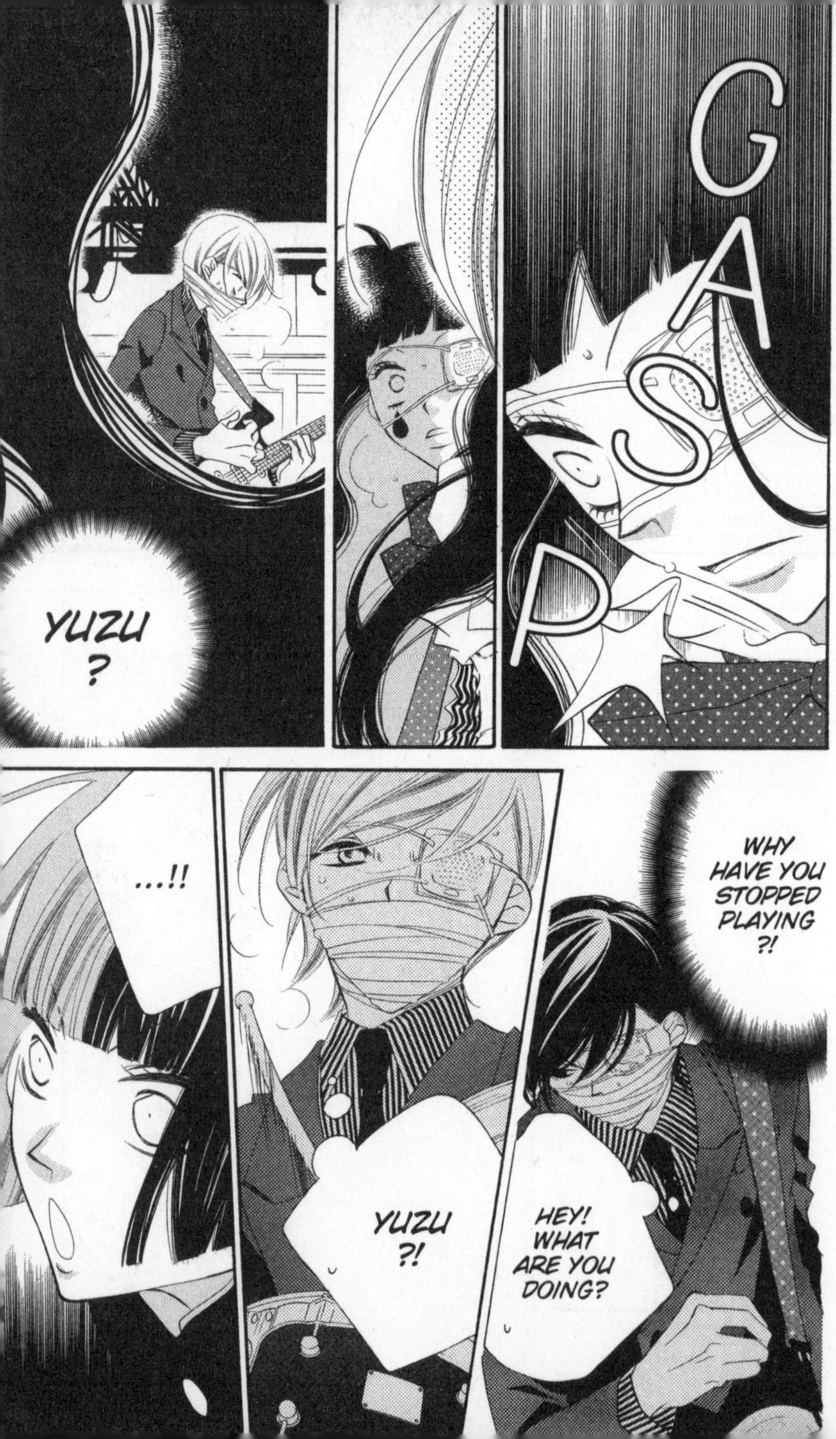
GASP
YUZU ?
WHY HAVE YOU STOPPED PLAYING ?!
HEY! WHAT ARE YOU DOING?
YUZU ?!
...!!

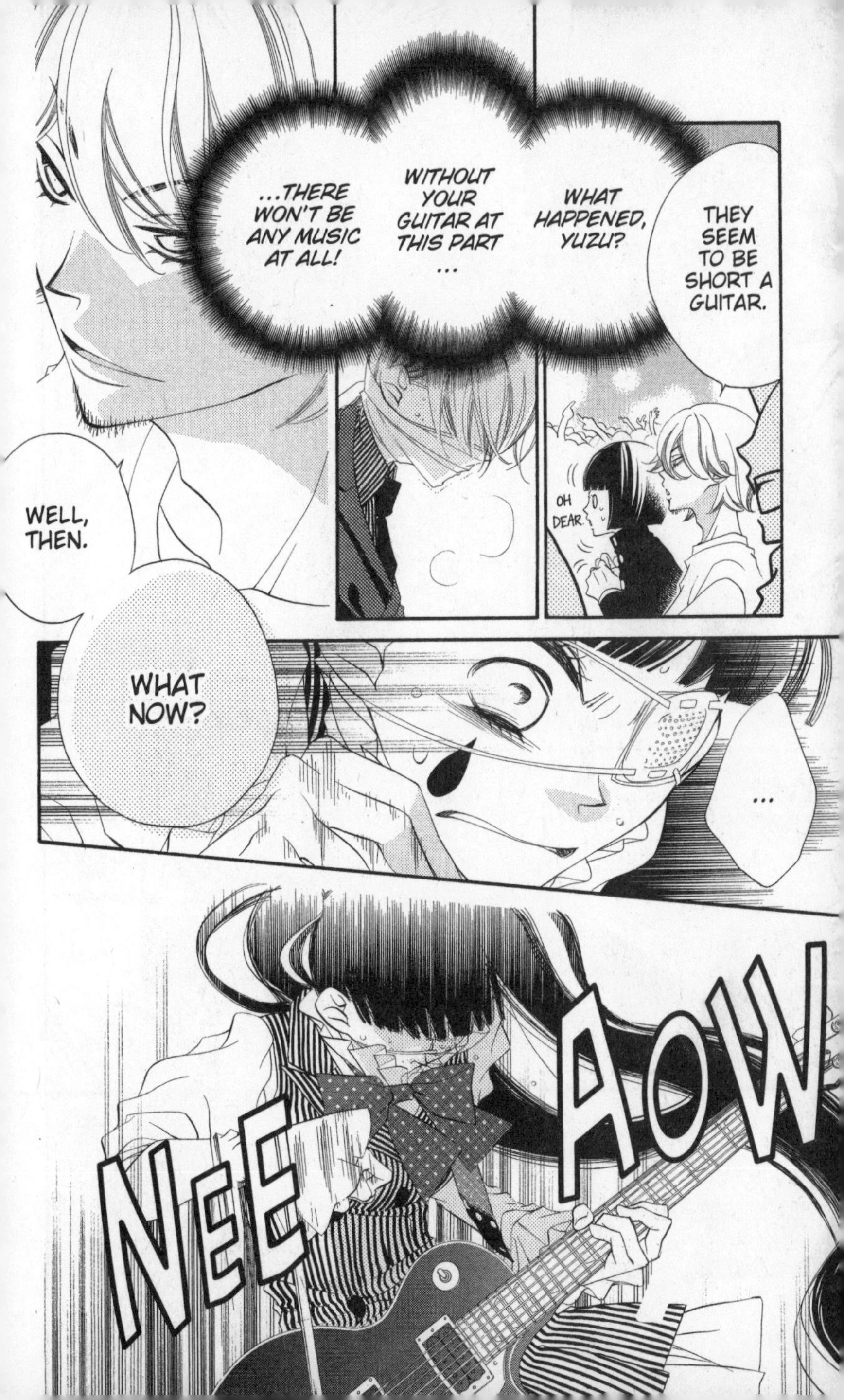
THEY SEEM TO BE SHORT A GUITAR.
OH DEAR.
WHAT HAPPENED, YUZU?
WITHOUT YOUR GUITAR AT THIS PART ...
...THERE WON'T BE ANY MUSIC AT ALL!
WELL, THEN.
WHAT NOW?
...
NEE AOW

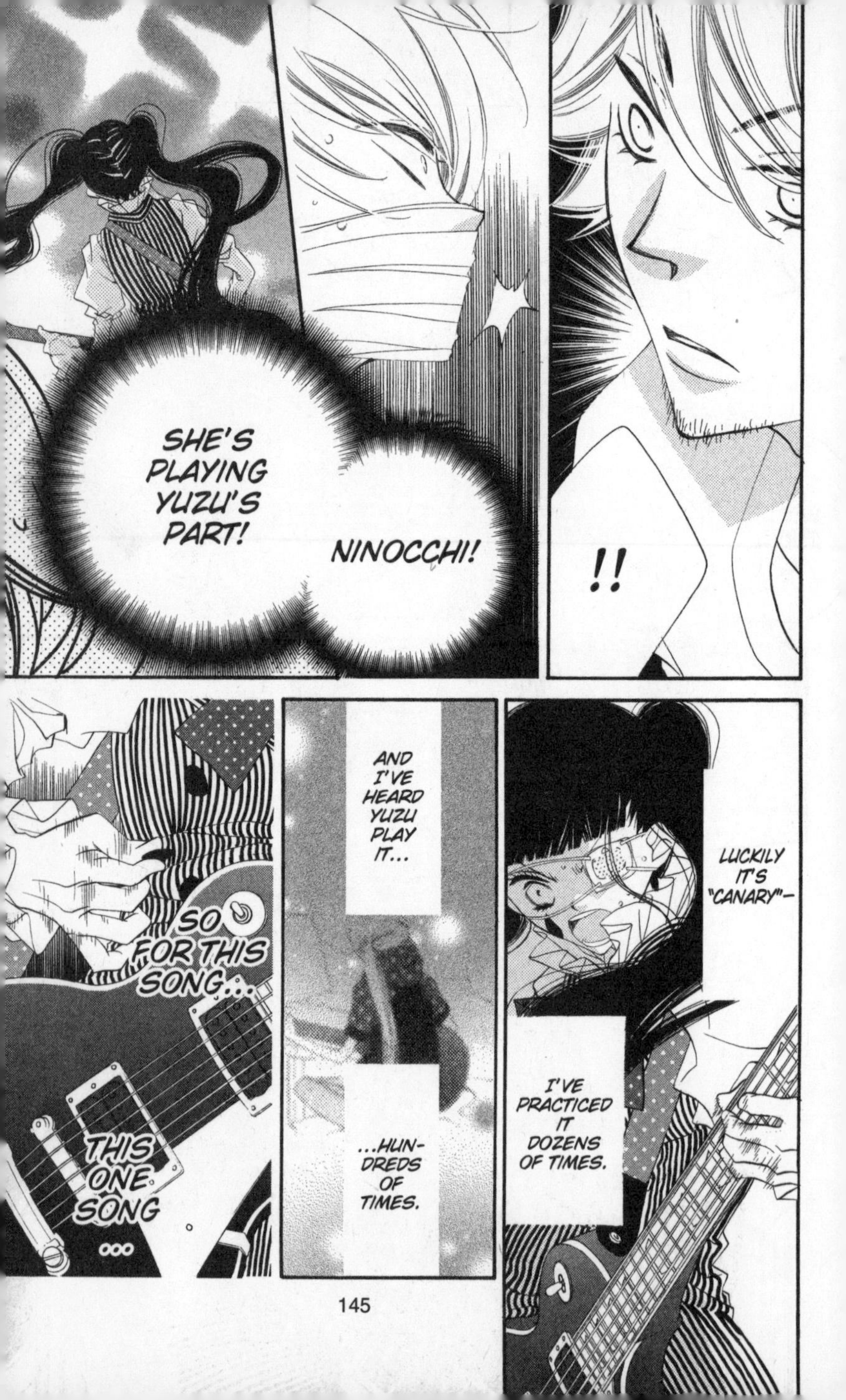
!!
NINOCCHI!
SHE'S PLAYING YUZU'S PART!
LUCKILY IT'S "CANARY"—
I'VE PRACTICED IT DOZENS OF TIMES.
AND I'VE HEARD YUZU PLAY IT...
...HUNDREDS OF TIMES.
SO FOR THIS SONG...
THIS ONE SONG...

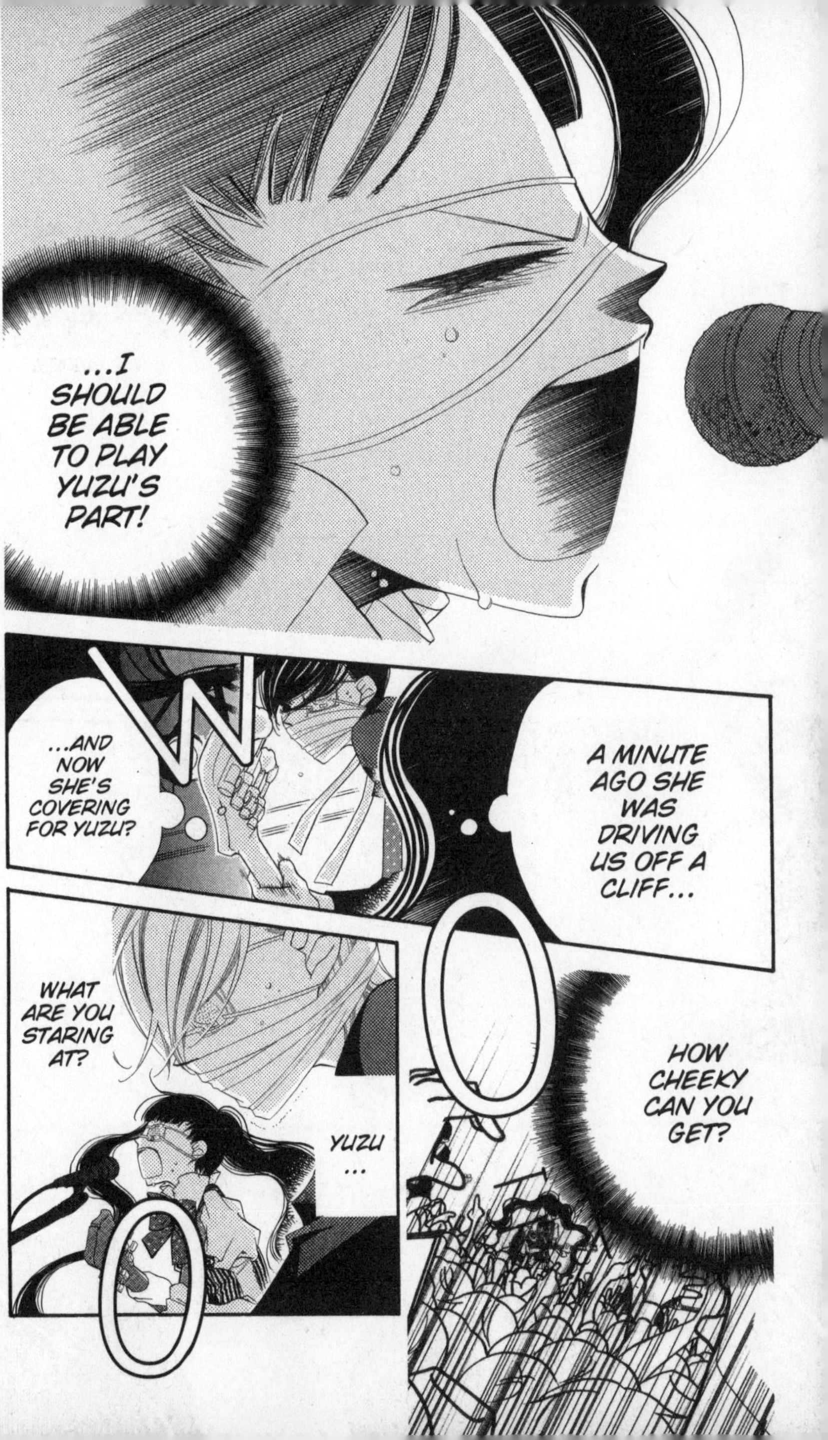
...I SHOULD BE ABLE TO PLAY YUZU'S PART!
A MINUTE AGO SHE WAS DRIVING US OFF A CLIFF...
...AND NOW SHE'S COVERING FOR YUZU?
HOW CHEEKY CAN YOU GET?
WHAT ARE YOU STARING AT?
YUZU ...

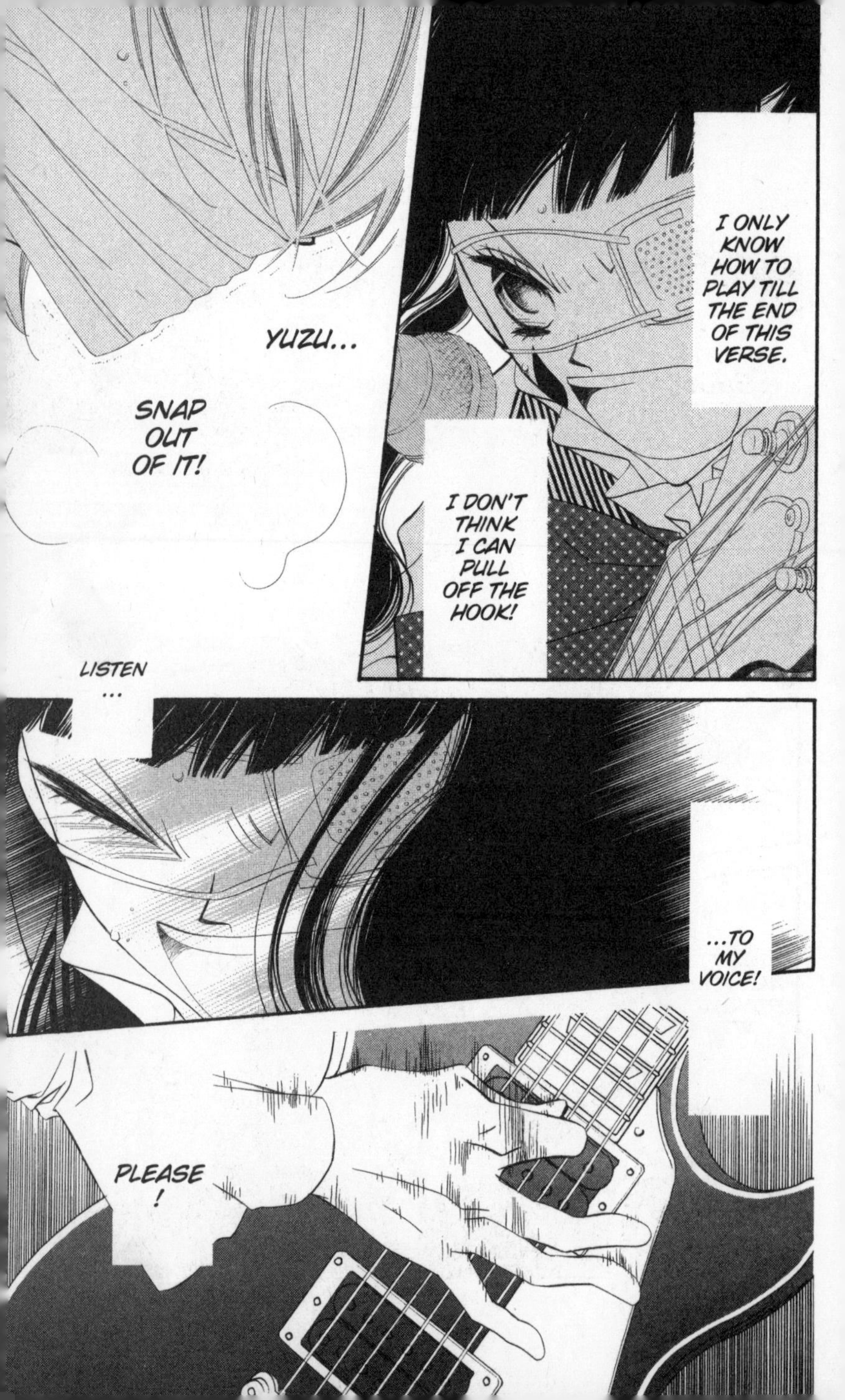
I ONLY KNOW HOW TO PLAY TILL THE END OF THIS VERSE.
I DON'T THINK I CAN PULL OFF THE HOOK!
YUZU...
SNAP OUT OF IT!
LISTEN...
...TO MY VOICE!
PLEASE!

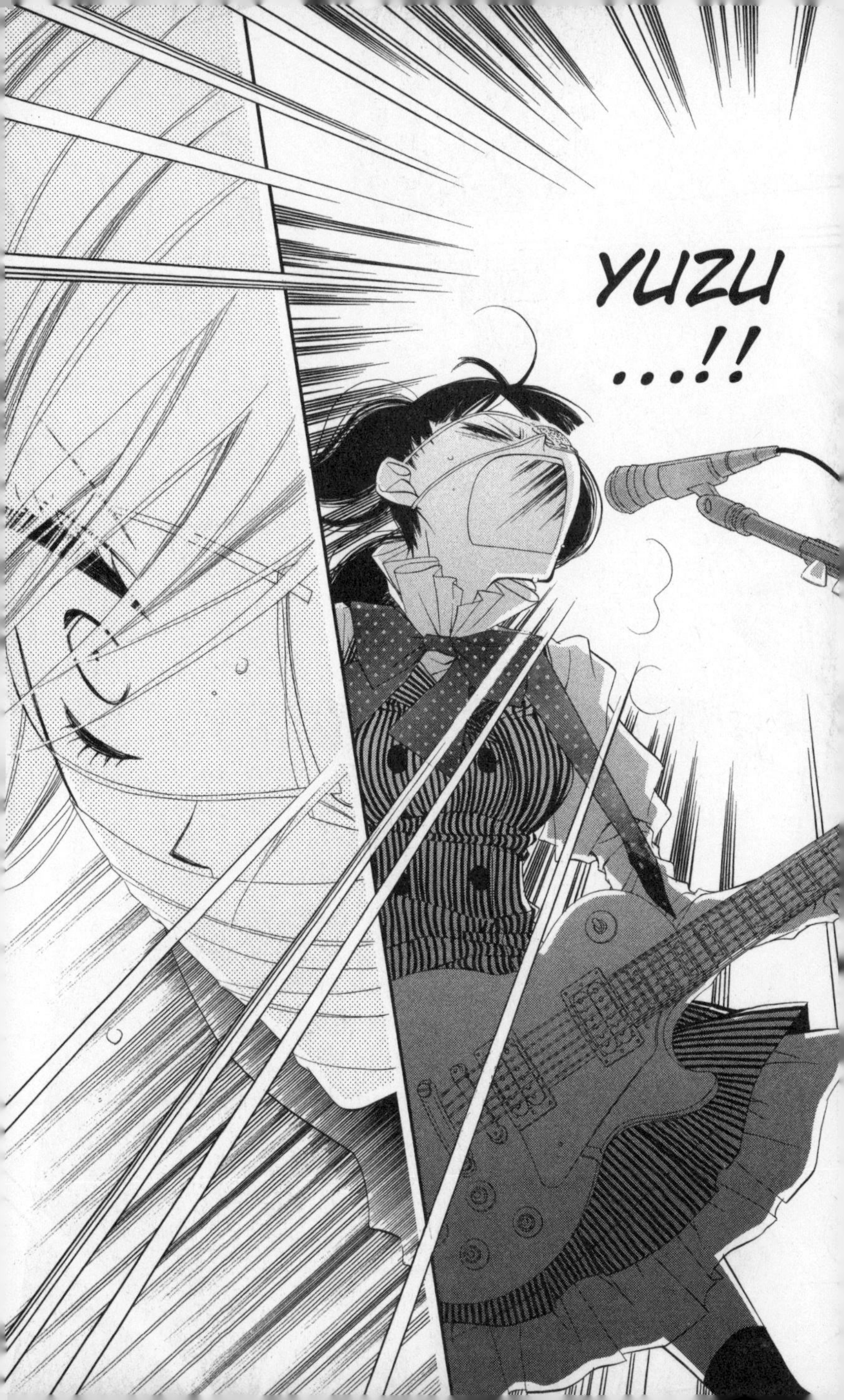
YUZU ...!!

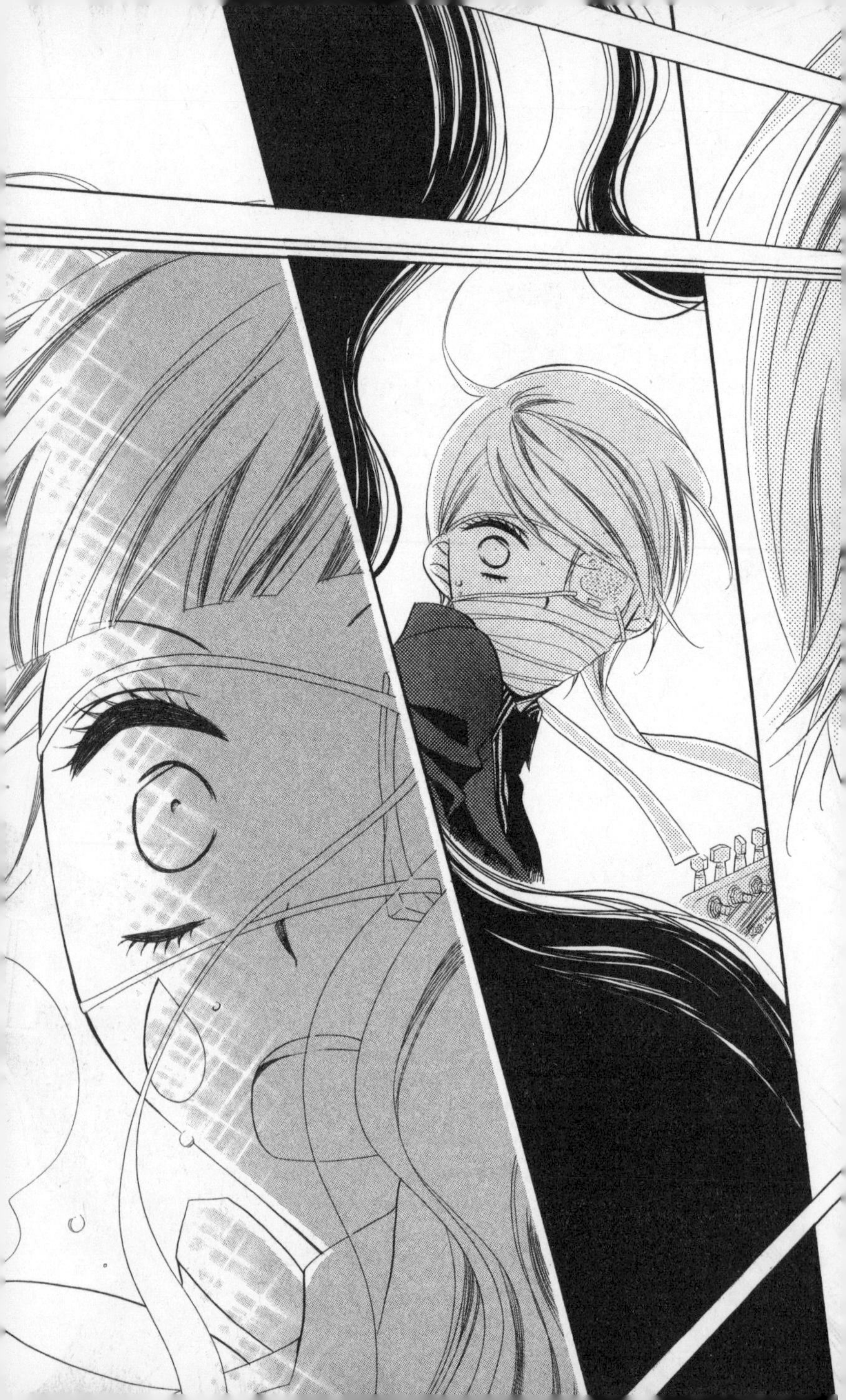

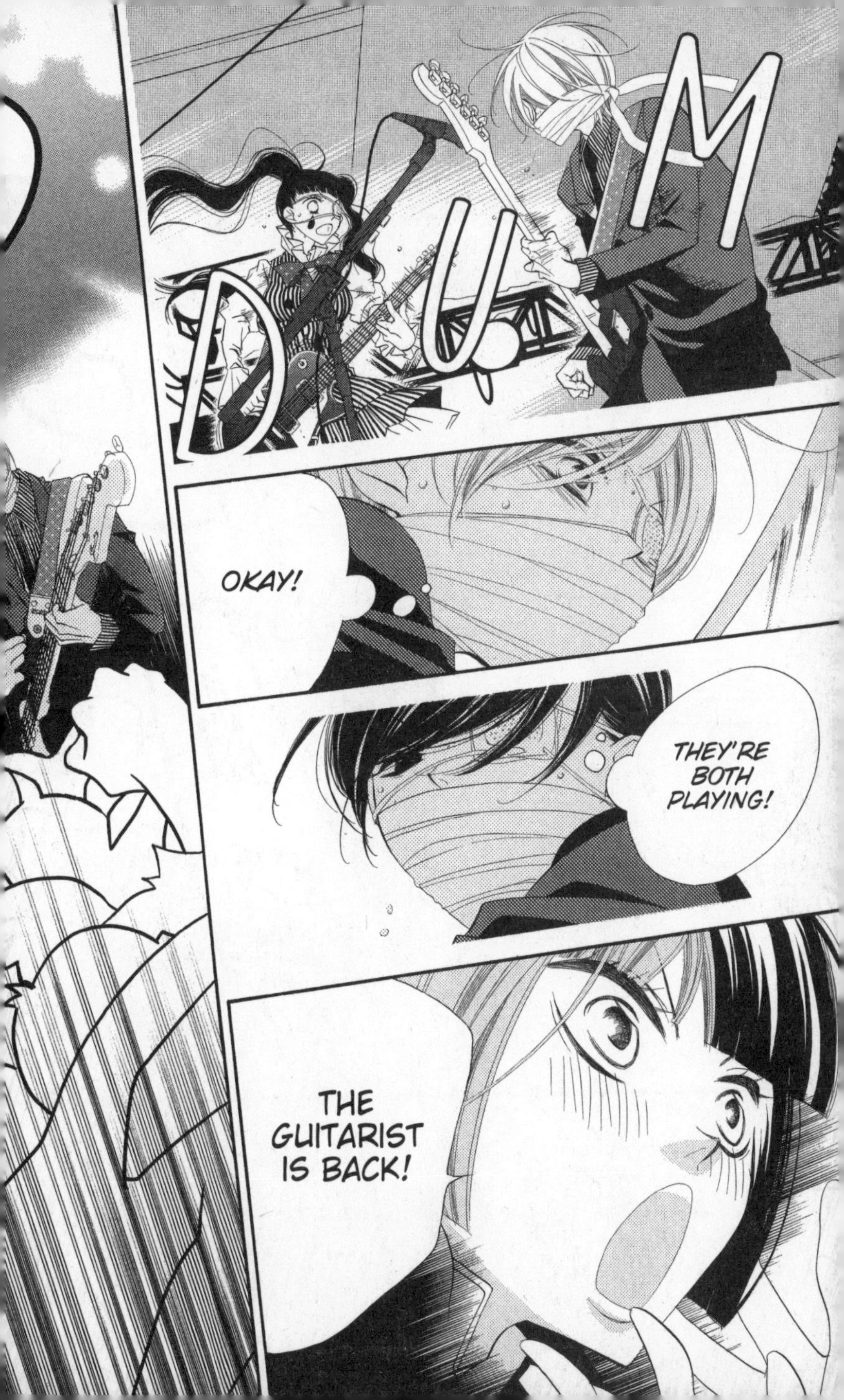
DUM
OKAY!
THEY'RE BOTH PLAYING!
THE GUITARIST IS BACK!

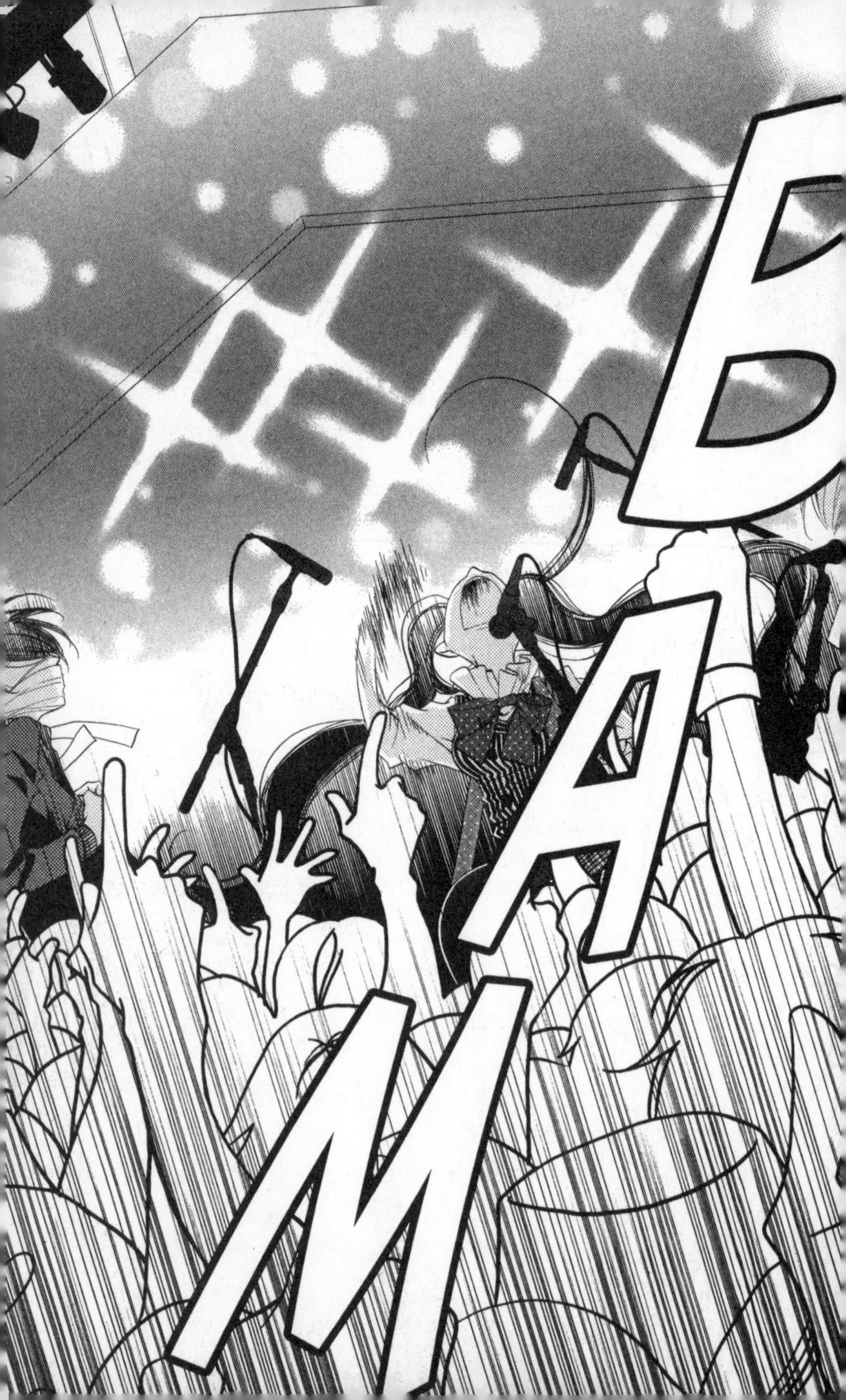
BAM

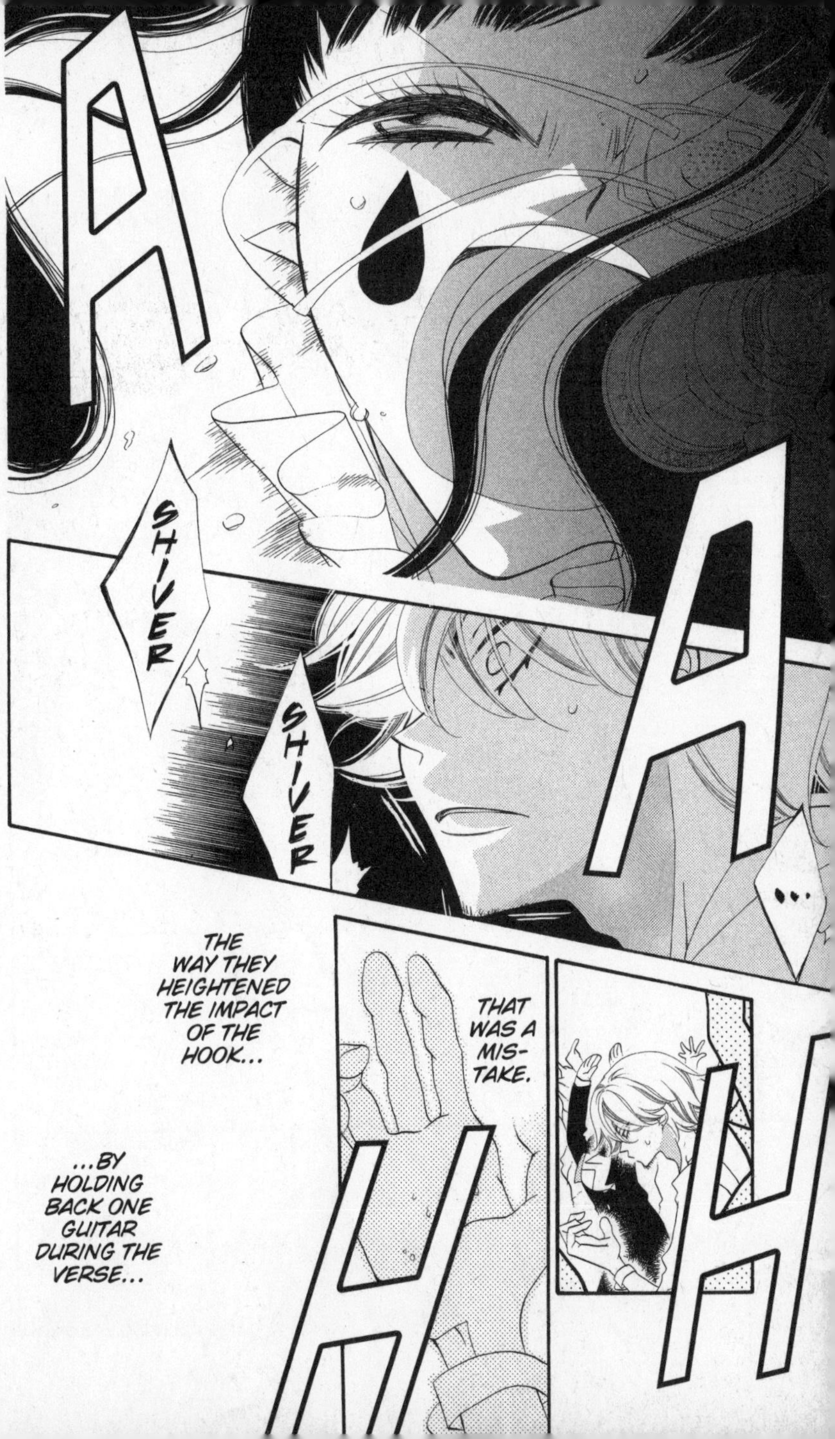
AAHHH
SHIVER
SHIVER
...
THAT WAS A MIS-TAKE.
THE WAY THEY HEIGHTENED THE IMPACT OF THE HOOK...
...BY HOLDING BACK ONE GUITAR DURING THE VERSE...

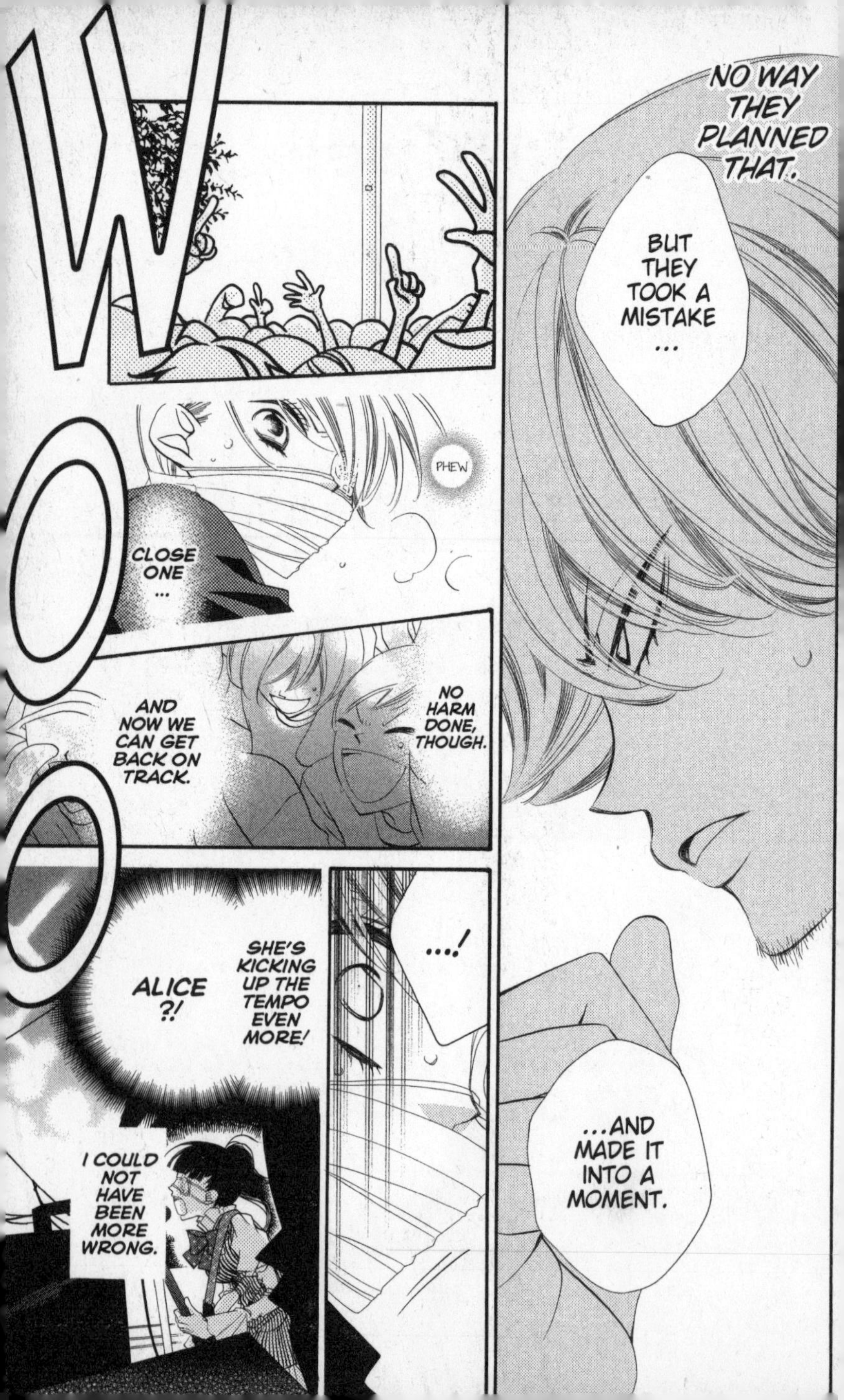
NO WAY THEY PLANNED THAT.
BUT THEY TOOK A MISTAKE...
...AND MADE IT INTO A MOMENT.
WOO
PHEW
CLOSE ONE...
NO HARM DONE, THOUGH.
AND NOW WE CAN GET BACK ON TRACK.
...!
SHE'S KICKING UP THE TEMPO EVEN MORE!
ALICE?!
I COULD NOT HAVE BEEN MORE WRONG.

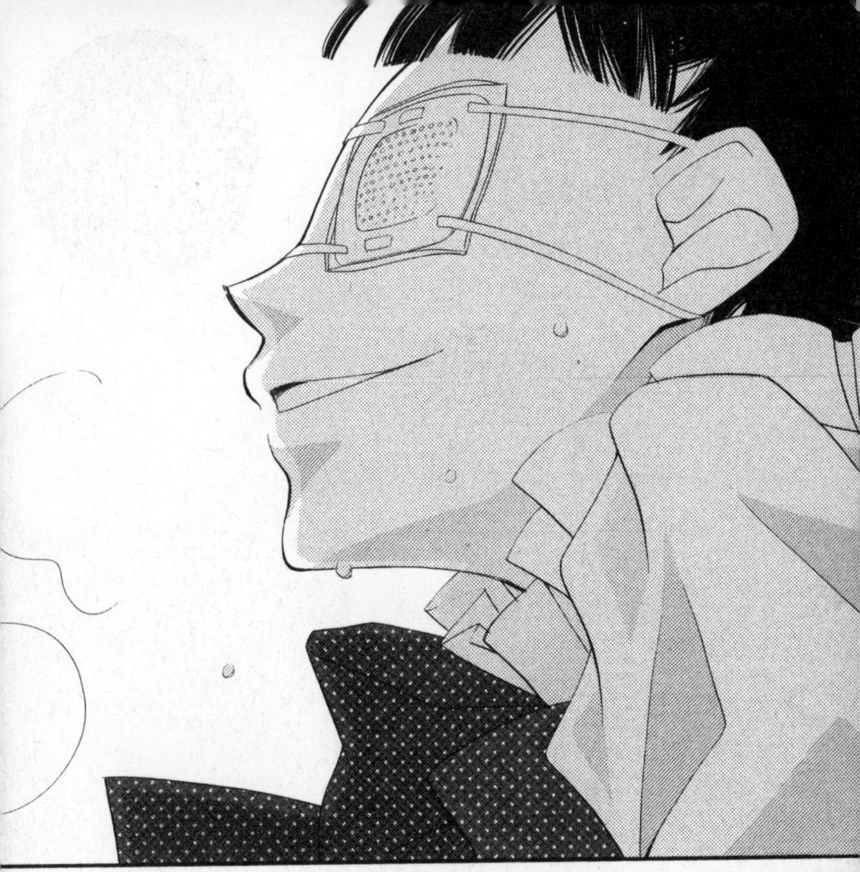

THE MONSTER'S CONCERT
HAD ONLY JUST BEGUN.

SONG 28

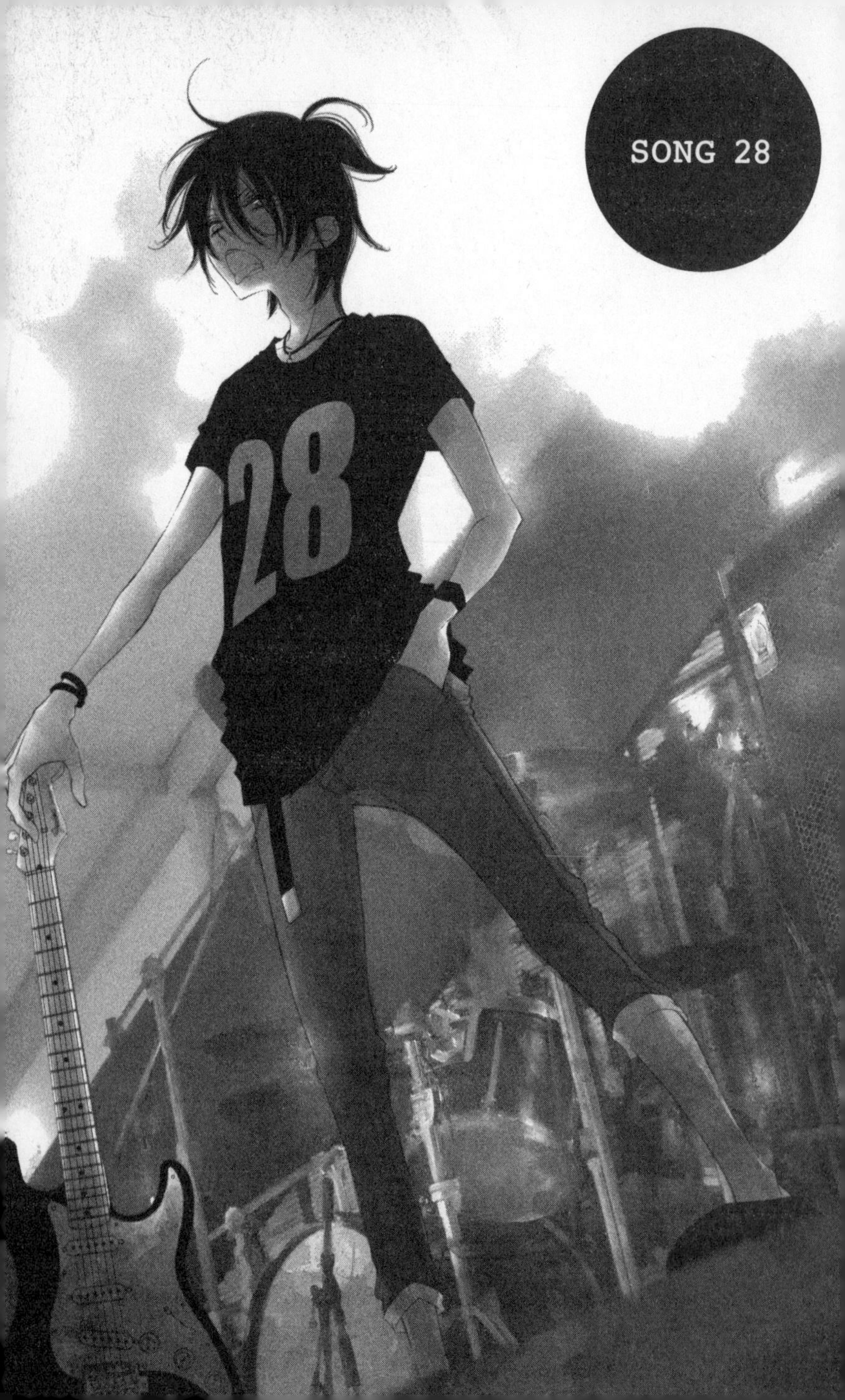
28

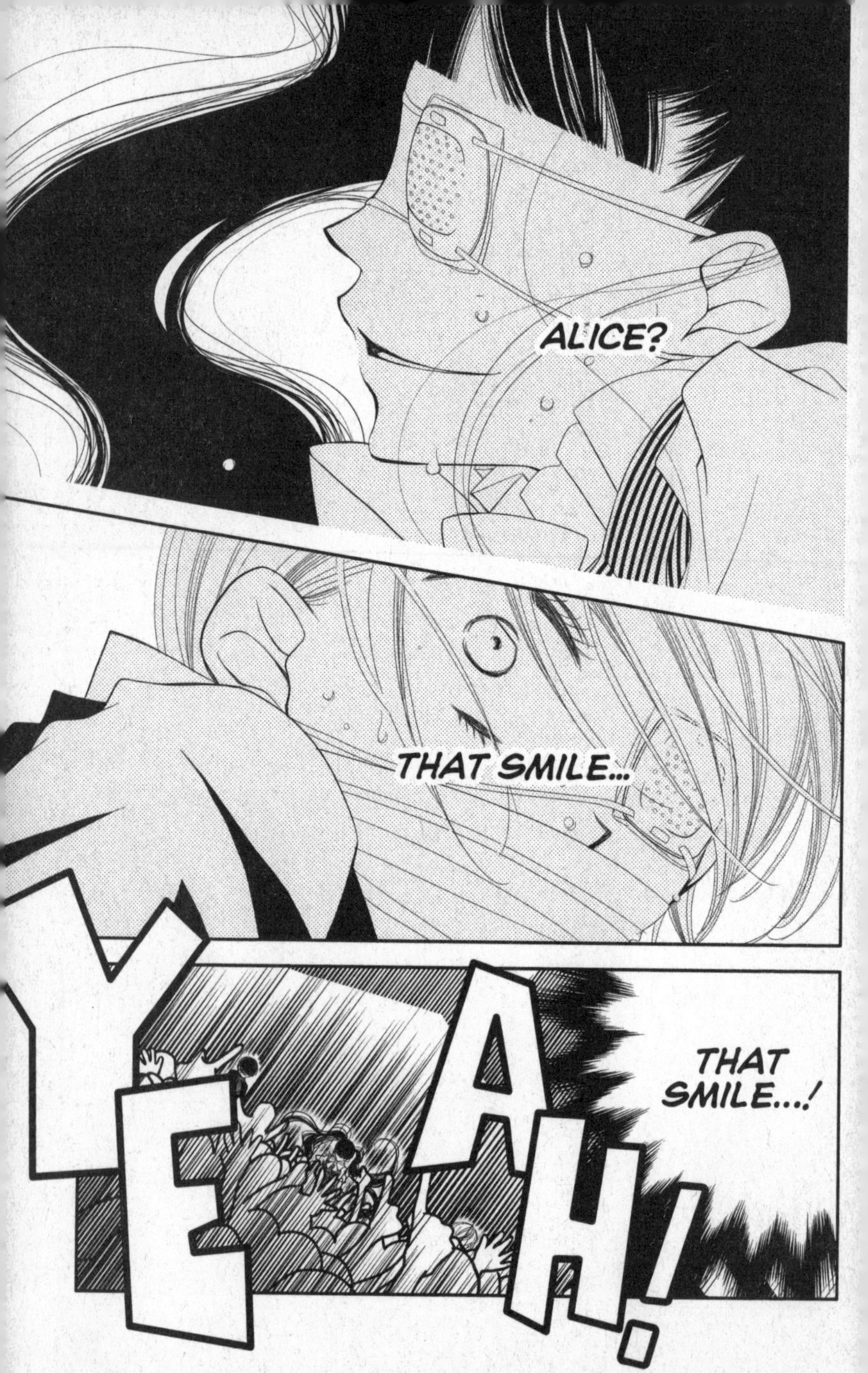
ALICE?
THAT SMILE...
THAT SMILE...!
YEAH!

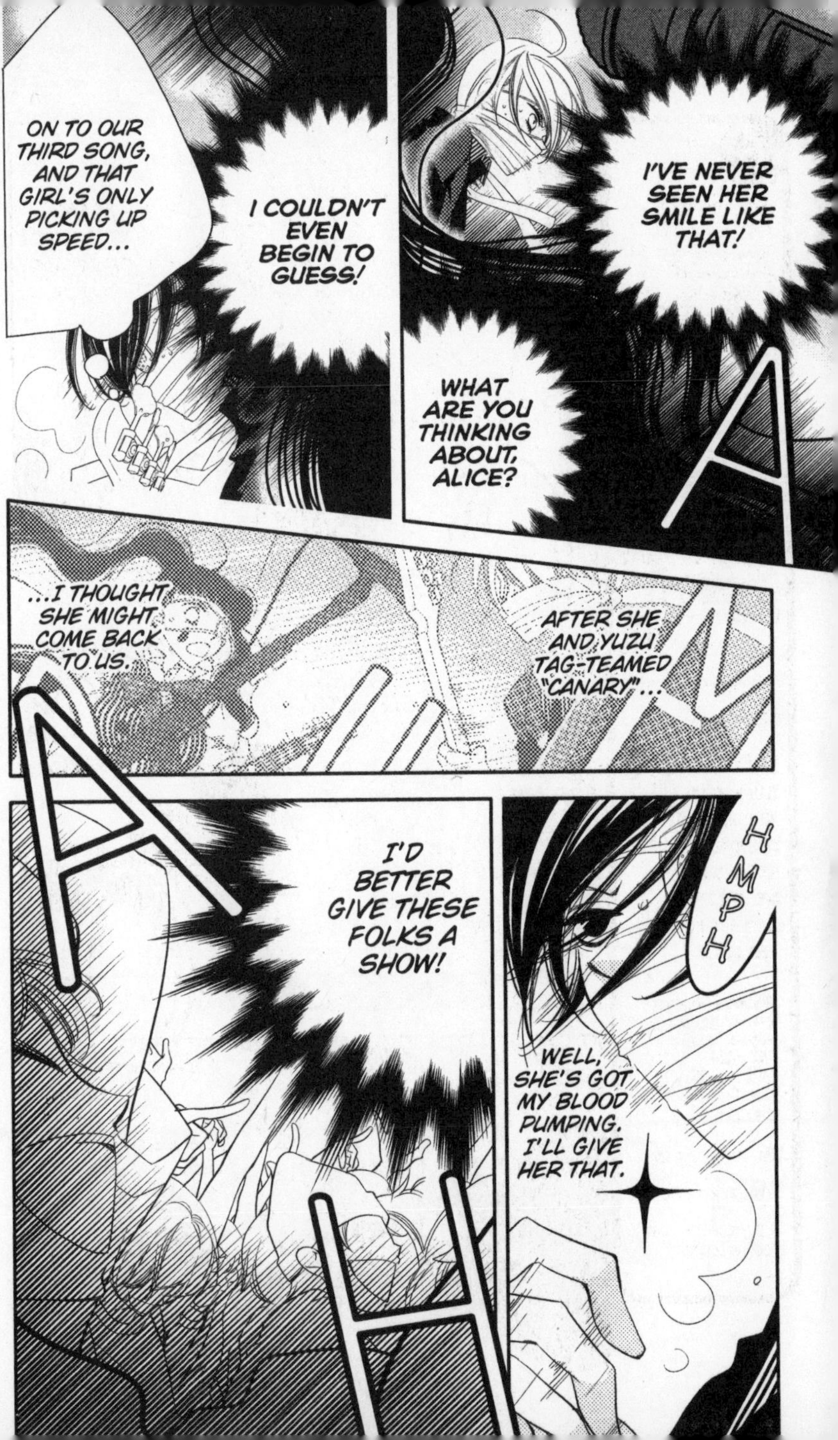
I'VE NEVER SEEN HER SMILE LIKE THAT!
WHAT ARE YOU THINKING ABOUT, ALICE?
I COULDN'T EVEN BEGIN TO GUESS!
ON TO OUR THIRD SONG, AND THAT GIRL'S ONLY PICKING UP SPEED...
AFTER SHE AND YUZU TAG-TEAMED "CANARY"...
...I THOUGHT SHE MIGHT COME BACK TO US.
HMPH
WELL, SHE'S GOT MY BLOOD PUMPING. I'LL GIVE HER THAT.
I'D BETTER GIVE THESE FOLKS A SHOW!

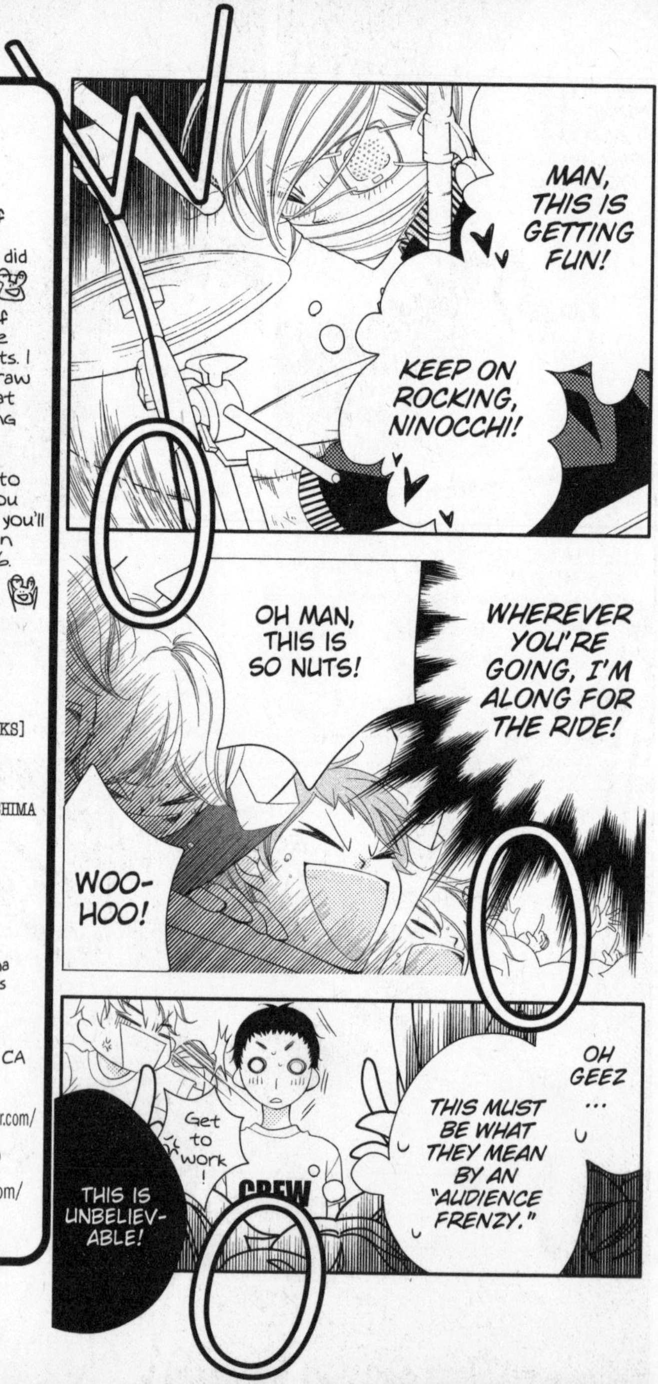
MAN, THIS IS GETTING FUN!
KEEP ON ROCKING, NINOCCHI!
WHEREVER YOU'RE GOING, I'M ALONG FOR THE RIDE!
OH MAN, THIS IS SO NUTS!
WOO-HOO!
OH GEEZ...
THIS MUST BE WHAT THEY MEAN BY AN "AUDIENCE FRENZY."
Get to work!
CREW
THIS IS UNBELIEVABLE!

6

And that's volume 5 of Anonymous Noise! How did you like it?

I had a lot of fun with the concert parts. I hope I can draw more of that sort of thing soon!

I can't wait to hear what you think! I hope you'll join me again for volume 6. Until then...

-Ryoko Fukuyama

1/20/15

[SPECIAL THANKS]
IZUMI HIOU
MINI KOMATSU
TAKAYUKI NAGASHIMA
KENJU NORO
MY FAMILY
MY FRIENDS
AND YOU!!

Ryoko Fukuyama
c/o Anonymous Noise Editor
VIZ Media
P.O. Box 77010
San Francisco, CA 94107

http://ryoconet.tumblr.com/

@ryocoryocoryoco

http://facebook.com/ryocoryocoryoco/

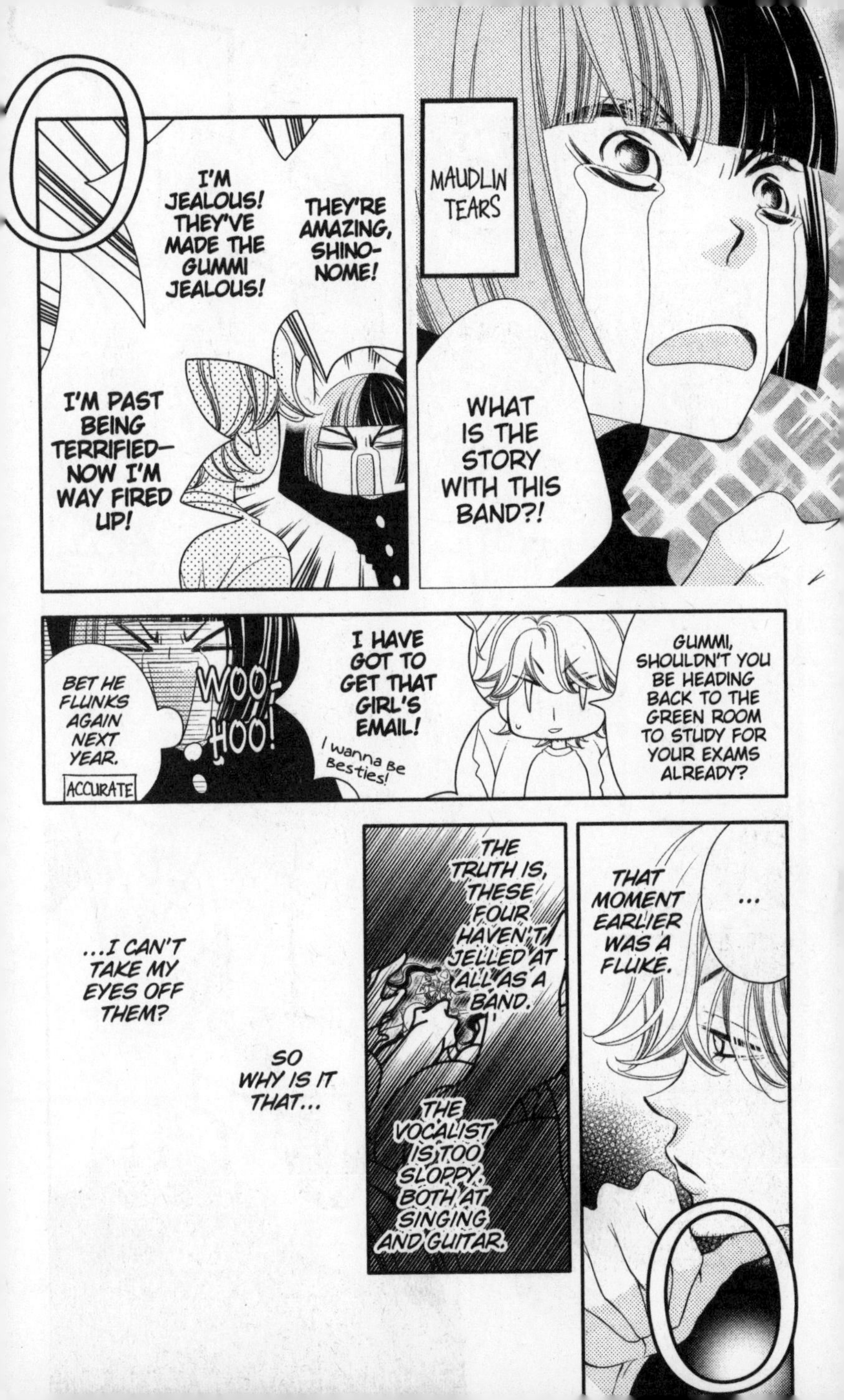
MAUDLIN TEARS
WHAT IS THE STORY WITH THIS BAND?!
THEY'RE AMAZING, SHINO-NOME!
I'M JEALOUS! THEY'VE MADE THE GUMMI JEALOUS!
I'M PAST BEING TERRIFIED—NOW I'M WAY FIRED UP!
GUMMI, SHOULDN'T YOU BE HEADING BACK TO THE GREEN ROOM TO STUDY FOR YOUR EXAMS ALREADY?
I HAVE GOT TO GET THAT GIRL'S EMAIL!
I wanna Be Besties!
WOO-HOO!
BET HE FLUNKS AGAIN NEXT YEAR.
ACCURATE
...
THAT MOMENT EARLIER WAS A FLUKE.
THE TRUTH IS, THESE FOUR HAVEN'T JELLED AT ALL AS A BAND.
THE VOCALIST IS TOO SLOPPY. BOTH AT SINGING AND GUITAR.
SO WHY IS IT THAT...
...I CAN'T TAKE MY EYES OFF THEM?

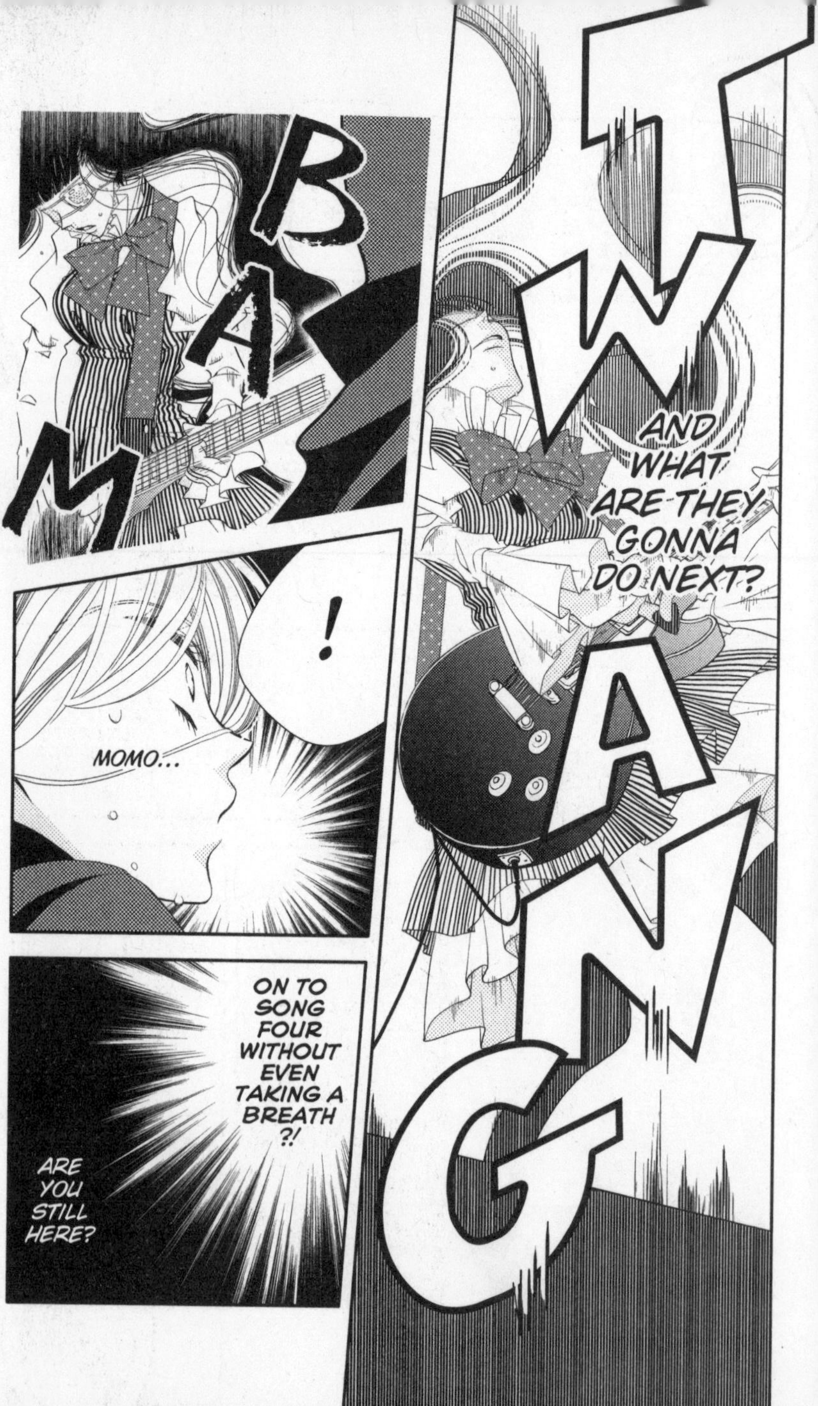
TWANG
AND WHAT ARE THEY GONNA DO NEXT?
BAM
!
MOMO...
ON TO SONG FOUR WITHOUT EVEN TAKING A BREATH?!
ARE YOU STILL HERE?

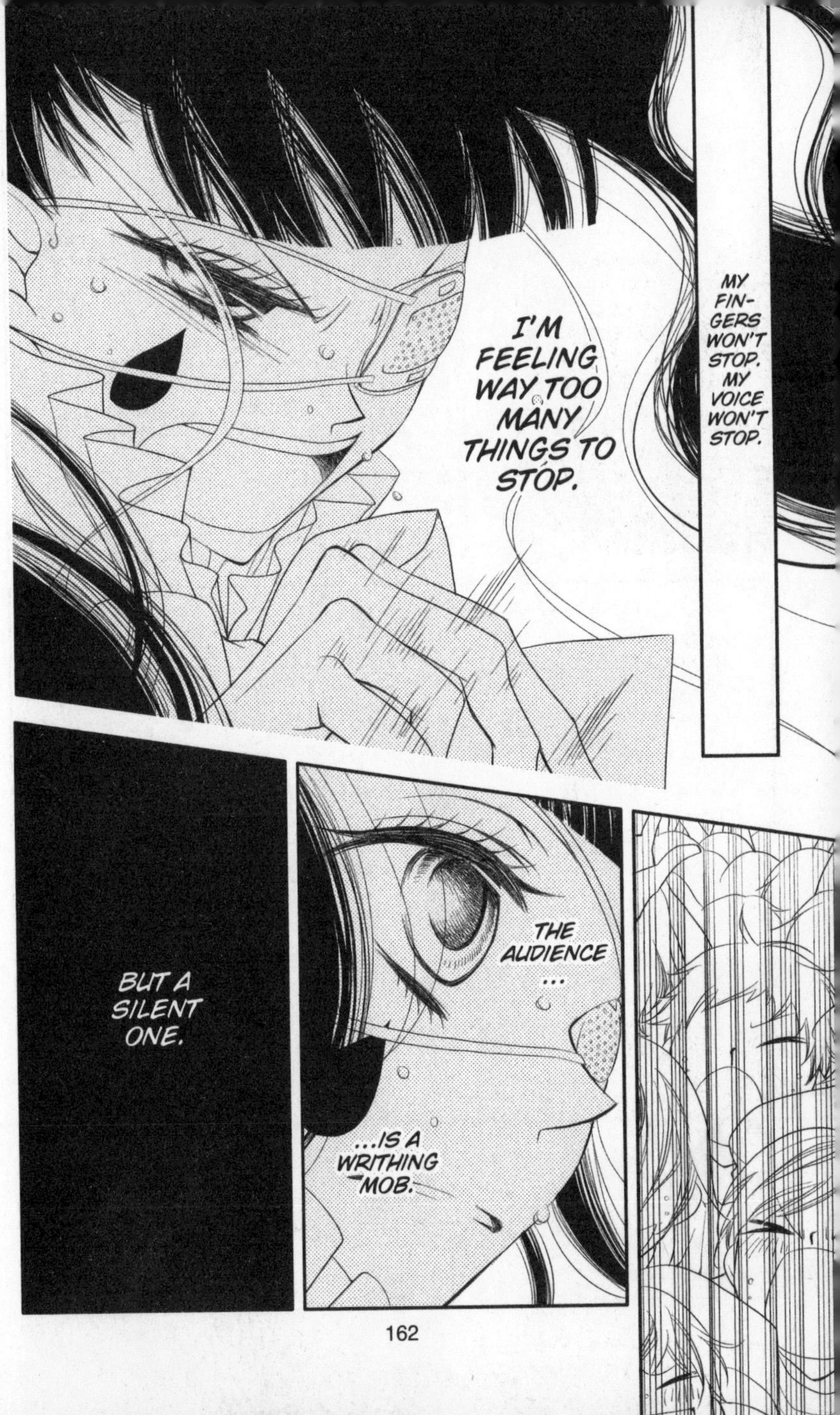
MY FIN-GERS WON'T STOP. MY VOICE WON'T STOP.
I'M FEELING WAY TOO MANY THINGS TO STOP.
THE AUDIENCE ...
...IS A WRITHING MOB.
BUT A SILENT ONE.

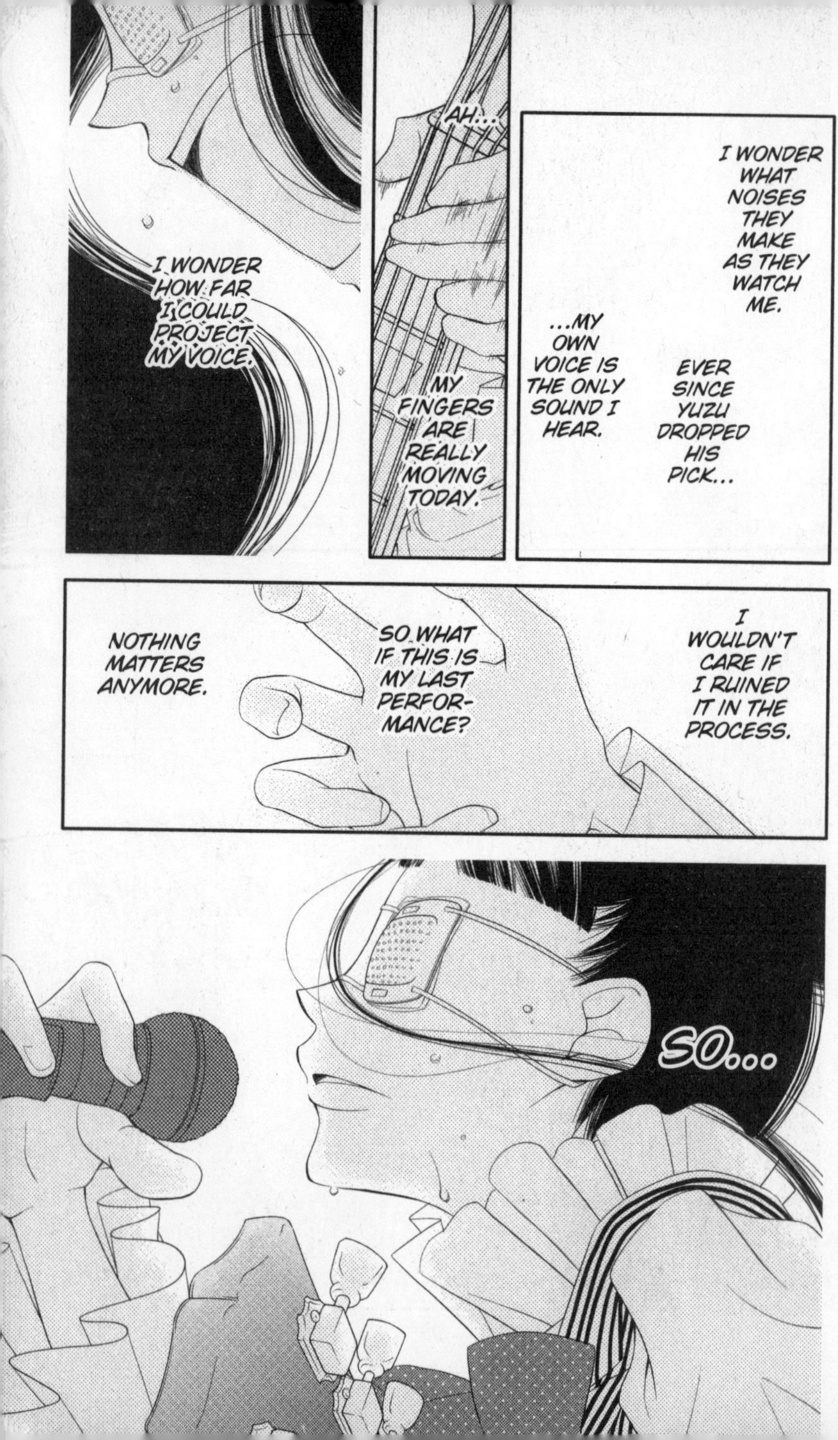
I WONDER WHAT NOISES THEY MAKE AS THEY WATCH ME.
EVER SINCE YUZU DROPPED HIS PICK...
...MY OWN VOICE IS THE ONLY SOUND I HEAR.
AH...
MY FINGERS ARE REALLY MOVING TODAY.
I WONDER HOW FAR I COULD PROJECT MY VOICE.
I WOULDN'T CARE IF I RUINED IT IN THE PROCESS.
SO WHAT IF THIS IS MY LAST PERFORMANCE?
NOTHING MATTERS ANYMORE.
SO...

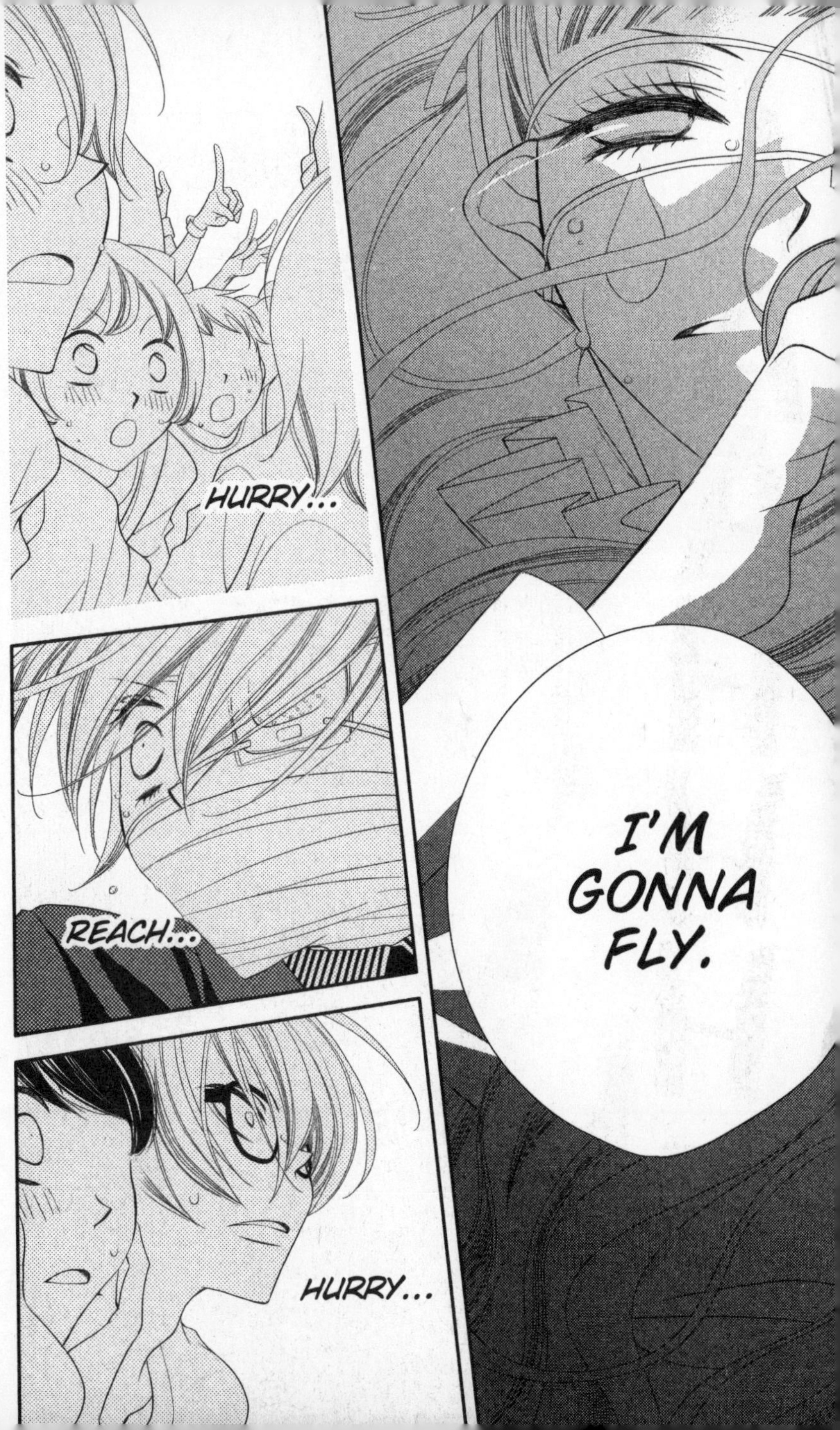
I'M GONNA FLY.
HURRY...
REACH...
HURRY...

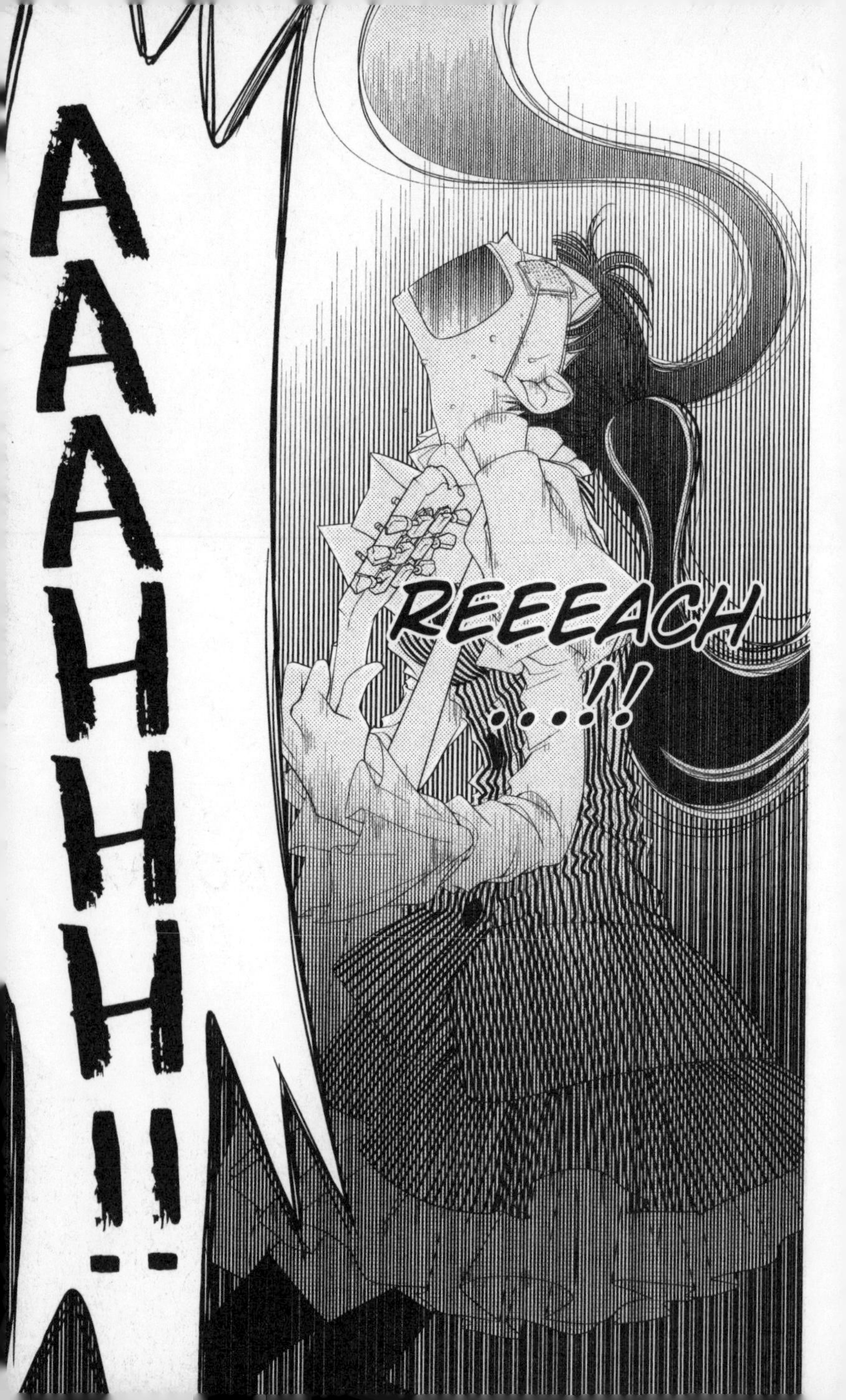
AAAHHHH!!
REEEACH ...!!

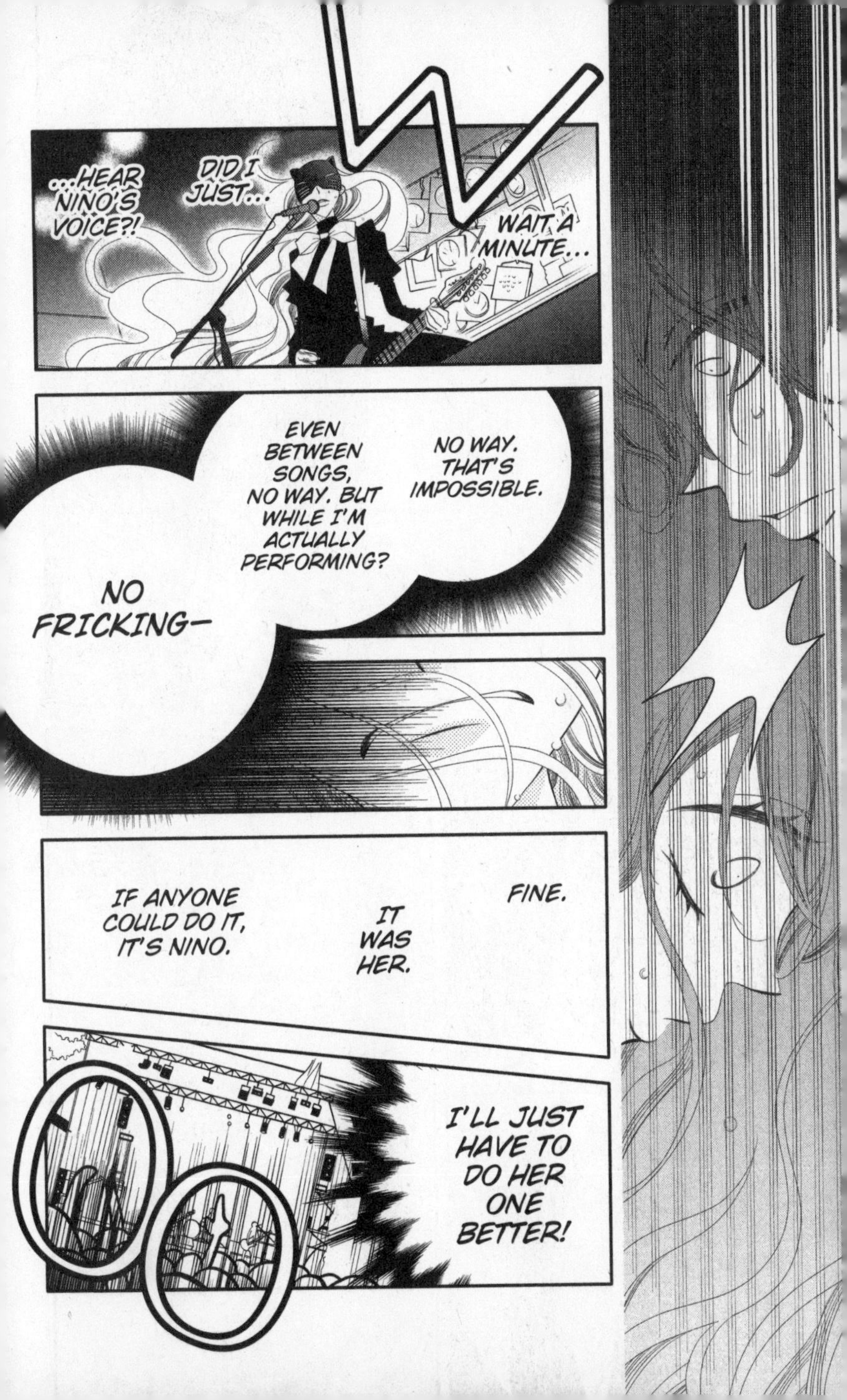
WAIT A MINUTE...
DID I JUST...
...HEAR NINO'S VOICE?!
NO WAY. THAT'S IMPOSSIBLE.
EVEN BETWEEN SONGS, NO WAY. BUT WHILE I'M ACTUALLY PERFORMING?
NO FRICKING—
FINE.
IT WAS HER.
IF ANYONE COULD DO IT, IT'S NINO.
I'LL JUST HAVE TO DO HER ONE BETTER!

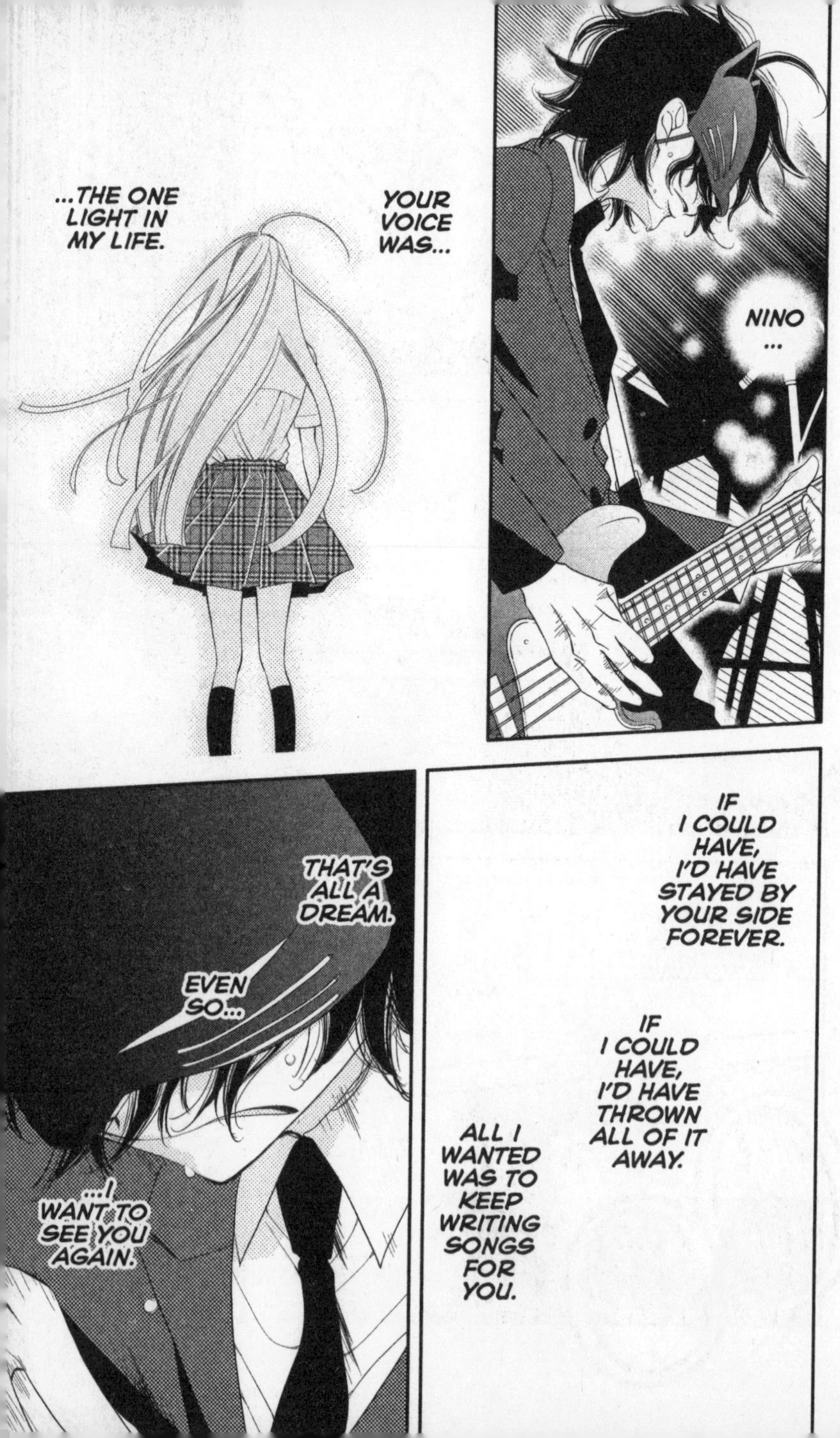
NINO...
YOUR VOICE WAS...
...THE ONE LIGHT IN MY LIFE.
IF I COULD HAVE, I'D HAVE STAYED BY YOUR SIDE FOREVER.
IF I COULD HAVE, I'D HAVE THROWN ALL OF IT AWAY.
ALL I WANTED WAS TO KEEP WRITING SONGS FOR YOU.
THAT'S ALL A DREAM.
EVEN SO...
...I WANT TO SEE YOU AGAIN.

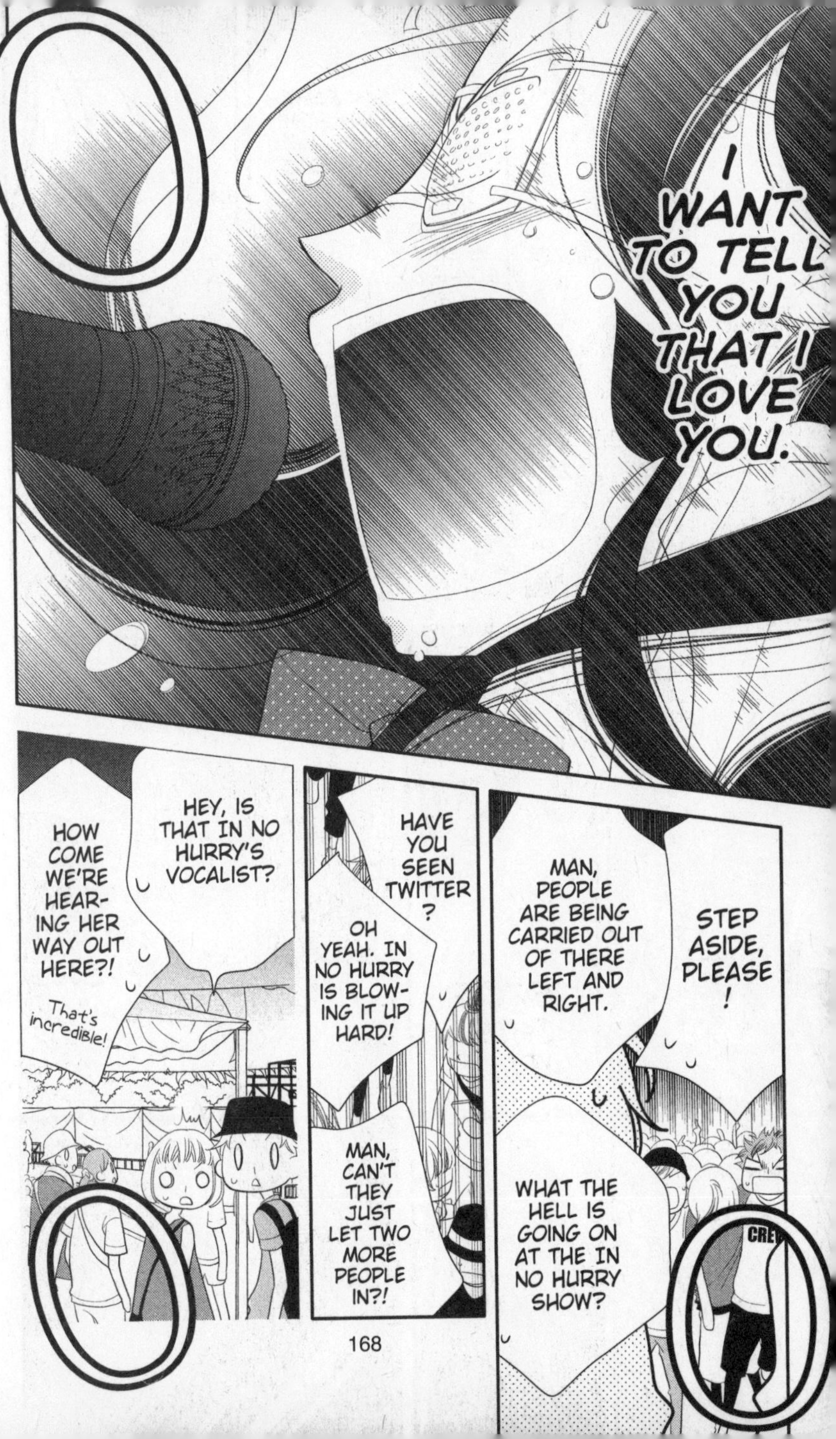
I WANT TO TELL YOU THAT I LOVE YOU.
STEP ASIDE, PLEASE!
MAN, PEOPLE ARE BEING CARRIED OUT OF THERE LEFT AND RIGHT.
WHAT THE HELL IS GOING ON AT THE IN NO HURRY SHOW?
HAVE YOU SEEN TWITTER?
OH YEAH. IN NO HURRY IS BLOWING IT UP HARD!
MAN, CAN'T THEY JUST LET TWO MORE PEOPLE IN?!
HEY, IS THAT IN NO HURRY'S VOCALIST?
HOW COME WE'RE HEARING HER WAY OUT HERE?!
That's incredible!

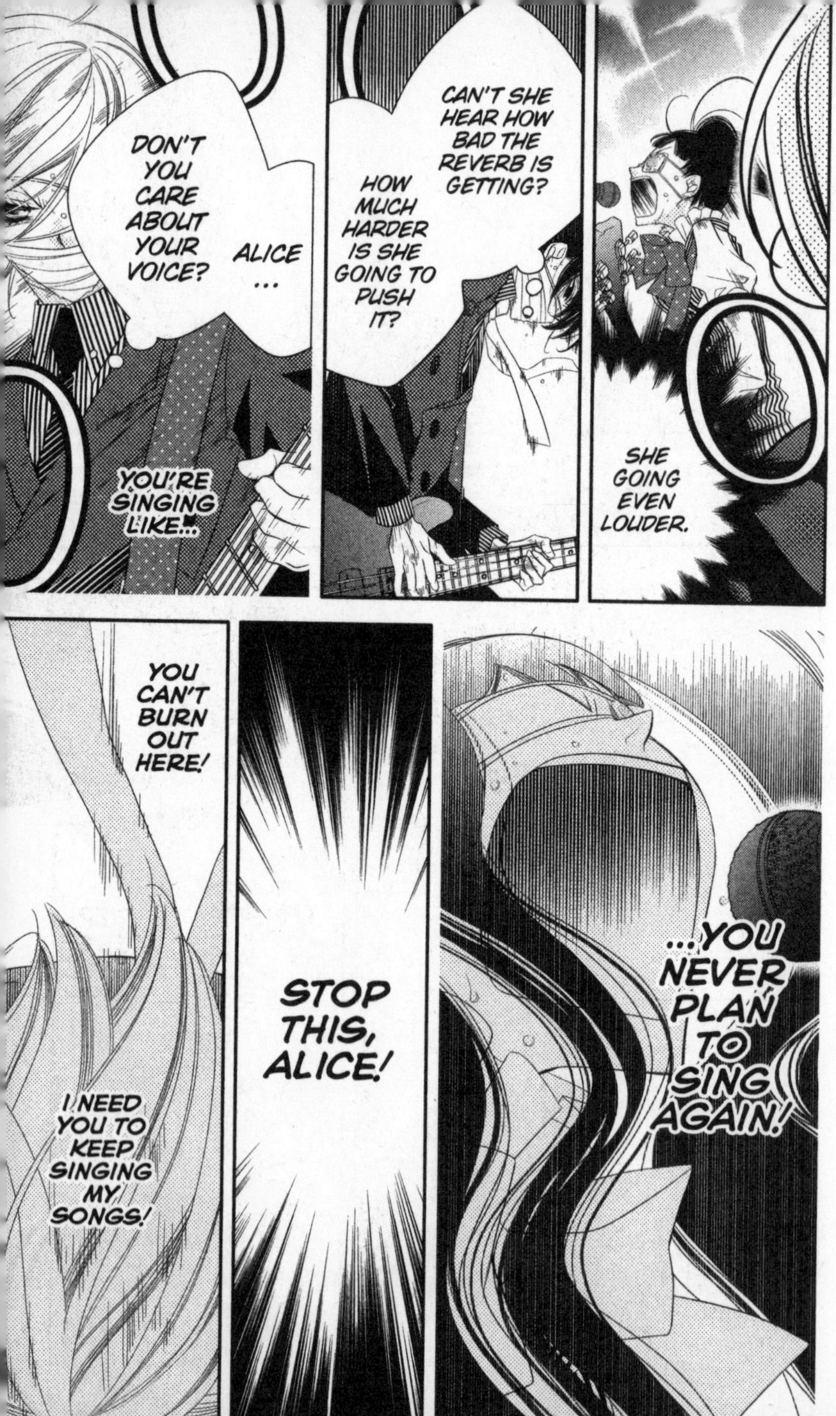
SHE GOING EVEN LOUDER.
CAN'T SHE HEAR HOW BAD THE REVERB IS GETTING?
HOW MUCH HARDER IS SHE GOING TO PUSH IT?
ALICE ...
DON'T YOU CARE ABOUT YOUR VOICE?
YOU'RE SINGING LIKE...
...YOU NEVER PLAN TO SING AGAIN!
STOP THIS, ALICE!
YOU CAN'T BURN OUT HERE!
I NEED YOU TO KEEP SINGING MY SONGS!

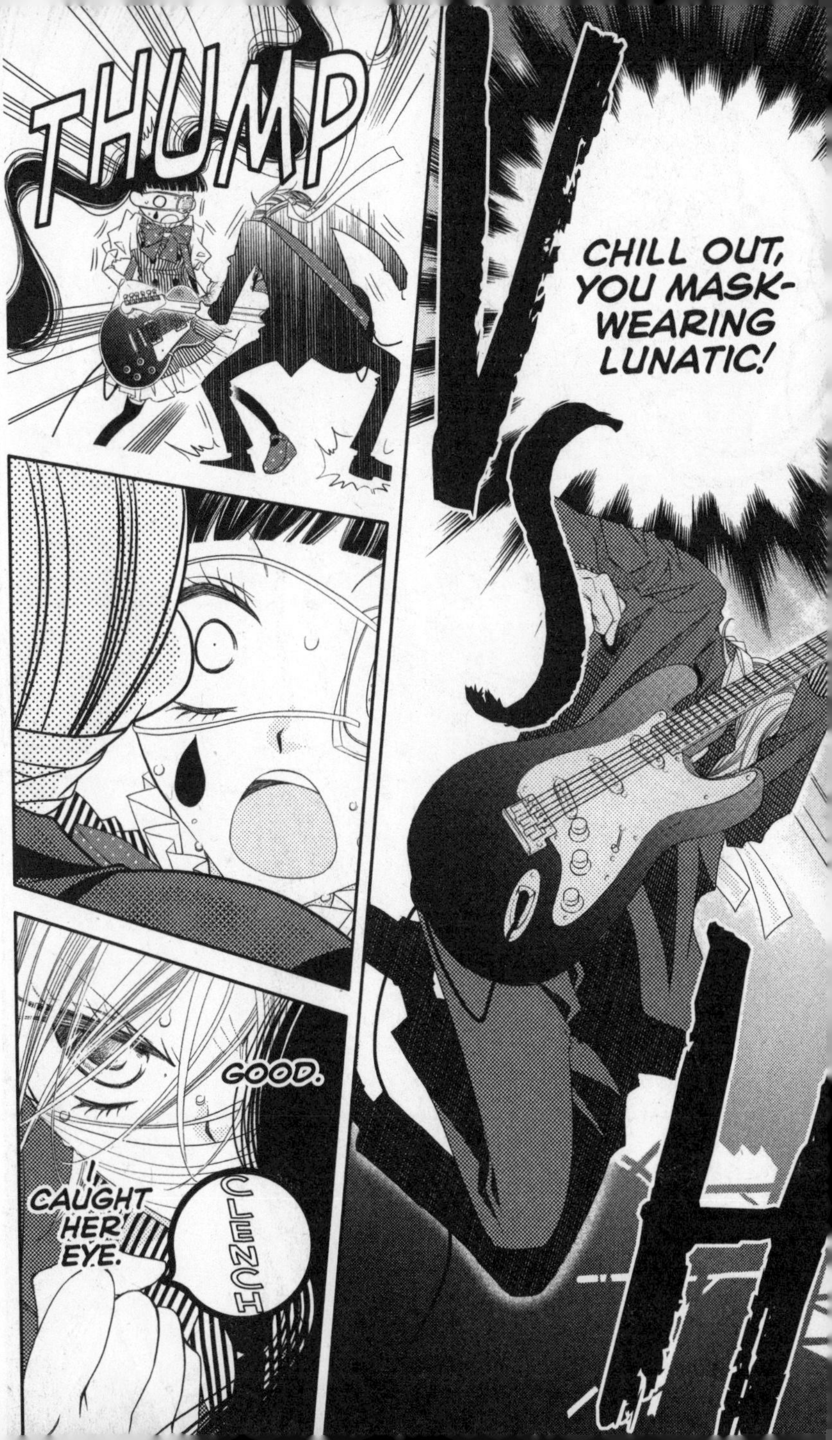
CHILL OUT, YOU MASK-WEARING LUNATIC!
THUMP
GOOD.
CLENCH
I CAUGHT HER EYE.

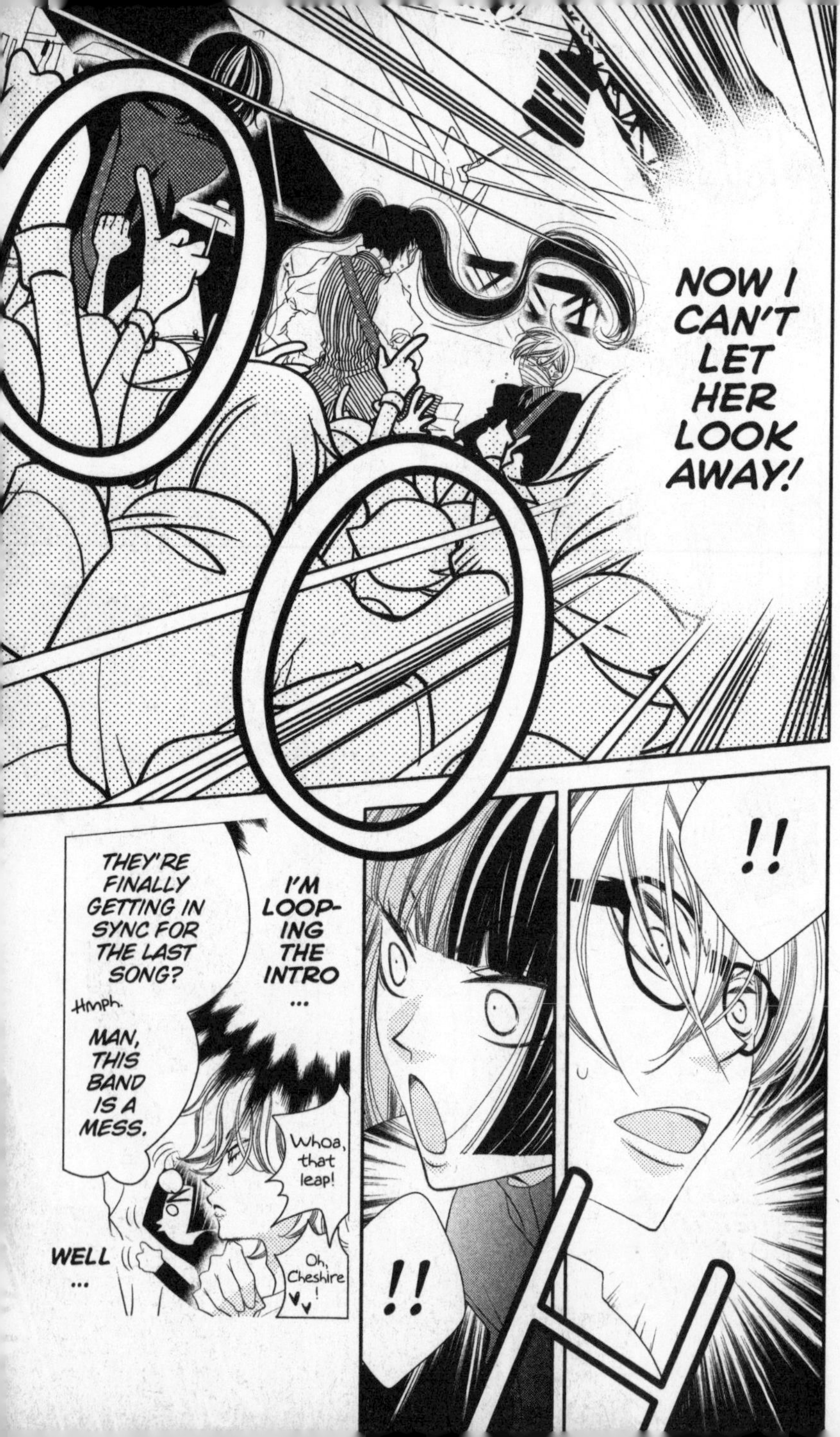
NOW I CAN'T LET HER LOOK AWAY!
!!
!!
I'M LOOPING THE INTRO...
THEY'RE FINALLY GETTING IN SYNC FOR THE LAST SONG?
Hmph.
MAN, THIS BAND IS A MESS.
Whoa, that leap!
Oh, Cheshire! ♥
WELL...

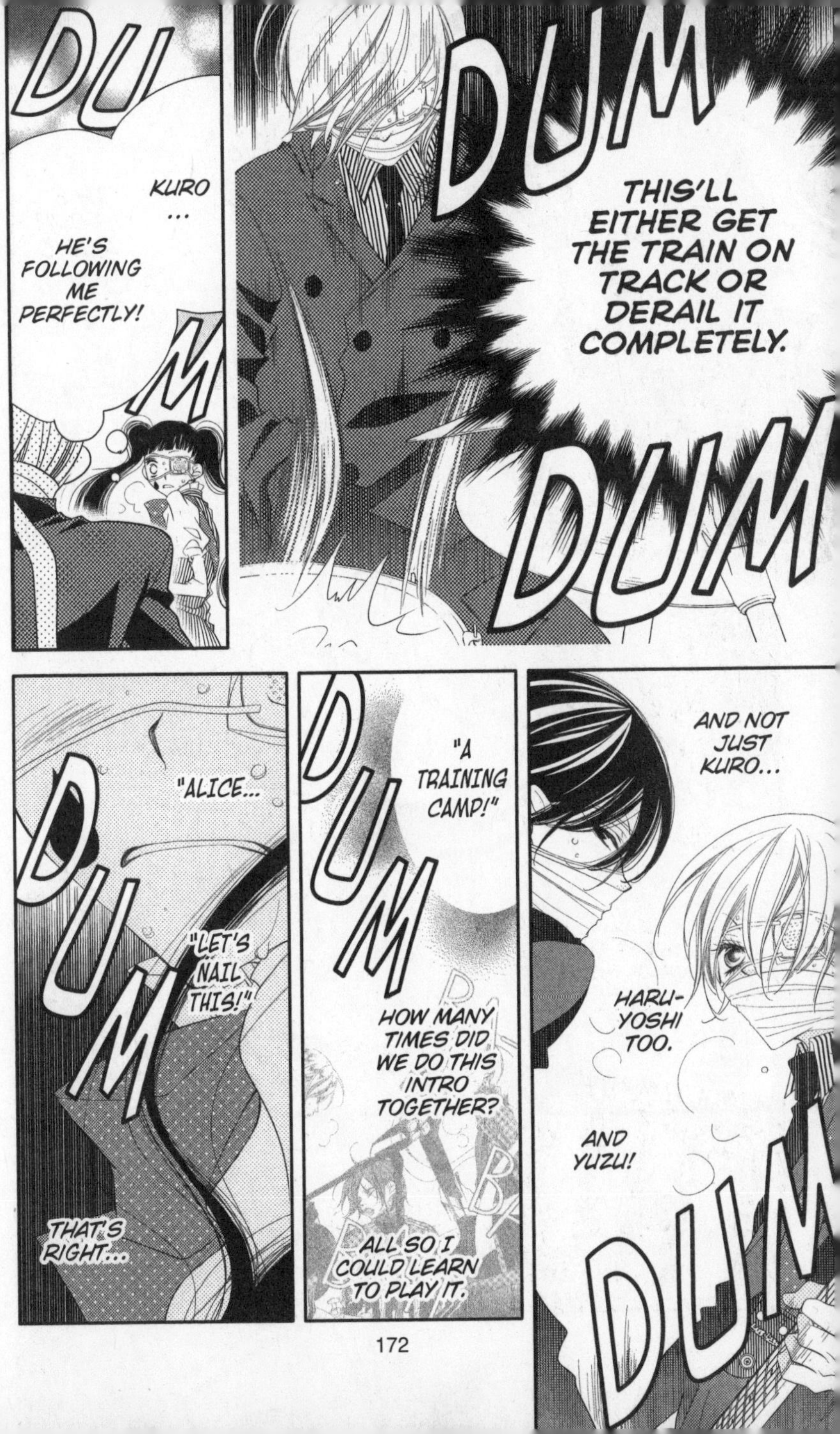
DUM
THIS'LL EITHER GET THE TRAIN ON TRACK OR DERAIL IT COMPLETELY.
DUM
DU
M
KURO ...
HE'S FOLLOWING ME PERFECTLY!
AND NOT JUST KURO...
HARU-YOSHI TOO.
AND YUZU!
DUM
"A TRAINING CAMP!"
DUM
HOW MANY TIMES DID WE DO THIS INTRO TOGETHER?
ALL SO I COULD LEARN TO PLAY IT.
"ALICE...
DUM
"LET'S NAIL THIS!"
THAT'S RIGHT...

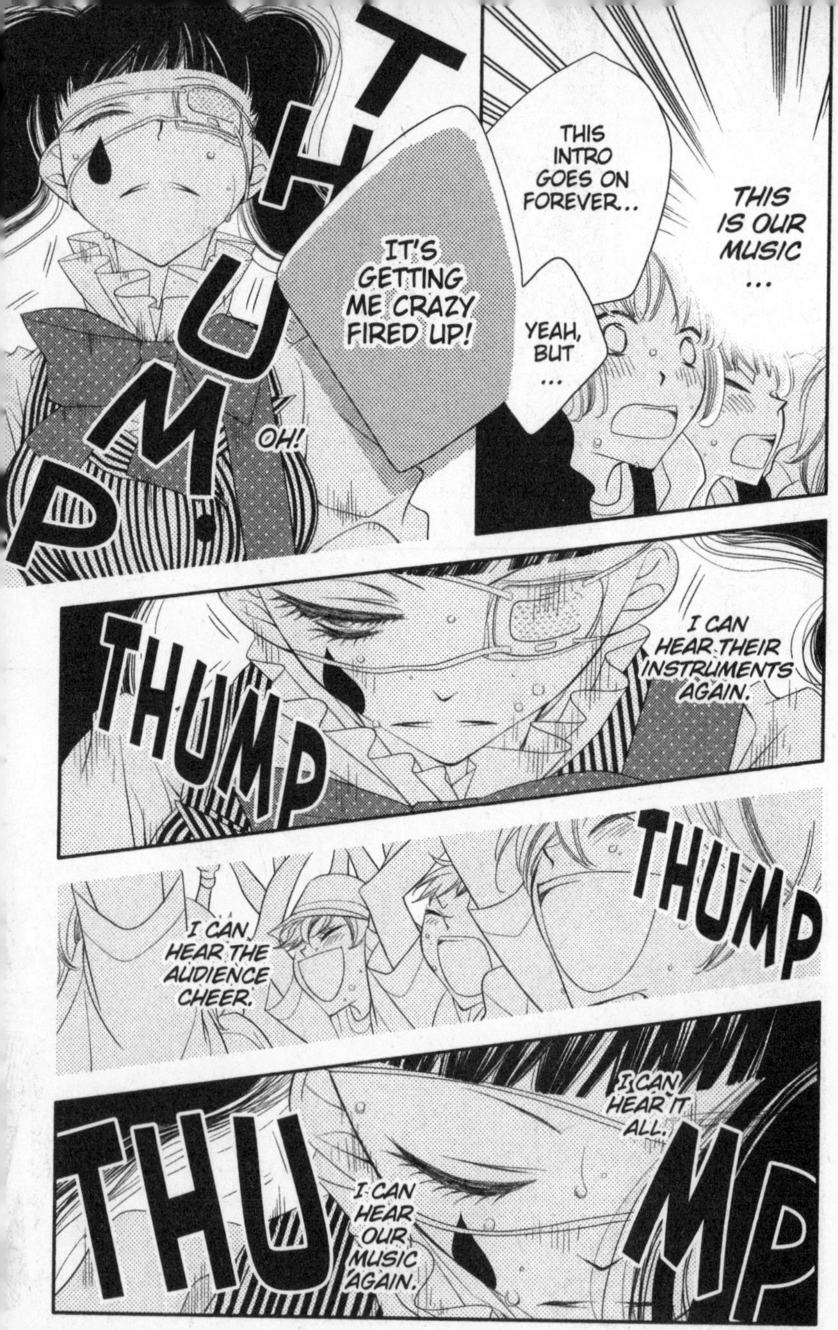
THIS IS OUR MUSIC ...
THIS INTRO GOES ON FOREVER...
IT'S GETTING ME CRAZY FIRED UP!
YEAH, BUT ...
THUMP
OH!
I CAN HEAR THEIR INSTRUMENTS AGAIN.
THUMP
THUMP
I CAN HEAR THE AUDIENCE CHEER.
I CAN HEAR IT ALL.
THUMP
I CAN HEAR OUR MUSIC AGAIN.

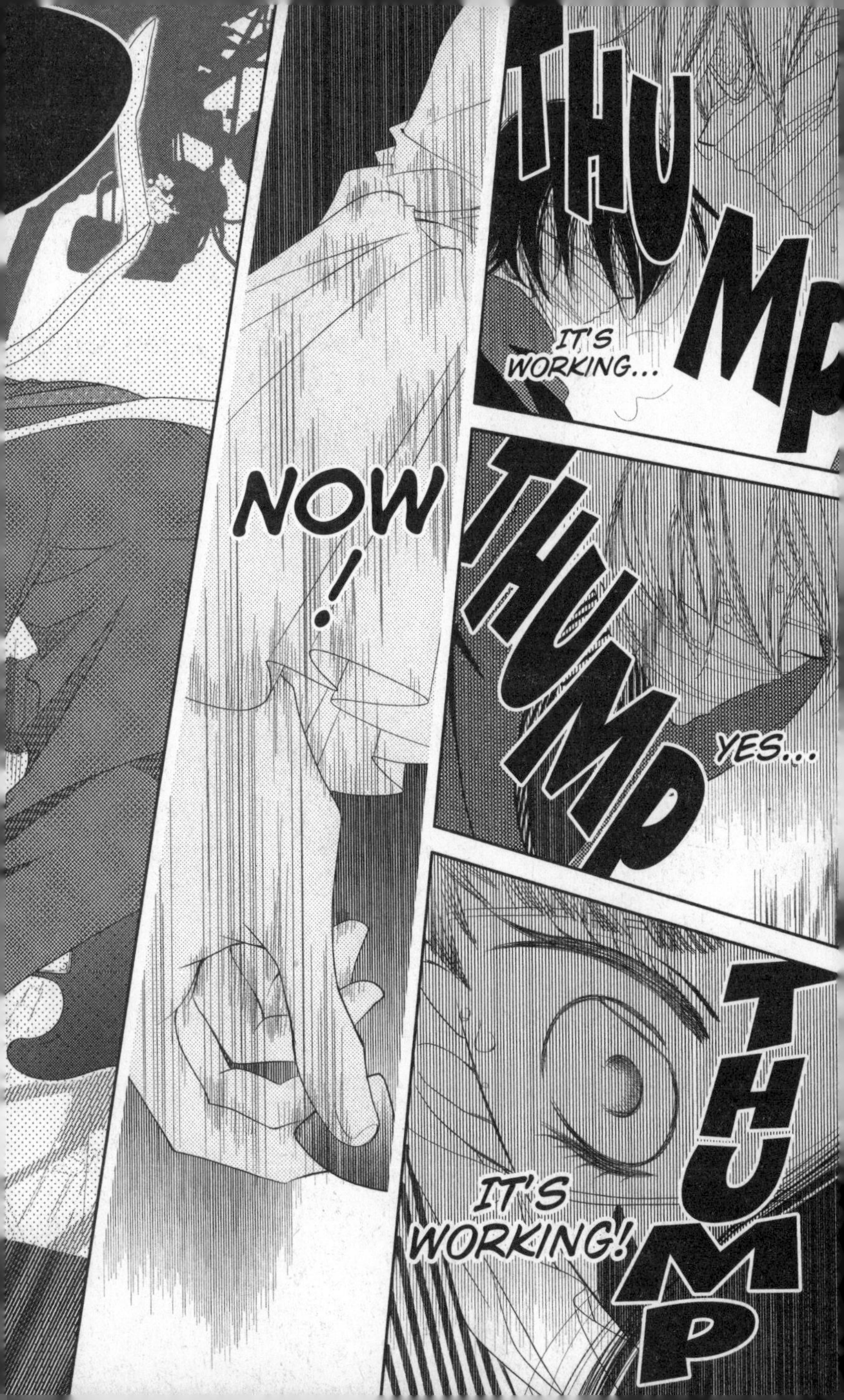
THUMP
IT'S WORKING...
THUMP
YES...
THUMP
IT'S WORKING!
NOW!

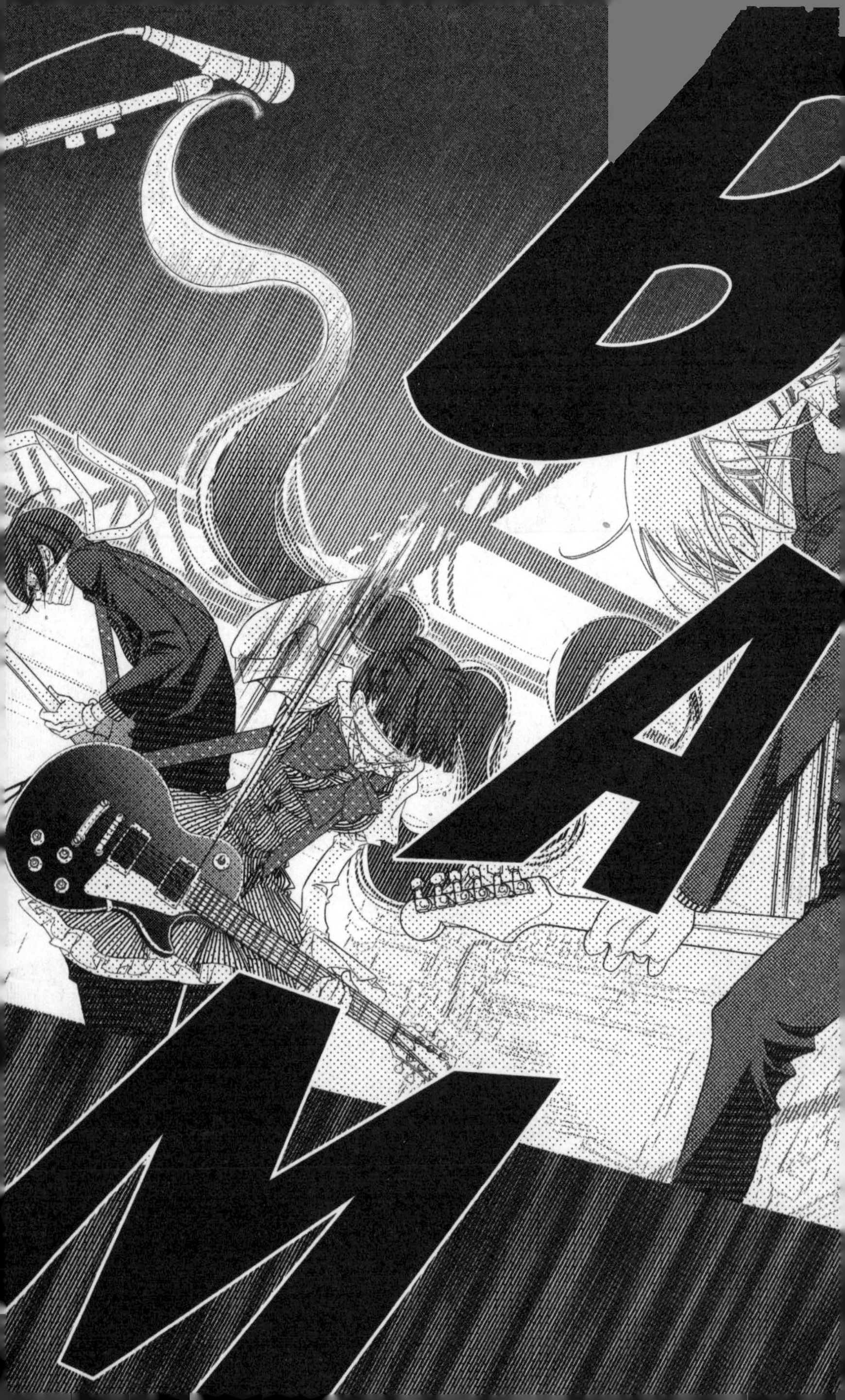
BAM

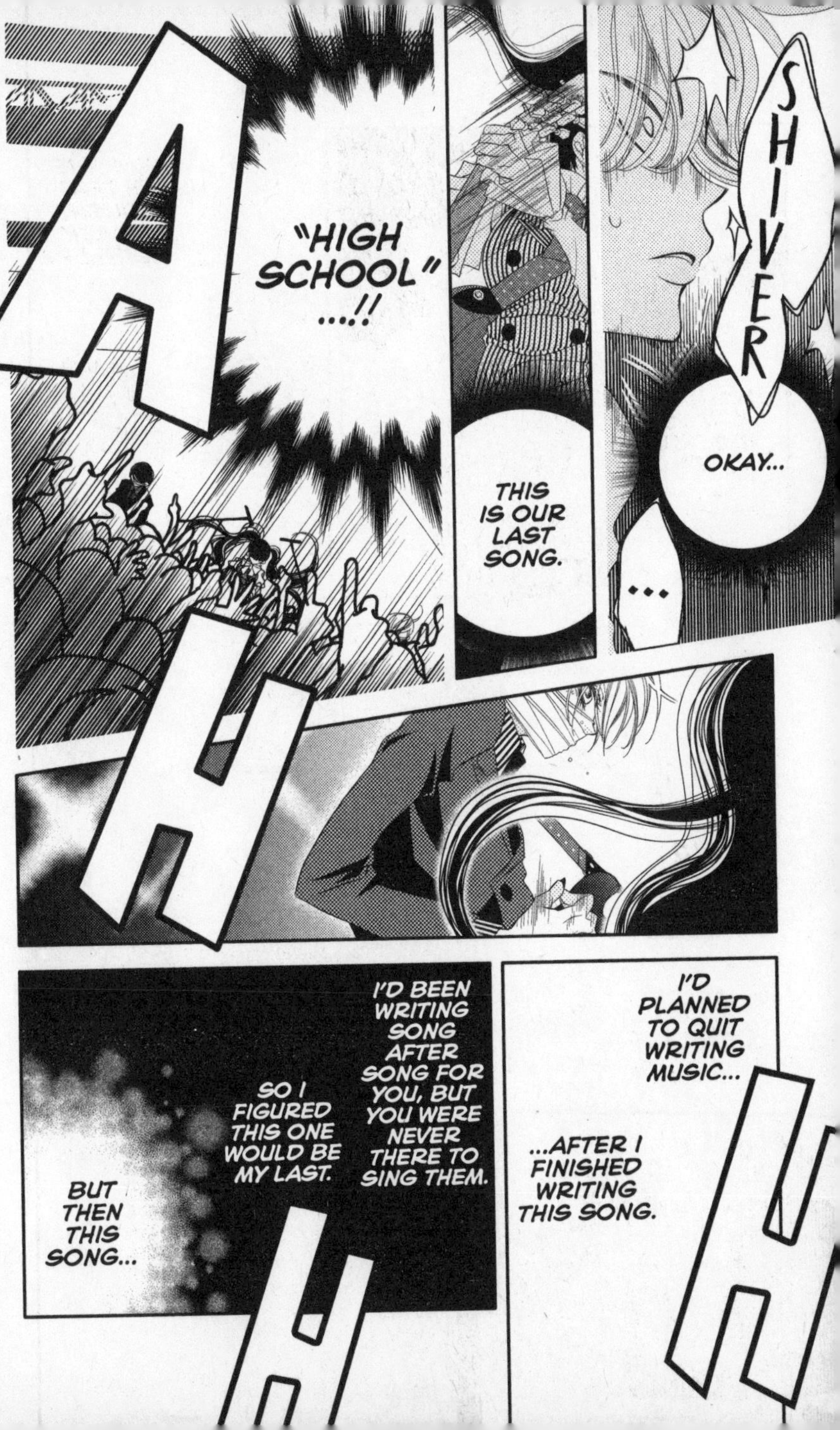
SHIVER
OKAY...
...
THIS IS OUR LAST SONG.
AHHH
"HIGH SCHOOL" ...!!
I'D PLANNED TO QUIT WRITING MUSIC...
...AFTER I FINISHED WRITING THIS SONG.
I'D BEEN WRITING SONG AFTER SONG FOR YOU, BUT YOU WERE NEVER THERE TO SING THEM.
SO I FIGURED THIS ONE WOULD BE MY LAST.
BUT THEN THIS SONG...

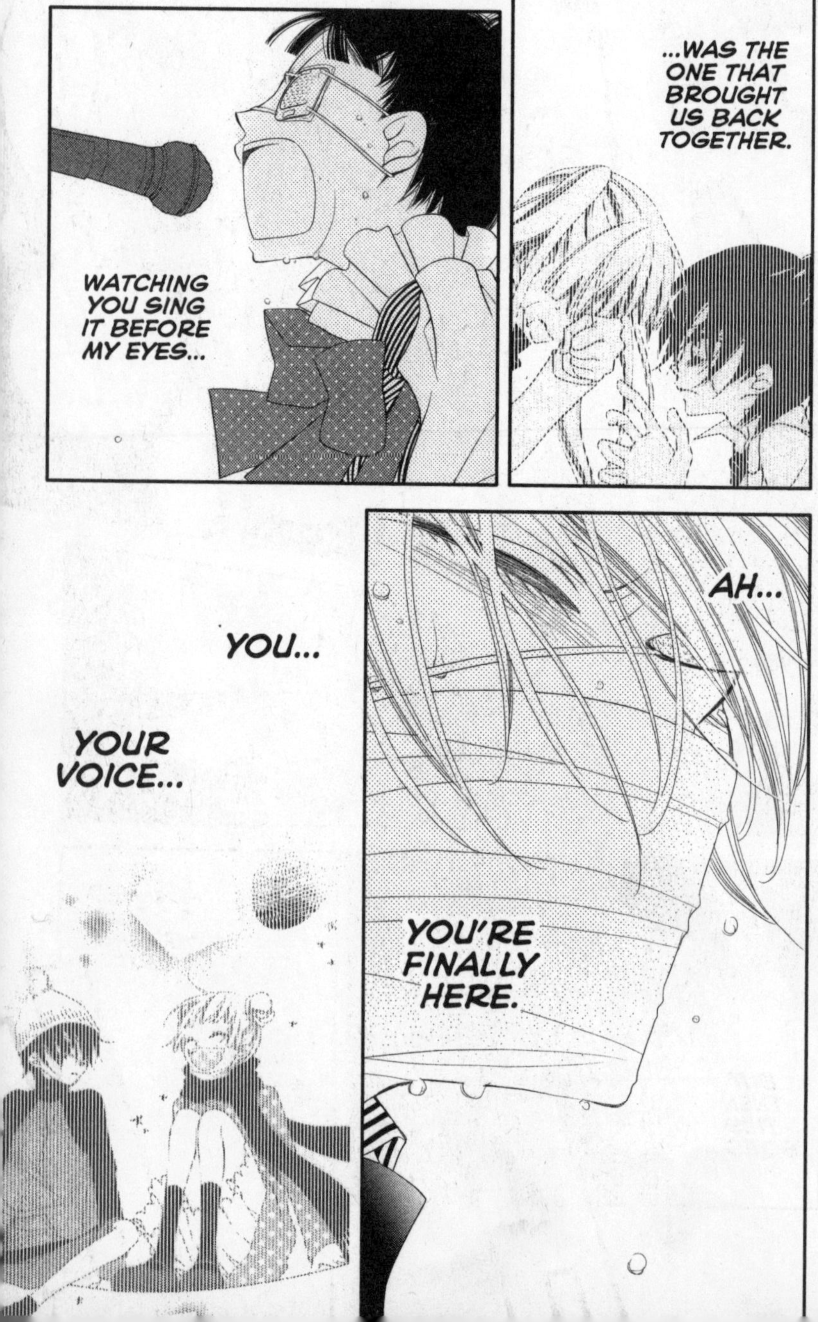
...WAS THE ONE THAT BROUGHT US BACK TOGETHER.
WATCHING YOU SING IT BEFORE MY EYES...
AH...
YOU'RE FINALLY HERE.
YOU...
YOUR VOICE...

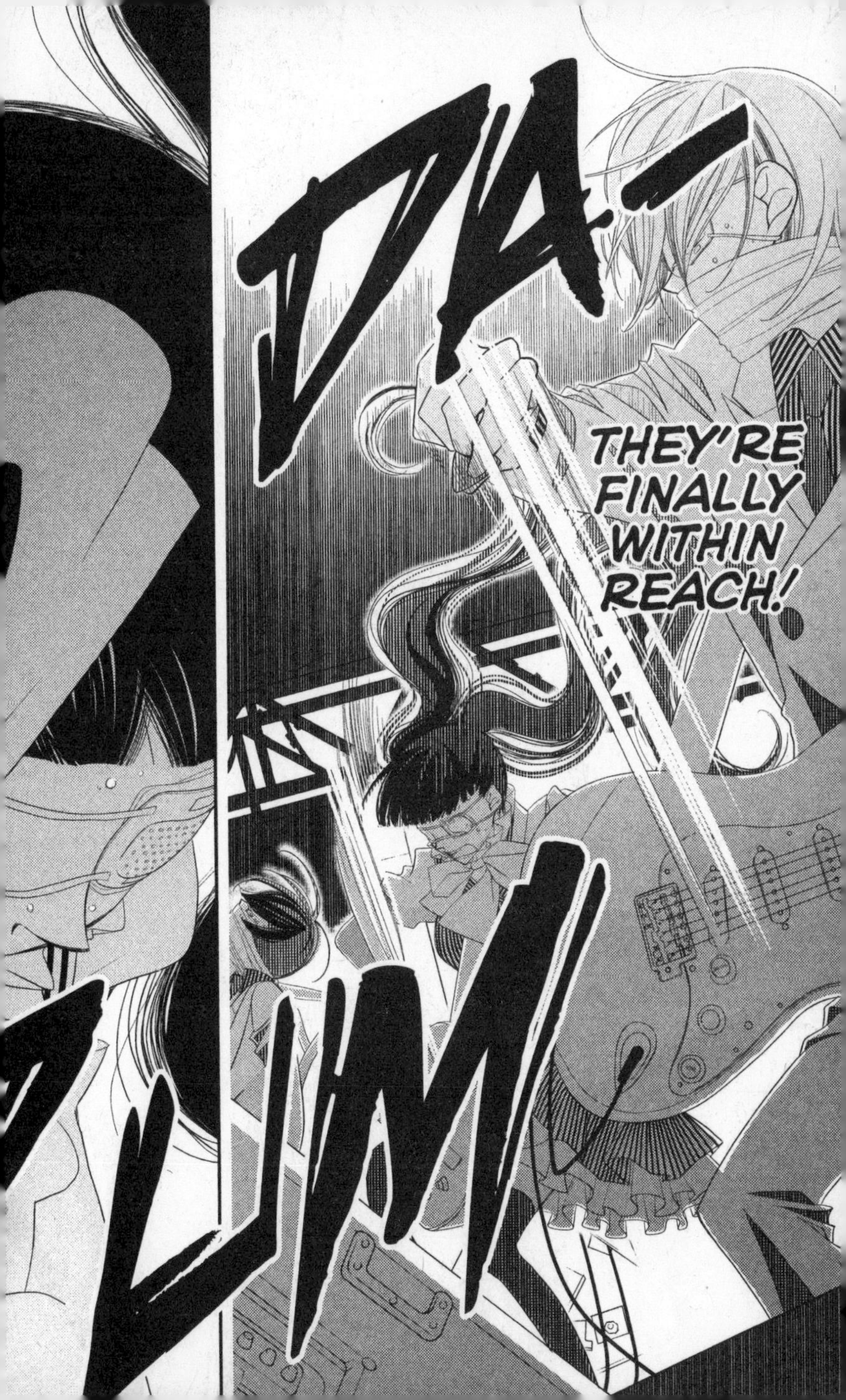
DA-
THEY'RE FINALLY WITHIN REACH!
DUN!

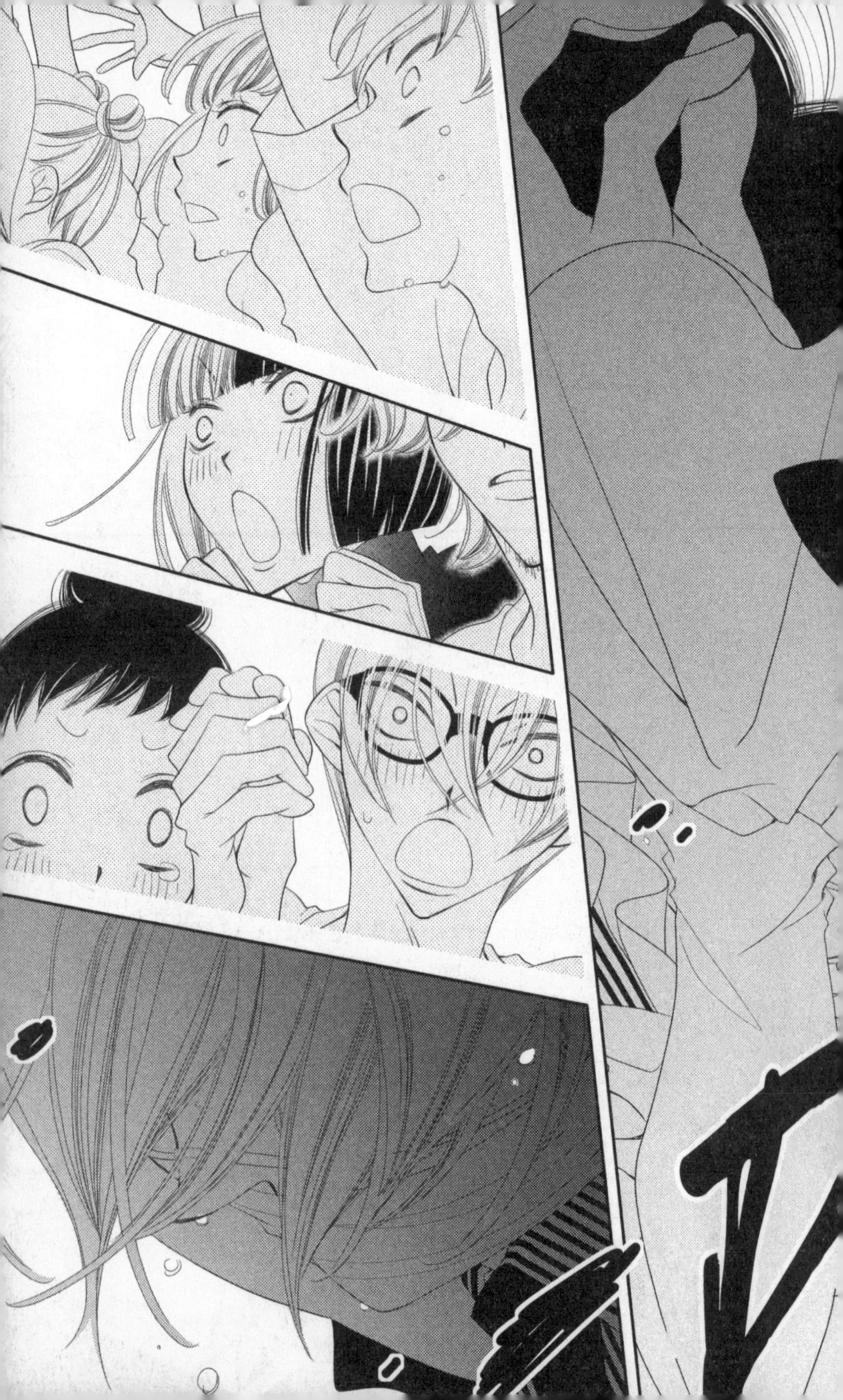

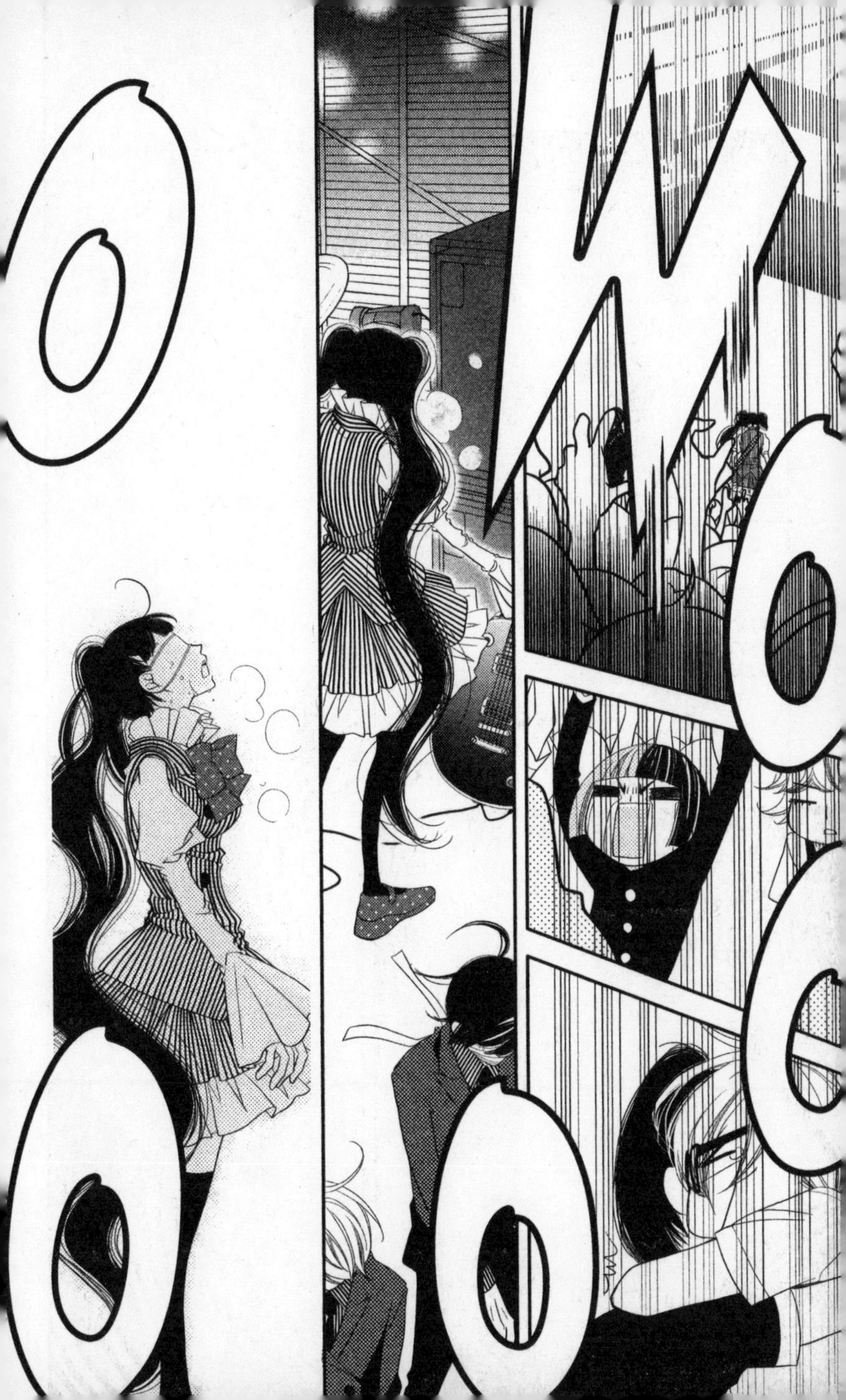
WOOOOO

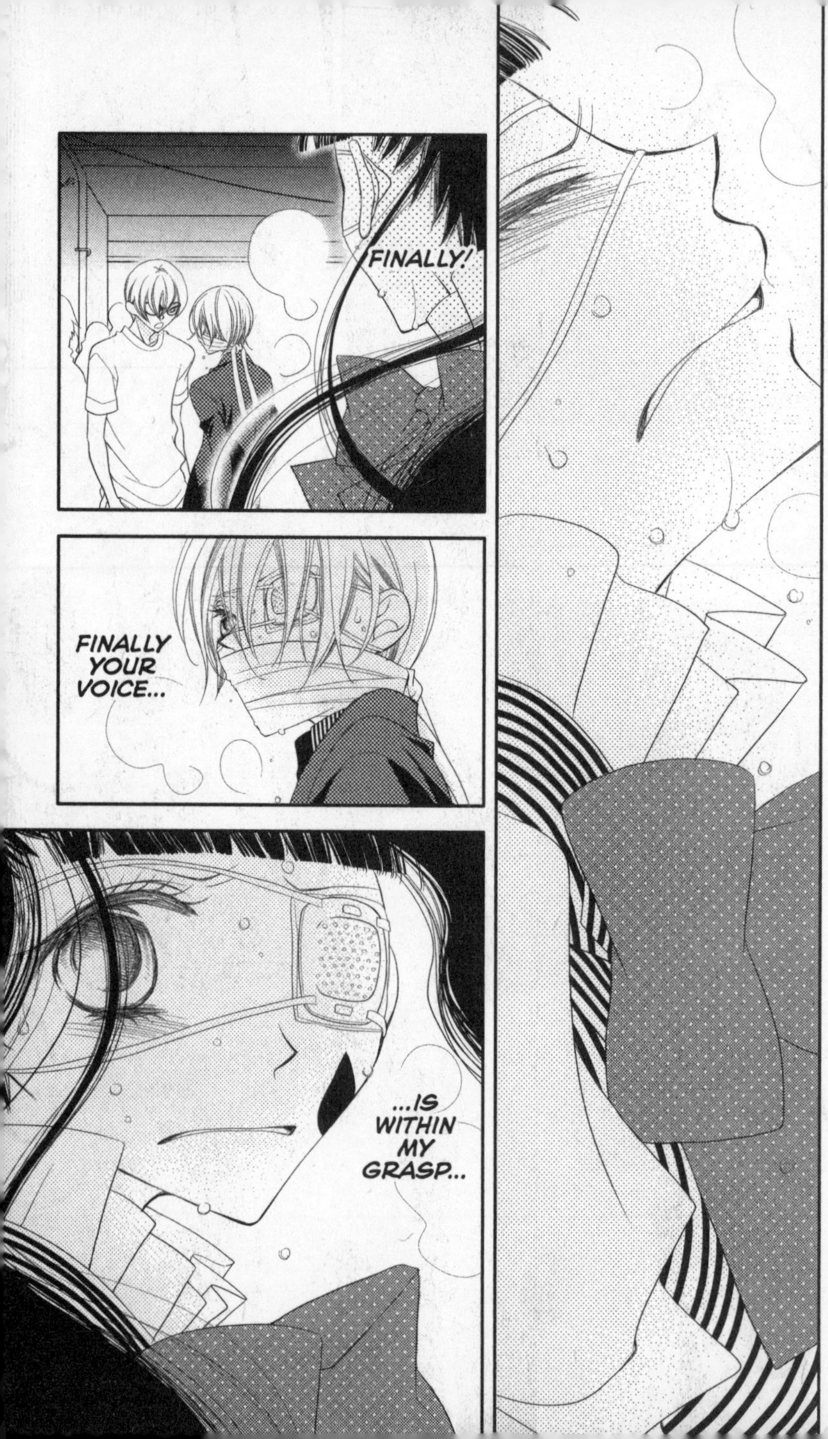
FINALLY!
FINALLY YOUR VOICE...
...IS WITHIN MY GRASP...

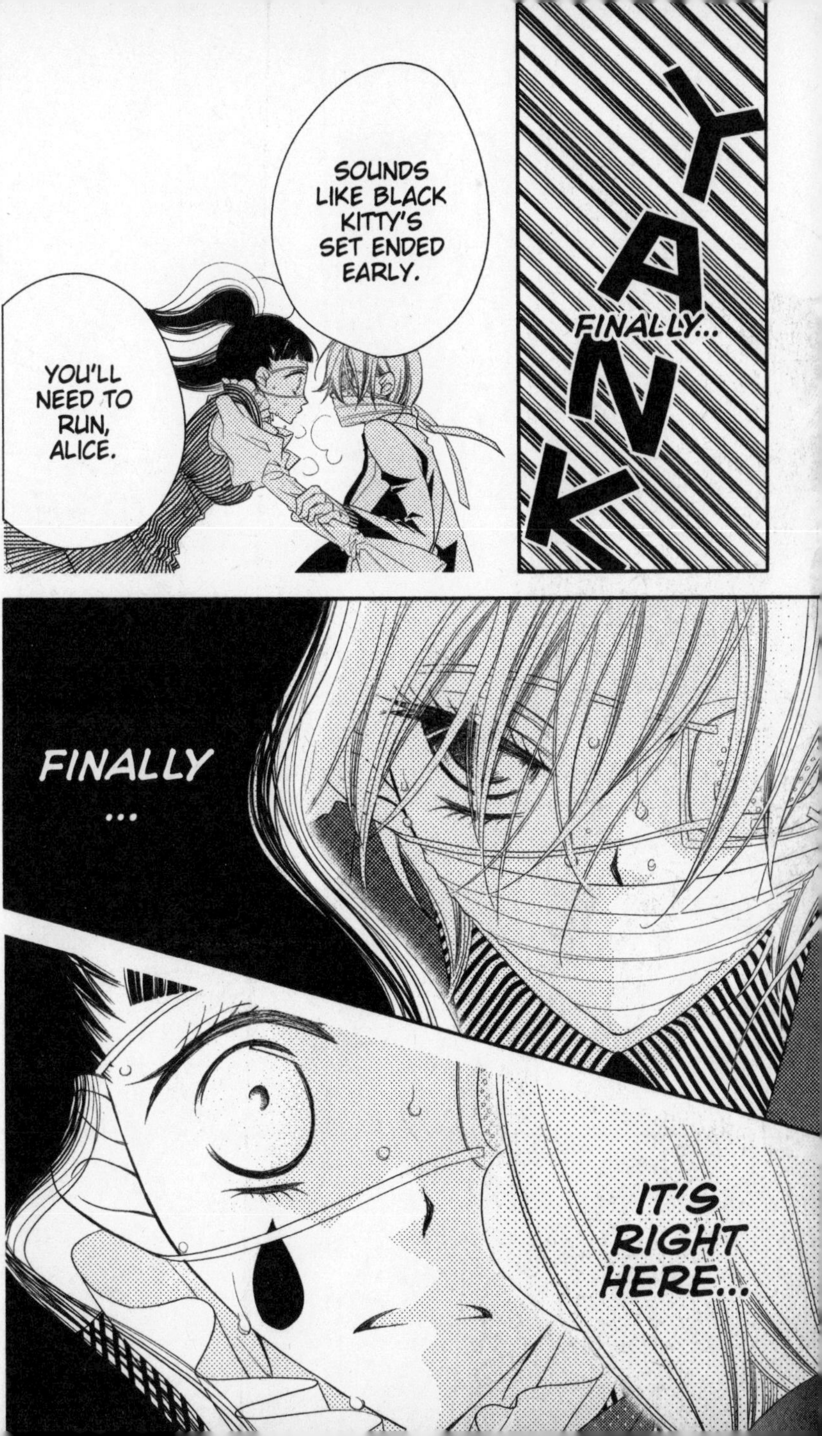
YANK
FINALLY...
SOUNDS LIKE BLACK KITTY'S SET ENDED EARLY.
YOU'LL NEED TO RUN, ALICE.
FINALLY ...
IT'S RIGHT HERE...

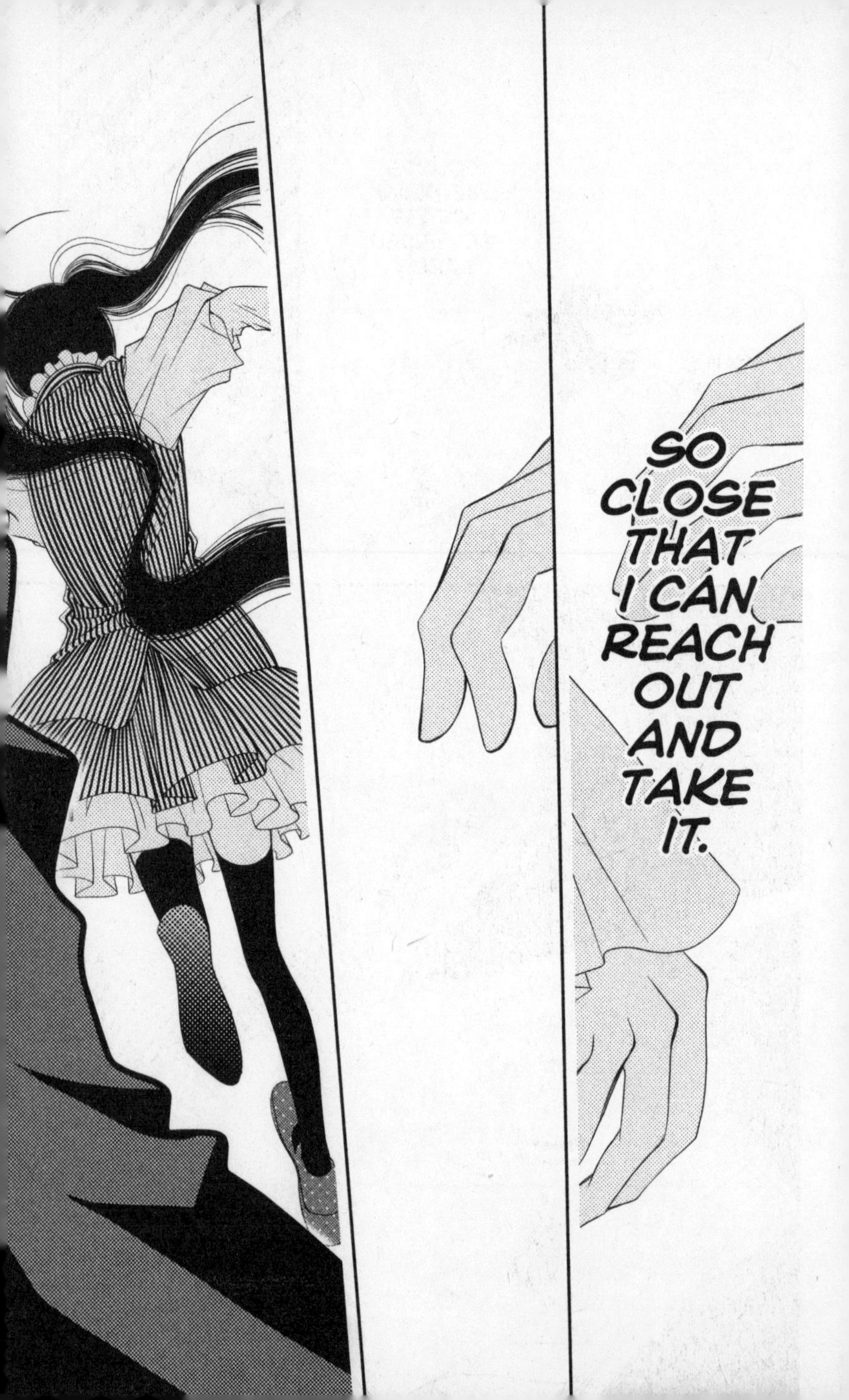
SO CLOSE THAT I CAN REACH OUT AND TAKE IT.

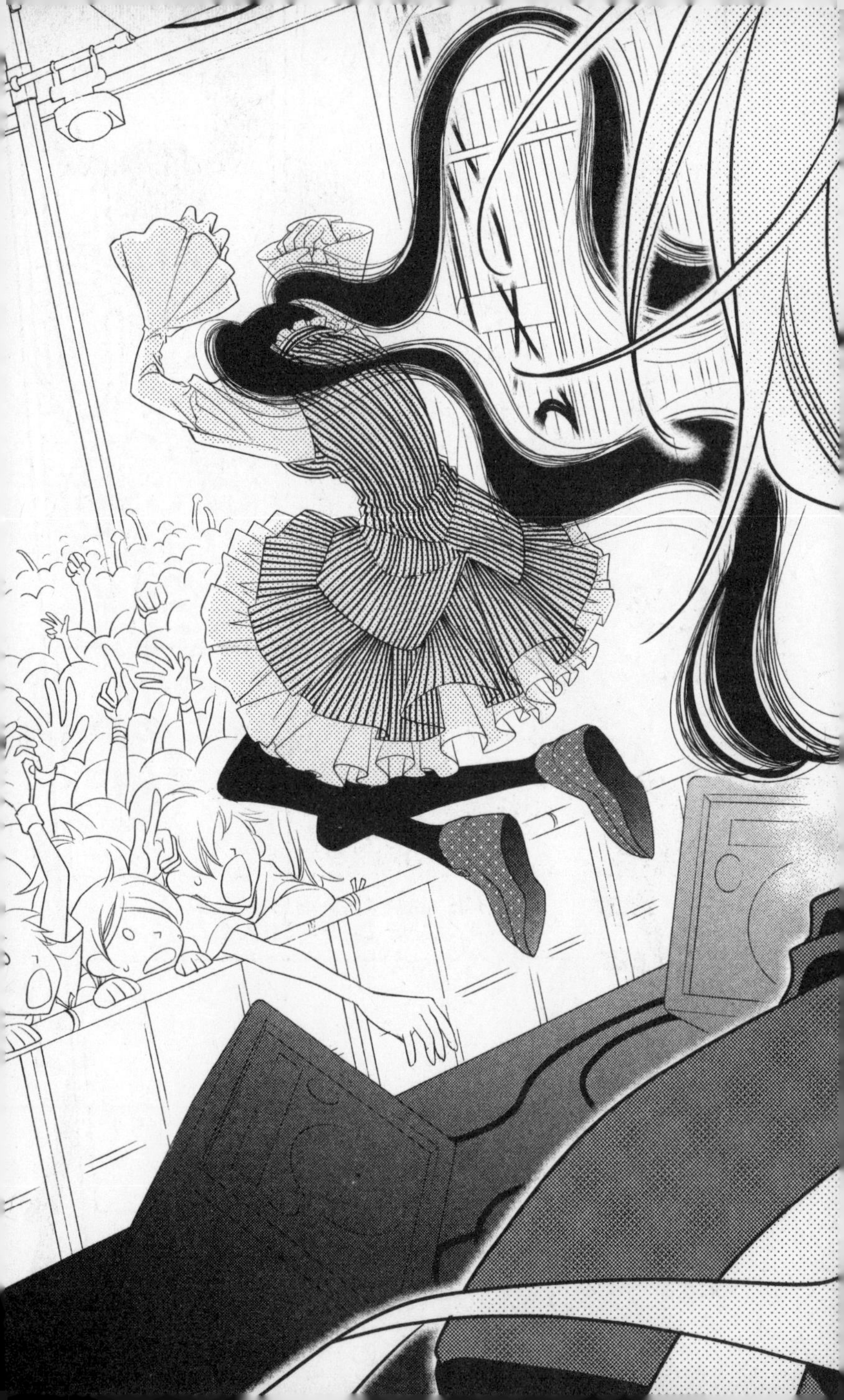

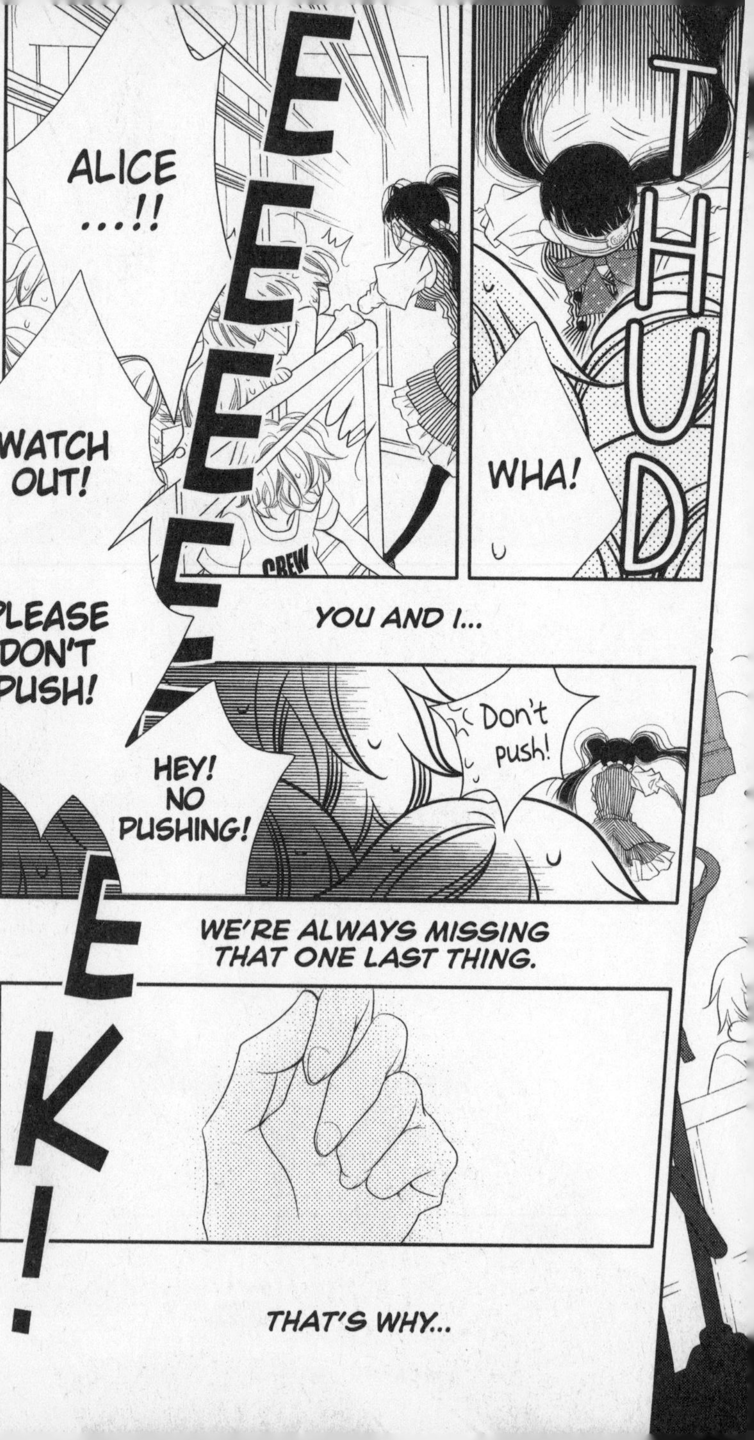
THUD
WHA!
ALICE ...!!
WATCH OUT!
EEEEEEEK!
YOU AND I...
Don't push!
HEY! NO PUSHING!
PLEASE DON'T PUSH!
WE'RE ALWAYS MISSING THAT ONE LAST THING.
THAT'S WHY...

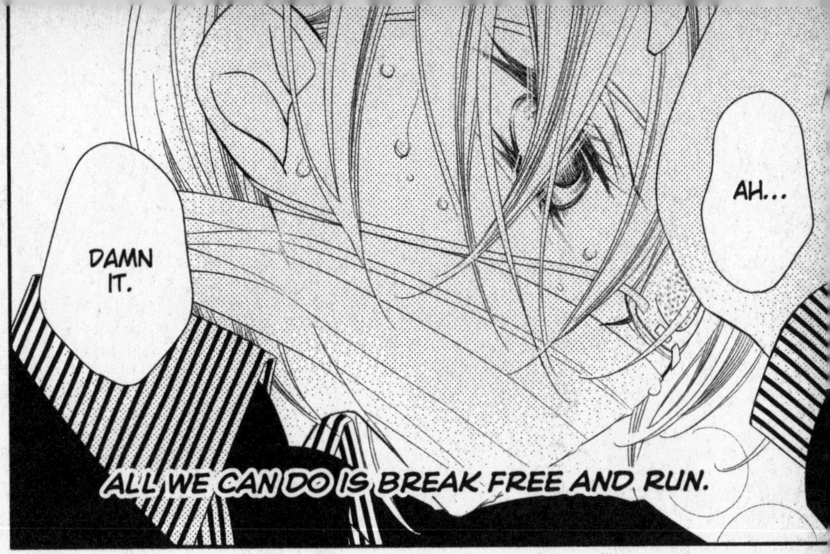
AH...
DAMN IT.
ALL WE CAN DO IS BREAK FREE AND RUN.

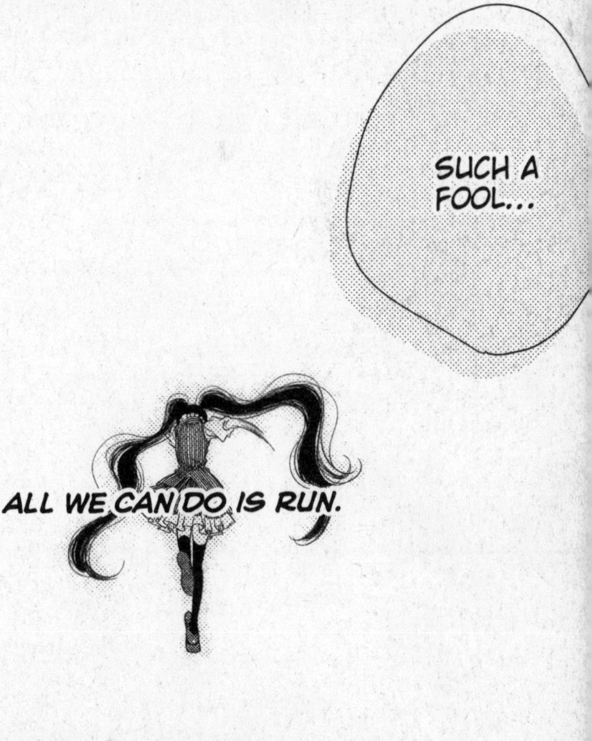
SUCH A FOOL...
ALL WE CAN DO IS RUN.

ANONYMOUS NOISE ⑤ / THE END

TO BE CONTINUED IN ANONYMOUS NOISE 6

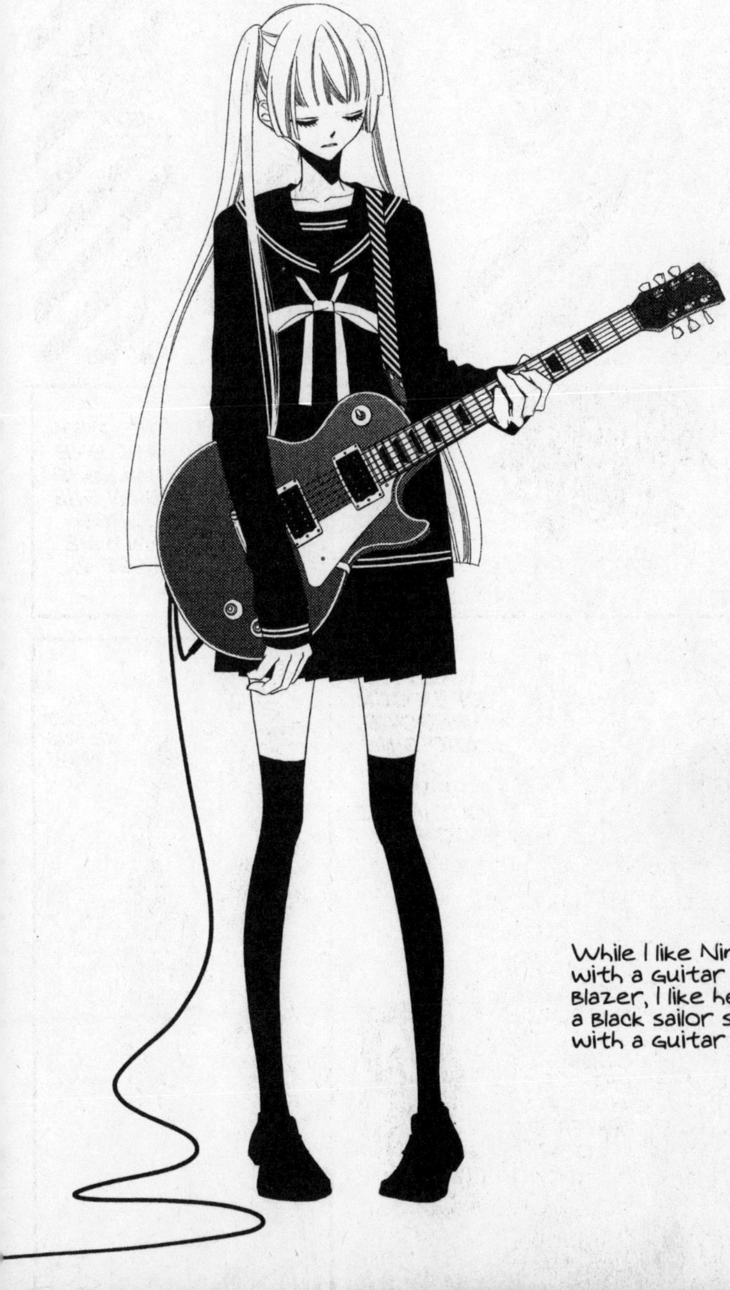

While I like Nino with a Guitar and a Blazer, I like her in a Black sailor suit with a Guitar too.

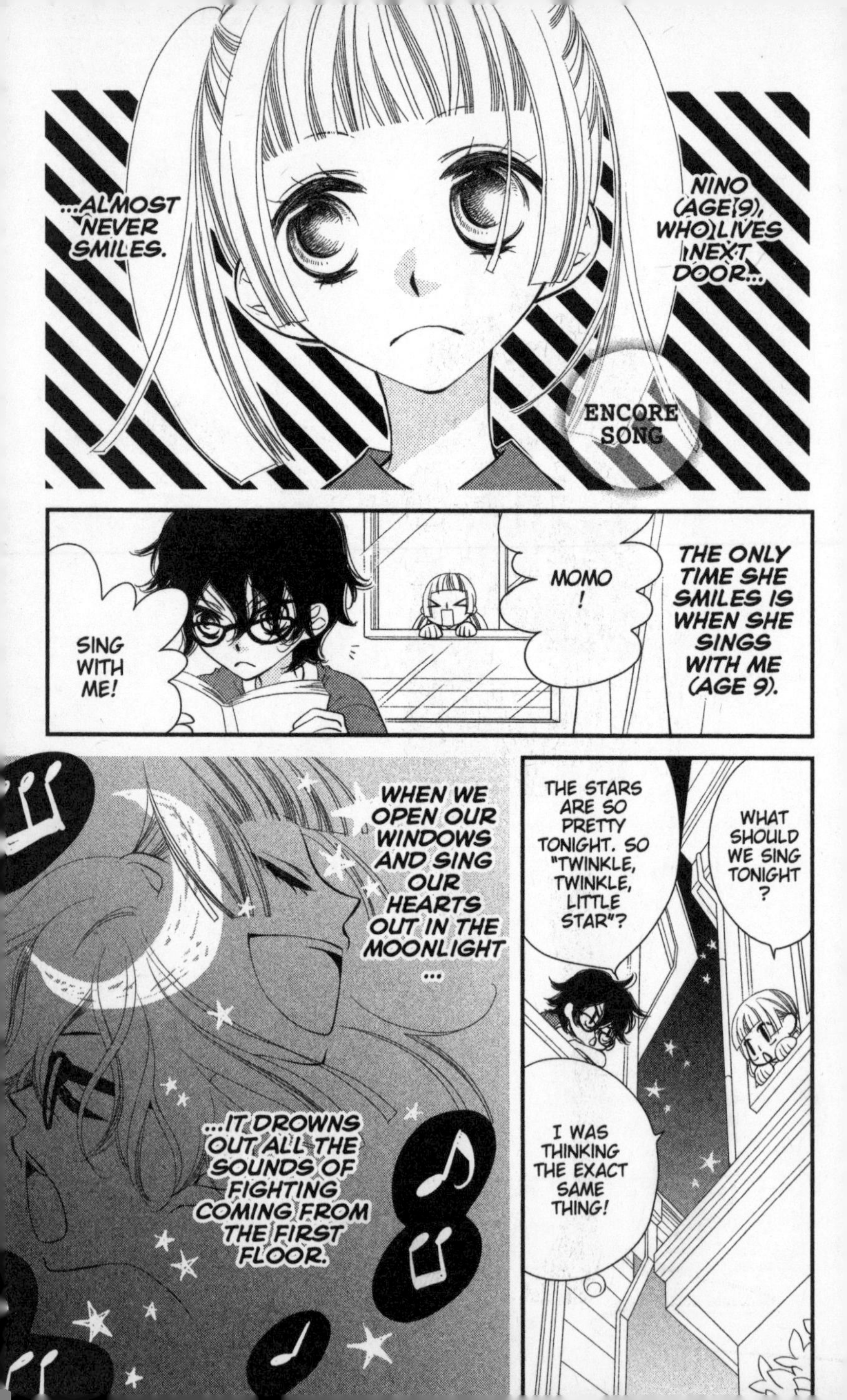
NINO (AGE 9), WHO LIVES NEXT DOOR...
...ALMOST NEVER SMILES.
ENCORE SONG
THE ONLY TIME SHE SMILES IS WHEN SHE SINGS WITH ME (AGE 9).
MOMO!
SING WITH ME!
WHAT SHOULD WE SING TONIGHT?
THE STARS ARE SO PRETTY TONIGHT. SO "TWINKLE, TWINKLE, LITTLE STAR"?
I WAS THINKING THE EXACT SAME THING!
WHEN WE OPEN OUR WINDOWS AND SING OUR HEARTS OUT IN THE MOONLIGHT...
...IT DROWNS OUT ALL THE SOUNDS OF FIGHTING COMING FROM THE FIRST FLOOR.

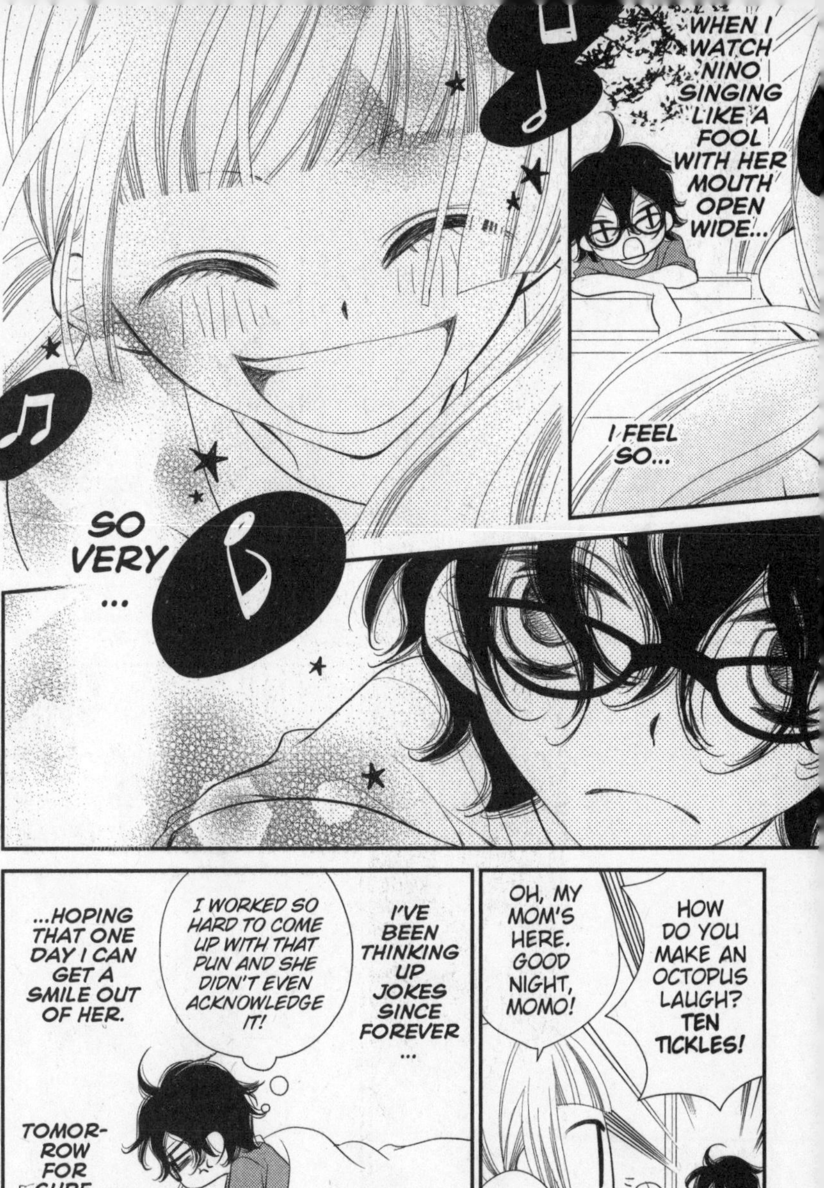
WHEN I WATCH NINO SINGING LIKE A FOOL WITH HER MOUTH OPEN WIDE...
I FEEL SO...
SO VERY ...
HOW DO YOU MAKE AN OCTOPUS LAUGH? TEN TICKLES!
OH, MY MOM'S HERE. GOOD NIGHT, MOMO!
OH ...
I'VE BEEN THINKING UP JOKES SINCE FOREVER ...
I WORKED SO HARD TO COME UP WITH THAT PUN AND SHE DIDN'T EVEN ACKNOWLEDGE IT!
...HOPING THAT ONE DAY I CAN GET A SMILE OUT OF HER.
TOMOR-ROW FOR SURE.
PUN NOTES

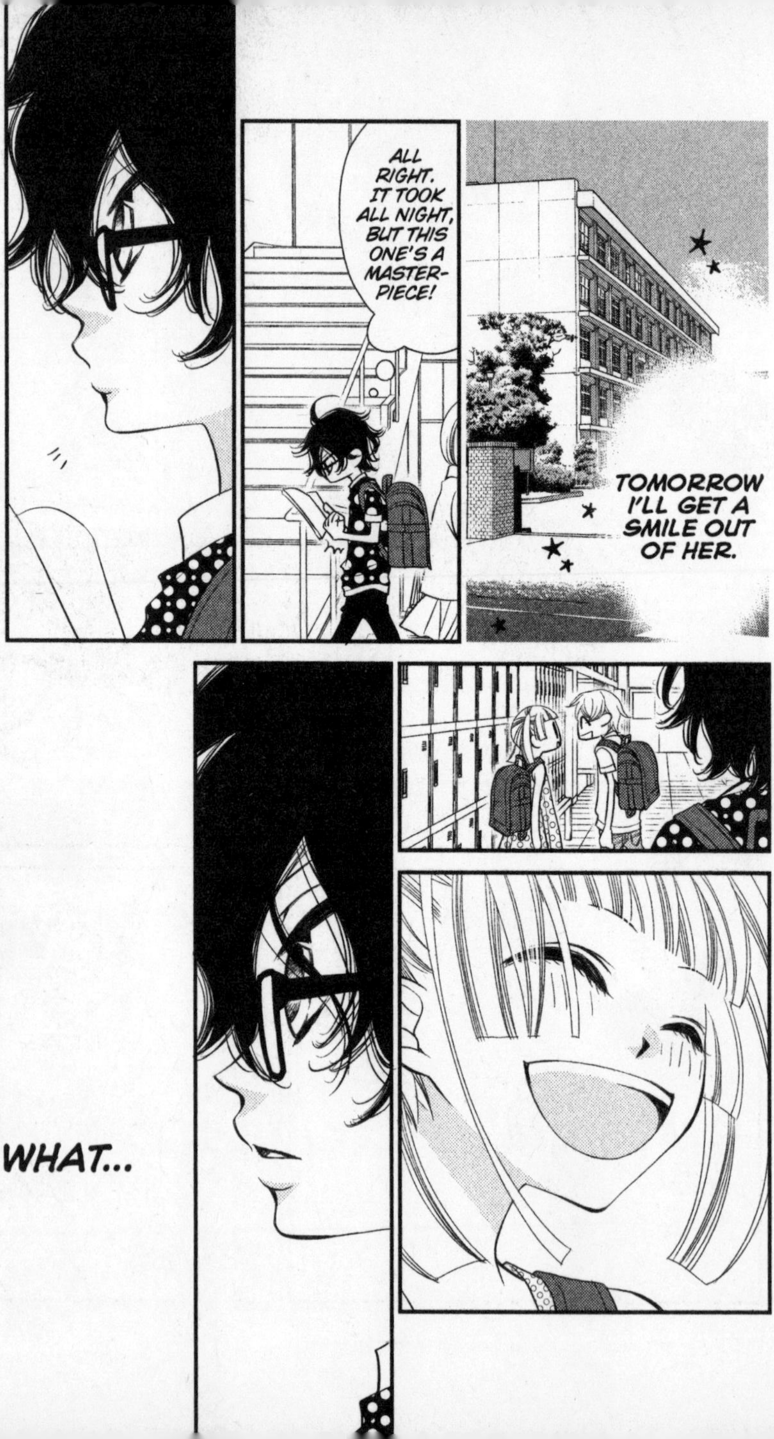
TOMORROW I'LL GET A SMILE OUT OF HER.
ALL RIGHT. IT TOOK ALL NIGHT, BUT THIS ONE'S A MASTER-PIECE!
WHAT...

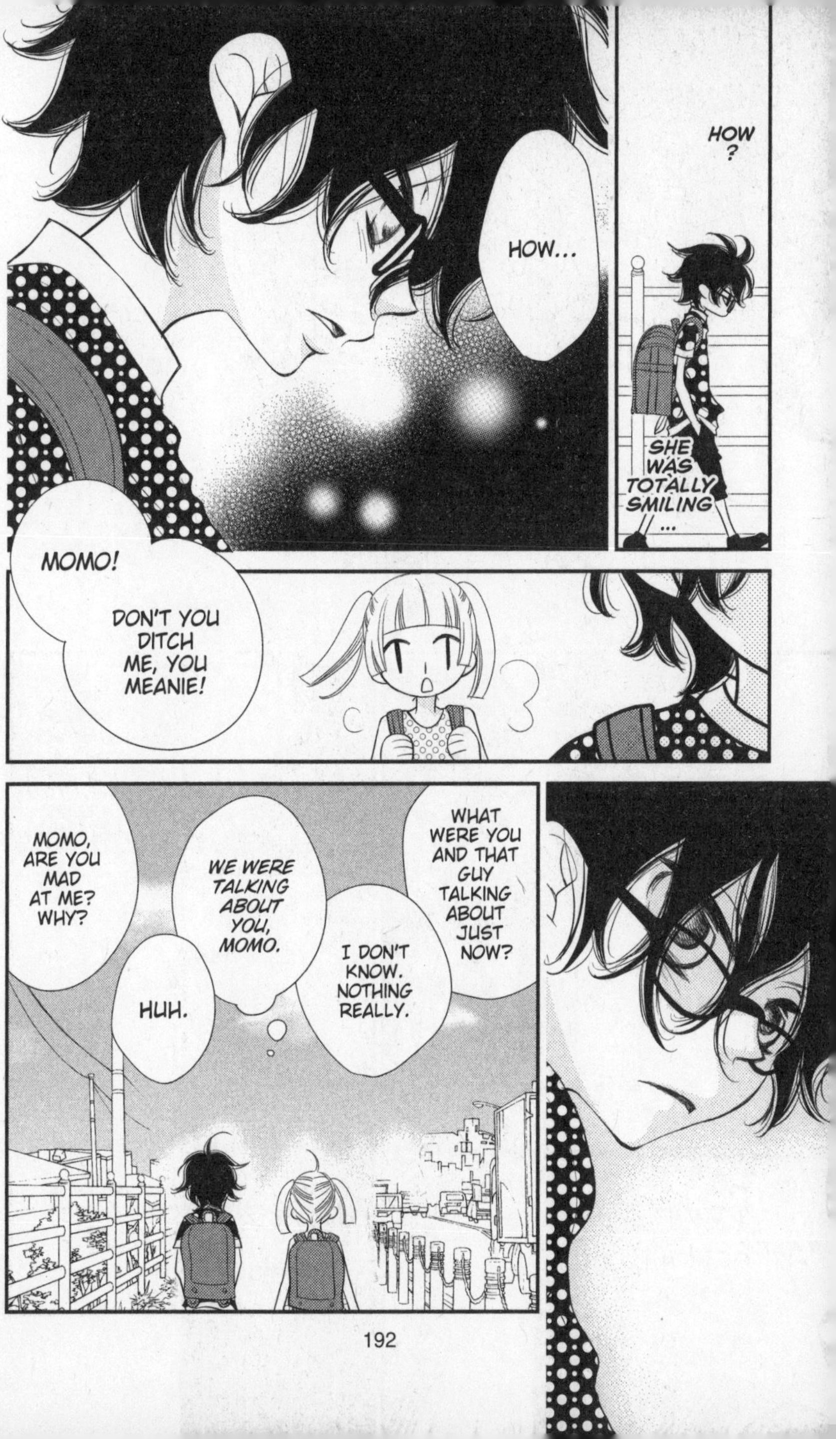
HOW ?
SHE WAS TOTALLY SMILING ...
HOW...
MOMO!
DON'T YOU DITCH ME, YOU MEANIE!
WHAT WERE YOU AND THAT GUY TALKING ABOUT JUST NOW?
WE WERE TALKING ABOUT YOU, MOMO.
I DON'T KNOW. NOTHING REALLY.
HUH.
MOMO, ARE YOU MAD AT ME? WHY?

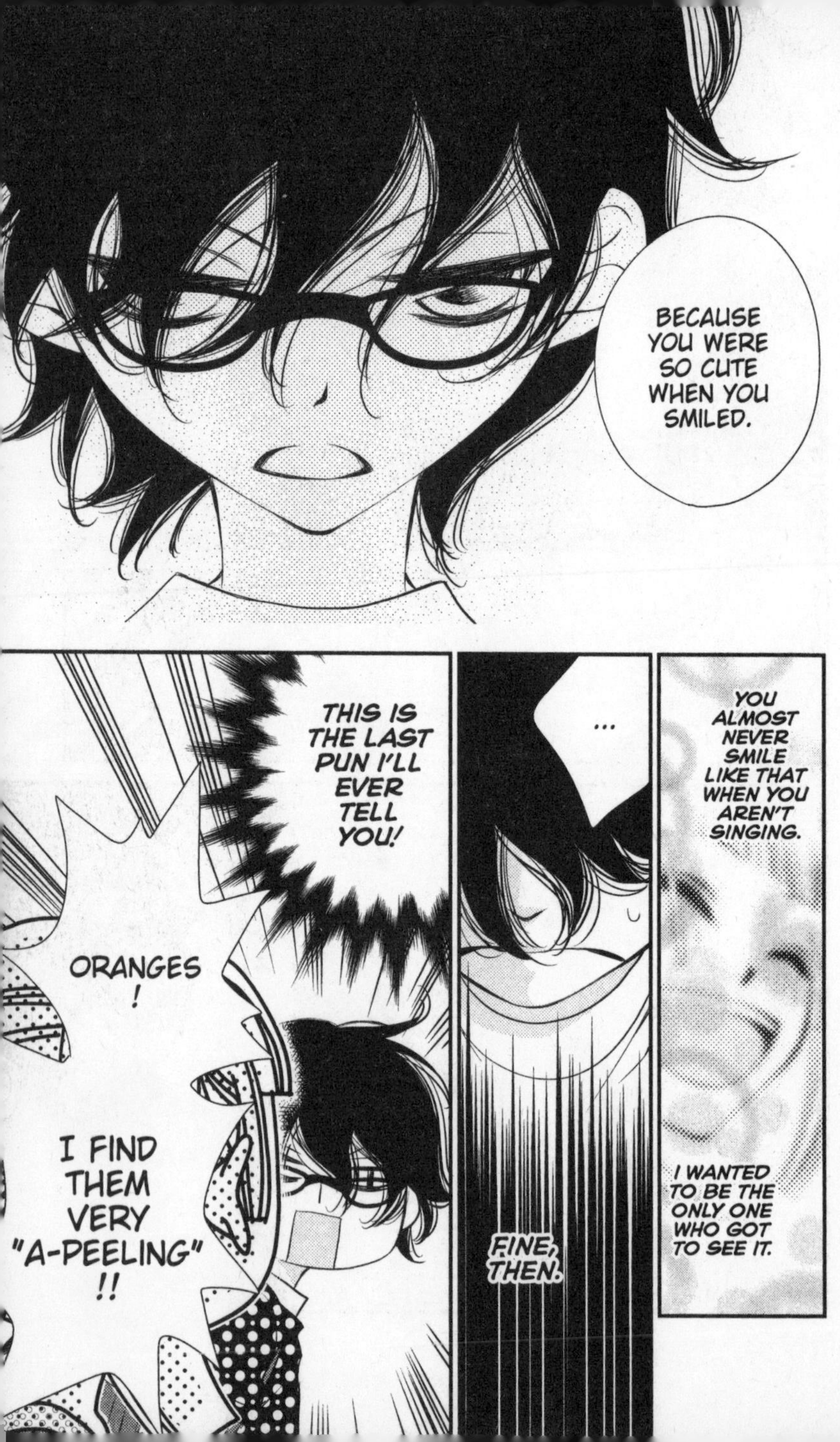
BECAUSE YOU WERE SO CUTE WHEN YOU SMILED.
YOU ALMOST NEVER SMILE LIKE THAT WHEN YOU AREN'T SINGING.
I WANTED TO BE THE ONLY ONE WHO GOT TO SEE IT.
...
FINE, THEN.
THIS IS THE LAST PUN I'LL EVER TELL YOU!
ORANGES!
I FIND THEM VERY "A-PEELING"!!

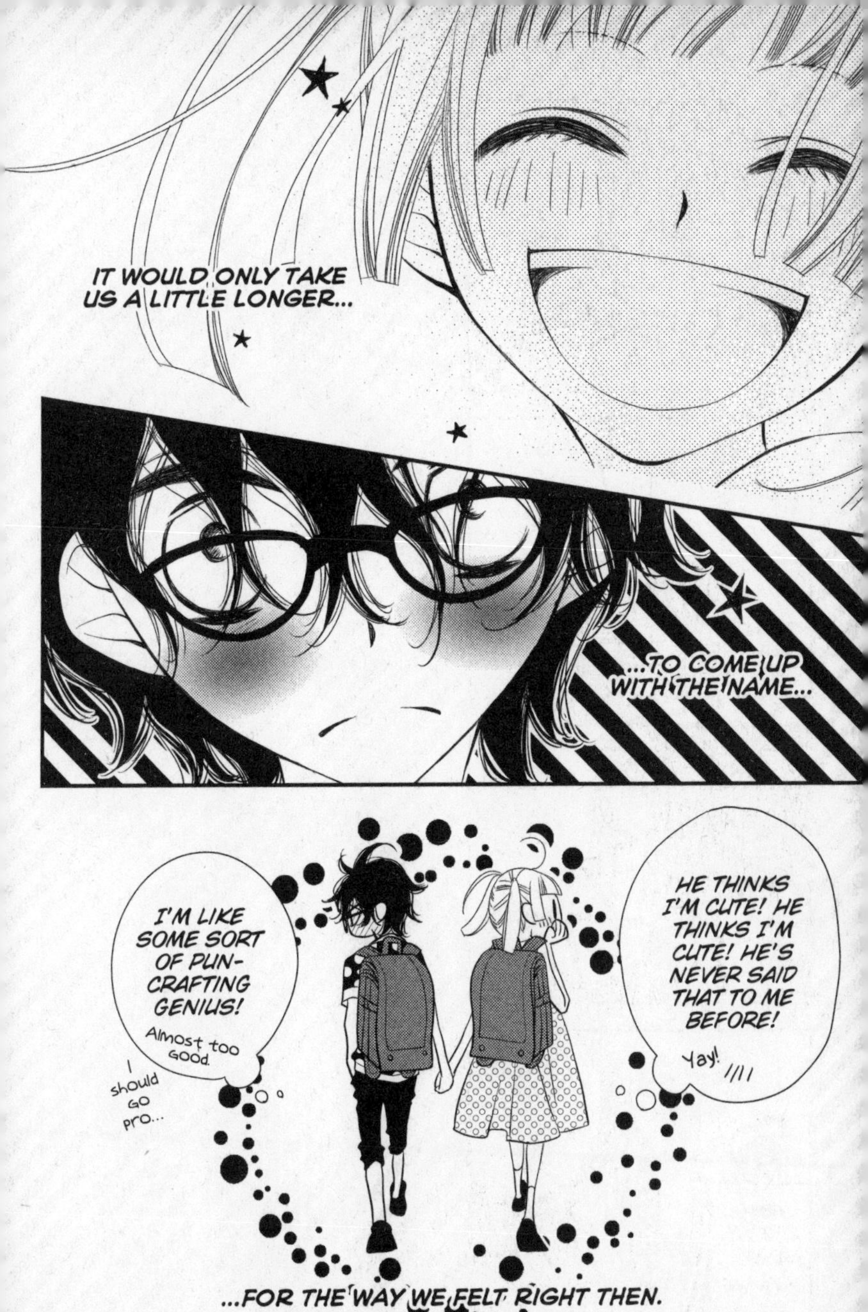
IT WOULD ONLY TAKE US A LITTLE LONGER...
...TO COME UP WITH THE NAME...
HE THINKS I'M CUTE! HE THINKS I'M CUTE! HE'S NEVER SAID THAT TO ME BEFORE!
Yay! ////
I'M LIKE SOME SORT OF PUN-CRAFTING GENIUS!
Almost too good.
I should go pro...
...FOR THE WAY WE FELT RIGHT THEN.

ENCORE SONG / THE END

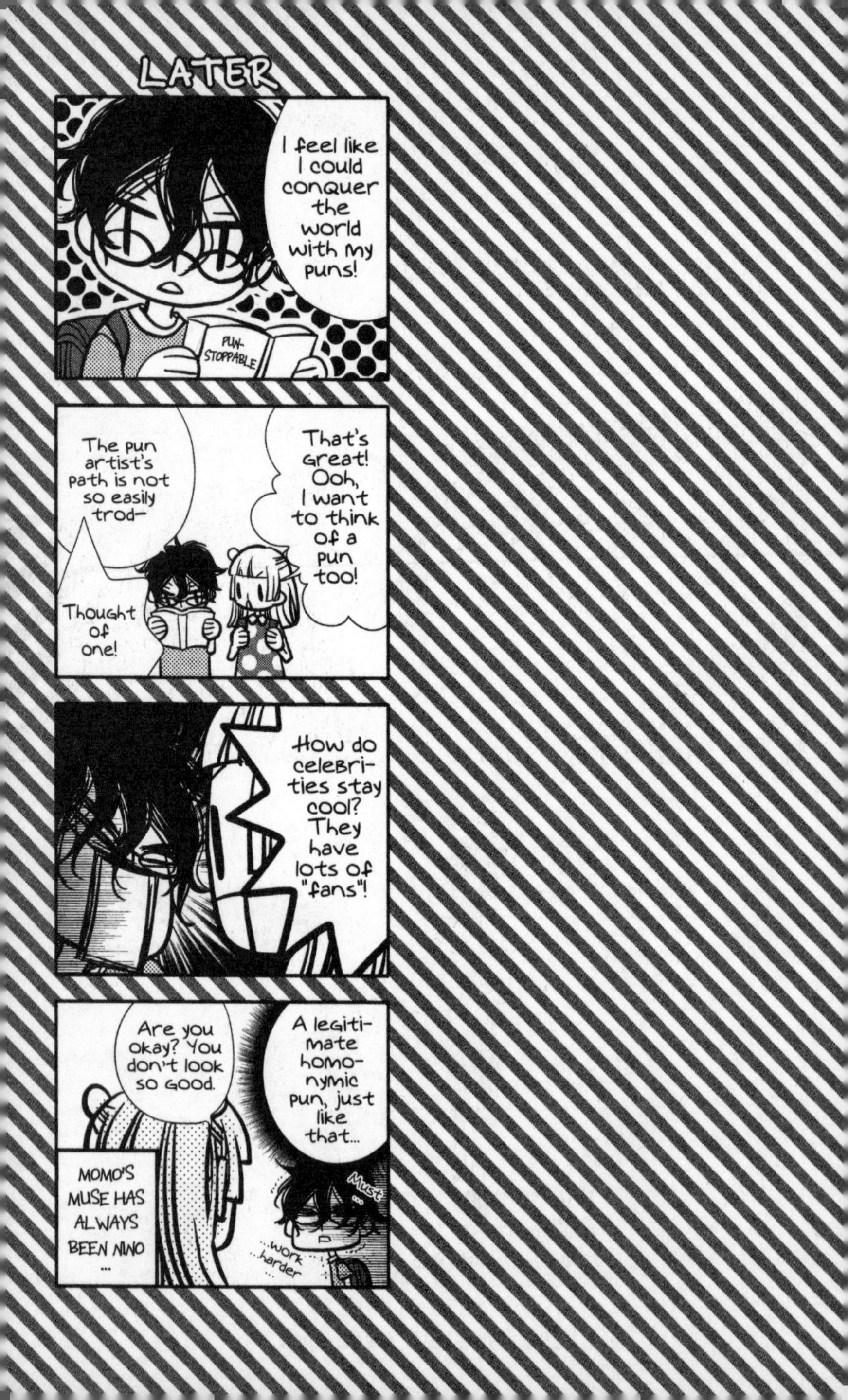
LATER
I feel like I could conquer the world with my puns!
PUN-STOPPABLE
That's great! Ooh, I want to think of a pun too!
The pun artist's path is not so easily trod—
Thought of one!
How do celebrities stay cool? They have lots of "fans"!
A legitimate homonymic pun, just like that...
Are you okay? You don't look so good.
Must... ...work ...harder ...
MOMO'S MUSE HAS ALWAYS BEEN NINO ...

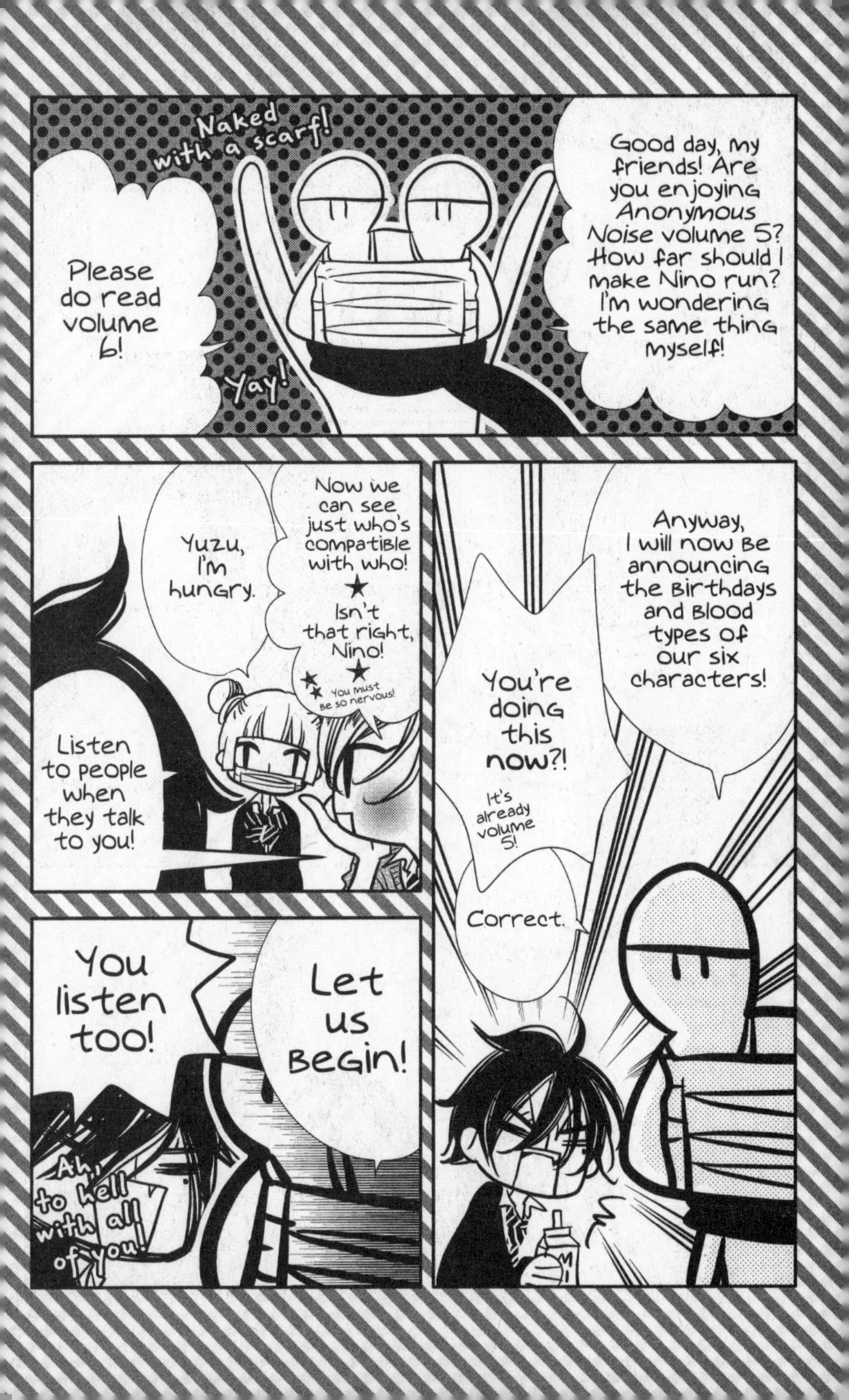
Good day, my friends! Are you enjoying Anonymous Noise volume 5? How far should I make Nino run? I'm wondering the same thing myself!
Naked with a scarf!
Please do read volume 6!
Yay!
Anyway, I will now be announcing the birthdays and blood types of our six characters!
You're doing this now?!
It's already volume 5!
Correct.
Now we can see just who's compatible with who! ★ Isn't that right, Nino! ★
You must be so nervous!
Yuzu, I'm hungry.
Listen to people when they talk to you!
Let us begin!
You listen too!
Ah, to hell with all of you!

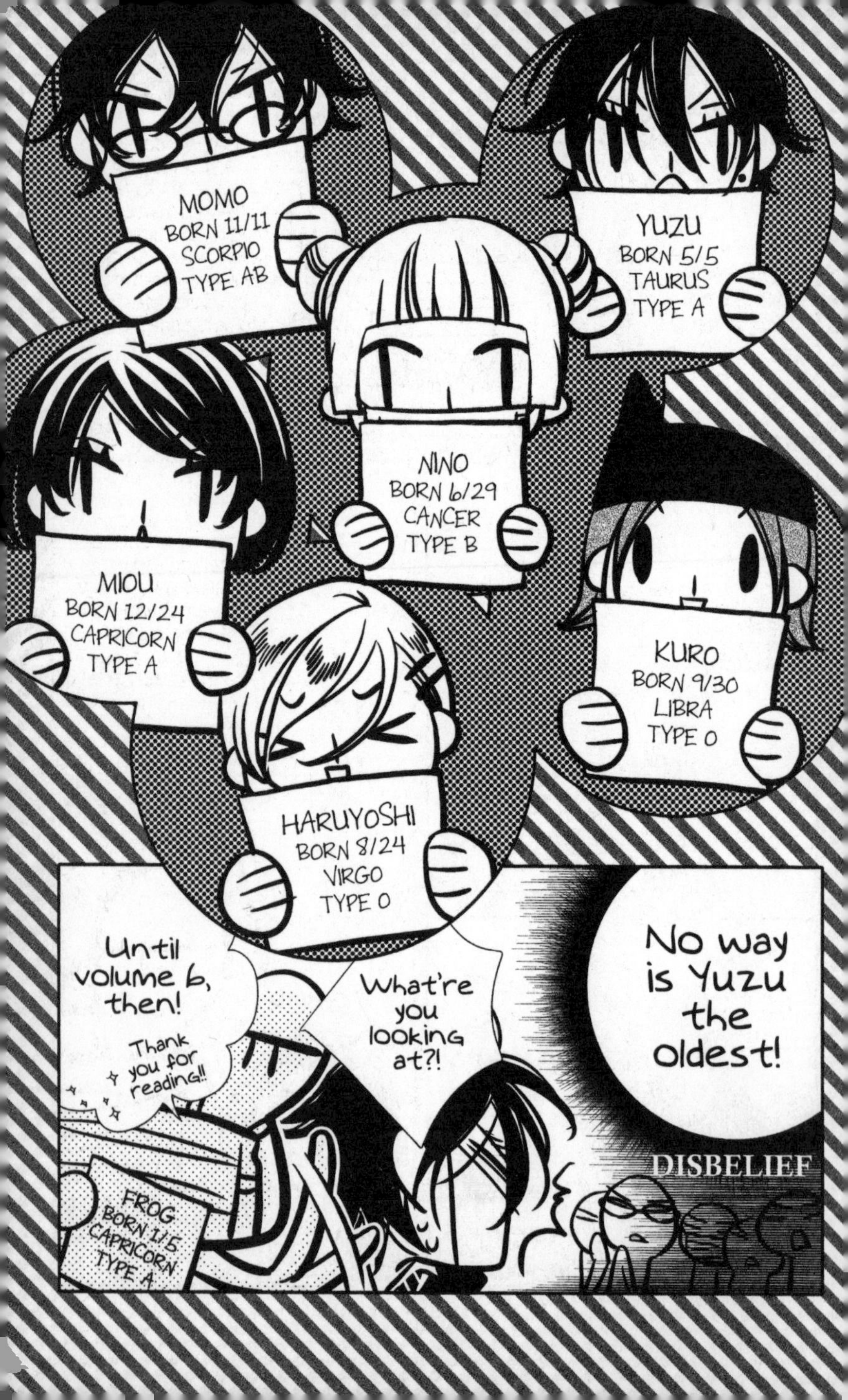
YUZU BORN 5/5 TAURUS TYPE A
MOMO BORN 11/11 SCORPIO TYPE AB
NINO BORN 6/29 CANCER TYPE B
KURO BORN 9/30 LIBRA TYPE O
MIOU BORN 12/24 CAPRICORN TYPE A
HARUYOSHI BORN 8/24 VIRGO TYPE O
No way is Yuzu the oldest!
DISBELIEF
What're you looking at?!
Until volume 6, then!
Thank you for reading!!
FROG BORN 1/5 CAPRICORN TYPE A

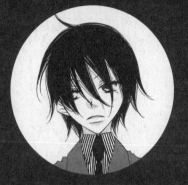

Before I began this project, my biggest fear
was that I wouldn't be able to depict the live
performances well, but now they're among my
favorite things to draw. Nino's performances
are always so passionate! I'd love to draw one
that's more relaxed...but that's up to her
and how she develops!

- Ryoko Fukuyama

Born on January 5 in Wakayama Prefecture in Japan,
Ryoko Fukuyama debuted as a manga artist after
winning the Hakusensha Athena Shinjin Taisho Prize
from Hakusensha's *Hana to Yume* magazine. She is also
the author of *Nosatsu Junkie*. *Anonymous Noise* was
adapted into an anime in 2017.

ANONYMOUS NOISE
Vol. 5
Shojo Beat Edition

STORY AND ART BY
RYOKO FUKUYAMA

English Translation & Adaptation/Casey Loe
Touch-Up Art & Lettering/Joanna Estep
Design/Yukiko Whitley
Editor/Amy Yu

Fukumenkei Noise by Ryoko Fukuyama
© Ryoko Fukuyama 2015
All rights reserved.
First published in Japan in 2015 by HAKUSENSHA, Inc., Tokyo.
English language translation rights arranged with HAKUSENSHA, Inc., Tokyo.

Printed in Canada

Published by VIZ Media, LLC
P.O. Box 77010
San Francisco, CA 94107

10 9 8 7 6 5 4 3 2 1
First printing, November 2017

www.viz.com

www.shojobeat.com

Surprise!

You may be reading the wrong way!

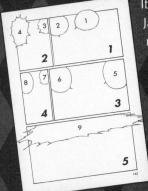

It's true: In keeping with the original Japanese comic format, this book reads from right to left—so action, sound effects and word balloons are completely reversed. This preserves the orientation of the original artwork—plus, it's fun! Check out the diagram shown here to get the hang of things, and then turn to the other side of the book to get started!

P9-CCW-513

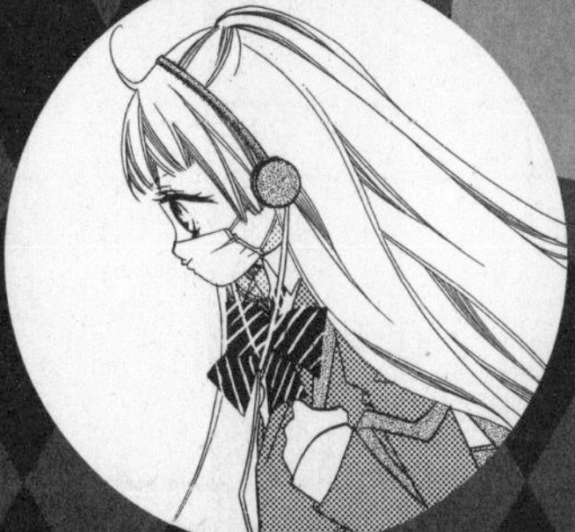